UKCH Religious Trends No. 5 2005/2006
The Future of the Church

Edited by Dr Peter Brierley

Assistant Editor: Kim Miles

CHRISTIAN RESEARCH

Vision Building, 4 Footscray Road, London SE9 2TZ

Tel: 020 8294 1989 Fax: 020 8294 0014

Email: admin@christian-research.org.uk

Websites: www.christian-research.org.uk   www.ukchristianhandbook.org.uk

Dedication

To those who have encouraged the dissemination of Christian statistics to enable church leadership to think more strategically about the future

British Library Cataloguing in Publication Data

UK Christian Handbook Religious Trends No. 5 – 2005/2006
1. Great Britain Christian Church
I. Brierley, Peter, 1938
ISBN 1 85321 160 5

Christian Research aims to provide Christian leaders with factual information, surveys, and other resource material to help them in the long-term in their strategic planning for evangelism and growth, and in the short-term with leadership training for greater efficiency, effectiveness, and cost-effectiveness. Christian Research also publishes and distributes related books and papers. The Christian Research Association is a registered charity, Number 1017701.

Material similar to that in *Religious Trends* is published every other month in the Christian Research Association's bulletin, *Quadrant*. This is available only to members. Details of membership may be obtained from Gwen Gowers, Christian Research, Vision Building, 4 Footscray Road, Eltham, London SE9 2TZ. Email: admin@christian-research.org.uk.
Websites: www.christian-research.org.uk and www.ukchristianhandbook.org.uk

Typeset by Paul Jones Associates, 98 Eden Way, Beckenham, Kent BR3 3DH.
Printed for Christian Research at the above address by Goodman Baylis, The Trinity Press, London Road, Worcester WR5 2JH.

by Dr Peter Brierley, Editor

GK Chesterton once wrote, "five times in the last 2,000 years the church has to all appearance gone to the dogs. In each case it was the dogs that died."[1] The UK may be approaching a sixth time, and the statistics given in this volume suggest that the dogs may temporarily be gaining the upper hand!

This fifth edition of *Religious Trends* focuses on the future. While every previous edition has always extrapolated the basic figures 2, 5 or even 10 years ahead, in this volume virtually every statistic is forecast through to 2020, and in the final section these figures are cumulated and then drawn forward to the year 2040.

The context of the UK figures is given against the background of the world picture painted in Section 1. Two main trends dominate world Christianity at this time – the emergence of the Christian majority in the Third World (away from the First World), and the growing emergence of evangelicals. These are growing as a proportion of the total in the First World because the non-evangelicals are declining faster than they are, but evangelicals are growing in the Third World because of conversion. The only other religious group growing as rapidly is Islam.

Section 2 has coloured maps showing the UK's religious community and its diversity, and also looks at the discrepancy between a high Christian percentage (72%) against a low rate of attendance (8%). The last part of the Section gives the overall figures for church membership, ministers, churches and Sunday attendance up to 2020. By then church membership is likely to be 7% of the population against 10% in 2000, and Sunday attendance at 4% instead of 8%. The detail of Section 2 is broken down in Section 8 (for the Institutional churches: Anglicans, Catholics, Orthodox and Presbyterians, deemed "institutional" because in some countries they are the state church) and Section 9 (for the Free Churches: Baptist, Independent, Methodist, New Church, Pentecostal and Others).

Section 3 looks at Mission and shows how the overall number of Mission Workers is declining, and looks likely to continue declining if present trends among young people leaving the church remain, since young Christian men and women in their 20s and 30s simply won't be around to volunteer for missionary or ministerial service.

Section 4 gives population and other demographic information in detail for the years ahead, and in outline to 2070. The proportion of births outside marriage is likely to increase rapidly, as is the age of first-time mothers. There are likely to be 39,000 centenarians in 2036 against 7,000 in 2001. Marriages in church are likely to drop drastically as the popularity of other "approved premises" grows, from 36% of the total in 2000 to 15% by 2020.

Section 5 looks at other statistics from a number of different studies, including the date of Easter over 6 centuries, the average income of a local church, and some of the characteristics of older people. Section 6 gives information about Christian bookshops and religious books, which unlike the market they serve, continue both to flourish and expand. Section 7 gives the details of numerous recent research reports on a myriad of topics, with a special subject index at the end.

Section 10 gives information for the non-Trinitarian churches and other religions. The non-Christian religions are growing, as a glance at Figure 12.14 will show, with Islam set to increase rapidly over the next two generations in the UK (nearly a three-fold increase between 2000 and 2040, Table 12.14.1). Section 11 gives the final series of maps by John Whitehorn of denominational boundaries and their relationship to current civil boundaries throughout the UK.

Some of the Christian churches are growing, especially the Pentecostals, largely due to the black majority churches which are mainly close to London (Tables 9.12.1, 9.12.14 and 9.17.5); the New Churches (House Churches), whose growth is driven by the continued expansion of Newfrontiers and the Association of Vineyard Churches (Tables 9.9.1, 9.10.5 and 9.9.3). The various overseas national churches (Table 9.20.2) are likewise set to grow further, doubling in size between 2000 and 2020, making the Other Denominations category expand slightly (Table 9.18.1). The Orthodox churches are also growing, though much more slowly (Table 8.8.1).

Elsewhere, however, the situation is bleak. If nothing changes, Presbyterian members are forecast to drop 42% in the period 2000 to 2020 (Table 8.10.1), Methodists 37% (Table 9.8.1), Anglicans 31% (Table 8.2.1), Catholics 28% (Table 8.5.1), Independents 22% (Table 9.6.1), and the Baptists 17% (Table 9.4.1). This accumulated forecast decline is of some 1.6 million church members, which the growing groups do not reverse since collectively the Orthodox, New Churches, Pentecostals and Other Denominations only add 288,000 members between them. Thus in 20 years 1.3 million members are predicted to leave from a 2000 total of 5.9 million, a loss of 23% (Table 2.23.1), a discouraging outlook.

Church closures and ministerial losses are expected to decline at a slower rate than membership. However, church attendance may drop even faster than membership, moving from 11% of the population in 1980, through 8% in 2000 to an expected 2% by 2040. Some will say, "but suppose another Billy Graham comes on the scene," or "we are praying for revival," and God may well intervene in these ways, but the figures must alert the Church to action in the meantime.

Suppose in 2005 a revival occurred in which, say, 75% of all the evangelical churches in the country doubled their congregation that year and 25% of all the non-evangelical churches. That would mean that church attendance would increase from 6.8% of the population to 9.8%, putting the percentage back to what it was in the late 1980s, an encouraging situation, but not a revolution for the church.

On the other hand, while the decline is real it is not as rapid as some expect. When John Major declared in 1995 that "fifty years from now Britain will still be the country of long shadows on county grounds, warm beer, invincible green suburbs, dog lovers and pool fillers and – as George Orwell said – 'old maids cycling to Holy Communion through the morning mist'"[2] he was probably correct, and so was George Orwell! However of the 2% of the population still going to church then, two-thirds, 65%, will be 65 or over (Table 12.9.2).

So what can be done? A major survey reported in part on Page 5.7 and in *Religious Trends* No 4 Pages 5.2 and 5.3 showed that the key for growth was clear vision, or having specific objectives, or knowing where one was going. However, Sir Terry Leahy, chief executive of Tesco, said in a conference that strategic planning is only part of the battle. "The difference between success and failure is the difference between implementing, say, 80% or only 50% of your plans."[3] Such vision has to be implemented by leaders who are capable of making things happen.

The conclusions on Page 12.13 show that the obstacles are formidable. There are likely to be huge losses by the institutional churches and a dramatic decline of young people. The implications of this get worse with every passing decade if it is not corrected. There will be large numbers of non-viable rural churches with single digit congregations, and a rate of decrease which is accelerating not lessening. Most leaders would blanch at such a challenge! Meanwhile the larger churches will continue to flourish and become the key units of operation.

Who will fill the gap by developing and implementing strategic, God-given plans that will give the church a future, not just a history? Are there men and women who can do the impossible? Or rather are there men and women who are so close to Christ that with Him they can know, "With God all things are possible" (Mark 10:27), and then say, "Here am I! Send me" (Isa 6:8)?

[1] *The Everlasting Man*, GK Chesterton, Part 2, Chapter 6. [2]Quoted in *The Daily Telegraph*, November 2004, Page 12.
[3] Quoted in *Management Today*, December 2004, Page 27.

Contents

How to use *Religious Trends*

Religious Trends is primarily a reference book for those wanting information about church life in the UK or wider afield. It is not a book to read straight through! Like any resource book, the Index (Section 13) is a good place to start, especially as this gives cumulative references to the previous three volumes.

All the sections listed on the Contents Page 0.5 are flagged by bleeds at the edge of each page. Hold the book closed, and you will see them on the edge. The book operates around these sections (plus a fourteenth, numbered zero, which comprises the necessary introductory pages). Page numbers are given in terms of these sections, and are continuous within each section but not beyond it, since each new section begins with its own page 1.

This edition has a number of special features, apart from those mentioned in the Preview:
- Section 1 looks at the growth in World Christianity both geographically and by churchmanship.
- Section 4 resumes the demographic overview of the UK population, but also forecasts most of these figures through to 2020. The total population is given up to 2071.
- Sections 6 and 11 are re-instated having been omitted from the previous edition because of lack of space. Section 6 gives data about Christian and religious books and bookshops, and Section 11 gives maps of the various denominational boundaries.
- The coloured maps in Section 2 focus on the religious identity by county or council in each of the four constituent countries of the UK, as well as maps of all the Local and Unitary Authority Districts.
- Sections 8 to 10 give a vast amount of individual denominational statistics (Sections 8 and 9) and Other Religions statistics (Section 10) for the years 2000 to 2003, and forecasts these forward in every case for 2005, 2010 and 2020. These are all summarised on Pages 2.22 and 2.23, the latter containing the main UK summary.
- Section 7 continues to list other religious research published in the past 2 years of which we are aware, and has its own subject index at the end of that section.

Each edition of *Religious Trends* is at least 90% different from the previous one. Number 4 is still in print should any reader wish to purchase a copy. As with the previous editions, this is published separately from the *UK Christian Handbook*, although it is still linked to that volume by its title.

Dr Peter Brierley
June 2005

Notes and definitions for statistics in sections 2, 8, 9 and 10

Page 2.23 is a **total summary** of all the data given in Sections 8 and 9. A repeat of the denominational totals are given on Pages 2.22 for ease of reference.

Membership figures were given in answer to the following request: "Total number of adult (aged 15 and over) members/adherents in the UK." Definitions of membership vary according to the church denomination or religious group in question. Adult church membership is defined as appropriate to each particular group, so that for example the Electoral Roll (not to be confused with the Local Authority Electoral Register) has been used for the Church of England, whilst because there is no comparable equivalent to the Protestant definitions of membership, Roman Catholic adult mass attendance figures have mostly been used. Where adherents are defined as non-communicant members, as with some Scottish denominations, these have been added to the true members.

Active membership is normally taken as half the community where actual membership is unknown. For religions other than Christianity, the results of the 2001 Population Census have been used where necessary.

Ministers are full-time active clergy, ordained officials (including those in administration, chaplaincies, etc.) or other recognised leaders. Many of the Afro-Caribbean clergy are part-time.

Churches (or equivalent buildings for religions other than Christianity) are those religious buildings in regular use, normally wholly owned by the organisations. Numbers of buildings do not necessarily correspond to the number of congregations or groups within the particular denomination so the number of congregations has been used in some tables as indicated.

Estimates indicated by footnotes are always editorial estimates, rather than ones made by the individual denominations themselves, which are not identified in these tables.

Estimates **for the year 2005** are based on the data for the previous years shown in the text and on other information where available, generally using a dampened linear regression.

Revised figures refer to changes from the previous edition of *Religious Trends*.

Extensive **footnotes** are sometimes supplied to help those requiring more information.

Projections are sometimes made using a dampened linear regression (that is, not strictly a straight line), but other times use alternatives. 37% of the projections to 2020 were provided by individual denominations.

World Christianity and Growth

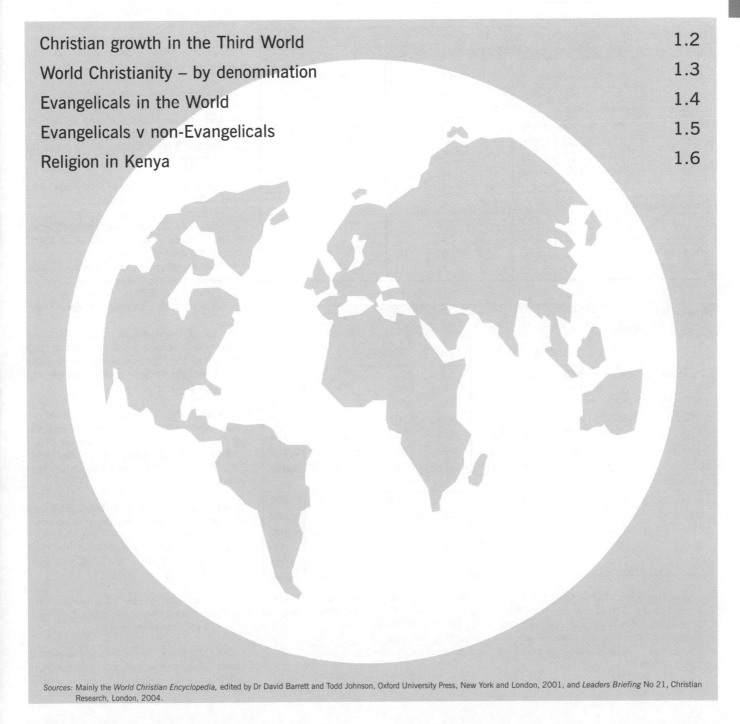

Sources: Mainly the *World Christian Encyclopedia,* edited by Dr David Barrett and Todd Johnson, Oxford University Press, New York and London, 2001, and *Leaders Briefing* No 21, Christian Research, London, 2004.

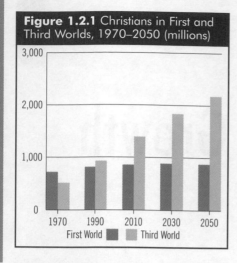

Figure 1.2.1 Christians in First and Third Worlds, 1970–2050 (millions)

First World / Third World

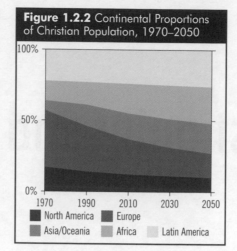

Figure 1.2.2 Continental Proportions of Christian Population, 1970–2050

North America / Europe / Asia/Oceania / Africa / Latin America

Two major changes have been in progress in world Christianity across the 20th century which will create a big impact on the 21st century church:

- The progress towards a Third World domination of Christianity, and
- The progress towards a world Christianity dominated by evangelicals.

These two trends are of course related to each other and impact upon each other; the second is considered on **Page 1.4**. The basis of these trends is Dr David Barrett's hugely valuable *World Christian Encyclopedia (WCE)*, the second edition of which was published in two volumes by Oxford University Press in 2001.

Comparisons of trends are easiest if the break points are evenly spaced; we have therefore taken David Barrett's figures and from linear extrapolation taken figures for 2010 and 2030 as well as his 2050.

Definitions of Christian and Continents

In this context "Christians" are defined as: "Followers of Jesus Christ as Lord, of all kinds, all traditions and confessions, and all degrees of commitment."

The terms "First World" and "Third World" used here reflect the UN definitions:

- "First World" groups the continents of Europe, North America and Oceania (what are effectively the Western nations); and
- "Third World" groups the continents of Africa, Asia and South (or Latin) America.

World Christianity compared to the population

The overall population of the world and the number of Christians divided between the Third World and the First World are given in **Table 1.2.1**, and the Christian numbers are graphed in **Figure 1.2.1**.

Table 1.2.1 shows that the Third World has not only exceeded the First World in total numbers of Christians (fewer in 1970, more in 1990) but the number of Christians in the Third World in 2050 is more than twice those in the First World.

The third band of columns in **Table 1.2.1** shows that while the Christian proportion of the world remains static at 33% or 34%, the reality is of a steadily increasing proportion of the Third World who are Christian, and a fast decreasing proportion of the First World.

The bottom part of **Table 1.2.1** translates the figures in the top portion into the change that is taking place on a daily basis.

Table 1.2.2 breaks down the middle segment of **Table 1.2.1** by individual continent, and these are then graphed in **Figure 1.2.2** (where Oceania is not shown separately as it is so small).

Table 1.2.1
Population of the World and the Christian Community, 1970–2050

Year/period	Population in millions			Christians in millions			Christians as % of Population		
	First World	Third World	TOTAL	First World	Third World	TOTAL	First World	Third World	TOTAL
1970	907	2,789	3,696	722	514	1,236	80	18	33
1990	1,030	4,236	5,266	813	934	1,747	79	22	33
2010	1,284	5,467	6,751	855	1,390	2,245	67	25	33
2030	1,462	6,646	8,108	887	1,836	2,723	61	28	34
2050	1,546	7,363	8,909	876	2,176	3,052	57	30	34
Daily increase in thousands									
1970–1990	17	198	215	13	57	70	76	29	33
1990–2010	35	168	203	6	62	68	17	37	33
2010–2030	24	162	186	4	61	65	17	38	35
2030–2050	11	99	110	–2	47	45	–18	47	41

Table 1.2.2
Christian Community in Millions by Continent, 1970–2050

Year	First World				Third World				World Total
	Europe	North America	Oceania	Total	Latin America	Africa	Asia	Total	
1970	493	211	18	722	269	144	101	514	**1,236**
1990	550	241	22	813	409	276	249	934	**1,747**
2010	556	271	28	855	544	472	374	1,390	**2,245**
2030	554	300	33	887	679	652	505	1,836	**2,723**
2050	526	314	36	876	776	793	607	2,176	**3,052**
% of total									
1970	40	17	1	58	22	12	8	42	**100**
1990	32	14	1	47	23	16	14	53	**100**
2010	25	12	1	38	24	21	17	62	**100**
2030	20	11	1	32	25	24	19	68	**100**
2050	17	10	1	28	26	26	20	72	**100**

The story in the bottom half of **Table 1.2.2**, and shown in **Figure 1.2.2**, is that the proportions of Christians in both North and Latin America are changing relatively slowly, while the proportions in Europe, Asia and Africa are changing extremely rapidly.

The Third World was already over 50% of the world's Christians by 1990 (53%), and by 2010 will be 62%. By 2050, if present trends continue, they will total 72%, nearly three-quarters of the Christian community.

Source: Leaders' Briefing No 21, *Evangelicals in the world of the 21st century,* Dr Peter Brierley, Christian Research, London, May 2004.

Two large Lausanne Congresses were held in 1974 and in 1989. The change in the Christian scene around the world between these dates is sometimes attributed to the acceptance of many evangelicals of social action as part of the Gospel. This is strongly emphasised in the Lausanne Covenant, a key result of Lausanne I, the fifth section of which declares "evangelism and socio-political involvement are both part of our Christian duty".

A second key change among evangelicals in this period was the expansion of their emphasis of reaching "unreached peoples". This also may be attributed to Lausanne I.

Table 1.3.1 and **Figure 1.3.1** show:

- The increasing proportion of Christians in the Independent churches across the world,
- The slowly declining proportion of the Roman Catholic Church, and
- The total of the other five groups (Protestant, Orthodox, Anglican, Marginal and Unaffiliated) keeping about the same proportion.

To find the reasons for these changes we have to look at the denominations which are not growing. They are nearly all institutional groups, and such churches have a number of problems. Some of these are identified in **Table 12.6.2**.

In the First World, the Independent groups were 6% of the total in 1970, rising to 11% in 1990, forecast to grow steadily to a projected 21% by 2050, as shown in **Figure 1.3.2**.

Table 1.3.2 shows that while the First World is busy starting denominations, the Third World plants churches.

Sources: *The Tide is Running Out*, Dr Peter Brierley, Christian Research, London, UK, 2000, Page 150; Article *"Southern bound: the church moves out of the cold"* by Dr Don Posterski, Envision, World Vision Canada, Volume 4, Number 1, Spring 2004, Page 15. *Operation World*, Patrick Johnstone, OM Publishing, Carlisle, and WEC International, Gerrards Cross, Bucks, UK, 1993, Page 643.

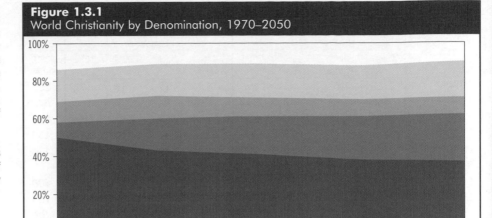

Figure 1.3.1
World Christianity by Denomination, 1970–2050

Legend: Roman Catholic | Independent | Orthodox | Protestant | All others

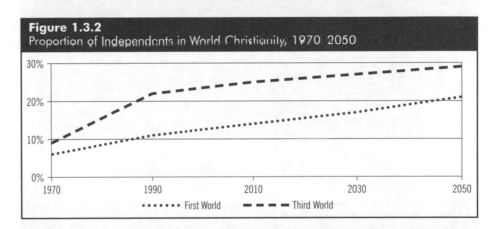

Figure 1.3.2
Proportion of Independents in World Christianity, 1970–2050

Legend: First World •••••• | Third World ━ ━ ━

Table 1.3.1
Christian Community in Millions by Denomination, 1970–2050

Year	Anglican	Independent	Orthodox	Protestant	Roman Catholic	Marginal	Unaffiliated	World Total
1970	48	96	140	211	624	11	106	**1,236**
1990	68	302	204	296	753	22	102	**1,747**
2010	97	460	226	399	910	36	117	**2,245**
2030	123	627	258	496	1,046	49	124	**2,723**
2050	146	753	267	574	1,125	62	125	**3,052**
% of total								
1970	*4*	*8*	*11*	*17*	*50*	*1*	*9*	*100*
1990	*4*	*17*	*12*	*17*	*43*	*1*	*6*	*100*
2010	*4*	*20*	*10*	*18*	*41*	*2*	*5*	*100*
2030	*5*	*23*	*9*	*18*	*38*	*2*	*5*	*100*
2050	*5*	*24*	*9*	*19*	*37*	*2*	*4*	*100*

Table 1.3.2 Number of Congregations and Denominations in the First and Third Worlds, 1970–2010

	Congregations		Denominations	
Year	First World	Third World	First World	Third World
1970	882,000	567,400	4,780	11,290
1990	1,122,700	1,532,200	9,320	19,310
2010	1,428,900	4,137,400	18,160	33,010
% increase each 20 years				
	+27	*+170*	*+95*	*+71*

Table 1.3.3
Number of National Mission Workers from the First and Third Worlds, 1990–2000

	First World				Third World				
Year	Europe	North America	Oceania	Total	Latin America	Africa	Asia	Total	World Total
1990	19,915	64,378	6,211	**90,504**	12,829	23,958	4,744	**41,531**	132,035
2000	22,897	71,088	9,452	**103,437**	12,442	69,203	10,192	**91,837**	195,274
% increase	*+15*	*+10*	*+52*	*+14*	*–3*	*+189*	*+115*	*+121*	*+48*

National mission workers are defined as those "working within their own home country. This includes field missionaries and also those in a supportive role, but with missionary status."

Table 1.4.1
Evangelical/Pentecostal Christians in millions by continent, 1970–2050

| Year | First World | | | | Third World | | | | |
	Europe	North America	Oceania	TOTAL	Latin America	Africa	Asia	TOTAL	WORLD TOTAL
1970	129	52	4	185	12	17	43	72	257
1990	185	99	8	292	119	94	137[1]	350	642
2010	201	119	10	330	168	168	217	553	883
2030	211	146	12	369	235	245	310	790	1,159
2050	226	168	15	409	302	321	382	1,005	1,414
% of total									
1970	50	20	2	72	5	6	17	28	100
1990	29	15	1	45	19	15	21	55	100
2010	23	13	1	37	19	19	25	63	100
2030	18	13	1	32	20	21	27	68	100
2050	16	12	1	29	21	23	27	71	100

[1] Estimate

Figure 1.4.1
Continental Proportions of Evangelicals/Pentecostals, 1970–2050

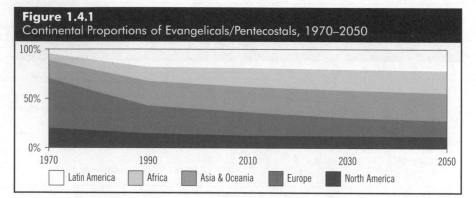

Latin America — Africa — Asia & Oceania — Europe — North America

Table 1.4.2 Percentage of Evangelicals or Pentecostals/Charismatics in the Christian Community by Continent, 1970–2050

| Year | First World | | | | Third World | | | | WORLD TOTAL % |
	Europe %	North America %	Oceania %	TOTAL %	America %	Africa %	Asia %	TOTAL %	
1970	26	25	22	25	4	12	43	14	21
1990	34	41	36	36	29	34	55	37	37
2010	36	44	36	39	31	36	58	41	39
2030	38	49	36	42	35	38	61	43	43
2050	43	54	42	47	39	40	63	46	46

Figure 1.4.2
Percentage of Evangelicals/Pentecostals in the Christian community, 1970–2050

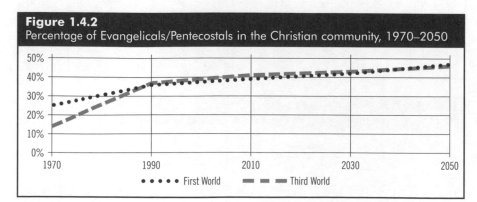

•••• First World   === Third World

Sources: World Christian Encyclopedia, Dr David Barrett, Oxford University Press, New York and London, 2001; Leaders' Briefing No 21, Evangelicals in the world of the 21st century, Dr Peter Brierley, Christian Research, London, May 2004.

[1] Forbidden Revolutions, Pentecostalism in Latin America, Catholicism in Eastern Europe, Prof David Martin, Gospel & Culture, SPCK, 1996.
[2] Report in idea, German Evangelical News Agency, English Edition, Volume 3, Number 4, 2nd December 2003, Page 1.

In his excellent assessment of Pentecostalism in Latin America, *Forbidden Revolutions*[1], David Martin gives a picture of an ever-increasing evangelicalism. He says it is growing in numbers in Latin America from 44 million in 1990 to 52 million 10 years later, but as a proportion of the total Christian community it remains at 11%.

The World Evangelical Alliance "is in contact with two million local churches with up to 400 million members in 123 countries"[2]. The previous General Secretary, Gary Edmonds, said the "fastest growth is happening in Latin America. Each year millions of Catholics join Pentecostal and Charismatic churches. In some regions of Brazil, evangelicals account for 40% of the population."

The WCE counted 80 million Pentecostals in Brazil in 2000, 47% of the population, and 51% of the Christian community, but numbered only 24 million evangelicals. In Latin America as a whole in 2000 David Barrett records 52 million evangelicals but 141 million Pentecostals/Charismatics. In Africa there were 91 million evangelicals in 2000 according to Barrett but 126 million Pentecostals. In the other four continents the number of evangelicals is greater than his number of Pentecostals/Charismatics.

Many would consider, however, that Pentecostals/Charismatics are evangelical, so **Table 1.4.1** therefore uses the number of Pentecostals/Charismatics for Africa and Latin America, but the larger number of evangelicals for the other continents.

The trends in **Table 1.4.1** are very similar to those in **Table 1.2.2**. Africa and Asia's proportion increases, Asia's more than Africa's (the opposite of **Table 1.2.2**), but Europe and North America's proportions drop.

Figure 1.4.1 shows that Third World evangelicalism really grew rapidly between 1970 and 1990. Could that have had some relation to the social work emphasis enshrined in the Lausanne Covenant produced at the 1974 gathering? Others might see it as the long term results of the impetus given to evangelicalism by Billy Graham from the 1950s onwards.

The percentage of evangelicals or Pentecostals/ Charismatics within the Christian community are shown by continent in **Table 1.4.2**. The figures show a rise in the first half of the 21st century, with almost half, 46%, of the Christian community either evangelical or Pentecostal by 2050 if present trends continue. After 2010 the proportions are expected to grow more rapidly than between 1990 and 2010.

The total percentages for the First and Third Worlds are shown in **Figure 1.4.2**. On these figures, First World experience is very similar to that of the Third World, confirming that the Christian community as a whole is becoming more evangelical/Pentecostal in the 21st century.

David Barrett gives a further important piece of information in his *World Christian Encyclopedia*. He breaks down the change in the number of adherents in the last decade in the 20th century between natural (or 'biological') growth and 'conversion' growth.

Thus the number of Christians increased from 1,747.5 million in 1990 to 1,999.6 million in 2000. He estimates this increase of 252 million people was made up of 227 million biological increase and 25 million conversion increase. These numbers may be expressed as percentages, shown in **Table 1.5** as 1.29% and 1.04% respectively. Some of the figures in **Table 1.5** are charted in **Figure 1.5**.

Table 1.5 is rather complicated but does three things – it breaks these percentages down between First and Third World, and between evangelicals and non-evangelicals, and it also compares them with the overall population.

The figures cannot be directly compared with the Tables on the previous pages because David Barrett only gives this data for the year 2000. The total number of Christians in the year 2000 in **Table 1.5** comes between the 1990 figure of 1,747 million and the 2010 figure of 2,245 million given in **Table 1.2.2**. Likewise for the First and Third World figures.

Table 1.5 shows that the Christian population is increasing annually faster than the world population in both the First and Third Worlds (1.15% is greater than 1.09% in the First World and 1.35% is greater than 1.33% in the Third World). However worldwide the overall rate of increase of Christians compared to the world population is slower (1.29% compared with 1.31% in the Total column) because there is a negative conversion rate in the First World, that is, people are leaving the Christian faith faster than they are joining it. This loss is sufficiently large to cancel out the overall increase of Christians from biological growth compared to the population generally.

The difference (which is not shown in **Table 1.5**) in birth rates (or biological growth) between Christians and non-Christians is however very finely balanced, and this is also true between evangelicals and non-evangelicals. Overall, non-evangelicals have slightly more children than evangelicals (1.30% is greater than 1.27%), but this is because there are more non-evangelical births in the Third World proportionately than evangelical births (1.36% to 1.34%). In the First World there are slightly more evangelical births than non-evangelical (1.17% to 1.14%), but because the numbers in the Third World are greater the overall balance goes the Third World way.

The evangelical conversion rate, however, is positive in the First World and even greater in the Third World (1.09% and 1.22%). The First World's problem is the non-evangelicals who are leaving, whereas in the Third World the non-evangelicals have a positive conversion

Table 1.5
Types of Christian Growth, Annual Rate, 1990–2000

	First World			Third World			Total World		
Group	Biological growth rate %	Conversion growth rate %	TOTAL (millions) in 2000	Biological growth rate %	Conversion growth rate %	TOTAL (millions) in 2000	Biological growth rate %	Conversion growth rate %	TOTAL (millions) in 2000
Evangelicals	1.17	1.09	376	1.34	1.22	271	1.27	1.16	648
Non-evangelicals	1.14	−1.04	469	1.36	1.01	883	1.30	−0.08	1,352
Total Christians	1.15	−0.77	845	1.35	1.11	1,154	1.29	1.04	2,000
Total population	1.09	n/a	1,054	1.33	n/a	5,001	1.31	n/a	6,055

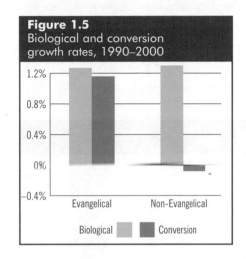

Figure 1.5
Biological and conversion growth rates, 1990–2000

Evangelical — Non-Evangelical

Biological / Conversion

rate, though lower than that of evangelicals (−1.04% and 1.01%).

What this all means is that evangelicals are growing across the world, both because of conversions and because of children being born into evangelical families. Of these two causes for growth, the family percentages are greater in both the First and the Third World.

Non-evangelicals are also growing, far faster biologically than through conversion, and in the First World the numbers leaving the faith are greater than those joining it by conversion

(giving the negative conversion rate −1.04%). So many are leaving in the First World that they cancel out conversion gains in the Third World. Therefore, across the world as a whole, non-evangelicals are leaving the faith rather than joining it (the negative total figure of −0.08%).

Evangelical conversions however are sufficient to outnumber the non-evangelical losses, so that Christianity grows worldwide primarily through children being born into Christian families, but also because overall there is a positive conversion rate.

[1] *Mission After Christendom*, David Smith, Darton, Longman and Todd, London, UK, 2003, Page 99.
[2] Ibid., Page 123.
[3] *The Church Inside Out*, J C Hoekendijk, SCM Press, London, UK, 1967.
[4] *Religion in Modern Europe*, The Putative Memory, Dr Grace Davie, Oxford University Press, Oxford, UK, 2000.
[5] *ChurchNext*, Professor Eddie Gibbs and Rev Dr Ian Coffey, IVP, Nottingham, UK, 2000, Page 225.
[6] Including *Mission-shaped Church*, Working Party chaired by Rt Rev Graham Cray, Bishop of Maidstone, Church House Publishing, 2004. *Coming Up Trumps! – Four ways into the Future*, Dr Peter Brierley, Authentic Media, Carlisle, and Christian Research, London, UK, 2004.
[7] Article *"Proven Principles for Change Leaders and Managers"* by Dr Larry Johnston, in McConkey/Johnston, Inc. Newsletter, Fall 2003, Page 2.

Two types of change are happening; **Page 1.2** described the growth of Third World Christianity, and **Page 1.4** the growth of evangelicalism. Such uniformity is happening in other aspects of global life also. David Smith says it "has led sociologists to employ the term *glocalisation* in order to describe the complex inter-relation... of both the increasing uniformity of institutions and behaviour around the world and the appearance and growth of rediscovered local identities, cultures and religions."[1]

The danger is that the similarities in the trends can lead to the conclusion that the Western, First World, model will dominate. Not at all! The figures on **Page 1.2** describe an increasing Third World Christianity. First World Christianity has enormous problems which the Third World must try to avoid. These problems are explained by David Smith: "Western Christians need to experi-

ence a mental, conceptual and spiritual transformation ... Received ideas concerning evangelism, which are based on Christendom assumptions that the church and the world share a basically common world-view, simply will no longer do."[2] He quotes the European theologian Hoekendijk: *"There is nothing left that can be called into memory, nothing that can be awakened."* [3]

The idea of memory has been taken further by sociologist Grace Davie in one of her books on European Christianity.[4]

This argues for a radical approach to church life in the First World, looking for "mission-shaped" churches, or "missional churches" as Professor Eddie Gibbs calls them.[5] There are many books urging radical strategic thinking.[6] The management guru Tom Peters urges First World Christians to "eradicate 'change' from our vocabulary, and substitute 'revolution'".[7]

Table 1.6 Christians in Kenya by denomination, 1970–2050 (millions)

Denomination	1970	1990	2010	2030	2050
Anglicans	0.6	2.3	3.6	5.0	6.5
R Catholics	1.9	5.0	7.7	10.3	13.0
Independents	1.6	4.8	7.2	9.8	12.3
Protestants	1.7	4.4	7.1	9.8	12.5
Others	1.5	1.9	2.3	2.7	3.1
TOTAL	**7.3**	**18.4**	**27.9**	**37.6**	**47.4**
Population	11.5	23.6	34.5	45.5	56.5
% Christians	63%	78%	81%	83%	84%
% Charismatics	9%	27%	29%	31%	32%
% Charis/Chris.	14%	34%	36%	38%	39%

Pages 1.2 and **1.4** describe two major changes which will create a big impact on the 21st century church: a) the progress towards a Third World domination of Christianity, and b) the progress towards a world Christianity dominated by evangelicals. Kenya illustrates both trends.

Part of the huge increase in African Christianity is seen in Kenya, whose numbers, given in **Table 1.6**, are broken down by denomination and shown in **Figure 1.6.1**, where 'Protestants' include Baptists, Methodists, Presbyterians and other largely non-charismatic denominations, 'Independents' are the Pentecostals and the many African indigenous charismatic groups, and 'Others' include the Orthodox and those whom David Barrett defines as "unaffiliated", not belonging to any denomination.

While all groups see growth, the fastest growth is among the Anglicans, who are growing at the rate of 3.0% per year, against 2.5% a year each for the Protestants and Independents, 2.4% for the Roman Catholics and 0.9% for the Others.

The percentage of the Kenyan population who are Christian increases also, from 63% in 1970, to 78% in 1990, to 81% in 2010 and 84% by 2050, if present trends continue. The largest group belonging to other religions in 2010 will be the Muslims at 7% of the population, the Bahá'ís at 1% and all other religions at 1% (half of whom are Hindus), leaving just 10% of the population not belonging to any specific religion, but whom David Barrett defines as "ethno-religionists", that is, "followers of a non-Christian or pre-Christian religion tied closely to a specific ethnic group with membership restricted to that group; usually animists, polytheists, shamanists, pagans, heathens or tribal religionists".

Figure 1.6.2 shows that Christianity grew especially in Kenya between 1970 and 1990; this growth almost entirely due to the growth in the charismatic or evangelical part. The non-charismatic group remains virtually the same percentage of the population throughout the 80-year period of the chart.

Table 5.11.2 lists the 10 countries in Africa where the AIDS rate is highest. Three of the 4 countries with the highest rates of HIV (over 30%) have fewer than 400,000 with the disease. The two countries with most sufferers, South Africa and Kenya, are 7th and 9th respectively. Which takes priority – the areas where there are the most people affected, or those places where the rate is highest and thus where AIDS is spreading more and more rapidly?

The problem eats at the living heart of African community life today, and if not careful will kill it for tomorrow, and what place then the Christian faith held by so many?

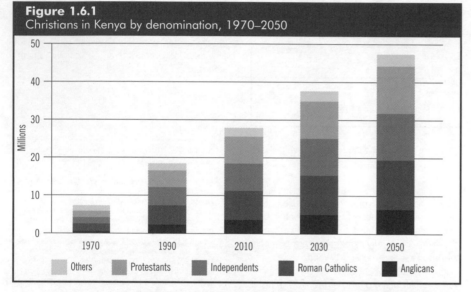

Figure 1.6.1
Christians in Kenya by denomination, 1970–2050

Legend: Others, Protestants, Independents, Roman Catholics, Anglicans

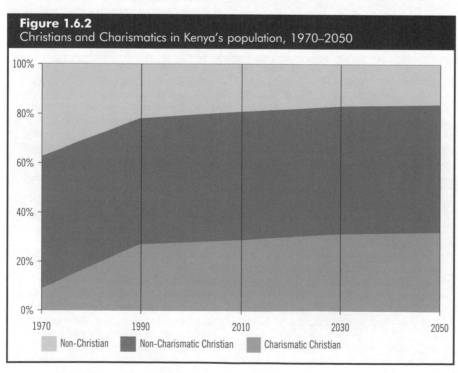

Figure 1.6.2
Christians and Charismatics in Kenya's population, 1970–2050

Legend: Non-Christian, Non-Charismatic Christian, Charismatic Christian

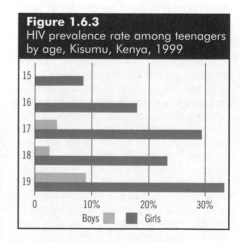

Figure 1.6.3
HIV prevalence rate among teenagers by age, Kisumu, Kenya, 1999

Legend: Boys, Girls

Sources: Work/Reference Manuals and other material from Dr Bernard, Director of Epidemiology in Human Reproduction, Aids Feedback, Liaison for UN and NG organisations, 22, Avenue Riant-Parc, 1209 Geneva, Switzerland, and the *World Christian Encyclopedia*, Dr David Barrett, Oxford University Press, New York and London, 2001. Fig 1.6.3: National AIDS Programme, Kenya and the Population Council in 1999, World Health Organisation and UNAIDS on 1st July 2002; www.unaids.org/html/pub/topics/epidemiology/slides06/Kenya_HIVprevteenag

Churches in the UK

Sources: Individual denominations, Population Census, 2001, *Religious Trends* No 4, English Church Attendance Survey 1998, Office for National Statistics, Research and Statistics Dept., Archbishops' Council and their publications

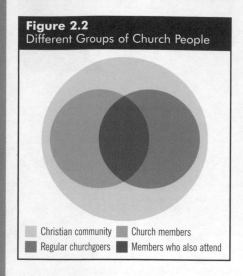

Figure 2.2
Different Groups of Church People

- ⬜ Christian community
- ⬛ Church members
- ⬛ Regular churchgoers
- ⬛ Members who also attend

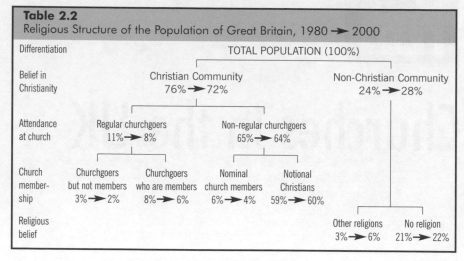

Table 2.2
Religious Structure of the Population of Great Britain, 1980 ➡ 2000

Differentiation						
			TOTAL POPULATION (100%)			
Belief in Christianity		Christian Community 76% ➡ 72%			Non-Christian Community 24% ➡ 28%	
Attendance at church		Regular churchgoers 11% ➡ 8%	Non-regular churchgoers 65% ➡ 64%			
Church member-ship	Churchgoers but not members 3% ➡ 2%	Churchgoers who are members 8% ➡ 6%	Nominal church members 6% ➡ 4%	Notional Christians 59% ➡ 60%		
Religious belief					Other religions 3% ➡ 6%	No religion 21% ➡ 22%

There are three broad measures for describing Christian people, at least in the Western nations, and **Figure 2.2** (not drawn to scale) illustrates how the sub-groups of membership and churchgoers (an overlapping grouping) may be accommodated.

The three circles in this diagram – the outer circle, and the two overlapping circles inside it, which in practice overlap much more – represent three ways of measuring people attached to Christianity. This analysis could of course be applied to any religious group.

Community

The Christian Community has been defined as "all those who would positively identify with belonging to a church even if they may only attend irregularly, or were just baptised as a child"[1] Some take the religious community as the one into which you were born or baptised. Another definition is "those who belong to a particular denomination, however loosely. If Anglican, Roman Catholic, Lutheran, Orthodox or Presbyterian, they will usually approximate to the number baptised in that country".[2] The Methodists keep a 'Community Roll' of such people for each church.

This Christian 'Community' might simply be taken as the total number who ticked "Christian" in the 2001 Population Census. Some equate the Christian Community to Christian "adherents"[3]. The broad thrust of these definitions is clear – all those in a particular country who call themselves Christian. The public's definition of "Christian" is much wider than the church's definition!

In Britain people going into hospital or prison are asked their religion. Many people simply reply "CofE" (Church of England), or "Methodist" or "RC" (Roman Catholic) even if they have no current connection with that particular church. When the Home Office published its figures for the religious affiliation of the prison population in 1990 the percentages were 78% Christian; 6% Other religions and 16% no religion[4], very close to the 2001 Census figures.

De-churched not unchurched

The faintest shaded area in **Figure 2.2** can be labelled "nominal Christians" to show the large percentage of those who call themselves Christians who are outside the regular church community. The percentages in **Table 2.2** show how the groups reflected in those various circles have been changing:

The first of each pair of percentages in **Table 2.2** relates to the year 1980 and the second to 2000. The first line splits the population into Christian v non-Christian, with the 72% from 2001 shown under the Christian Community, having come down from an estimated 76% in 1980.

The line labelled "Attendance" splits that Christian Community into regular churchgoers and those who don't attend regularly. The first group shows the 8% revealed by the 1998 survey having come down from 11% in 1980. This means (by subtraction) that non-regular churchgoers have declined only marginally in these 20 years, and remain the bulk of those who call themselves "Christian".

The third line labelled "Membership" divides these churchgoers/non-goers into whether they are members or not. Many, but not all, of the churchgoers are members: 6% of the 8% in 2000, and 8% of the 11% in 1980. The remaining 2% of churchgoers in 2000 and 3% in 1980 are not members (or perhaps more correctly not *yet* members). This proportion, which is estimated, is becoming a greater proportion of churchgoers. In other words, regular churchgoers are less willing to become church members (especially if they are younger people), reflecting the growing modern trend of being wary in giving commitment.

The "Nominal church members" are so called because they retain church membership but are not regularly attending church (though will very likely go at Easter and Christmas). Their percentage is known since the percentage of members is known, 14% in 1980 and 10% in 2000. Thus the 8% "churchgoers who are members" and the 6% "nominal church

members" for 1980 add to 14%, and the 6% and 4% add to 10% for 2000. These latter people, an increasingly elderly group, are literally dying out, as younger people dislike membership. The small movement recorded here between 1980 and 2000 is likely to accelerate in the next 20 years.

The "Notional Christians" percentages come from subtracting the "nominal church member" percentages from the figures for "non-regular churchgoers" in the line above. This group is growing, albeit slowly over the past 20 years, but will grow more quickly as the nominal Christians decrease. One of the sad things implicit in this percentage is that many of these people have interacted with the church in days gone by. The numbers who used to attend Sunday School attest to that.

The movement reflected in **Table 2.2** is that the proportion of Christians in the population is decreasing. The two main reasons for this are the declining attendance on the one hand and a decreasing number of nominal church members on the other. Both figures in the 72% ➡ 8% gap between those calling themselves Christian and those who go to church are likely to decrease. As **Table 12.3** indicates, by 2020 it is likely to be 50% ➡ 4.4%.

The final line in **Table 2.2** shows both the increasing proportion of the population belonging to other religions and those avowing no religion at all. The other religion percentage is growing by far the most rapidly and is likely to continue to do so as the government forecasts a continuing high number of immigrants coming into the UK over the next 20 years.

[1] Lawson, Mary, editor, 1991, *Austrian Christian Handbook,* MARC Europe, London, Page 15.
[2] *World Churches Handbook,* edited by Peter Brierley, 1997, Christian Research and Lausanne Committee for World Evangelization, London, Page 10.
[3] Such as Johnstone, Patrick, 1993, *Operation World,* OM Publishing, Carlisle.
[4] Figures given in *Religious Trends* No 1, 1998/1999,

The 2001 Population Census showed that 72% of the UK population described themselves as Christian. The percentage varied: it was 72% in both England and Wales but 65% in Scotland and 86% in Northern Ireland. Some have contested the accuracy of the 72% figure; others maintain it is very reasonable. On this page are given arguments for and against.

ARGUMENTS AGAINST

Reporting uncertainty

The Office for National Statistics (ONS) had to adjust its initial estimates for the population because of some counting discrepancies. Could these have included people's religion?

Methodological variations

People in different parts of the UK were asked different questions (see *Religious Trends* No 4 Page 2.2). Both the Scottish and Irish questions made reference to "belonging" which might carry *conceptual* overtones not present in the English and Welsh question.

Different context

In Scotland the question on ethnicity immediately preceded the question on religion, whereas they were separated by other questions on the English and Welsh form.

The Scottish and Irish questions asked about specific denominational allegiance, which the English and Welsh did not.

Social context

In Scotland the proportion of those of other religions even when present, forms a far smaller part of the local community. In England there are particular areas where Asians form a large percentage of the local population. Shortly before the 2001 Census there had been race riots in some of these areas. Steve Bruce would argue this made people tend to tick "Christian" to distance themselves from the alternatives, when otherwise they might not have done so.

Different from other studies

The British Social Attitudes annual study is based on over 3,400 personal interviews. It reported in 2002 41% saying they had no religion, 54% Christian, 4% other religions and 1% not answered. These answers have changed since the study began in 1983. Then they found 31% with no religion, 66% Christian, 2% other religions, 1% not answered. The wording was the same both years: "Do you regard yourself as belonging to any particular religion? If Yes, which?" Could respondents exaggerate to an interviewer?

Steve Bruce would argue that if 41% of a thoroughly representative sample of people can say they have no religion in 2002, how come only 15% nationally said so in 2001?

Imposition by the Head of Household?

The "Head of Household" may ascribe identities to other members of the household rather than specifically ask each of them. However, the figures in **Table 4.4.4** indicate that 65% of their children aged 17 or 18 were Christian but only 55% of their children aged 0 to 2 . This suggests respondents tried to identify their children's religion accurately.

A Christian country: the default option

An old lady had said to Steve Bruce, "I put down Church of Scotland because I wanted to say this is a Christian country." Could this be true of others?

This is close to Professor Philip Jenkins' suggestion in *The Next Christendom*: "People living in ... historical Christian strongholds may default to the word "Christian," simply because they don't identify strongly with any other group."

ARGUMENTS IN FAVOUR

Christian belief

Professor Robin Gill has analysed all the various opinion polls which have asked a question about God since market research surveys first began in 1937. The wording naturally varies from survey to survey, but while the proportion saying they believe in God has decreased across the last half of the 20th century, the percentage is still 67%, not the same as the 72% saying they are Christian, or 78% claiming a religion, but clearly of the same order of magnitude. (See *Religious Trends* No 2 Page 5.9 and No 3 Page 5.7 for details).

Christian values

In 2002, 28% of all Primary pupils were in Church schools, and 15% of all Secondary school pupils. This popularity of Church schools stems partly from their academic excellence, but also from the morals taught in them. Traditional morality is regarded as hugely important by many, and it may well be that Census respondents, believing in such values, and appreciating that they stem from Christian beliefs ticked "Christian" because they wished to be associated with such values.

Baptism statistics

Some denominations baptise or christen infants. Details are given in **Table 4.4.1**. While the percentage of babies being christened is less than the 72%, it remains a high percentage, virtually half of all births. The majority of parents bringing children for infant baptism will be in the 25 to 35 age-group, an age band marked by being more absent than present in the church, so the high baptism rate indicates that those being baptised come from numerous families not attending church regularly. This suggests a favourable disposition towards Christianity in the population at large, of which 72% might perhaps be a reasonable indication.

Marriage statistics

Religious marriages as a proportion of the total of all marriages in England have dropped from 50% in 1991 to 35% in 2000; details are in **Table 4.5.1**. This is partly due to an increasing number of second marriages (most of which do not take place in a church) and the opportunity to be married in "approved premises". **Figure 4.5.2** shows the importance of the latter.

First marriages in church have dropped from 66% in 1991 to 43% in 2003. Most first marriages are by those in their 20s, and the fact that half wish to marry in church suggests a wider affiliation to Christianity.

Funerals

No firm figures are collected on the type of ceremony used at funerals, but the large majority of these are conducted with a religious ceremony, frequently at a crematorium. In one recent survey, 59% of respondents said they had been to a church for a funeral in the past year. That again is of a similar order of magnitude as the 72%.

Economic assessment

In 1995 Littlewoods heavily promoted the FA Cup Final (which they were sponsoring) by designating it "Songs of Praise", and describing the match (in lettering invoking religious symbolism) as "the quest for the Holy Grail". A 1997 series of advertisements for Audi cars involved religious themes. One had a picture of one of their cars as if it were an altar with two tall candles, one at each end, with the slogan "Worship here".

These are but two examples of advertisements by major companies using religious themes. They would not have spent money on them if they didn't recognise that the underlying religious connotations would be understood by those who saw them.

Religious Books

The number of religious books published increased from 2,600 in 1993 to 4,400 in 1994, remaining at about that figure each year since (details *Religious Trends* No 3 Table 6.2.4). No other category of book has seen such a level of increase. This number represents about 4% of books published.

The market must be sustained by the volume of sales, and this indicates many will read a Christian book, irrespective of whether they attend church regularly.

Songs of Praise

During the 1990s the *Songs of Praise* average audience was 4.9 million people each Sunday, slightly more than the average Sunday church attendance! (Details *Religious Trends* No 2 Page 6.5). Half the audience is 65 or over, these 2 million people being twice the number of churchgoers that age.

Sunday School

Part of the attraction of *Songs of Praise* is the fact that many older people in Britain attended Sunday School when they were children, as may be seen in Figure 2.15 of *Religious Trends* No 2. 48% of children born in 1930 attended, for example. Many of these were still alive in 2001, most of whom would certainly have indicated they were Christian in the Census.

Religious or Spiritual?

Did the 2001 Census measure a person's religion or their spirituality? The question without doubt aimed to ask their religion. The Soul of Britain survey, undertaken by the BBC in mid-2000, showed a third, 31%, saying they were "spiritual" and a further 27% who said they were "religious". In the absence of explicit "spiritual" language, most Census respondents had to use the more formal religious wording.

In view of all the above, it may be argued that the 72% figure revealed by the 2001 Population Census is probably as accurate as any other Census statistic, and has a wide degree of affirmation from many other measurements of religious behaviour.

Sources: Implicit Religion: 72% Christian, 8% Attendance, Leaders Briefing No 20, Dr Peter Brierley, Christian Research, London, May 2004; Professor Steve Bruce, Aberdeen University, Letter, *Quadrant,* Christian Research, London, September 2003; *Religion and Social Capital,* Professor Leslie Francis, Chapter 4 in *Public Faith,* SPCK, London, Ed P Avis, 2003.

2

(AVON)
1 Bath & NE Somerset UA
2 City of Bristol UA
3 North Somerset UA
4 South Gloucestershire UA
BEDFORDSHIRE
1 Bedford
2 Luton UA
3 Mid Bedfordshire
4 South Bedfordshire
BERKSHIRE
1 Bracknell Forest UA
2 Reading UA
3 Slough UA
4 West Berkshire UA
5 Windsor & Maidenhead UA
6 Wokingham UA
BUCKINGHAMSHIRE
1 Aylesbury Vale
2 Chiltern
3 Milton Keynes UA
4 South Buckinghamshire
5 Wycombe
CAMBRIDGESHIRE
1 Cambridge
2 East Cambridgeshire
3 Fenland
4 Huntingdonshire
5 Peterborough UA
6 South Cambridgeshire
CHESHIRE
1 Chester
2 Congleton
3 Crewe & Nantwich
4 Ellesmere Port & Neston
5 Halton UA
6 Macclesfield
7 Vale Royal
8 Warrington UA
(CLEVELAND)
1 Hartlepool UA
2 Middlesbrough UA
3 Redcar & Cleveland UA
4 Stockton-on-Tees UA
CORNWALL
1 Caradon
2 Carrick
3 Kerrier
4 North Cornwall
5 Penwith
6 Restormel
7 Isles of Scilly
CUMBRIA
1 Allerdale
2 Barrow-in-Furness
3 Carlisle
4 Copeland
5 Eden
6 South Lakeland
DERBYSHIRE
1 Amber Valley
2 Bolsover
3 Chesterfield
4 Derby UA
5 Derbyshire Dales
6 Erewash
7 High Peak
8 North East Derbyshire
9 South Derbyshire
DEVON
1 East Devon
2 Exeter
3 Mid Devon
4 North Devon
5 Plymouth UA
6 South Hams
7 Teignbridge
8 Torbay UA
9 Torridge
10 West Devon

DORSET
1 Bournemouth UA
2 Christchurch
3 East Dorset
4 North Dorset
5 Poole UA
6 Purbeck
7 West Dorset
8 Weymouth & Portland
DURHAM
1 Chester-le-Street
2 Darlington UA
3 Derwentside
4 Durham
5 Easington
6 Sedgefield
7 Teesdale
8 Wear Valley
EAST SUSSEX
1 Brighton & Hove UA
2 Eastbourne
3 Hastings
4 Lewes
5 Rother
6 Wealden
EAST YORKSHIRE
1 City of Kingston upon Hull UA
2 East Riding of Yorkshire UA
ESSEX
1 Basildon
2 Braintree
3 Brentwood
4 Castle Point
5 Chelmsford
6 Colchester
7 Epping Forest
8 Harlow
9 Maldon
10 Rochford
11 Southend-on-Sea UA
12 Tendring
13 Thurrock UA
14 Uttlesford
GLOUCESTERSHIRE
1 Cheltenham
2 Cotswold
3 Forest of Dean
4 Gloucester
5 Stroud
6 Tewkesbury
GREATER LONDON
1 City of London
2 Islington
3 Hackney
4 Tower Hamlets
5 Greenwich
6 Lewisham
7 Southwark
8 Lambeth
9 Wandsworth
10 Hammersmith
11 Kensington & Chelsea
12 City of Westminster
13 Camden
14 Haringey
15 Enfield
16 Waltham Forest
17 Redbridge
18 Newham
19 Barking & Dagenham
20 Havering
21 Bexley
22 Bromley
23 Croydon
24 Sutton
25 Merton
26 Kingston upon Thames
27 Richmond
28 Hounslow
29 Hillingdon

30 Ealing
31 Harrow
32 Brent
33 Barnet
GREATER MANCHESTER
1 Bolton
2 Bury
3 Manchester
4 Oldham
5 Rochdale
6 Salford
7 Stockport
8 Tameside
9 Trafford
10 Wigan
HAMPSHIRE
1 Basingstoke & Deane
2 East Hampshire
3 Eastleigh
4 Fareham
5 Gosport
6 Hart
7 Havant
8 New Forest
9 Portsmouth UA
10 Rushmoor
11 Southampton UA
12 Test Valley
13 Winchester
HEREFORDSHIRE UA
HERTFORDSHIRE
1 Broxbourne
2 Dacorum
3 East Hertfordshire
4 Hertsmere
5 North Hertfordshire
6 St Albans
7 Stevenage
8 Three Rivers
9 Watford
10 Welwyn Hatfield
ISLE OF WIGHT UA
KENT
1 Ashford
2 Canterbury
3 Dartford
4 Dover
5 Gravesham
6 Maidstone
7 Medway UA
8 Sevenoaks
9 Shepway
10 Swale
11 Thanet
12 Tonbridge & Malling
13 Tunbridge Wells
LANCASHIRE
1 Blackburn with Darwen UA
2 Blackpool UA
3 Burnley
4 Chorley
5 Fylde
6 Hyndburn
7 Lancaster
8 Pendle
9 Preston
10 Ribble Valley
11 Rossendale
12 South Ribble
13 West Lancashire
14 Wyre
LEICESTERSHIRE
1 Blaby
2 Charnwood
3 Harborough
4 Hinckley & Bosworth
5 Leicester UA
6 Melton
7 North West Leicestershire
8 Oadby & Wigston

9 Rutland UA
LINCOLNSHIRE
1 Boston
2 East Lindsey
3 Lincoln
4 North East Lincolnshire UA
5 North Kesteven
6 North Lincolnshire UA
7 South Holland
8 South Kesteven
9 West Lindsey
MERSEYSIDE
1 Knowsley
2 Liverpool
3 St Helens
4 Sefton
5 Wirral
NORFOLK
1 Breckland
2 Broadland
3 Great Yarmouth
4 Kings Lynn & West Norfolk
5 North Norfolk
6 Norwich
7 South Norfolk
NORTH YORKSHIRE
1 Craven
2 Hambleton
3 Harrogate
4 Richmondshire
5 Ryedale
6 Scarborough
7 Selby
8 York UA
NORTHAMPTONSHIRE
1 Corby
2 Daventry
3 East Northamptonshire
4 Kettering
5 Northampton
6 South Northamptonshire
7 Wellingborough
NORTHUMBERLAND
1 Alnwick
2 Berwick-upon-Tweed
3 Blyth Valley
4 Castle Morpeth
5 Tynedale
6 Wansbeck
NOTTINGHAMSHIRE
1 Ashfield
2 Bassetlaw
3 Broxtowe
4 Gedling
5 Mansfield
6 Newark & Sherwood
7 Nottingham UA
8 Rushcliffe
OXFORDSHIRE
1 Cherwell
2 Oxford
3 South Oxfordshire
4 Vale of White Horse
5 West Oxfordshire
SHROPSHIRE
1 Bridgnorth
2 North Shropshire
3 Oswestry
4 Shrewsbury & Atcham
5 South Shropshire
6 Telford & Wrekin UA
SOMERSET
1 Mendip
2 Sedgemoor
3 South Somerset
4 Taunton Deane
5 West Somerset
SOUTH YORKSHIRE
1 Barnsley
2 Doncaster

3 Rotherham
4 Sheffield
STAFFORDSHIRE
1 Cannock Chase
2 East Staffordshire
3 Lichfield
4 Newcastle-under-Lyme
5 Stafford
6 Staffordshire Moorlands
7 South Staffordshire
8 Stoke-on-Trent UA
9 Tamworth
SUFFOLK
1 Babergh
2 Forest Heath
3 Ipswich
4 Mid Suffolk
5 St Edmundsbury
6 Suffolk Coastal
7 Waveney
SURREY
1 Elmbridge
2 Epsom & Ewell
3 Guildford
4 Mole Valley
5 Reigate & Banstead
6 Runnymede
7 Spelthorne
8 Surrey Heath
9 Tandridge
10 Waverley
11 Woking
TYNE & WEAR
1 Gateshead
2 Newcastle upon Tyne
3 North Tyneside
4 South Tyneside
5 Sunderland
WARWICKSHIRE
1 North Warwickshire
2 Nuneaton & Bedworth
3 Rugby
4 Stratford-upon-Avon
5 Warwick
WEST MIDLANDS
1 Birmingham
2 Coventry
3 Dudley
4 Sandwell
5 Solihull
6 Walsall
7 Wolverhampton
WEST SUSSEX
1 Adur
2 Arun
3 Chichester
4 Crawley
5 Horsham
6 Mid Sussex
7 Worthing
WEST YORKSHIRE
1 Bradford
2 Calderdale
3 Kirklees
4 Leeds
5 Wakefield
WILTSHIRE
1 Kennet
2 North Wiltshire
3 Salisbury
4 Swindon UA
5 West Wiltshire
WORCESTERSHIRE
1 Bromsgrove
2 Malvern Hills
3 Redditch
4 Worcester
5 Wychavon
6 Wyre Forest

NORTHERN IRELAND
ANTRIM
1 Antrim
2 Ballymena
3 Ballymoney
4 Belfast
5 Carrickfergus
6 Larne
7 Lisburn
8 Moyle
9 Newtonabbey
ARMAGH
1 Armagh
2 Craigavon
DOWN
1 Ards
2 Banbridge
3 Castlereagh
4 Down
5 Newry & Mourne
6 North Down
FERMANAGH
1 Fermanagh
LONDONDERRY
1 Coleraine
2 Derry
3 Limavady
4 Magherafelt
TYRONE
1 Cookstown
2 Dungannon
3 Omagh
4 Strabane

SCOTLAND
1 City of Aberdeen
2 City of Dundee
3 City of Edinburgh
4 City of Glasgow
5 Clackmannanshire
6 East Ayrshire
7 East Dunbartonshire
8 East Lothian
9 East Renfrewshire
10 Falkirk
11 Inverclyde
12 Midlothian
13 North Ayrshire
14 North Lanarkshire
15 Renfrewshire
16 South Ayrshire
17 South Lanarkshire
18 West Dunbartonshire
19 West Lothian

WALES
1 Isle of Anglesey UA
2 Blaenau Gwent UA
3 Bridgend UA
4 Caerphilly UA
5 Cardiff UA
6 Carmarthenshire UA
7 Ceredigion UA
8 Conwy UA
9 Denbighshire UA
10 Flintshire UA
11 Gwynedd UA
12 Merthyr Tydfil UA
13 Monmouthshire UA
14 Neith Port Talbot UA
15 Newport UA
16 Pembrokeshire UA
17 Powys UA
18 Rhondda, Cynon, Taff UA
19 Swansea UA
20 Torfaen UA
21 Vale of Glamorgan UA
22 Wrexham UA

FOR KEYS, SEE PAGE 2.4

For Scotland, see *Religious Trends* No 4 Page 2.4

GREATER LONDON

2

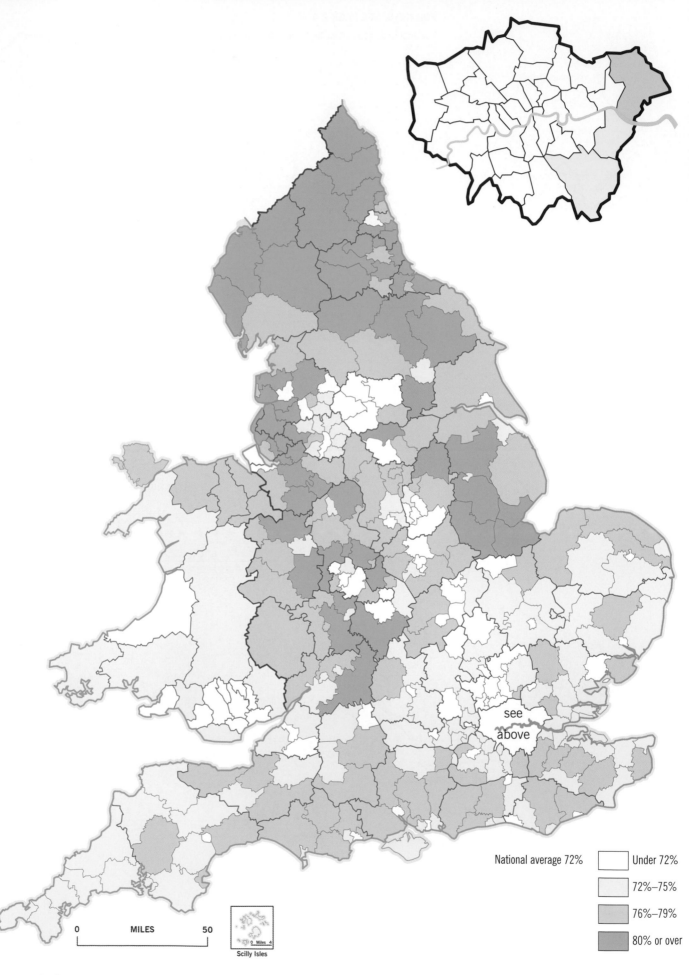

National average 72%

Under 72%

72%–75%

76%–79%

80% or over

see above

0 MILES 50

0 Miles 4
Scilly Isles

2

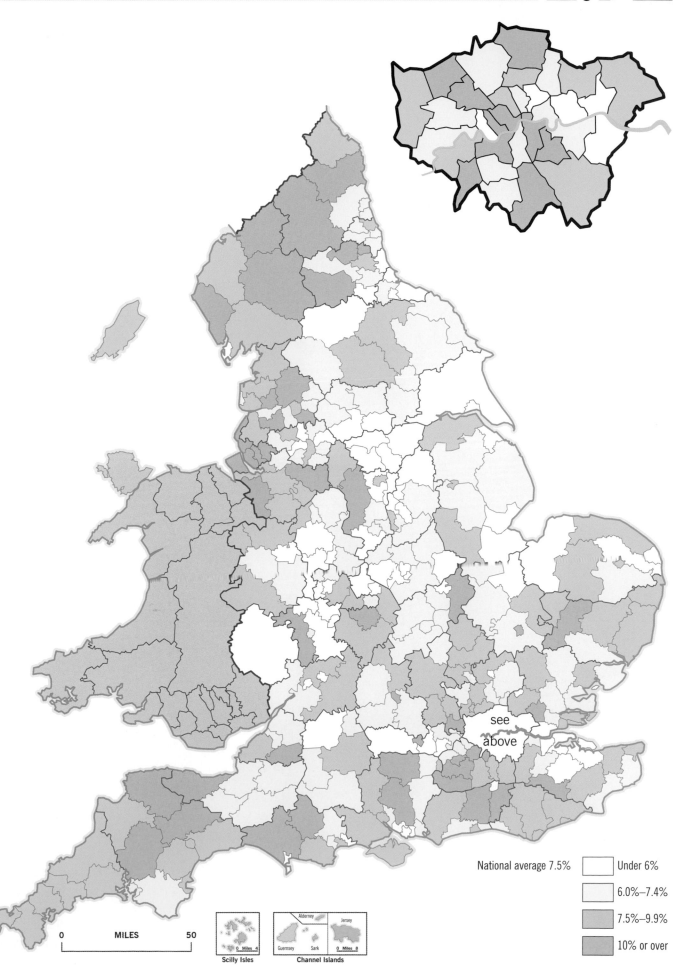

National average 7.5%

- Under 6%
- 6.0%–7.4%
- 7.5%–9.9%
- 10% or over

MILES

0   50

Scilly Isles   Channel Islands

Alderney

Guernsey   Sark   Jersey

2

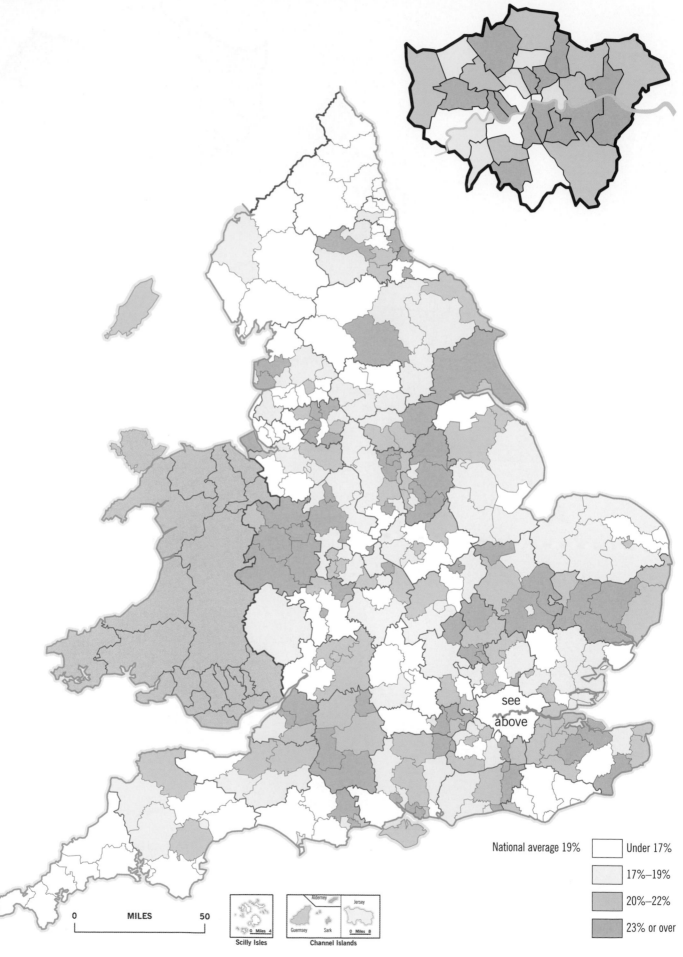

see
above

National average 19%

Under 17%

17%–19%

20%–22%

23% or over

0   MILES   50

0 Miles 4
Scilly Isles

Alderney
Jersey
Guernsey   Sark
0 Miles 8
Channel Islands

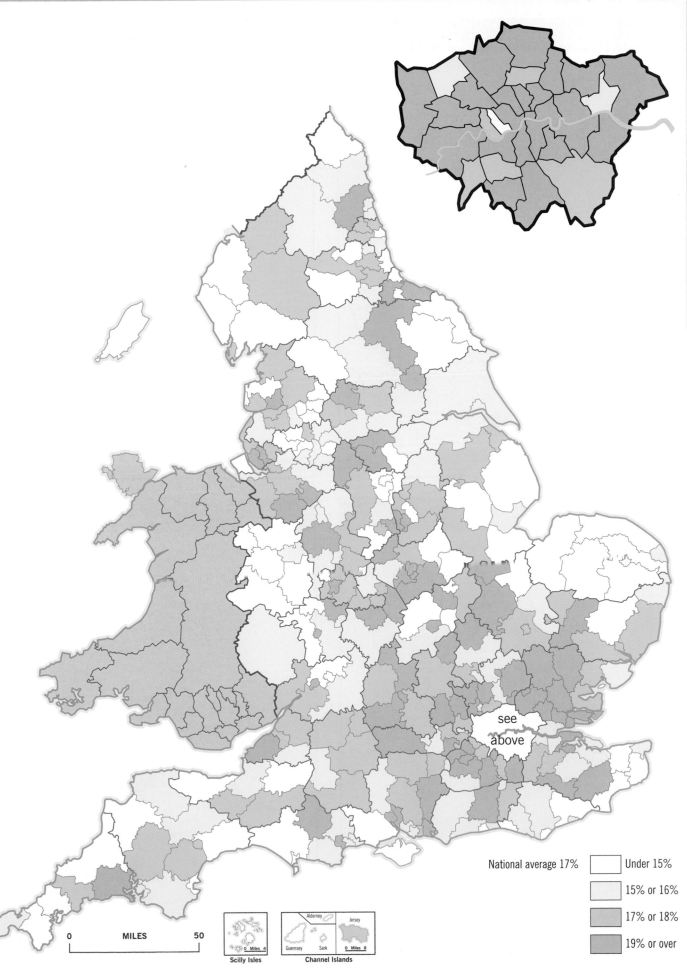

National average 17%

	Under 15%
	15% or 16%
	17% or 18%
	19% or over

MILES

0   50

Scilly Isles

Alderney   Jersey

Guernsey   Sark

Channel Islands

see
above

Figure 2.10.1
Christians as a Percentage of the Population, 2001

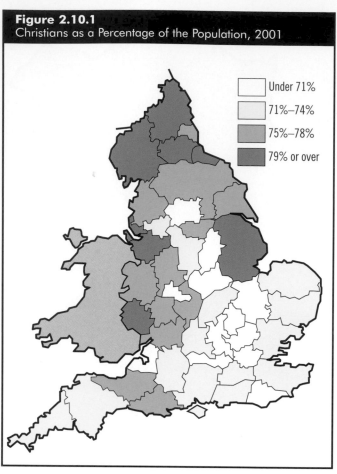

Under 71%

71%–74%

75%–78%

79% or over

Figure 2.10.2
Muslims as a Percentage of the Population, 2001

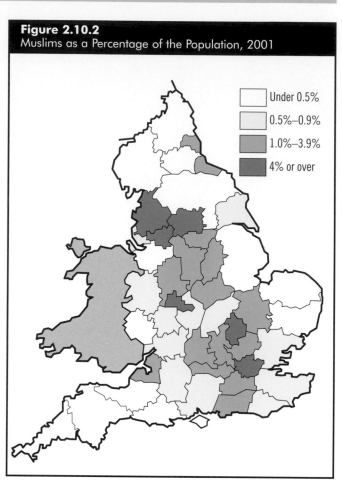

Under 0.5%

0.5%–0.9%

1.0%–3.9%

4% or over

Figure 2.10.3
Buddhists as a Percentage of the Population, 2001

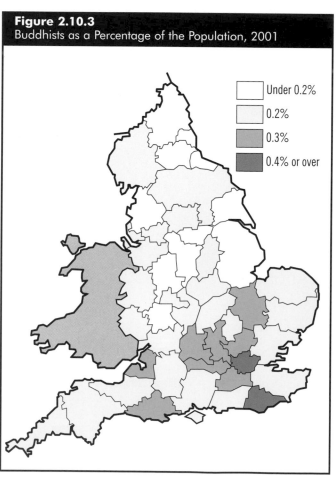

Under 0.2%

0.2%

0.3%

0.4% or over

Figure 2.10.4
Hindus as a Percentage of the Population, 2001

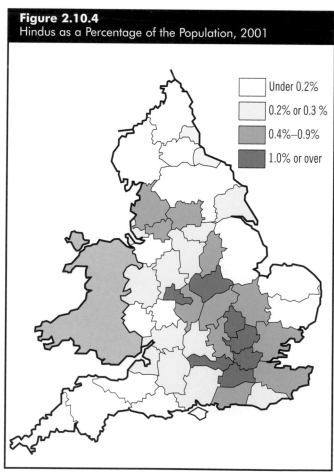

Under 0.2%

0.2% or 0.3 %

0.4%–0.9%

1.0% or over

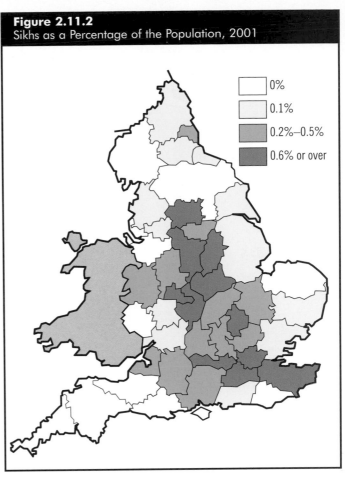

Figure 2.11.1
Jews as a Percentage of the Population, 2001

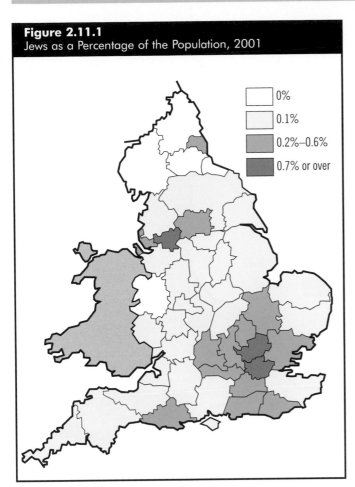

0%
0.1%
0.2%–0.6%
0.7% or over

Figure 2.11.2
Sikhs as a Percentage of the Population, 2001

0%
0.1%
0.2%–0.5%
0.6% or over

2

Figure 2.11.3
Other Religions as a Percentage of the Population, 2001

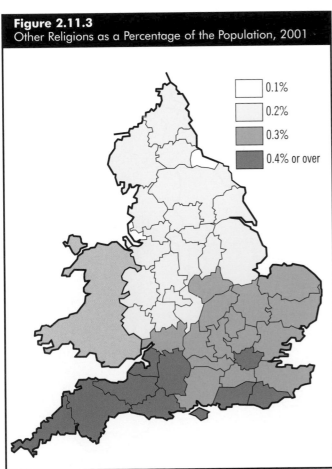

0.1%
0.2%
0.3%
0.4% or over

Figure 2.11.4
No Religion as a Percentage of the Population, 2001

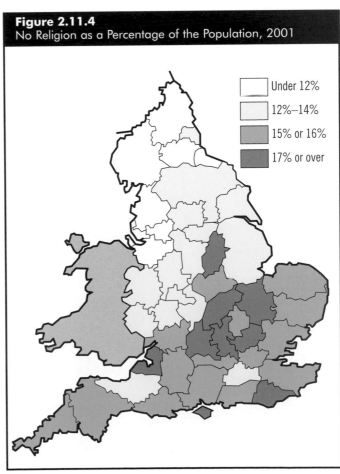

Under 12%
12%–14%
15% or 16%
17% or over

Figure 2.12.1
Christians as a Percentage of the Population, 2001

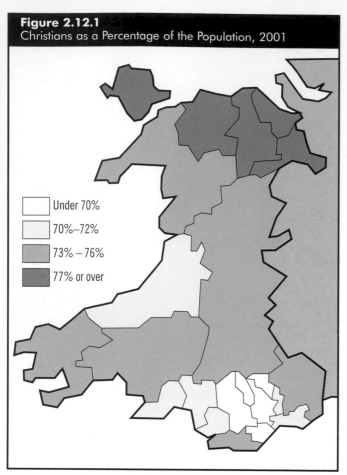

Under 70%

70%–72%

73% – 76%

77% or over

Figure 2.12.2
Muslims as a Percentage of the Population, 2001

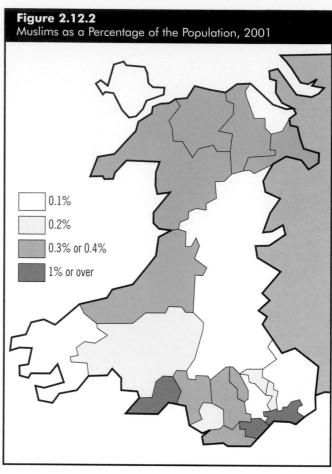

0.1%

0.2%

0.3% or 0.4%

1% or over

Figure 2.12.3
Buddhists as a Percentage of the Population, 2001

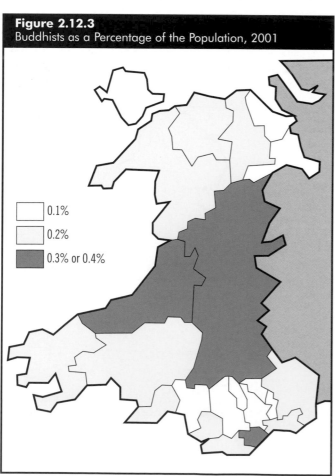

0.1%

0.2%

0.3% or 0.4%

Figure 2.12.4
Hindus as a Percentage of the Population, 2001

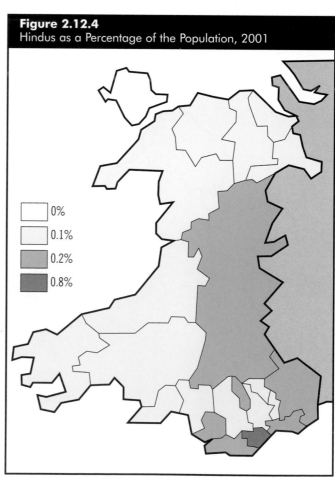

0%

0.1%

0.2%

0.8%

Figure 2.13.1
Jews as a Percentage of the Population, 2001

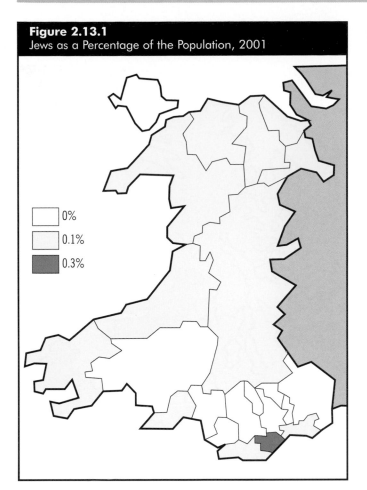

- 0%
- 0.1%
- 0.3%

Figure 2.13.2
Sikhs as a Percentage of the Population, 2001

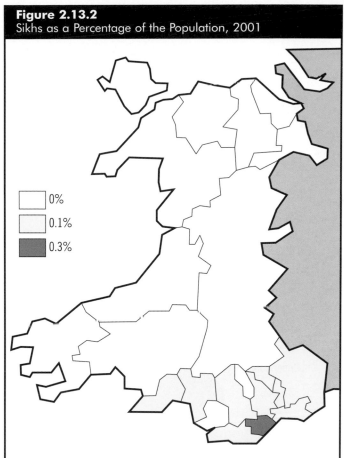

- 0%
- 0.1%
- 0.3%

Figure 2.13.3
Other Religions as a Percentage of the Population, 2001

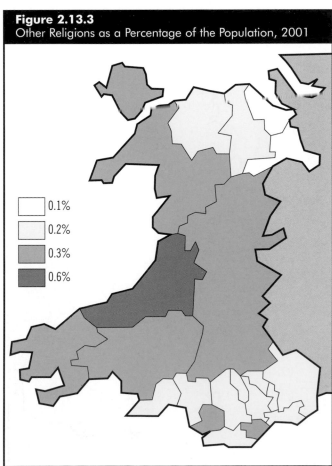

- 0.1%
- 0.2%
- 0.3%
- 0.6%

Figure 2.13.4
No Religion as a Percentage of the Population, 2001

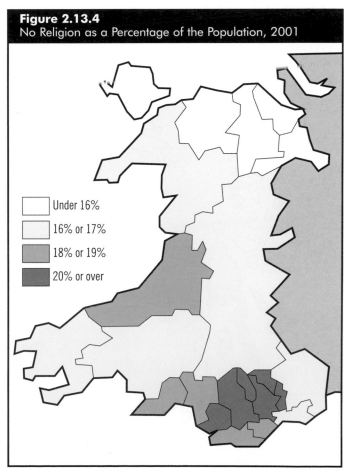

- Under 16%
- 16% or 17%
- 18% or 19%
- 20% or over

Figure 2.14.1
Christians as a Percentage of the Population, 2001

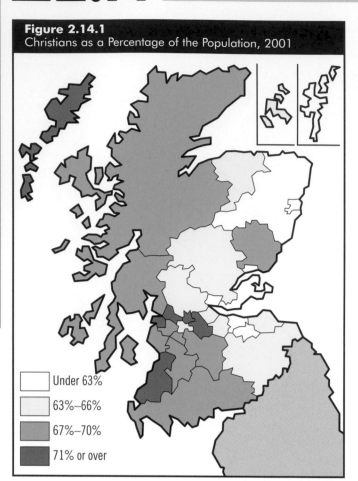

Under 63%

63%–66%

67%–70%

71% or over

Figure 2.14.2
Muslims as a Percentage of the Population, 2001

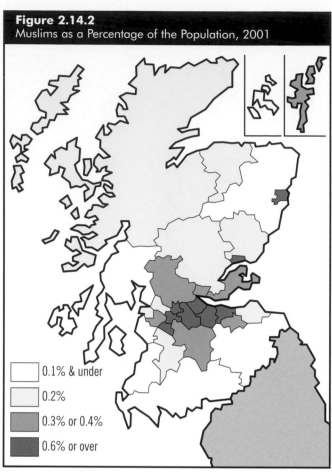

0.1% & under

0.2%

0.3% or 0.4%

0.6% or over

Figure 2.14.3
Buddhists as a Percentage of the Population, 2001

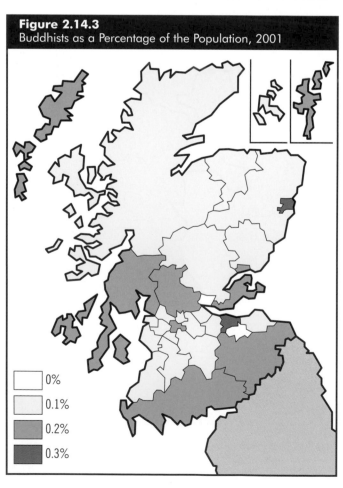

0%

0.1%

0.2%

0.3%

Figure 2.14.4
Hindus as a Percentage of the Population, 2001

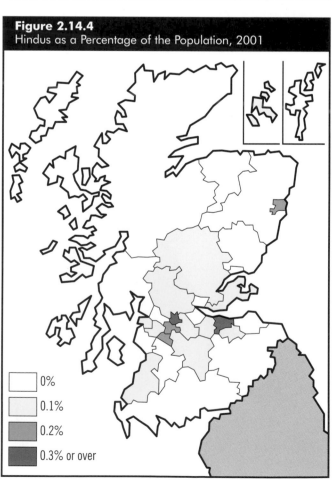

0%

0.1%

0.2%

0.3% or over

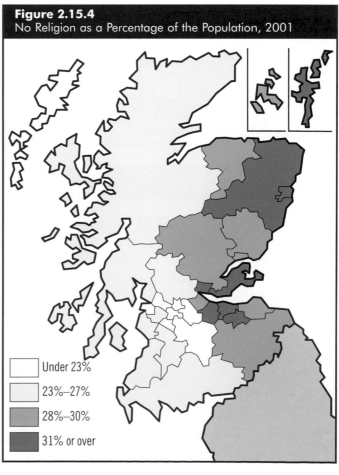
Figure 2.15.1
Jews as a Percentage of the Population, 2001

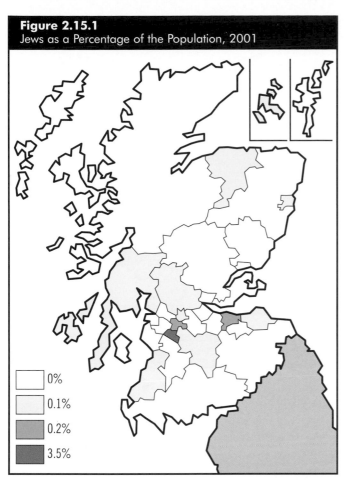

- 0%
- 0.1%
- 0.2%
- 3.5%

Figure 2.15.2
Sikhs as a Percentage of the Population, 2001

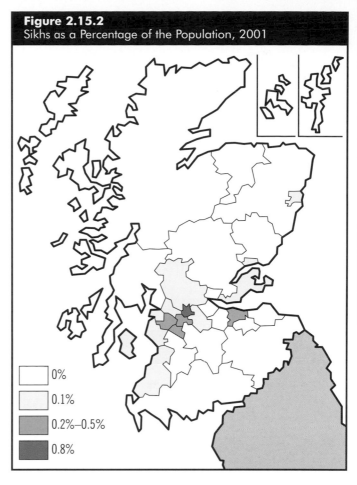

- 0%
- 0.1%
- 0.2%–0.5%
- 0.8%

Figure 2.15.3
Other Religions as a Percentage of the Population, 2001

- 0.2% or 0.3%
- 0.4%
- 0.5%
- 0.6% or over

Figure 2.15.4
No Religion as a Percentage of the Population, 2001

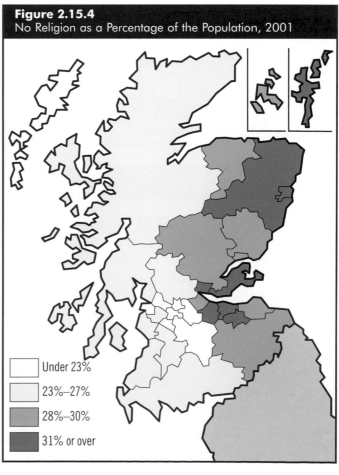

- Under 23%
- 23%–27%
- 28%–30%
- 31% or over

Figure 2.16.1
Roman Catholics as a Percentage of the Population, 1991

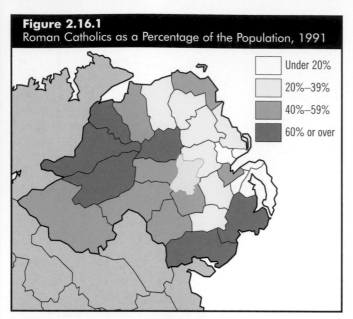

Under 20%
20%–39%
40%–59%
60% or over

Figure 2.16.2
Roman Catholics as a Percentage of the Population, 2001

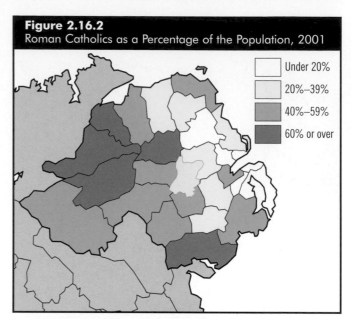

Under 20%
20%–39%
40%–59%
60% or over

Figure 2.16.3 Presbyterian Church of Ireland
as a Percentage of the Population, 1991

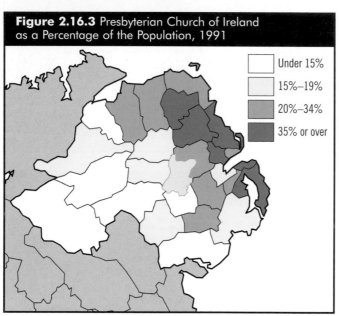

Under 15%
15%–19%
20%–34%
35% or over

Figure 2.16.4 Presbyterian Church of Ireland
as a Percentage of the Population, 2001

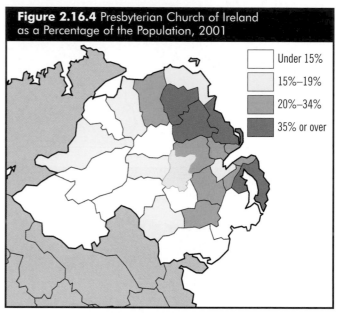

Under 15%
15%–19%
20%–34%
35% or over

Figure 2.16.5 Church of Ireland
as a Percentage of the Population, 1991

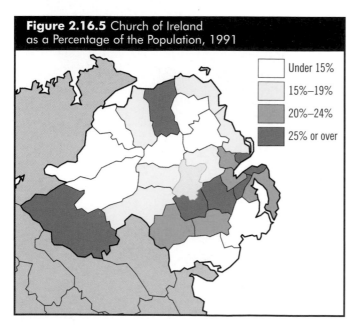

Under 15%
15%–19%
20%–24%
25% or over

Figure 2.16.6 Church of Ireland
as a Percentage of the Population, 2001

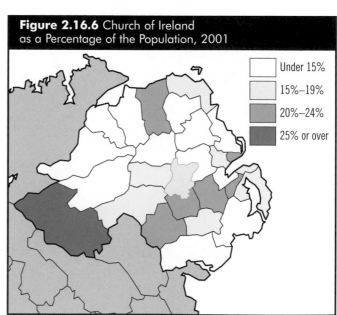

Under 15%
15%–19%
20%–24%
25% or over

Figure 2.17.1
Methodists as a Percentage of the Population, 1991

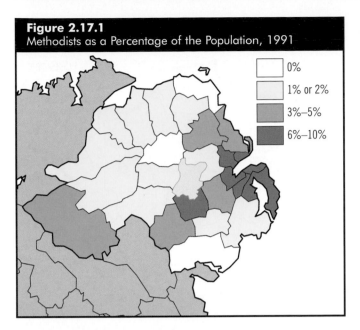

	0%
	1% or 2%
	3%–5%
	6%–10%

Figure 2.17.2
Methodists as a Percentage of the Population, 2001

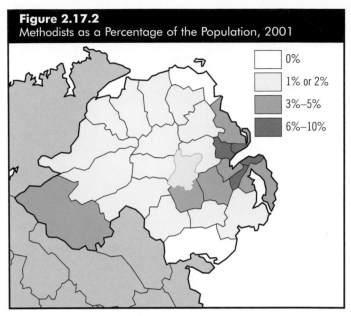

	0%
	1% or 2%
	3%–5%
	6%–10%

Figure 2.17.3
Other Christian as a Percentage of the Population, 1991

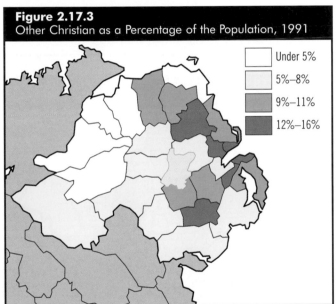

	Under 5%
	5%–8%
	9%–11%
	12%–16%

Figure 2.17.4
Other Christian as a Percentage of the Population, 2001

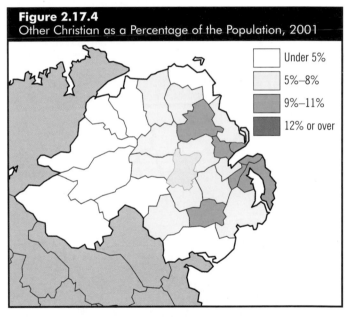

	Under 5%
	5%–8%
	9%–11%
	12% or over

Figure 2.17.5
No Religion as a Percentage of the Population, 1991

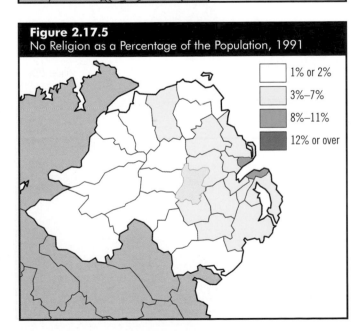

	1% or 2%
	3%–7%
	8%–11%
	12% or over

Figure 2.17.6
No Religion as a Percentage of the Population, 2001

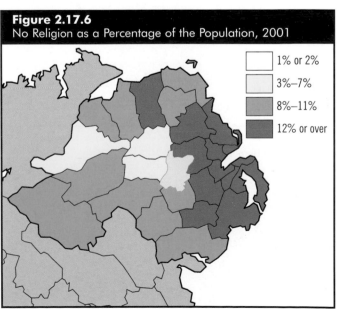

	1% or 2%
	3%–7%
	8%–11%
	12% or over

Figure 2.18.1
Christians as a Percentage of the Population, 2001

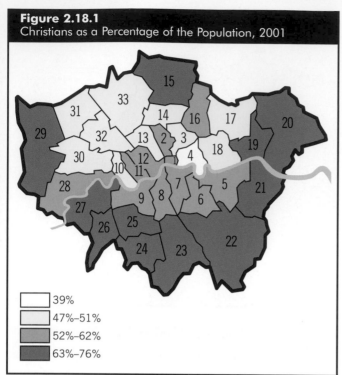

☐	39%
☐	47%–51%
▨	52%–62%
▨	63%–76%

Figure 2.18.2
Muslims as a Percentage of the Population, 2001

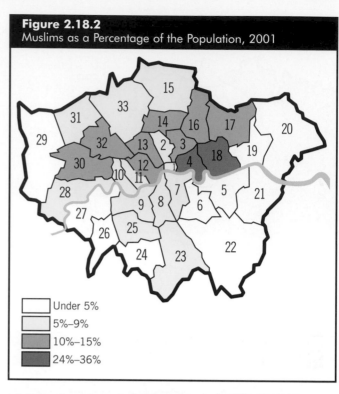

☐	Under 5%
☐	5%–9%
▨	10%–15%
▨	24%–36%

Figure 2.18.3
Buddhists as a Percentage of the Population, 2001

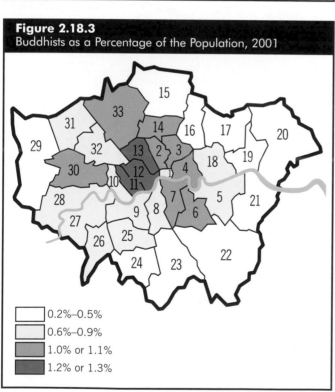

☐	0.2%–0.5%
☐	0.6%–0.9%
▨	1.0% or 1.1%
▨	1.2% or 1.3%

Figure 2.18.4
Hindus as a Percentage of the Population, 2001

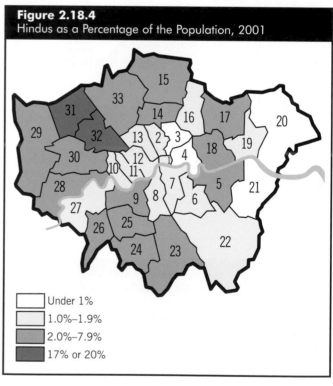

☐	Under 1%
☐	1.0%–1.9%
▨	2.0%–7.9%
▨	17% or 20%

Greater London Boroughs

1	City of London	12	City of Westminster	23	Croydon
2	Islington	13	Camden	24	Sutton
3	Hackney	14	Haringey	25	Merton
4	Tower Hamlets	15	Enfield	26	Kingston upon Thames
5	Greenwich	16	Waltham Forest	27	Richmond
6	Lewisham	17	Redbridge	28	Hounslow
7	Southwark	18	Newham	29	Hillingdon
8	Lambeth	19	Barking & Dagenham	30	Ealing
9	Wandsworth	20	Havering	31	Harrow
10	Hammersmith	21	Bexley	32	Brent
11	Kensington & Chelsea	22	Bromley	33	Barnet

The figures underlying these maps are given in *Religious Trends* No 4 2003/2004 Page 4.4

Figure 2.19.1
Jews as a Percentage of the Population, 2001

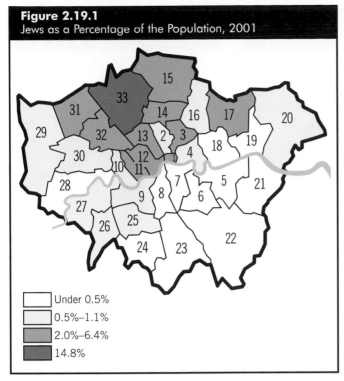

Under 0.5%
0.5%–1.1%
2.0%–6.4%
14.8%

Figure 2.19.2
Sikhs as a Percentage of the Population, 2001

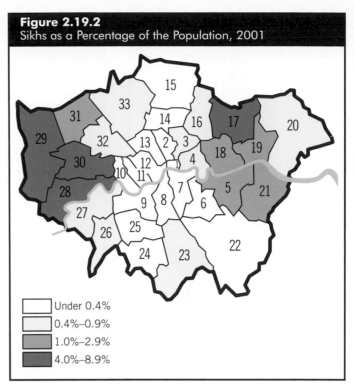

Under 0.4%
0.4%–0.9%
1.0%–2.9%
4.0%–8.9%

Figure 2.19.3
Other Religions as a Percentage of the Population, 2001

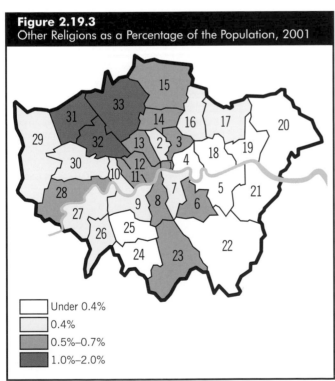

Under 0.4%
0.4%
0.5%–0.7%
1.0%–2.0%

Figure 2.19.4
No Religion as a Percentage of the Population, 2001

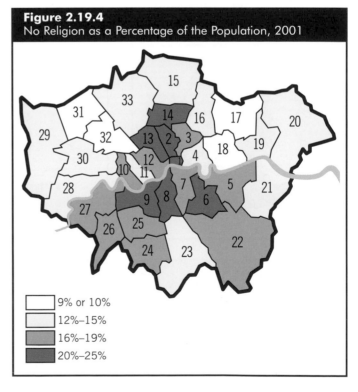

9% or 10%
12%–15%
16%–19%
20%–25%

The figures underlying these maps are given
in *Religious Trends* No 4 2003/2004 Page 4.4

Figure 2.20.1
Percentage of Infants Baptised in the C of E under 1 year of age, 1992

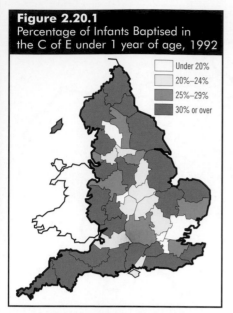

Under 20%
20%–24%
25%–29%
30% or over

Figure 2.20.2
Percentage of Infants Baptised in the C of E under 1 year of age, 1997

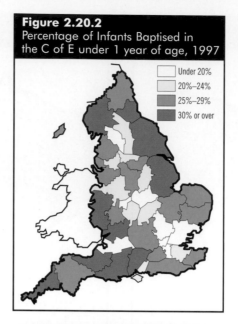

Under 20%
20%–24%
25%–29%
30% or over

Figure 2.20.3
Percentage of Infants Baptised in the C of E under 1 year of age, 2002

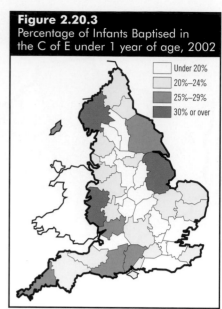

Under 20%
20%–24%
25%–29%
30% or over

Figure 2.20.4
Recurring Income less Expenditure in 2002

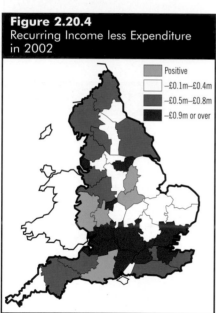

Positive
−£0.1m–£0.4m
−£0.5m–£0.8m
−£0.9m or over

Figure 2.20.5 Number of churches with usual Sunday Attendance of 350 or more, 2003

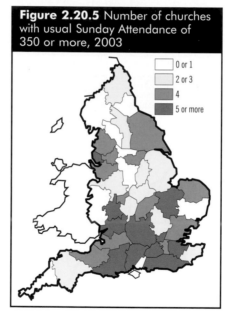

0 or 1
2 or 3
4
5 or more

Figures 2.20.1–3 trace the reducing proportion of babies who are baptised over the years 1992-2002. The average percentage of 26% in 1992 had fallen to 23% by 1997 and to 18% by 2002, indicating an accelerating rate of decline.

Figure 2.20.4 takes from the unrestricted recurring income in each Diocese in 2002 the recurring expenditure. For all but five Dioceses (shown in green) the result was negative, that is, recurring expenditure exceeded income. In a quarter of the Dioceses, 11, shown in dark red, the difference was £0.9 million or more. These Dioceses are likely to be either urban or located in the south or south east.

The numbers for **Figures 2.20.1–5** are given in **Table 8.3.3**.

Figure 2.20.6
Archidiaconal Areas of the Church of England

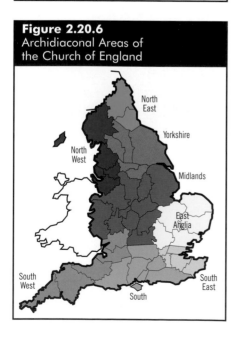

North East
Yorkshire
North West
Midlands
East Anglia
South West
South
South East

Figure 2.20.7
Dioceses of the Church of England

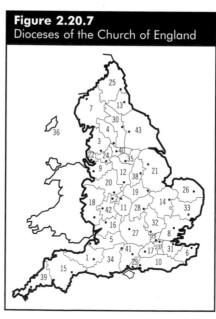

Table 2.20
Dioceses of the Church of England

1 Bath & Wells	16 Gloucester	31 Rochester
2 Birmingham	17 Guildford	32 St Albans
3 Blackburn*	18 Hereford	33 St Edmundsbury
4 Bradford*	19 Leicester	& Ipswich
5 Bristol	20 Lichfield	34 Salisbury
6 Canterbury	21 Lincoln	35 Sheffield*
7 Carlisle*	22 Liverpool*	36 Sodor & Man*
8 Chelmsford	23 London	37 Southwark
9 Chester*	24 Manchester*	38 Southwell and
10 Chichester	25 Newcastle*	Nottingham*
11 Coventry	26 Norwich	39 Truro
12 Derby	27 Oxford	40 Wakefield*
13 Durham*	28 Peterborough	41 Winchester
14 Ely	29 Portsmouth	42 Worcester
15 Exeter	30 Ripon & Leeds*	43 York*
		44 Europe
		(not shown)

*indicates Northern Province

Table 2.21.1 — ENGLAND
Sunday Church Attendance in England by Age and Gender, 1980–2010

Age	MALE							FEMALE						
	1980	1985	1990	1995	2000	2005	2010	1980	1985	1990	1995	2000	2005	2010
<15	612,900	535,500	496,100	382,600	323,700	231,600	127,900	612,200	546,200	520,500	432,600	345,500	274,400	189,100
15–19	171,500	145,000	123,300	93,600	64,900	46,700	27,800	225,700	200,400	181,800	154,400	128,800	85,500	57,600
20–29	227,000	196,000	177,400	139,200	108,500	76,900	46,500	292,000	275,200	261,300	240,200	221,600	195,400	152,800
30–44	349,500	320,400	302,000	258,600	218,000	173,100	136,800	444,500	446,200	450,700	423,100	400,400	377,000	350,300
45–64	418,700	393,500	381,300	353,700	330,000	320,300	305,500	539,400	543,000	554,400	542,300	536,200	546,800	546,100
65/65+	320,300	323,200	330,700	312,200	340,900	384,600	416,000	525,000	530,100	538,700	532,000	535,200	552,600	563,400
Total	2,099,900	1,913,600	1,810,800	1,539,900	1,386,000	1,233,200	1,060,500	2,638,800	2,541,100	2,507,400	2,324,600	2,167,700	2,031,700	1,859,300
Grand Total (Male + Female)								4,738,700	4,454,700	4,318,200	3,864,500	3,553,700	3,264,900	2,919,800

Table 2.21.2 — WALES
Sunday Church Attendance in Wales by Age and Gender, 1980–2010

Age	MALE							FEMALE						
	1980	1985	1990	1995	2000	2005	2010	1980	1985	1990	1995	2000	2005	2010
<15	43,900	32,640	21,370	15,300	11,230	9,040	6,850	59,390	47,050	34,720	27,040	22,090	19,310	16,540
15-19	11,330	9,360	7,400	5,690	4,890	4,030	3,160	15,700	13,950	12,190	10,830	9,630	8,630	7,620
20-29	13,120	12,810	12,500	9,840	8,250	6,820	5,390	18,660	19,610	20,560	17,310	15,800	13,960	12,110
30-44	21,800	20,060	18,310	14,360	12,470	10,420	8,370	33,820	33,690	33,560	29,760	27,250	24,660	22,060
45-64	34,070	29,130	24,200	19,210	16,740	14,730	12,720	52,840	48,600	44,350	39,550	36,570	35,050	33,540
65/65+	32,640	27,870	23,100	19,620	17,070	14,730	12,380	58,530	53,370	48,210	44,560	41,790	38,880	35,970
Total	156,860	131,870	106,880	84,020	70,650	59,770	48,870	238,940	216,270	193,590	169,050	153,130	140,490	127,840
Grand Total (Male + Female)								395,800	348,140	300,470	253,070	223,780	200,260	176,710

Table 2.21.3 — SCOTLAND
Sunday Church Attendance in Scotland by Age and Gender, 1980–2010

Age	MALE							FEMALE						
	1980	1985	1990	1995	2000	2005	2010	1980	1985	1990	1995	2000	2005	2010
<15	100,290	87,630	74,660	61,080	47,320	32,420	18,520	124,540	107,960	90,980	73,240	57,250	35,910	18,860
15-19	18,280	16,980	15,660	14,220	12,770	10,970	9,420	27,800	24,530	21,180	17,660	15,100	11,160	9,570
20-29	26,610	24,600	22,540	20,320	18,070	15,340	12,960	56,690	48,750	40,620	32,140	24,500	15,380	8,790
30-44	45,500	42,810	40,050	37,050	34,010	30,030	26,710	93,020	84,750	76,260	67,250	55,110	42,410	29,930
45-64	77,540	74,580	71,540	68,100	64,610	59,280	55,220	133,720	126,140	118,350	109,830	99,210	83,670	68,300
65/65+	58,230	59,190	60,170	60,870	61,570	59,480	57,530	124,880	122,040	119,090	115,520	112,880	114,850	116,390
Total	326,450	305,790	284,620	261,640	238,350	207,520	180,360	560,650	514,170	466,480	415,640	364,050	303,380	251,840
Grand Total (Male + Female)								887,100	819,960	751,100	677,280	602,400	510,900	432,200

Table 2.21.4 — TOTAL: GREAT BRITAIN
Sunday Church Attendance in Great Britain by Age and Gender, 1980–2010

Age	MALE							FEMALE						
	1980	1985	1990	1995	2000	2005	2010	1980	1985	1990	1995	2000	2005	2010
<15	757,090	655,770	592,130	458,980	382,250	273,060	153,270	796,130	701,210	646,200	532,880	424,840	329,620	224,500
15-19	201,110	171,340	146,360	113,510	82,560	61,700	40,380	269,200	238,880	215,170	182,890	153,530	105,290	74,790
20-29	266,730	233,410	212,440	169,360	134,820	99,060	64,850	367,350	343,560	322,480	289,650	261,900	224,740	173,700
30-44	416,800	383,270	360,360	310,010	264,480	213,550	171,880	571,340	564,640	560,520	520,110	482,760	444,070	402,290
45-64	530,310	497,210	477,040	441,010	411,350	394,310	373,440	725,960	717,740	717,100	691,680	671,980	665,520	647,940
65/65+	411,170	410,260	413,970	392,690	419,540	458,810	485,910	708,410	705,510	706,000	692,080	689,870	706,330	715,760
Total	2,583,210	2,351,260	2,202,300	1,885,560	1,695,000	1,500,490	1,289,730	3,438,390	3,271,540	3,167,470	2,909,290	2,684,880	2,475,570	2,238,980
% pop	9.7	8.8	8.1	6.9	6.1	5.3	4.5	12.2	11.5	11.0	10.0	9.2	8.2	7.3
Overall (Male + Female)								11.0	10.2	9.6	8.5	7.6	6.8	6.0

Table 2.22.1
TOTAL Institutional Churches[2]

	Membership	Churches	Ministers
2000	4,673,035	28,734	20,559
2001	4,618,747	28,686	20,352
2002	4,510,255	28,621	19,882
2003	4,440,602	28,518	19,777
2005	4,372,260	28,270	19,202
2010	3,973,666	27,702	17,328
2020	3,278,480	25,406	14,146

Table 2.22.2
Total Anglican Churches[4]

	Membership	Churches	Ministers
2000	1,663,848	18,600	10,735
2001	1,653,296	18,598	10,702
2002	1,492,410	18,593	10,514
2003	1,524,875	18,546	10,655
2005	1,542,613	18,460	10,406
2010	1,397,311	18,299	9,404
2020	1,141,605	16,670	7,923

Table 2.22.3
Total Catholic Churches[5]

	Mass Attendance	Churches	Priests
2000	1,771,121	4,741	6,926
2001	1,741,677	4,730	6,756
2002	1,809,736	4,727	6,505
2003	1,730,323	4,731	6,379
2005	1,681,519	4,705	6,103
2010	1,529,525	4,647	5,498
2020	1,275,590	4,442	4,257

Table 2.22.4
Total Orthodox Churches[6]

	Membership	Churches	Priests
2000	245,186	253	260
2001	252,428	259	269
2002	259,969	265	274
2003	262,443	273	287
2005	271,158	278	307
2010	276,240	293	311
2020	284,975	311	330

Table 2.22.5
Total Presbyterian Churches[7]

	Membership	Churches	Ministers
2000	992,880	5,140	2,638
2001	971,346	5,099	2,625
2002	948,140	5,036	2,589
2003	922,961	4,968	2,456
2005	876,970	4,827	2,386
2010	770,590	4,463	2,115
2020	576,310	4,073	1,636

Table 2.22.6
TOTAL Free Churches[3]

	Membership	Churches	Ministers
2000	1,240,537	19,516	13,978
2001	1,243,904	19,734	14,194
2002	1,256,359	19,544	14,262
2003	1,260,026	19,455	14,799
2005	1,262,064	19,365	15,247
2010	1,261,805	19,033	16,129
2020	1,281,071	18,394	17,493

Table 2.22.7
Total Baptist Churches[8]

	Membership	Churches	Ministers
2000	206,416	3,475	2,714
2001	204,387	3,467	2,827
2002	202,872	3,433	2,871
2003	201,875	3,433	2,846
2005	199,171	3,512	2,906
2010	188,040	3,519	2,923
2020	170,750	3,491	2,919

Table 2.22.8
Total Independent Churches[9]

	Membership	Churches	Ministers
2000	180,418	3,184	1,258
2001	178,656	3,164	1,257
2002	176,012	3,126	1,248
2003	176,332	3,083	1,255
2005	171,993	3,015	1,255
2010	158,850	2,809	1,265
2020	140,535	2,369	1,287

Table 2.22.9
Total Methodist Churches[10]

	Membership	Churches	Ministers
2000	353,562	6,552	2,452
2001	345,427	6,764	2,451
2002	336,155	6,537	2,345
2003	324,023	6,433	2,320
2005	303,973	6,139	2,186
2010	274,850	5,635	2,095
2020	221,620	4,785	1,797

Table 2.22.10
Total New Churches[11]

	Attendance	Congregations	Leaders
2000	133,662	1,799	2,048
2001	137,219	1,836	2,089
2002	143,019	1,922	2,161
2003	147,698	1,972	2,241
2005	153,900	2,000	2,331
2010	163,290	2,112	2,494
2020	186,350	2,293	2,762

Table 2.22.11
Total Pentecostal Churches[12]

	Membership	Congregations	Ministers
2000	226,413	2,348	3,356
2001	238,591	2,374	3,425
2002	258,257	2,395	3,511
2003	269,094	2,413	3,996
2005	288,183	2,570	4,419
2010	327,524	2,846	5,287
2020	405,800	3,249	6,691

Table 2.22.12
Total Other Denominations[13]

	Membership	Churches	Ministers
2000	140,066	2,158	2,150
2001	139,624	2,129	2,145
2002	140,044	2,131	2,126
2003	141,004	2,121	2,141
2005	144,844	2,129	2,150
2010	149,251	2,112	2,115
2020	156,016	2,207	2,041

[1] For grand total of all denominations see Table 2.23.1
[2] Total of Tables 2.22.2–5
[3] Total of Tables 2.22.7–12
[4] Repeat of Table 8.2.1
[5] Repeat of Table 8.5.1
[6] Repeat of Table 8.8.1
[7] Repeat of Table 8.10.1
[8] Repeat of Table 9.4.1
[9] Repeat of Table 9.6.1
[10] Repeat of Table 9.8.1
[11] Repeat of Table 9.9.1
[12] Repeat of Table 9.12.1
[13] Repeat of Table 9.18.1

Table **2.23.1** gives an overview of the total church membership, churches and ministers in the UK. The figures from 2000 onwards are the sum of **Tables 2.22.1** and **2.22.6** on the previous page, which in turn are the sum of all the churches listed by individual denomination in Sections 8 and 9. In this edition of *Religious Trends* some 258 distinct denominations are behind these totals.

Table **2.23.1** also repeats the figures for 1990 and 1995 from the previous edition of *Religious Trends* for comparison. It may be seen that the number of churches especially dropped between 1995 and 2000, the beginning perhaps of many closures, though subsequent numbers drop less rapidly. The same is true of the number of ministers.

Table **2.23.2** gives the only known counts of the number of denominations in the UK. The number increased substantially in the 1980s, and is likely to continue to increase perhaps quite rapidly in the years 2010 to 2020 (which would be in line with global expectations; see **Table 1.3.2**). This implies that as the number of church members decreases the church splits into more and more units!

It is obvious from **Figure 2.23.1** that church membership is dropping. Between 1990 and 1995, church membership dropped at an average rate of 1.0% per year, between 1995 and 2000 this increased to 1.3% per annum, but between 2000 and 2005 the rate of decline has slowed to an average 0.9% per year. However after 2005 the decline is expected to increase, almost doubling to a rate of 1.7% per year between 2005 and 2010, and more or less keeping to that rate with an average per annum rate of change of -1.6% between 2010 and 2020.

If these figures are correct (and 96 of the 258 denominations, 37%, provided their own forecasts for one or more years) then it means that the UK church has perhaps 3 or 4 years of comparative stability before membership numbers begin to drop relatively rapidly.

The same pattern of decline may be seen in the percentage that UK church membership is of the total population. In 1990 one person in 9 in the population was a church member, by 2020 it will be just one person in 14.

How meaningful is this decline? Is not institutional membership in general decline? Yes, the membership of Trade Unions and the political parties are also in decline, and, if anything, faster than that of the churches. Why? Although an age profile of membership is not generally available, almost certainly it consists of a much larger number of older people than younger people. The commitment of older people is not going to change; the decline in **Table 2.23.1** has more to do with mortality than anything else.

The Sunday attendance figures in **Table 2.23.1** are taken from **Table 2.21.4** but do not include Northern Ireland for which such data is unavail-

able. The figures for 2001–2003 and 2020 are extrapolations from the other data. It is clear from both **Table 2.23.1** and **Figure 2.23.2** that these are decreasing very rapidly, and, if these trends prove true, Sunday attendance is set to more than halve in the 30 years 1990 to 2020. Only a tenth of the buildings in which worship takes place close in this period, and the number of ministers reduces by the same proportion (though more will be unpaid and part-time than paid and full-time), but it is the people who simply will not be present. *That* is the critical factor behind these numbers.

Table 2.23.1
Total UK Church Statistics

Year	Membership		Churches	Ministers	Sunday attendance	
	Total in UK	% of pop			Total in GB	% of pop
1990	6,634,335	*11.5*	49,321[2]	35,558[2]	5,369,770	9.6
1995	6,303,726	*10.8*	48,999[2]	35,074[2]	4,794,850	8.5
2000	5,913,572	*10.0*	48,250	34,537	4,379,880	7.6
2001	5,862,651	*9.9*	48,420	34,546	4,315,040[1]	7.3
2002	5,766,614	*9.7*	48,165	34,144	4,224,220[1]	7.1
2003	5,700,628	*9.6*	47,973	34,576	4,133,400[1]	6.9
2005	5,634,324	*9.4*	47,635	34,449	3,976,060	6.8
2010	5,190,471	*8.6*	46,735	33,457	3,528,710	6.0
2020	4,559,551	*7.2*	43,890	31,639	2,683,950	4.4

[1] Estimate (see text) [2] Revised figure

Figure 2.23.1
Total UK Church Membership, 1990–2020

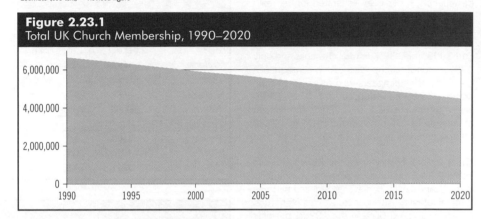

Figure 2.23.2
Rates of Decline in Christian Numbers

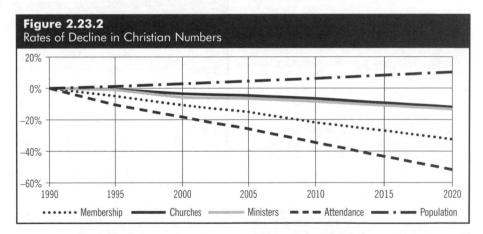

······ Membership   —— Churches   ▬▬ Ministers   – – – Attendance   —·— Population

Table 2.23.2
Number of Denominations listed in the *UK Christian Handbook* and/or *Religious Trends*

1977	97
1987	140
1992	208
1994	222
1996	243
1998	247
2000	250
2003	258
2005[1]	270
2010[1]	290
2020[1]	340

[1] Estimate [2] A denomination is taken as "a Christian organisation uniting a number of local congregations" (John Adair, *The Becoming Church*, SPCK, 1977).

2

Church attendance was measured in England through the English Church Census in 1989 and the English Church Attendance Survey in 1998. Tables on **Page 2.13** of *Religious Trends* No 2 broke down the 1989 figures by Environment, and Tables on **Page 2.24** of *Religious Trends* No 3 did the same for the 1998 figures. The figures on this page use those Tables and others to estimate the 2010 figures and analyse the trends in them in more detail.

In both surveys rural church attendance was broken down into two groups: Commuter Rural and Remoter Rural. Church leaders were asked to self-designate which of these their church was in, and this designation is the one used. 67% of churches were given an environmental designation; it has been estimated for the rest.

Table 2.24.1 shows that while church attendance generally dropped 22% between 1989 and 1998, it fell 39% in rural churches and only 17% in non-rural churches. As a consequence the 22% of churchgoers who attended in rural areas in 1989 had dropped to 17% by 1998. These trends are likely to continue and worsen at least up to 2010, by which time only 12% of churchgoers will be in rural areas.

Table 2.24.2 breaks down the Rural figures in **Table 2.24.1** by three parameters: commuter v rural, evangelical v non-evangelical and by three denominations. Attendance at remoter rural churches dropped 50% in the 1990s, but only 29% in commuter rural areas; both are set to decline further in the first decade of the 21st century. Rural attendance declined 47% in non-evangelical churches but only 11% in evangelical churches, but both percentages are set to increase. The denominational variations were smaller, but Anglican attendance dropped most, and is forecast to drop further still.

Table 2.24.3 gives the number of churches (as opposed to attendance) in rural areas broken down by the same parameters in **Table 2.24.2**. It shows that the number of evangelical churches increased in the 1990s, and this was actually in both the commuter rural areas and the remoter rural areas. This was much less because of new churches being started, but because some (about 3%) previously non-evangelical churches became evangelical. The increase in Anglican and Catholic congregations took place entirely in the commuter rural areas; the number of their remoter rural congregations declined in the 1990s. The proportion of rural churches which are Anglican continues to increase, largely because many Anglican

churches are listed and cannot be easily closed; at some stage, however, alternative funding support will need to become available as Dioceses will not be able to maintain them.

Given the number of churchgoers and the number of churches, the average congregation may be worked out. These numbers are given in **Tables 2.24.4** and **5** respectively for the Commuter and Remoter Rural churches. They

show that congregations have declined in the 1990s by all the different parameters, though in 1998 the average evangelical congregation was slightly larger than the non-evangelical, a trend which continues in 2010. The average Anglican congregation in remoter rural areas had dropped to just 14 people by 1998 and to only 3 by 2010, which must have implications for long-term viability for these parishes.

Table 2.24.1
Attendance by Environment

Year	All Churches	Rural	Non-Rural
1989	**4,742,800**	1,043,400	3,699,400
% change	*−22%*	*−39%*	*−17%*
1998	**3,714,700**	631,500	3,083,200
% change	*−24%*	*−47%*	*−19%*
2010	**2,829,800**	333,700	2,496,100
1989	*100%*	*22%*	*78%*
1998	*100%*	*17%*	*83%*
2010	*100%*	*12%*	*88%*

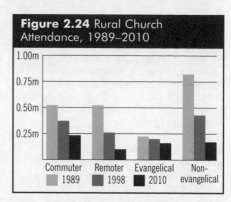

Figure 2.24 Rural Church Attendance, 1989–2010

Legend: 1989 / 1998 / 2010 — Commuter, Remoter, Evangelical, Non-evangelical

Table 2.24.2
Attendance by Rural Environment

Year	Rural Churches	Commuter	Remoter	Evangelical	Non-evangelical	Anglican	Roman Catholic	All others
1989	**1,043,400**	521,700	521,700	223,500	819,900	443,200	223,100	377,100
% change	*−39%*	*−29%*	*−50%*	*−11%*	*−47%*	*−45%*	*−39%*	*−33%*
1998	**631,500**	371,500	260,000	199,500	432,000	245,200	135,300	251,000
% change	*−47%*	*−37%*	*−61%*	*−19%*	*−60%*	*−54%*	*−48%*	*−41%*
2010	**333,700**	232,600	101,100	161,100	172,600	113,800	71,000	149,000
Percentage in:								
1989	*100%*	*50%*	*50%*	*21%*	*79%*	*43%*	*21%*	*36%*
1998	*100%*	*59%*	*41%*	*32%*	*68%*	*39%*	*21%*	*40%*
2010	*100%*	*70%*	*30%*	*48%*	*52%*	*34%*	*21%*	*45%*

Table 2.24.3
Number of Churches by Rural Environment

Year	Rural Churches	Commuter	Remoter	Evangelical	Non-evangelical	Anglican	Roman Catholic	All others
1989	**16,980**	5,980	11,000	4,150	12,830	9,000	915	7,065
% change	*−7%*	*+ 1%*	*−11%*	*+ 10%*	*−12%*	*+ 1%*	*+ 2%*	*−18%*
1998	**15,830**	6,030	9,800	4,570	11,260	9,120	934	5,776
% change	*−10%*	*− 1%*	*−16%*	*+ 10%*	*−19%*	*−2%*	*+ 1%*	*−26%*
2010	**14,180**	5,960	8,220	5,030	9,150	8,960	950	4,270
Percentage in:								
1989	*100%*	*35%*	*65%*	*24%*	*76%*	*53%*	*5%*	*42%*
1998	*100%*	*38%*	*62%*	*29%*	*71%*	*58%*	*6%*	*36%*
2010	*100%*	*42%*	*58%*	*35%*	*65%*	*63%*	*7%*	*30%*

Table 2.24.4
Average Size of Congregation in Commuter Rural Areas

Year	Commuter Rural	Evangelical	Non-Evangelical	Anglican	Roman Catholic	All others
1989	**87**	77	91	70	283	76
% change	*−29%*	*−13%*	*−35%*	*−30%*	*−42%*	*−20%*
1998	**62**	67	59	49	163	61
% change	*−37%*	*−21%*	*−47%*	*−44%*	*−48%*	*−26%*
2010	**39**	53	31	27	84	45

Table 2.24.5
Average Size of Congregation in Remoter Rural Areas

Year	Remoter Rural	Evangelical	Non-Evangelical	Anglican	Roman Catholic	All others
1989	**47**	42	49	38	208	43
% change	*−43%*	*−31%*	*−47%*	*−63%*	*−40%*	*−23%*
1998	**27**	29	26	14	124	33
% change	*−54%*	*−41%*	*−62%*	*−77%*	*−47%*	*−21%*
1998	**12**	17	10	3	66	26

UK Mission Overseas

Sources: Statistics provided by UK mission agencies of all denominations in a special survey specifically designed for publication in this volume, plus previous editions of *Religious Trends,* the *UK Christian Handbook* and a private survey by Christian Research. Pages 3.2 to 3.6 were compiled by Judi Stirling.

Table 3.2.1 Total Mission Workers

Country	Position	2004	2003	2001	1999	1997	1995	1993	1991
France	1	230	249	190	268	268	298	284	236
Kenya	2	210	293	270	349	248	306	295	293
Spain	3	136	154	139	134	159	142	134	109
South Africa	4	134	140	159	192	229	240	260	245
Zambia	5	124	151	124	151	189	201	211	164
Brazil	6	122	173	140	180	199	207	212	210
Nepal	=7	119	127	170	190	240	227	179	156
North Africa	=7	119	55	48	50	55	40	34	24
Tanzania	9	107	125	84	150	170	167	198	209
Zimbabwe	10	94	121	107	144	165	206	217	247

The 10 countries with the most British mission workers are given in **Table 3.2.1** in total and in **Tables 3.2.2–5** by different denominational groupings. These all exclude those serving in the UK. The total taken is of the number of UK serving members.

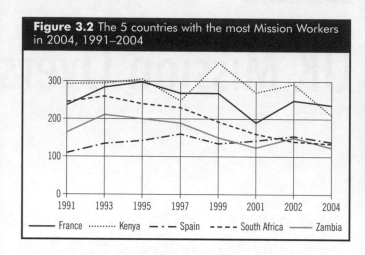

Figure 3.2 The 5 countries with the most Mission Workers in 2004, 1991–2004

France ·········· Kenya — · — Spain — — — South Africa ——— Zambia

Table 3.2.2 Anglican Mission Workers

Country	Position	2004	2003	2001	1999	1997	1995	1993	1991
France	1	45	49	49	26	31	26	26	21
Tanzania	2	40	47	49	54	75	68	63	84
Spain	3	35	40	38	10	10	13	15	22
Uganda	4	33	70	59	72	73	62	63	67
Kenya	5	28	42	37	46	31	31	36	38
South Africa	6	23	21	17	19	32	34	35	35
Paraguay	7	22	19	22	19	16	22	20	23
Zimbabwe	8	18	19	19	27	28	28	40	30
China	9	17	17	14	14	0	0	0	0
Chile	10	15	15	30	21	13	19	25	28

Table 3.2.3 Roman Catholic Mission Workers

Country	Position	2004	2003	2001	1999	1997	1995	1993	1991
South Africa	1	50	68	71	90	104	107	118	102
Zimbabwe	2	47	56	57	54	72	43	61	148
Kenya	3	40	90	61	77	41	101	86	98
Peru	=4	26	25	28	30	35	35	38	46
Zambia	=4	26	34	25	29	40	68	80	43
Tanzania	6	21	25	32	34	34	21	33	32
Nigeria	7	20	24	34	35	44	64	69	96
Cameroon	8	13	41	22	23	15	31	31	22
India	9	12	23	19	25	28	35	34	26
Argentina	10	11	3	3	5	4	4	4	6

Table 3.2.4 Other Denominations' Mission Workers

Country	Position	2004	2003	2001	1999	1997	1995	1993	1991
Kenya	1	37	56	45	61	49	36	45	44
Spain	2	34	31	34	36	38	39	33	24
Peru	3	32	31	29	17	18	18	24	19
Brazil	4	29	35	48	51	60	65	64	69
USA	5	28	67	28	60	64	61	57	55
Nepal	6	28	38	57	66	69	63	44	45
France	7	24	28	36	33	38	32	37	22
Malawi	8	23	38	42	37	25	26	32	29
Ireland	9	22	21	21	16	16	12	12	32
Zimbabwe	10	21	29	31	29	32	40	59	51

Table 3.2.5 Interdenominational Mission Workers

Country	Position	2004	2003	2001	1999	1997	1995	1993	1991
North Africa	1	110	49	46	45	49	35	33	24
Kenya	2	101	101	127	139	122	122	105	102
France	=3	88	92	105	122	124	131	102	88
Nepal	=3	88	86	113	108	150	142	115	98
Middle East	5	72	107	81	118	190	192	188	87
Spain	6	63	62	67	69	77	65	61	55
USA	7	62	60	58	50	46	35	79	21
Brazil	8	54	89	92	89	85	88	109	96
Philippines	=9	52	62	73	73	85	67	71	76
Papua New Guinea	=9	52	78	77	61	28	26	39	47

Figure 3.3.1 and **Table 3.3.1** show that the number of British mission workers has declined across all types of Society or Agency. The most marked drop is in "Roman Catholic" personnel, which fell by 22% between 2003 and 2004. "Other Denominations" were not far behind with a 17% decline, partly due to the closure of World-Wide Advent Missions.

Anglican mission agencies fell by 7% between 2003 and 2004, with several of the larger Anglican agencies reducing their number of overseas mission workers.

Interdenominational mission agencies saw the least decline between 2003 and 2004 as well as experiencing the least percentage change across the seven year period 1997 to 2004, just 7%. **As Figure 3.3.2** illustrates, 61% of mission workers were interdenominational in 2004 compared with 55% in 1997, a trend which is likely to continue, with it being 66% by 2010 and 77% by 2020 if present trends continue.

Table 3.3.2 shows that much of the decline experienced by mission agencies between 2003 and 2004 is in UK based personnel (such as secondments and home staff) rather than those working overseas.

If present trends continue, the number of mission workers is set to halve from their 1997 number by 2020.

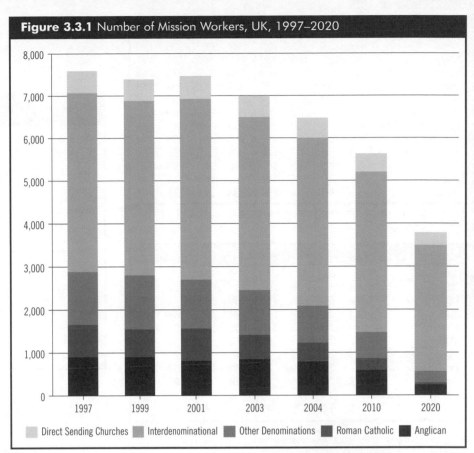

Figure 3.3.1 Number of Mission Workers, UK, 1997–2020

Legend: Direct Sending Churches ▪ Interdenominational ▪ Other Denominations ▪ Roman Catholic ▪ Anglican

3

Table 3.3.1 Total British Mission Workers 1997–2020

Denomination	1997	1999	2001	2003	2004	2010E	2020E
Anglican	906	907[1]	813	851[1]	792	591	244
Roman Catholic	754	642	757	562	439	278	47
Other Denominations	1,239[1]	1,261[1]	1,156[1]	1,036[1]	859	610	271
Interdenominational	4,189[1]	4,094[1]	4,221[1]	4,070[1]	3,935	3,738	2,946
Direct Sending Churches	529	513	535	496[1]	468	429	295
TOTAL	**7,617**	**7,417**	**7,482**	**7,015**	**6,493**	**5,646**	**3,803**

[1] Revised figure   E = Estimate, if present trends continue

Table 3.3.2
Mission Workers by Type of Work, 1997–2020

Mission workers	1997	1999	2001	2003	2004	2010E	2020E
Overseas[2]	5,759	5,416	5,281	4,788	4,772	3,764	2,409
Cross-culture UK	292	257	383	270	213	221	154
Own culture UK	901	979	1,099	978	768	845	736
Secondments	216	234	108	114	35	5	0
UK Home staff[1,2]	} 449	} 531	} 611	498	363	487	297
UK Executive staff				367	342	324	207
Total: Serving Members	**7,617**	**7,417**	**7,482**	**7,015**	**6,493**	**5,646**	**3,803**
UK Office staff	897	1,071	1,175	960	1,034	564	342
Associates	257	303	232	409	388	253	124
Retired personnel	1,895	2,079	2,380	1,431	1,174	912	600
Total: Mission Workers	**10,666**	**10,870**	**11,269**	**9,815**	**9,089**	**7,375**	**4,869**
Number of Societies	227	227	233	228	225	195	118

[1] Adjusted figures   [2] Including those on Furlough or Home Assignment   E = Estimate, if present trends continue

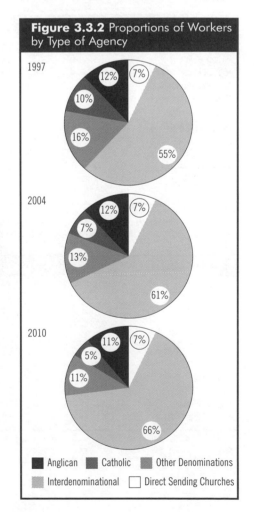

Figure 3.3.2 Proportions of Workers by Type of Agency

1997

2004

2010

Legend: ■ Anglican ■ Catholic ■ Other Denominations ■ Interdenominational □ Direct Sending Churches

Table 3.4.1 All Societies

Agency	Position	2004	2003	2001	1999	1997	1995	1993
YWAM	1	486	486	486	486	486	486	451
Operation Mobilisation	2	403	403	407	366	379	370	295
Echoes of Service[1]	3	383	404	402	404	416	407	378
Wycliffe Bible Translators	4	230	260	284	255	320	287	308
Church Mission Society	5	220	229	161	257	287	269	267
OMF International (UK)	6	216	266	266	266	218	218	273
WEC International	7	207	173	290	312	388	388	398
World Horizons	8	156	167	108	170	218	220	224
BMS World Mission	9	143	142	187	186	304	255	170
Interserve	=10	140	136[2]	156	138	146	159	148
SIM UK	=10	140	158	191	228	123	111	111

[1] Echoes of Service is counted as a Direct Sending Church, but these are too few to be listed separately.
[2] Revised figure.

Table 3.4.2 Anglican Societies

Agency	Position	2004	2003	2001	1999	1997	1995	1993
CMS	1	220	229	161	257	287	269	267
ICS	2	137	135	153	56	71	71	71
USPG	3	128	128	124	124	163	163	159
Crosslinks	4	106	100	110	105	105	109	110
SAMS	5	75	99	81[1]	162	75	100	102
Right Hand Trust	6	37	34	36	44	47	20	10
The Mission to Seamen	7	33	33	33	33	54	39	61
CMS Ireland	8	24	28	28	28	31	27	26
PNG Church Partnership	=9	14	13	10	14	18	10	14
CMJ	=9	14	19	47	44	40	45	47

CMS = Church Mission Society. ICS = Intercontinental Church Society. USPG = United Society for the Propagation of the Gospel. SAMS = South American Mission Society. PNG = Papua New Guinea. CMJ = Church's Ministry Among Jewish People. [1] Estimate

Table 3.4.3 Roman Catholic Societies

Agency	Position	2004	2003	2001	1999	1997	1995	1993
Society of Jesus	1	43	60	53	51	62	57	57
Mill Hill Missionaries	2	38	45	46	49	n/a	n/a	n/a
Missionaries of Africa	3	26	26	30	32	85	46	52
FMDM	4	22	24	37	28	102	204	204
Fidei Domum Priests	5	21	27	31	31	40	39	51
Salesian Frs and Bros.	6	18	19	22	24	24	37	38
FMM	7	15	18	18	24	130	44	44
SNDN	8	13	15	23	19	24	29	29
Redemptorists	9	10	12	10	11	14	17	25
MMM	=10	9	7	13	15	16	n/a	n/a
CM (VF)	=10	9	9	9	5	5	13	15

FMDM = Franciscan Missionaries of Divine Motherhood. Salesians Frs and Bros. = Salesian Fathers and Brothers. FMM = Franciscan Missionaries of Mary. SNDN = Sisters of Notre Dame de Namur. MMM = Medical Missionaries of Mary. CM(VF) = Comboni Missionaries (Verona Fathers).

Table 3.4.4 Other Denominations

Agency	Position	2004	2003	2001	1999	1997	1995	1993
BMS World Mission	1	143	142	187	186	304	255	170
AOGWM	2	113	92	119	121	120	134	142
FPCUMB	3	96	96	96	59	59	59	59
Salvation Army	4	82	108[1]	135	135	162	182	185
Elim Interntnl Missions	5	72	72	71	52	48	30	43
MCWCO	6	60	72	73	85	93	115	115
CoSBoWM	7	59	70	72	125	106	136	110
PCIOB	8	49	70	88	88	56	51	61
Baptist Missions	9	44	46	46	20	19	20	31
Grace Baptist Mission	10	41	41	55	50	49	46	43

BMS = Baptist Missionary Society. AOGWM = Assemblies of God World Mission. FPCUMB = Free Presbyterian Church of Ulster Mission Board. MCWCO = Methodist Church World Church Office. CoSBoWM = Church of Scotland Board of World Mission. PCIOB = Presbyterian Church in Ireland Overseas Board. [1] Estimate

Table 3.4.5 Interdenominational Societies

Agency	Position	2004	2003	2001	1999	1997	1995	1993
YWAM	1	486	486	486	486	486	486	451
Operation Mobilisation	2	403	403	407	366	379	370	295
Wycliffe Bible Translators	3	230	260	284	255	320	287	308
OMF International (UK)	4	216	246[1]	266	266	218	218	273
WEC International	5	207	173	290	312	388	388	398
World Horizons	6	156	167	108	170	218	220	224
Interserve	=7	140	136[1]	156	138	146	159	148
SIM UK	=7	140	158	191	228	123	111	111
The Navigators	9	139	139	146	91	89	100	60
CLC	10	130	67	144	85	104	113	122

YWAM = Youth With A Mission. CLC = Christian Literature Crusade. [1] Revised figure.

The 10 Societies or Agencies with the most British mission workers are given in **Table 3.4.1** in total and in **Tables 3.4.2–5** by denominational groupings. The total is taken as the number of UK serving members.

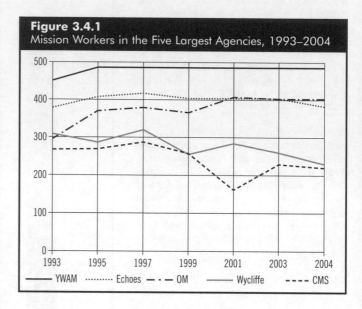

Figure 3.4.1
Mission Workers in the Five Largest Agencies, 1993–2004

Legend: YWAM ⸺ Echoes ⋯⋯ OM — · — Wycliffe ⸺ CMS - - -

Table 3.5.1 Length of Service by Gender, 2003 and 2004

Length in years	Male 2003 %	Male 2004 %	Female 2003 %	Female 2004 %	Overall 2003 %	Overall 2004 %	Male proportion 2003 %	Male proportion 2004 %
Under 2	17	20	20	17	19	19	39	50
2 to 4	20	18	19	17	20	17	43	48
5 to 8	19	30	20	28	19	29	41	48
9 to 12	13	12	14	12	14	12	41	49
13 & over	31	20	27	26	28	23	46	40
Base	1,047	1,590	1,421	1,818	2,468	3,408	42	47
Average length	8.0	7.0	7.6	7.7	7.7	7.3		

Table 3.5.2
Why Churches Support
Mission Agencies

We have a particular interest in ...

The kind of work they do	43%
An individual who works with them	28%
The country(ies) where they work	24%

Figure 3.5.1
Length of Service, 2003 & 2004

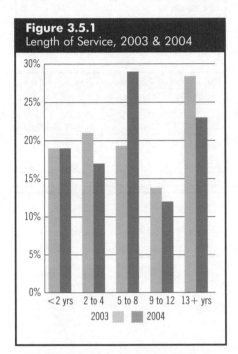

Figure 3.5.2 Churches with Member Serving as Mission Worker, by Size

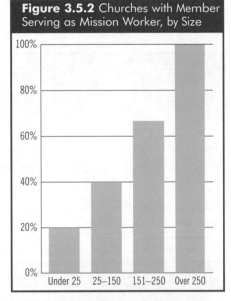

Table 3.5.3 Proportions of British Mission Workers by Continent, 1995–2004

Continent	1995 %	1997 %	1999 %	2003 %	2004 %
Africa	38	36	37	36	36
Americas	15	15	16	15	14
Asia	27	29	28	29	28
Europe	20	20	19	20	22

Figure 3.5.3 Church Support of Overseas Work, 2003

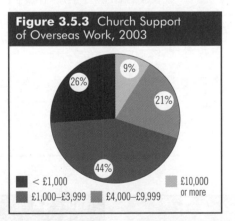

< £1,000
£1,000–£3,999
£4,000–£9,999
£10,000 or more

Table 3.5.4
Number of Mission Workers Worldwide, 1991–2004

	Other denominations[1] Number	Agencies	Interdenominational Number	Agencies	Roman Catholic Number	Agencies	All denominations Number	Agencies
1991	4,352	31	42,645	65	80,511	55	127,508	151
1993	3,851	31	42,449	66	84,544	54	130,844	151
1995	3,686	32	48,586	67	92,000	63	144,272	162
1997	3,674	33	49,121	74	89,000	59	141,795	166
1999	6,263	35	39,823	78	69,743	54	115,829	167
2003	5,725[2]	32	36,404[3]	80	49,000[2]	54	91,129	166
2004	2,871[3]	29	33,454[3]	78	48,500[2]	110	84,825	217

Previous to 2004, "Number of Agencies" is number of agencies giving details.
[1] Includes Anglican mission agencies. [2] Estimate [3] Includes estimates for missing data.

In 2003 data was collected for the first time on the length of service and gender of mission workers. Although it is too early to see any established trends, it is interesting to see some indications of possible future developments. The average length of service decreased slightly between 2003 and 2004, largely because a number of long serving men came home, as may be seen in **Table 3.5.1**.

Table 3.5.1 also shows that the percentage of mission workers who are men has increased by 5% across all ages, and that the percentage of men serving under 2 years has increased by 11%. Perhaps some of these "extra" men are new career mission workers rather than short term mission workers, who will replace those who left in the last year.

Figure 3.5.1 shows that the trends analysed in *Religious Trends* No 4 for length of service in 2003 have continued into 2004, with the exception of the number of mission workers serving 5-8 years.

Table 3.5.3 shows that there is very little change in the location of mission workers, from a continental viewpoint. However, there is more change from country to country year by year, which is analysed in **Table 3.2.1**. Specific details of locations of the mission workers in 2004 will be given in the next edition of the *UK Christian Handbook*.

Table 3.5.4 indicates that 57% of mission workers worldwide from agencies with a British sending base are Roman Catholic, compared with 63% in 1991.

A private survey by Christian Research for one large mission agency in 2003, USPG, showed that, on average, two churches in five, 40%, had a member serving as a mission worker. As might be expected however the likelihood of having such varied by the size of the church, as shown in **Figure 3.5.2**. Virtually all churches with a Sunday congregation in excess of 250 have a mission worker linked to them.

That same survey showed that the main reason churches support particular agencies was the work they do (**Table 3.5.2**). Churches on average gave about 7% of their income to overseas work of some kind, which in 2003 averaged £3,900. As **Figure 3.5.3** shows the large proportion of churches give under £4,000, and just 9% give £10,000 or more.

Source: Private research report for USPG, *The Image of USPG*, May 2003, quoted with permission.

Table 3.6.1 shows that overall there has been little change between 2002 and 2003 in where new mission workers come from, though there has been a decrease in the proportion of mission workers joining from training agencies.

Table 3.6.2 shows an increase in the percentage of mission workers who resigned in 2003, but rather fewer for other reasons. As classification in these circumstances is sometimes difficult, the increase in resignations may just reflect the drop in "other" reasons.

"Associates" are defined as those linked to a Mission Agency in some way (for prayer support, for example) but not financially supported nor under Agency leadership. Although the number of Associates varies from year to year as **Table 3.6.3** demonstrates, the number of Associates rose substantially in 2003, and has fallen back somewhat in 2004.

Table 3.6.4 shows that there has been a slight decrease in the number of overseas personnel involved in outreach in the UK. Three fifths of such workers are female.

Figure 3.6 and **Table 3.6.5** show the proportion of UK mission workers who come from agencies who are members of Global Connections. The percentage has increased markedly from 1995 to 2004, and is set to continue to do so.

Table 3.6.6 indicates that the proportion of men working overseas remained unchanged between 1997 and 2004. The largest drop is in the number of male mission workers in the UK, working either in their own culture or cross culturally. Although there has been an increase in the proportion of male secondments, the number in 2004 is much lower than in 1997. The proportion of male office staff has increased, narrowing the gap between men and women; the proportion of male executive staff remains high, with currently almost three quarters of UK executive staff being men.

Table 3.6.1
Joining Agencies, 2002 & 2003

Where people had joined from	2002 %	2003 %
Secular employment	47	48
An accredited training agency	20	11
As short-term or gap year	12	13
Another agency	11	10
Return after medical absence	1	1
Return after absence for children's education	1	3
Return after looking after parents	1/3	0
Other reasons	8	14
Base (=100%)	392	393

Table 3.6.2
Leaving Agencies, 2002 & 2003

Why people left	2002 %	2003 %
Resigned	23	32
Usual retirement	18	18
End of contract	18	14
Medical reasons	7	7
To look after their children	6	4
To undertake further study	4	3
Were asked to leave	2	5
To look after their parents	1	3
Early retirement	1	3
Other reasons	20	11
Base (= 100%)	255	366

Table 3.6.3
Associates by Gender, 1993–2004

Year	Male %	Female %	Base
1993	38	62	308
1995	58	42	264
1997	46	54	257
1999	n/a	n/a	303
2001	n/a	n/a	232
2003	45	55	409
2004	46	54	332

Table 3.6.4 Number of Overseas Personnel Working in the UK, 2001 and 2004

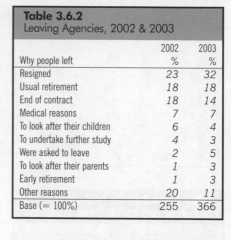

	2001	2004	% male in 2004	% female in 2004
Outreach	114	106	42	58
Admin	53	54	52	48
TOTAL	167	160	46	54

Table 3.6.5 GC[1] Member Societies v non-GC Member Societies[2], 1995–2004

Membership	GC Member Societies	non-GC Member Societies	% of total with GC Societies
1995	3,582	2,569	58
1997	3,993	2,210	64
1999	4,550	1,620	74
2001	4,818	1,307	79
2003	4,887	1,070	82
2004	4,735	851	85
2010E	4,568	371	92

[1] Global Connections, formerly the Evangelical Missionary Alliance
[2] Excludes Roman Catholic Societies and Direct Sending Churches
E = Estimate

Table 3.6.6
Mission Workers by Gender, 1997 and 2004

	Male %	Female %	Base 1997	Male %	Female %	Base 2004
Overseas	45	55	5,509	46	54	4,507
Cross-culture UK[1]	51	49	2,205	46	54	213
Own culture UK[1]				29	71	768
Secondments	43	57	216	54	46	35
UK Home staff	39	61	1,034	50	50	363
UK Executive staff	70	30		73	27	342
Total: Serving Members	**47**	**53**	**8,964**	**46**	**54**	**6,228**
UK Office staff	36	64	905	41	59	1,034
Associates	46	54	257	45	55	388
Retired personnel	30	70	2,005	34	66	1,174
Total: Mission Workers	**44**	**56**	**12,131**	**44**	**56**	**8,824**

[1] Previously this total was split between: cross culture overseas; own culture overseas; furlough/home leave.

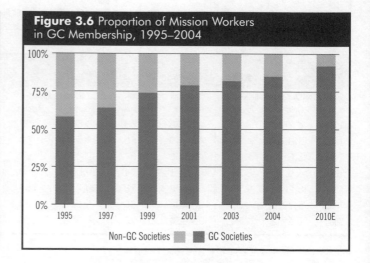

Figure 3.6 Proportion of Mission Workers in GC Membership, 1995–2004

Non-GC Societies | GC Societies

Figure 3.7.1
No. of Mission Workers Leaving p.a.

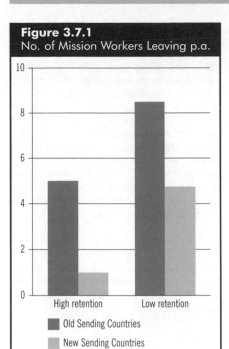

■ Old Sending Countries
■ New Sending Countries

Figure 3.7.2 Length of Service by Type of Agency, in Years

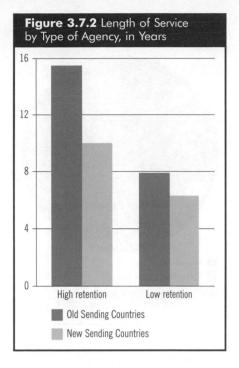

■ Old Sending Countries
■ New Sending Countries

Figure 3.7.3 Length of Pre-field Training by Type of Agency, in Years

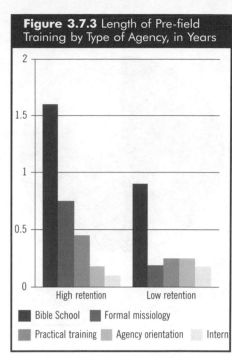

■ Bible School ■ Formal missiology
■ Practical training ■ Agency orientation ■ Intern

3

In February 1995 the Missions Commission of the World Evangelical Fellowship (now the World Evangelical Alliance) sought to answer the question as to why there were so many mission workers who came back home before they were expected to. An international survey was undertaken called "ReMAP" which stood for "Reducing Missionary Attrition Project", which was reported in detail with many articles applying the findings in the book *Too Valuable to Lose: Examining the Causes and Cures of Missionary Attrition* edited by Dr William Taylor and published by the William Carey Library, Pasadena, California in 1997.

A second survey

A follow-up survey was undertaken in early 2003. While the first study focused mainly on missionary attrition and especially personal reasons for their early return, ReMAP II centred on the flip-side of the coin: missionary retention.

ReMAP II was limited to long-term cross-cultural mission workers. A questionnaire was sent to all known evangelical mission agencies in 22 countries from the new sending countries (NSC) of Africa, Asia, and Latin America as well as some older sending countries (OSC) of Europe, North America and the Pacific. Their mission executives were asked about the organisational ethos of their agency, vision, values, practices and procedures as well as their personnel deployment, missionary attrition and retention data. More than 570 agencies with some 37,000 long-term mission workers participated, representing one fifth (20%) of evangelical mission workers globally. The agencies' response was multiplied by the number of their active mission workers in order to consider their agency's contribution to the national mission force.

Mission executives were also asked to indicate for each mission worker who left if this person harmoniously transferred to another agency, or returned for unpreventable reasons or for potentially preventable reasons. The respective annual retention rates were then calculated.

Findings

The findings showed that mission agencies are definitely not all the same. There are significant differences in how they operate and how long they keep their mission workers.

Figure 3.7.1 compares the average mission workers leaving per year for mission agencies in both OSC and NSC. Agencies were divided into two groups, those with a high retention rate (which meant that fewer workers left) and those with a low retention rate. By definition, the "high retention" agencies had fewer workers leave, but **Figure 3.7.1** shows that agencies in the NSC kept significantly more of their workers than those in the OSC.

Taking the numbers in **Figure 3.7.1** as a proportion of those in each type of agency and applying the probability of leaving on the existing mission force allows the number of mission workers who will still be with the agency in 10 or 20 years time to be calculated. Over such periods the annual attrition makes an increasing impact on the mission agency. **Table 3.7** shows how many would remain of every 10 mission workers serving with an agency if these proportions were applied. The Table shows how many mission workers would have remained by 1990 and 2000 if agencies had had 10 workers in 1980.

Figure 3.7.2 shows the average length of service of those returning home in each group.

Table 3.7 Number of Mission Workers still with Agency for given retention rates

	Old Sending Countries		New Sending Countries	
	High	Low	High	Low
1980	10	10	10	10
1990	9	7	10	8
2000	9	6	9	7

Whether with high or low retention, the OSC obtained longer lengths of service than the NSC. However, 15% of those returning in the High retention agencies returned for potentially preventable reasons compared with 90% in the Low retention agencies.

Why the differences

Some 88 factors potentially explaining the differences were surveyed. Of these, half revealed significant differences. One of the most important was training before a mission worker was sent overseas. Such "pre-field training" can be of different types, and **Figure 3.7.3** shows that of those who returned during 2001 and 2002 those who had served longest, especially in OSC, were much more likely to have had such training. Such training was most likely to have been at Bible School, or from having studied missiology, or other practical mission worker training. Having such training clearly helps mission workers stay on the field longer.

Source: Article written by Rob Hay, *Generating Change,* from whom further information on ReMAP II may be obtained. His phone number is 07813 136 826.

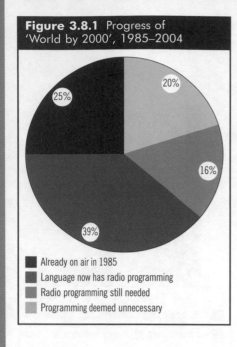

Figure 3.8.1 Progress of 'World by 2000', 1985–2004

- Already on air in 1985
- Language now has radio programming
- Radio programming still needed
- Programming deemed unnecessary

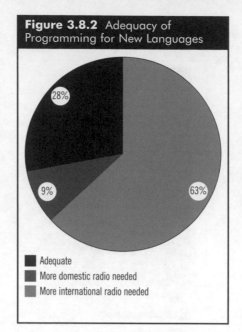

Figure 3.8.2 Adequacy of Programming for New Languages

- Adequate
- More domestic radio needed
- More international radio needed

Christian Radio

Christian broadcasting outside the USA in 1985 was mainly international short wave radio, largely on stations operated by Christians. A growing mission movement focused on completing the Great Commission, with the year 2000 as an attractive target date. In 1985 the major Christian broadcasters publicly committed their organisations to provide Gospel radio programmes for everyone in a language they could understand. Their declaration was called *World by 2000*. To have an achievable target for the year 2000, *World by 2000* chose languages spoken by 1 million or more – 372 in all.

Research revealed that a quarter, 25% or 93, of these languages had Christian broadcasts already. Another fifth, 20% or 75, were deemed lower priority or not needing broadcasts at all (such as some European minority languages, for example).

However, by 2004, two-fifths, 39% or 146, of these languages now have radio services. This leaves a sixth, 16% or 58, languages needing a radio programme to complete the 1985 commitment, several of which already have work in progress. These figures are illustrated in **Figure 3.8.1**.

A 30 minute daily programme is considered the minimum amount of programming in order to build an audience on international short wave transmissions. Not all of the languages which have been added have yet reached that minimum, as **Figure 3.8.2** indicates.

In almost 20 years, the radio scene has changed with more domestic stations becoming accessible. *World by 2000* has now become *World by Radio*, and the constituent organisations are already working on reaching people in the megacities of the world by radio and other electronic media.

Table 3.8
World Bible Translation Progress as at 2003

Translation state	Total Languages		Population	
	Number	% of total	Number	% of total
No Bible translation work at all	2,737	40	147,000,000	2
In progress (but no scripture yet)	1,717	25	233,000,000	4
Total languages WITHOUT scriptures	**4,454**	**65**	**380,000,000**	**6**
Some scripture (at least one book)	873	13	967,000,000[1]	15
New Testament	1,068	16	45,000,000[1]	1
Complete Bible	414	6	4,908,000,000[1]	78
Total languages WITH scriptures	**2,355**	**35**	**5,920,000,000**	**94**
TOTAL (= 100%)	**6,809**	**100**	**6,300,000,000**	**100**
Languages Wycliffe and SIL[2] are involved in	1,262	19	1,158,000,000	18

[1] Estimate
[2] SIL International is Wycliffe's primary international field partner overseas.

Bible translation

Table 3.8 and **Figure 3.8.3** illustrate that although 94% of the world's population have some part of the Bible (either a complete Bible, New Testament, or portion), 65% of the world's languages still do not have any part of the Bible. This equates to some 380 million people!

Wycliffe and SIL International are currently involved in 74% of all translation projects worldwide, which represents over 70 countries and 1.2 billion people. At the current pace of translation, by 2150 all languages will have a portion of Scripture; Wycliffe's vision, however, since 1999 has been to reach this target by 2025. Wycliffe is willing to consider helping any other individual or agency involved in Bible translation, and such has been the progress since 1999 that the target is now likely to be reached by 2021.

Sources: Tony Ford of Feba Radio for Radio detail; email: info@feba.org.uk, web: www.feba.org.uk, phone: 01903 237 281. Wycliffe Bible Translators for Bible information; email: askus@wycliffe.org, web: www.wycliffe.org.uk, phone: 01494 682 268

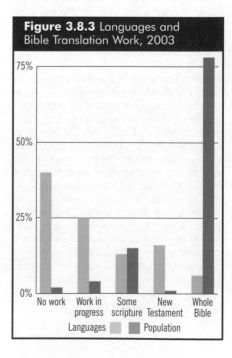

Figure 3.8.3 Languages and Bible Translation Work, 2003

(No work, Work in progress, Some scripture, New Testament, Whole Bible) — Languages / Population

4

UK Population

4

Sources: *Population Trends*, National Statistics, The Stationery Office, relevant issues; Government Actuary's Department, www.gad.gov.uk; Census 2001 Reports for England and Wales, National Statistics, 2004; *Older People*, www.statistics.gov.uk; Denominational statistics; Christian Research private surveys.

This section deliberately looks ahead, so that Christian leaders who wish to strategically plan for the next 20, 40 or 60 years may conveniently have some of the basic data by which to do so. The population of each of the four countries in the UK is given by age and gender up to 2041 on **Page 4.3**, and on this page for the UK as a whole to 2071. Births are given to 2050 on **Page 4.4**, together with the religion of children.

Civil and religious marriages are given to 2020 on **Page 4.5**, and the marital status of the population on **Pages 4.8** and **4.9**, one page for the data and one to illustrate it. The marital status for churchgoers is given for the first time on **Page 4.9**, Christian Research having now accumulated sufficient data to estimate it reasonably.

Deaths to 2070 are given on **Page 4.6**, along with the number of centenarians to 2030. All the secular data comes from the Government, and especially the Government Actuary's Department which is responsible for forecasting the population. Trends in marriage and divorce are given on **Page 4.7**, and household composition on **Page 4.10**.

Table 4.2.1
UK Population in Thousands by Age-group, 2046–2071 and Percentage of Men*

Age	2046	%	2051	%	2056	%	2061	%	2066	%	2071	%
0–9	6,719	51.1	6,756	51.1	6,756	51.1	6,707	51.1	6,640	51.1	6,594	51.1
10–14	3,349	51.0	3,344	51.0	3,368	51.0	3,382	51.0	3,368	51.0	3,333	51.0
15–19	3,460	51.0	3,393	51.0	3,388	51.0	3,412	51.0	3,426	51.0	3,412	51.0
20–29	7,642	49.9	7,529	49.9	7,376	49.9	7,304	49.9	7,324	49.9	7,363	49.9
30–44	11,688	48.9	11,849	48.9	11,953	49.0	11,901	49.0	11,724	48.9	11,568	48.9
45–64	15,966	48.6	15,728	48.6	15,292	48.5	15,077	48.4	15,154	48.4	15,292	48.5
65–74	6,767	47.3	6,909	47.3	7,403	47.7	7,498	47.7	7,159	47.5	6,878	47.4
75/75+	9,881	43.6	9,933	43.5	9,775	43.2	9,836	43.2	10,136	43.5	10,335	43.7
Total	**65,472**	**48.9**	**65,441**	**48.9**	**65,311**	**48.9**	**65,117**	**48.9**	**64,931**	**48.9**	**64,775**	**48.9**

* The percentages represent the proportion of men in that age-group.

Table 4.2.3
Age and Gender of Population and Churchgoers, England, 1985 and 2005

Age group	Population 1985 Male %	Female %	Total %	Churchgoers 1985 Male %	Female %	Total %	Population 2005 Male %	Female %	Total %	Churchgoers 2005 Male %	Female %	Total %
Under 15	10	9	19	12	12	24	9	9	18	7	8	15
15–19	4	4	8	3	5	8	3	4	7	2	2	4
20–29	8	8	16	5	6	11	6	6	12	2	6	8
30–44	10	10	20	7	10	17	11	11	22	5	12	17
45–64	11	11	22	9	12	21	13	12	25	10	17	27
65/65+	6	9	15	7	12	19	7	9	16	12	17	29
All ages	49	51	100	43	57	100	49	51	100	38	62	100

Churchgoing percentages are based on figures given in Table 2.21.1; population figures from the Office for National Statistics in *Religious Trends* No 1 (1985) and No 3 (2005).

Table 4.2.4
Age and Gender of Population and Churchgoers, Wales, 1985 and 2005

Age group	Population 1985 Male %	Female %	Total %	Churchgoers 1985 Male %	Female %	Total %	Population 2005 Male %	Female %	Total %	Churchgoers 2005 Male %	Female %	Total %
Under 15	10	9	19	9	14	23	9	9	18	5	9	14
15–19	4	4	8	3	4	7	4	3	7	2	4	6
20–29	8	7	15	4	5	9	6	6	12	4	7	11
30–44	10	10	20	6	10	16	10	10	20	5	12	17
45–64	11	11	22	8	14	22	13	13	26	7	18	25
65/65+	6	10	16	8	15	23	7	10	17	7	20	27
All ages	49	51	100	38	62	100	49	51	100	30	70	100

Churchgoing percentages are based on figures given in Table 2.21.1; population figures from the Office for National Statistics in *Religious Trends* No 1 (1985) and No 3 (2005).

Table 4.2.5
Age and Gender of Population and Churchgoers, Scotland, 1985 and 2005

Age group	Population 1985 Male %	Female %	Total %	Churchgoers 1985 Male %	Female %	Total %	Population 2005 Male %	Female %	Total %	Churchgoers 2005 Male %	Female %	Total %
Under 15	10	9	19	11	13	24	9	8	17	7	7	14
15–19	4	4	8	2	3	5	3	3	6	2	2	4
20–29	8	8	16	3	6	9	7	6	13	3	3	6
30–44	10	10	20	5	11	16	11	11	22	6	8	14
45–64	10	12	22	9	15	24	13	13	26	11	17	28
65/65+	6	9	15	7	15	22	6	10	16	12	22	34
All ages	48	52	100	37	63	100	49	51	100	41	59	100

Churchgoing percentages are based on figures given in Table 2.21.1; population figures from the Office for National Statistics in *Religious Trends* No 1 (1985) and No 3 (2005).

Table 4.2.2 Population of EU and Other European Countries

Country	Abb	Population (000s) 2000	2002	2025	% Xn 2025
Austria	A	8,110	8,130	8,390	87.0
Belgium	B	10,249	10,300	10,343	85.5
Cyprus	CY	755	814	864	92.4
Czech Republic	CZ	10,278	10,246	9,512	74.7
Denmark	DK	5,320	5,350	5,604	89.2
Estonia	EE	1,372	1,338	1,131	70.8
Finland	FIN	5,176	5,200	5,217	91.0
France	F	58,892	59,470	64,337	67.8
Germany	D	82,018	82,490	77,181	73.7
Greece	EL	10,010	10,970	11,365	93.8
Hungary	HU	10,043	9,923	8,900	90.8
Ireland	IRL	3,787	3,920	4,006	96.0
Italy	I	57,762	57,480	55,177	79.9
Latvia	LV	2,380	2,329	1,936	77.9
Lithuania	LT	3,699	3,465	3,399	92.9
Luxembourg	L	440	440	503	93.0
Malta	MT	389	393	430	97.6
Netherlands	NL	15,864	16,140	17,116	77.3
Poland	PL	38,654	38,622	39,069	97.9
Portugal	P	10,010	10,050	10,625	90.5
Slovakia	SK	5,399	5,398	5,409	88.5
Slovenia	SI	1,988	1,986	1,818	93.8
Spain	E	39,930	40,980	39,099	92.0
Sweden	S	8,862	8,980	9,313	66.3
United Kingdom	UK	58,817	59,232	60,388	69.2
Grand total	**EU-25**	**450,204**	**453,646**	**451,132**	**79.4**
Albania	AL	3,401	3,141	4,173	44.0
Bulgaria	BG	8,191	7,965	6,959	83.8
Croatia	HR	4,568	4,439	4,282	96.1
Iceland	IS	279	287	319	96.0
Macedonia	MK	2,022	2,046	2,256	62.0
Norway	NO	4,479	4,514	4,921	92.3
Romania	RO	22,456	22,387	20,060	90.9
Switzerland	CH	7,164	7,171	7,609	86.9
Turkey	TR	64,815	70,318	85,526	0.5
Yugoslavia[2]	YU	10,637	10,535	10,841	72.5
Grand Total	**EU-35**	**578,216**	**586,449**	**598,078**	**68.4**

Abb = Official abbreviation Xn = Christian
[1] Estimate [2] Serbia and Montenegro

Sources: Eurostat Yearbook, 2003, Eurostat, European Commission, 2003; *Statistical Yearbook on Candidate and South-east European countries*, Eurostat, European Commission, 2002; Office for National Statistics for UK statistics; Percentage of Christians from *World Christian Encyclopedia*, David Barrett, OUP, 2001; www.library.uu.n/wesp/populstat/Asia (for Cyprus), www.unicef.org/infobycountry.

Table 4.3 UK Population in Thousands by Age-group, 1991–2041
The percentages represent the proportion of men in that age group

UNITED KINGDOM

Age-group	1991	%	1996	%	2001	%	2006	%	2011	%	2016	%	2021	%	2026	%	2031	%	2036	%	2041	%
0–9	7,438	51.1	7,503	51.2	7,305	51.1	6,855	51.1	6,782	51.1	6,882	51.1	7,009	51.1	7,041	51.1	6,927	51.1	6,773	51.1	6,699	51.1
10–14	3,571	51.2	3,763	51.1	3,827	51.0	3,727	51.2	3,474	51.0	3,372	51.0	3,402	51.0	3,471	51.0	3,530	51.0	3,503	51.0	3,416	51.0
15–19	4,084	50.8	3,591	50.1	3,616	50.5	3,932	51.3	3,769	51.2	3,517	51.0	3,415	51.0	3,445	51.0	3,515	51.0	3,574	51.0	3,547	51.0
20–29	8,533	50.3	8,178	50.0	7,864	50.2	7,588	49.9	8,123	50.2	8,213	50.2	7,801	50.0	7,450	49.9	7,381	50.0	7,480	49.9	7,609	49.9
30–44	12,367	49.9	12,553	49.8	13,076	49.6	13,192	49.5	12,377	49.2	11,927	49.1	12,283	49.1	12,657	49.1	12,500	49.2	11,998	49.0	11,685	48.9
45–64	12,388	49.4	13,338	49.5	14,038	49.4	14,993	49.3	15,988	49.1	16,417	49.1	16,591	49.0	16,221	48.7	15,755	48.6	15,620	48.6	15,638	48.6
65–74	5,067	44.8	5,061	45.6	4,942	46.6	5,063	47.5	5,578	47.8	6,435	47.8	6,634	47.8	6,773	47.9	7,526	47.8	7,859	47.7	7,349	47.8
75/75+	3,993	34.0	4,155	35.0	4,419	36.6	4,644	38.5	4,930	40.4	5,372	41.9	6,102	42.6	7,118	43.3	7,701	43.3	8,410	43.5	9,259	43.5
Total	**57,441**	**47.7**	**58,142**	**47.8**	**59,087**	**48.1**	**59,994**	**48.5**	**61,021**	**48.8**	**62,135**	**48.9**	**63,237**	**49.0**	**64,176**	**49.0**	**64,835**	**49.0**	**65,217**	**49.0**	**65,402**	**49.0**

ENGLAND

Age-group	1991	%	1996	%	2001	%	2006	%	2011	%	2016	%	2021	%	2026	%	2031	%	2036	%	2041	%
0–9	6,163	51.1	6,246	51.2	6,096	51.2	5,775	51.1	5,753	51.1	5,855	51.1	5,975	51.1	6,022	51.1	5,949	51.1	5,841	51.1	5,802	51.1
10–14	2,943	51.2	3,119	51.1	3,176	51.2	3,110	51.2	2,906	51.0	2,848	51.0	2,886	51.0	2,950	51.0	3,006	51.0	2,996	51.0	2,934	51.0
15–19	3,386	50.8	2,969	50.1	3,002	50.5	3,277	51.2	3,148	51.2	2,946	51.0	2,887	51.0	2,925	51.0	2,990	51.0	3,046	51.0	3,036	51.0
20–29	7,116	50.3	6,823	50.1	6,598	50.3	6,381	49.9	6,851	50.2	6,952	50.1	6,623	50.0	6,364	49.8	6,346	49.8	6,448	49.9	6,569	49.9
30–44	10,363	49.9	10,500	50.1	10,985	49.8	11,155	49.7	10,527	49.5	10,177	49.3	10,492	49.2	10,833	49.3	10,737	49.2	10,357	49.1	10,143	49.0
45–64	10,319	49.6	11,131	49.6	11,709	49.5	12,500	49.4	13,341	49.3	13,736	49.3	13,959	49.3	13,718	49.0	13,379	48.9	13,308	48.9	13,315	48.8
65–74	4,222	45.0	4,212	45.8	4,108	46.9	4,208	47.7	4,651	47.9	5,379	47.9	5,530	47.9	5,635	48.1	6,285	48.1	6,606	48.0	6,223	48.2
75/75+	3,365	34.2	3,499	35.1	3,718	36.8	3,903	38.7	4,139	40.6	4,504	42.1	5,125	43.0	5,985	43.4	6,467	43.4	7,056	43.6	7,779	43.7
Total	**47,877**	**47.8**	**48,499**	**47.9**	**49,392**	**48.3**	**50,309**	**48.6**	**51,316**	**48.9**	**52,127**	**49.3**	**53,477**	**49.1**	**54,432**	**49.1**	**55,159**	**49.1**	**55,658**	**49.1**	**55,801**	**49.2**

WALES

Age-group	1991	%	1996	%	2001	%	2006	%	2011	%	2016	%	2021	%	2026	%	2031	%	2036	%	2041	%
0–9	373	51.2	370	50.8	359	51.3	330	51.2	321	51.4	328	50.9	332	51.2	327	51.4	318	51.3	309	51.1	303	51.2
10–14	182	51.1	190	51.1	191	51.3	189	51.3	176	51.1	164	51.2	168	51.2	171	50.9	171	51.5	167	51.5	162	51.2
15–19	197	50.5	176	50.3	178	50.0	199	51.3	191	51.3	178	51.1	167	50.9	170	51.2	173	51.4	174	51.1	170	51.2
20–29	398	50.0	381	49.9	361	49.3	350	49.4	377	50.4	381	50.7	361	50.7	336	50.6	328	50.6	335	50.4	339	50.7
30–44	590	49.7	584	49.4	592	48.8	583	47.9	535	46.7	514	46.3	537	47.3	556	48.0	549	47.9	516	47.9	497	47.5
45–64	640	49.4	688	49.6	724	49.3	770	49.0	804	48.5	803	47.9	788	47.2	759	46.5	731	46.0	723	46.2	741	46.6
65–74	284	45.1	279	45.9	264	47.0	272	47.8	304	48.0	353	48.2	361	47.6	357	47.6	385	47.3	391	46.5	356	45.5
75/75+	209	33.5	225	34.2	242	36.8	251	38.2	262	40.5	286	42.0	325	43.1	383	43.6	412	43.4	442	43.2	475	43.4
Total	**2,873**	**47.6**	**2,893**	**47.6**	**2,911**	**48.0**	**2,944**	**48.3**	**2,970**	**48.5**	**3,007**	**48.5**	**3,039**	**48.7**	**3,059**	**48.7**	**3,067**	**48.7**	**3,057**	**48.5**	**3,043**	**48.4**

SCOTLAND

Age-group	1991	%	1996	%	2001	%	2006	%	2011	%	2016	%	2021	%	2026	%	2031	%	2036	%	2041	%
0–9	641	51.2	636	50.6	591	51.1	528	51.1	494	51.0	484	51.0	485	50.9	479	50.9	455	51.2	428	50.9	407	51.1
10–14	317	51.1	322	50.9	315	51.1	305	50.8	276	50.7	252	50.8	241	50.6	242	50.8	243	50.6	234	50.9	220	50.5
15–19	373	50.5	326	50.2	317	50.3	325	51.1	307	50.8	278	50.7	254	50.4	244	50.4	244	50.4	246	50.4	237	50.6
20–29	771	50.0	725	49.6	665	49.3	623	50.2	645	50.2	636	50.2	590	49.8	538	49.8	504	49.4	493	49.7	495	49.5
30–44	1,094	49.5	1,121	49.2	1,130	48.5	1,083	48.1	968	48.0	890	48.4	894	49.0	900	49.0	862	48.8	794	48.4	732	48.2
45–64	1,118	48.2	1,184	48.6	1,241	49.0	1,323	48.7	1,406	48.2	1,420	47.7	1,376	47.2	1,285	47.0	1,192	49.2	1,133	47.5	1,125	47.7
65–74	441	43.5	448	44.2	447	44.7	455	45.5	477	46.5	540	47.0	570	47.0	592	46.5	643	45.9	642	45.5	562	45.2
75/75+	329	32.5	337	33.5	360	35.0	410	33.9	410	39.0	450	40.0	499	41.5	576	42.0	626	42.2	690	42.0	754	41.9
Total	**5,084**	**47.1**	**5,099**	**47.1**	**5,066**	**47.4**	**5,052**	**47.4**	**4,983**	**48.1**	**4,950**	**48.2**	**4,909**	**48.3**	**4,856**	**48.3**	**4,769**	**48.5**	**4,660**	**48.2**	**4,532**	**48.1**

NORTHERN IRELAND

Age-group	1991	%	1996	%	2001	%	2006	%	2011	%	2016	%	2021	%	2026	%	2031	%	2036	%	2041	%
0–9	262	51.0	256	51.2	243	51.2	223	51.1	214	50.9	215	50.7	217	50.7	213	50.7	204	51.5	196	51.0	189	51.3
10–14	130	51.2	133	51.1	128	51.2	124	50.8	116	50.9	108	50.9	107	50.5	109	50.5	109	50.5	106	50.0	100	51.0
15–19	128	51.2	122	50.8	120	50.8	132	51.5	123	51.2	115	51.3	107	50.5	106	50.9	108	50.9	108	50.9	105	50.5
20–29	248	50.4	251	50.2	242	50.0	233	50.2	251	51.0	244	51.2	227	51.1	212	51.4	204	50.5	204	51.0	207	50.7
30–44	320	50.0	349	49.6	370	49.2	372	48.7	349	48.4	346	48.6	357	49.0	366	49.7	352	49.7	328	49.1	312	49.0
45–64	311	48.2	336	48.8	364	49.2	399	49.4	434	49.1	460	48.5	468	47.6	459	47.5	454	47.6	454	47.8	458	48.0
65–74	120	44.2	123	43.9	123	45.5	129	46.5	146	47.3	163	47.2	173	48.0	189	47.6	212	46.7	220	46.8	208	46.2
75/75+	89	34.8	94	34.0	100	37.0	108	38.0	117	38.5	131	40.5	154	41.6	176	42.0	196	42.9	221	42.5	249	43.0
Total	**1,608**	**47.6**	**1,664**	**47.5**	**1,690**	**48.0**	**1,720**	**48.3**	**1,750**	**48.4**	**1,782**	**48.6**	**1,810**	**48.6**	**1,830**	**48.8**	**1,839**	**48.8**	**1,837**	**48.6**	**1,828**	**48.7**

Sources: Government Actuary's Department, Base year 2002. www.gad.gov.uk/Population/2002, *Population Trends* No 115, Spring 2004

Table 4.4.1
Baptisms of Children, by Denomination, UK, 1991–2001

	Church of England[1]	Roman Catholic[2]	Methodist[3]	Church of Scotland	Other Churches[4]	TOTAL	% of births
1991	217,000	77,352	27,414	15,541	66,700	**404,007**	*51*
1993	197,740	74,895	25,354	13,806	67,650	**379,445**	*50*
1995	186,380	75,200	23,426	12,737	70,060	**367,803**	*50*
1997	179,280	67,384	22,985	12,156	71,709	**353,514**	*49*
1999	168,910	62,166	21,363	10,460	70,001	**332,900**	*48*
2001	145,200	59,182	19,810	9,170	67,962	**301,324**	*45*

[1] Infants (under 1) and children (under 12) [2] In England and Wales [3] Excluding those baptised over the age of 13; taken from Minutes of the Methodist Conference [4] Estimate of infant baptisms in the Church in Wales, Scottish Episcopal Church, Church of Ireland (Northern Ireland), Roman Catholic Church in Scotland and Northern Ireland, Presbyterian Church of Wales, Free Church of Scotland, Free Church of Scotland (Continuing) for 2001, and United Free Church of Scotland.

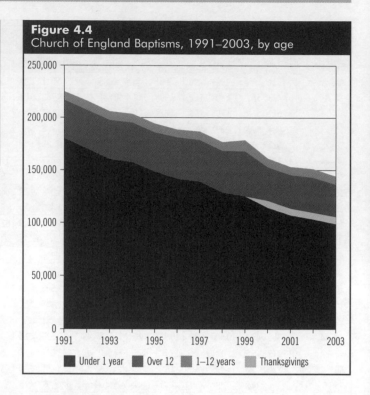

Figure 4.4
Church of England Baptisms, 1991–2003, by age

Legend: ■ Under 1 year ■ Over 12 ■ 1–12 years ■ Thanksgivings

Table 4.4.2
Births, UK, 1990–2050

Year	Number of births	% births outside marriage	% to women under 20[2]	% to women 35 or over[2]
1995	731,900	33.6	6.5	11.9
1996	733,200	35.5	6.9	12.6
1997	726,600	36.8	7.2	13.7
1998	716,900	37.6	7.6	14.5
1999	700,000	38.8	7.8	15.4
2000	679,000	39.5	7.6	16.6
2001	669,100	40.1	7.4	17.3
2002	668,800	40.6	7.3	18.1
2003	695,600	41.5	7.1	18.7
2004[3]	716,000	42.3	7.0	19.3
2005[1]	708,000	44	7.7	21
2010[1]	695,000	48	8.0	25
2020[1]	718,000	58	8.7	34
2030[1]	708,000	67	9	43
2040[1]	695,000	76	10	52
2050[1]	679,000	85	11	60

[1] Estimate [2] England and Wales only [3] Provisional
Source: ©Crown Copyright 2004. *Population Trends* No 116, Summer 2004, Page 39 and No 120, Summer 2005, Page 50. www.gad.gov.uk/Population. For earlier years see Table 4.4.1 in *Religious Trends* No 3.

Table 4.4.3 Baptisms by Age, Church of England, 1991–2002

Age: Year	Under 1	1–12	Over 12	Thanks-givings[1]
1991	180,000	36,980	8,020	–
1992	170,100	37,300	8,990	–
1993	160,300	37,440	8,250	–
1994	157,100	38,110	8,270	–
1995	148,000	38,380	7,920	–
1996	141,400	39,560	7,740	–
1997	138,900	40,380	8,150	–
1998	129,000	39,360	8,380	–
1999	125,600	43,310	10,130	–
2000	114,200	38,480	8,430	6,910
2001	106,900	38,300	8,100	6,800
2002	103,200	39,700	8,400	7,000
2003	99,000	37,100	8,300	6,900

[1] Not recorded prior to 2000
Source: Church Statistics, Research and Statistics Dept, Church House Publishing, for years indicated

In 1900, 65% of children born in England were baptised by the Church of England before they were one year old. Ninety years later that percentage was down to 27%, but as **Table 4.4.1** indicates the total numbers by other denominations is considerable, sufficient to make the total number of children baptised (some more than a year old) still about half of all those born in the UK. That pattern has broadly continued across the 1990s. If the number of births continues to decrease, as the numbers in **Table 4.4.2** suggest they will, then the number of infants christened will also drop.

Within the Church of England baptisms are recorded for those under one year of age, those between one and 12 years of age, and those older. While more than two-thirds, 70% in 2001, of the total baptisms are still of those under one year of age, **Figure 4.4** clearly shows that this proportion has changed over the 1990s.

While the number of baptisms among those over a year, and as adults, is broadly unchanged, as **Table 4.4.3** shows, it is the number of infants being baptised which is decreasing, newly introduced counts for thanksgivings not yet making a significant change in the downward pattern.

These trends are also reflected in the 2001 census statistics, as the percentage of children who were recorded as Christian rose from 55% for those aged 0–2, to 61% for those aged 3 or 4, and to 69% for those aged 10 or 11, as shown in **Table 4.4.4**.

Table 4.4.4
Religion of Children, by Age, 2001

Age	All dependent children	Cian %	Buddhist %	Hindu %	Jew %	Muslim %	Sikh %	Other %	None %	n/a %
0 to 2	1,811,608	55.3	0.2	1.1	0.5	5.8	0.7	0.1	23.1	13.2
3 or 4	1,279,439	61.0	0.2	1.0	0.5	5.5	0.7	0.1	19.8	11.2
5 to 7	1,945,633	65.8	0.2	1.1	0.4	5.1	0.7	0.1	16.7	9.9
8 or 9	1,358,612	68.3	0.2	1.1	0.4	4.6	0.7	0.1	15.4	9.2
10 or 11	1,380,278	69.4	0.2	1.1	0.4	4.5	0.7	0.1	14.9	8.7
12 to 14	2,014,759	69.4	0.2	1.2	0.4	4.5	0.8	0.2	15.2	8.1
15	650,764	68.7	0.2	1.3	0.4	4.7	0.9	0.2	15.8	7.8
16	553,116	68.7	0.2	1.6	0.4	4.8	1.0	0.2	16.3	6.8
17 or 18	671,057	65.4	0.3	2.2	0.6	6.2	1.4	0.3	16.9	6.7
OVERALL	**11,665,266**	**65.3**	**0.2**	**1.2**	**0.4**	**5.1**	**0.8**	**0.1**	**17.3**	**9.6**

Cian = Christian Other = Any other religion None = No religion n/a = Religion not stated
Source: Census 2001: National Report for England and Wales, Part 2, National Statistics, London, Spring 2004, Table T52, Page 245

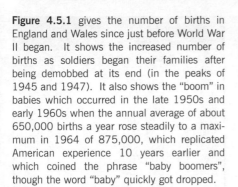

Figure 4.5.1 gives the number of births in England and Wales since just before World War II began. It shows the increased number of births as soldiers began their families after being demobbed at its end (in the peaks of 1945 and 1947). It also shows the "boom" in babies which occurred in the late 1950s and early 1960s when the annual average of about 650,000 births a year rose steadily to a maximum in 1964 of 875,000, which replicated American experience 10 years earlier and which coined the phrase "baby boomers", though the word "baby" quickly got dropped.

Thirty years later around 1990 there is clear evidence of a "mini-boom", which is where **Figure 4.5.2** begins, which shows evidence of a "mini-mini-boom" 30 years later in 2020. Both these diagrams show the increasing numbers being born outside marriage, the number increasing very substantially in the 1980s, but at a less rapid rate in the 1990s. **Figure 4.5.2** shows that the proportion grows steadily, however, the actual numbers being given in **Table 4.4.2**. The 50% mark is likely to be reached in 2012. It should be noted, however, that **Figure 4.5.1** gives numbers for England and Wales, whereas **Figure 4.5.2** illustrates UK figures.

Figure 4.5.3 shows the breakdown of UK marriages by age. While the number of those under 20 remains much the same (rising from 59,000 in 1990 to 67,000 by 2040), the proportion having children after the age of 35 rises rapidly. **Figures 4.5.4** and **4.5.5** explore the age dimension further, showing that majority of the increase in births outside marriage is with those under 30, whereas the greater number of multiple maternities is more likely among those 35 and over.

Source: Population Trends, National Statistics, Number 115, Spring 2004, Annual Update Births in 2002, England and Wales.

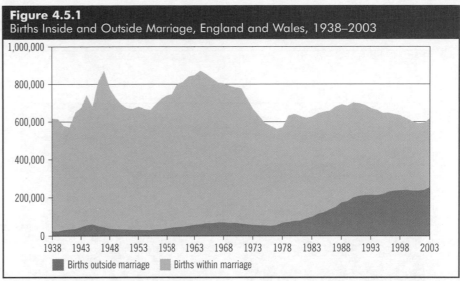

Figure 4.5.1
Births Inside and Outside Marriage, England and Wales, 1938–2003

Births outside marriage ■ Births within marriage ■

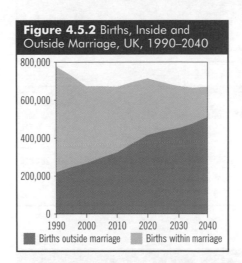

Figure 4.5.2 Births, Inside and Outside Marriage, UK, 1990–2040

■ Births outside marriage ■ Births within marriage

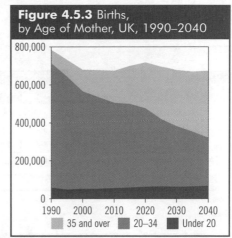

Figure 4.5.3 Births, by Age of Mother, UK, 1990–2040

■ 35 and over ■ 20–34 ■ Under 20

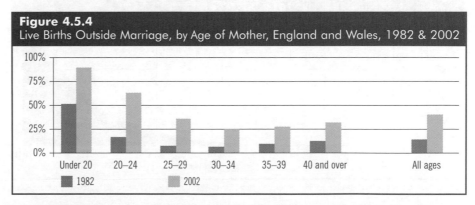

Figure 4.5.4
Live Births Outside Marriage, by Age of Mother, England and Wales, 1982 & 2002

■ 1982 ■ 2002

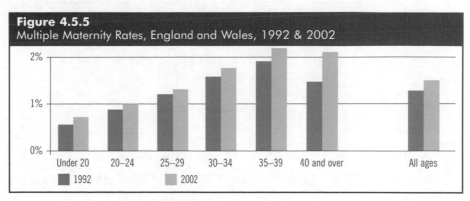

Figure 4.5.5
Multiple Maternity Rates, England and Wales, 1992 & 2002

■ 1992 ■ 2002

Table 4.5 Average Number of Liveborn Children per Woman by Age and Year of Birth, England and Wales, 1927–1982

Year of birth	Age of woman					
	20	25	30	35	40	45[1]
1927	0.17	0.87	1.55	1.97	2.17	2.20
1932	0.19	0.96	1.73	2.17	2.32	2.34
1937	0.23	1.13	1.95	2.29	2.37	2.39
1942	0.31	1.27	1.96	2.19	2.27	2.29
1947	0.34	1.14	1.71	1.98	2.06	2.08
1952	0.36	0.99	1.60	1.92	2.03	2.05
1957	0.27	0.88	1.49	1.85	1.99	2.01
1962	0.23	0.76	1.36	1.75	1.91	*1.93*
1967	0.21	0.71	1.27	1.67	*1.84*	*1.86*
1972	0.22	0.63	1.13	*1.62*	*1.77*	*1.79*
1977	0.21	0.59	*1.10*	*1.53*	*1.69*	*1.71*
1982	0.21	*0.56*	*1.08*	*1.60*	*1.78*	*1.80*

[1] Includes births at ages 45 and over, achieved up to the end of 2002.
Numbers in italic are Christian Research estimates.

4.6 Abortions and Deaths

Figure 4.6.1
Number of Deaths, UK, 1990–2070 (thousands)

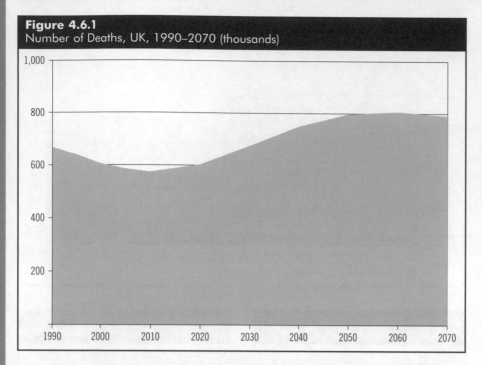

Table 4.6.1
Deaths, UK, 1995–2070

Year	Number of deaths	% cremations
1995	641,712	71.0
1996	636,000	69.7
1997	629,700	70.4
1998	629,200	69.4
1999	632,100	69.9
2000	608,400	71.5
2001	602,300	70.7
2002	606,200	71.9
2003	612,000	71.8[1]
2004[2]	584,800	71.8[1]
2005[1]	589,000	72
2010[1]	577,000	73
2020[1]	606,000	74
2030[1]	679,000	76
2040[1]	752,000	78
2050[1]	799,000	80
2060[1]	808,000	82
2070[1]	793,000	82

[1] Estimate [2] Provisional

Source: ©Crown Copyright 2004. *Population Trends* No 116, Summer 2004, Page 41 and No 120, Summer 2005, Page 47, and Cremation Society: www.srgw.demon.co.uk/CremSoc4. For earlier years see Table 4.8.1 in *Religious Trends* No 2.

Table 4.6.2
Number and Percentage of Deaths, by Age, UK, 2003

	<1	1–4	5–9	10–14	15–19	20–24	25–34	35–44	45–54	55–64	65–74	75–84	85/85+	TOTAL
M	1,830	310	200	260	850	1,350	3,480	6,440	12,700	28,300	55,100	89,600	54,100	**254,520**
F	1,480	280	160	210	370	490	1,640	3,880	8,600	18,000	39,000	92,700	118,000	**284,810**
M%	0.57	0.03	0.01	0.02	0.05	0.08	0.09	0.16	0.38	0.99	2.66	7.46	18.96	**0.99**
F%	0.49	0.02	0.01	0.01	0.02	0.03	0.04	0.10	0.25	0.61	1.68	5.19	16.21	**1.06**

Source: Population Trends, National Statistics, No 116, Summer 2004, Page 47.

Table 4.6.3 Life Expectancy, in Years, England and Wales

Year	Men	Women
1841	41	43
1901	45	49
1951	66	71
1976	70	75
2001	76	81
2026	81	85

Sources: www.statistics.gov.uk/cci, *Population Trends* National Statistics, Nos 116, Summer 2004, 118, Winter 2004 and www.barnett-waddingham.co.uk.

Figure 4.6.2
Number of Centenarians, UK, 1911–2031

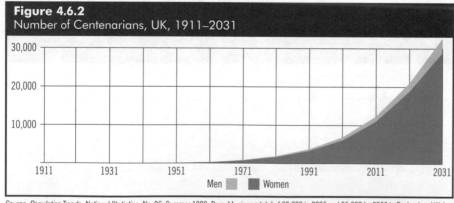

Men ▨ Women ▨

Source: Population Trends, National Statistics, No. 96, Summer 1999, Page 11, gives a total of 39,000 in 2036 and 95,000 by 2066 in England and Wales.

Table 4.6.4 Abortions, Residents in England and Wales, 1995–2005

Year	Number of abortions	Cumulative abortions since 1967 Act
1995	154,300	3,518,441
1996	167,900	3,686,341
1997	170,100	3,856,441
1998	177,332	4,033,733
1999	174,856	4,208,629
2000	174,109[1]	4,382,738
2001	177,086	4,559,824
2002	177,000	4,736,824
2005[1]	179,000	5,272,324

[1] Estimate
Source: Health Statistics, National Statistics.

Table 4.6.5
Major Causes of Death, by Sex and Age, England and Wales, 2002

	Men			Women		
Cause	50–64 %	65–84 %	85/85+ %	50–64 %	65–84 %	85/85+ %
Cancers	39	32	18	53	29	12
Circulatory system	36	41	43	22	40	42
Respiratory system	7	13	19	8	13	17
Digestive system	7	4	3	6	5	4
Injury and poisoning	4	1	2	3	1	2
Nervous system	2	3	3	3	3	3
Mental & behavioural	1	1	3	~	2	6
Other	4	5	9	5	7	14
Number of deaths (=100%)	35,600	144,600	53,600	23,000	129,600	116,300

Source: Older People, National Statistics, www.statistics.gov.uk/cci/nugget, Life Expectancy, July 2004.

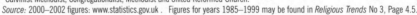

Table 4.7.1 Number of Marriages by Location, England and Wales, 2000–2020

Year	Total marriages	Registry Office	Approved Premises	Church
		Number which were held in		
2000	267,961	125,008	45,792	97,161
2001	249,227	110,089	50,149	88,989
2002	255,600	106,950	62,780	85,870
2005¹	238,800	84,800	84,300	69,700
2010¹	216,900	59,200	106,900	50,800
2020¹	173,300	26,700	121,100	26,500

¹Estimate   *Source:* www.statistics.gov.uk
Figures for years since 1985 may be found in *Religious Trends* No 3, Page 4.5

Table 4.7.2
Religious Marriages by Denomination, England and Wales, 2000–2020

Year	Total religious marriages	Anglican²	Roman Catholic	Non-conformist³	Other Christian	Others
2000	97,161	65,536	11,312	13,435	4,316	2,565
2001	88,989	60,878	10,518	11,163	4,047	2,383
2002	85,870	58,710	9,980	10,570	4,170	2,440
2005¹	69,700	47,400	8,200	9,000	3,200	1,900
2010¹	50,800	34,600	5,900	6,600	2,300	1,400
2020¹	26,500	18,000	3,100	3,400	1,200	800

¹Estimate   ²Church of England and Church in Wales; Church of England only are in Table 8.3.1. ³Defined by Office of National Statistics as Baptist, Calvinist Methodist, Congregationalist, Methodist and United Reformed Church.
Source: 2000–2002 figures: www.statistics.gov.uk .   Figures for years 1985–1999 may be found in *Religious Trends* No 3, Page 4.5.

Table 4.7.3 Divorces by Country within UK, 1995–2005

Year	Total UK	England	Wales	Scotland	N.I.
1995	170,000	147,500	8,000	12,200	2,300
1996	171,700	148,700	8,400	12,300	2,300
1997	161,100	138,700	8,000	12,200	2,200
1998	160,100	137,300	7,900	12,400	2,500
1999	158,700	137,000	7,500	11,900	2,300
2000	154,600	133,900	7,200	11,100	2,400
2001	156,800	136,400	7,400	10,600	2,400
2002	160,535	139,935	7,535	10,800	2,200
2003	165,900	145,800	7,700	10,100	2,300
2005¹	149,300	130,100	6,900	10,000	2,300

¹Estimate   *Source:* Relevant issues of *Population Trends.*

Table 4.7.2 and **Figure 4.7.1** show a fast declining number of religious marriages. The declining number of marriages in England and Wales is largely due to fewer getting married in church. If these figures are fulfilled, and they are but projections of present trends, they show that the number of religious marriages will fall by almost three-quarters, 73%, over the 20 years from 2000. This is roughly halving the number every 10 years, the pattern seen in **Figure 4.7.1** since 1990. This is twice the rate of decline of marriages in general, but this has more to do with the very rapid growth in "approved premises" shown in **Table 4.7.1** and **Figure 4.7.2**, than the decline in church weddings *per se* or the increasing unpopularity of marriage. Perhaps only 10% of church weddings are of people who regularly attend church.

The decline in marriages in different denominations in **Table 4.7.2** follows the decline in religious marriages. The numbers per denomination reflect the same proportion of the total as was the average across 2000–2002. The Anglican number averaged 4 per church in 2000; if present trends continue, the average will be only just above 1 per church in 2020. **Table 12.3** suggests a large decline in 'Occasional Offices' by 2020, except for funerals; **Table 4.7.2** shows how large that decline could be.

Table 4.7.3 shows that the number of divorces is gradually declining, at an average rate of 1.3% per year between 1995 and the estimated figure for 2005. This is largely because of the decreasing number of married people, only 50.7% of the population in the 2001 Census.

Figure 4.7.1
Religious and Civil Marriages, England and Wales, 1970–2020

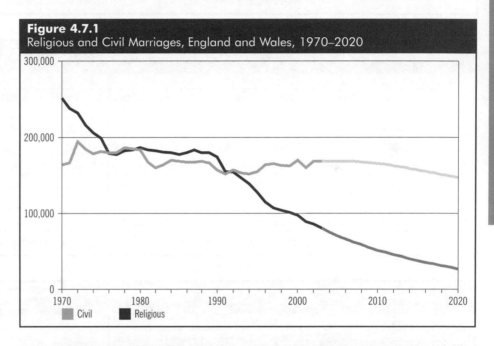

Civil   Religious

Figure 4.7.2
Location of Marriage, England and Wales, 1990–2020

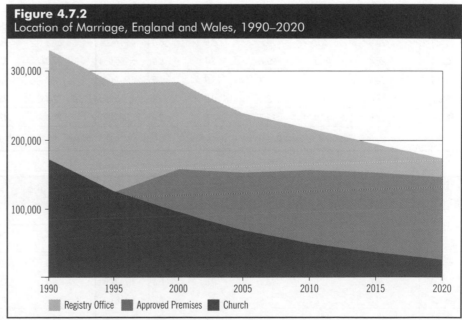

Registry Office   Approved Premises   Church

Sources: Population Trends 22 for 1970–1978 figures; religious marriages for 1979, 1981–1984 estimated; all marriages 2003 to 2020 estimated; *Population Trends* 116 for later figures, published by The Stationery Office, 2004.

Table 4.8.1
Age, Gender and Marital Status of Population in England and Wales, 1996 — **1996**

| | MEN | | | | | | WOMEN | | | | | |
Age	Single %	Married %	Cohabiting %	Sep/Div'd %	Widowed %	Base (=100%)	Single %	Married %	Cohabiting %	Sep/Div'd %	Widowed %	Base (=100%)
<16	100.0	0.0	0.0	0.0	0.0	5,395,000	100.0	0.0	0.0	0.0	0.0	5,163,000
16–29	71.6	14.7	13.2	0.5	0.0	4,767,000	58.2	23.7	16.5	1.6	0.0	4,794,000
30–44	18.8	62.4	11.9	6.7	0.2	5,532,000	11.9	69.0	9.8	9.0	0.3	5,604,000
45–64	8.2	77.9	2.9	9.4	1.6	5,861,000	5.0	75.1	2.0	11.4	6.5	5,952,000
65/65+	6.8	72.2	1.5	3.7	15.8	3,354,000	7.4	39.6	1.0	4.0	48.0	4,849,000
All 16+	**26.4**	**56.9**	**8.0**	**5.9**	**2.8**	**19,524,000**	**19.3**	**53.7**	**7.4**	**7.6**	**12.0**	**21,199,000**

Sep/Div'd = Separated/Divorced. Those who are separated, divorced or widowed and also cohabiting are included under "cohabiting"

Table 4.8.2
Age, Gender and Marital Status of Population in England and Wales, 2001 — **2001**

| | MEN | | | | | | WOMEN | | | | | |
Age	Single %	Married %	Cohabiting %	Sep/Div'd %	Widowed %	Base (=100%)	Single %	Married %	Cohabiting %	Sep/Div'd %	Widowed %	Base (=100%)
<16	100.0	0.0	0.0	0.0	0.0	5,174,000	100.0	0.0	0.0	0.0	0.0	5,098,000
16–29	74.9	10.9	13.9	0.3	0.0	4,627,000	62.3	17.9	18.8	1.0	0.0	4,567,000
30–44	20.9	58.9	15.9	4.2	0.1	5,898,000	14.4	63.6	13.5	8.0	0.5	5,959,000
45–64	9.0	75.5	4.3	9.6	1.6	6,153,000	5.3	72.8	2.8	13.3	5.8	6,281,000
65/65+	6.0	72.2	2.1	4.7	15.0	3,505,000	5.1	37.3	1.4	4.8	51.4	5,326,000
All 16+	**27.0**	**55.0**	**9.9**	**5.4**	**2.7**	**20,183,000**	**19.3**	**53.7**	**7.4**	**7.6**	**12.0**	**21,199,000**

Sep/Div'd = Separated/Divorced. Those who are separated, divorced or widowed and also cohabiting are included under "cohabiting"

Table 4.8.3
Age, Gender and Marital Status of Population in England and Wales, 2011 — **2011**

| | MEN | | | | | | WOMEN | | | | | |
Age	Single %	Married %	Cohabiting %	Sep/Div'd %	Widowed %	Base (=100%)	Single %	Married %	Cohabiting %	Sep/Div'd %	Widowed %	Base (=100%)
<16	100.0	0.0	0.0	0.0	0.0	4,537,000	100.0	0.0	0.0	0.0	0.0	5,287,000
16–29	76.6	8.0	14.8	0.6	0.0	4,997,000	64.8	14.0	20.8	0.4	0.0	4,902,000
30–44	28.4	45.5	20.7	5.4	0.0	5,460,000	20.0	52.0	19.8	8.2	0.0	5,602,000
45–64	12.5	65.0	7.0	13.9	1.6	6,967,000	8.2	65.3	5.0	17.0	4.5	7,178,000
65/65+	3.6	71.6	3.5	8.0	13.3	4,160,000	2.4	45.2	2.5	9.7	40.2	5,196,000
All 16+	**29.6**	**48.0**	**12.2**	**7.8**	**2.4**	**21,584,000**	**21.4**	**47.0**	**11.8**	**9.9**	**9.9**	**22,878,000**

Sep/Div'd = Separated/Divorced. Those who are separated, divorced or widowed and also cohabiting are included under "cohabiting"

Table 4.8.4
Age, Gender and Marital Status of Population in England and Wales, 2021 — **2021**

| | MEN | | | | | | WOMEN | | | | | |
Age	Single %	Married %	Cohabiting %	Sep/Div'd %	Widowed %	Base (=100%)	Single %	Married %	Cohabiting %	Sep/Div'd %	Widowed %	Base (=100%)
<16	100.0	0.0	0.0	0.0	0.0	5,161,000	100.0	0.0	0.0	0.0	0.0	5,756,000
16–29	76.0	8.0	15.4	0.6	0.0	4,740,000	63.4	15.0	21.3	0.3	0.0	4,687,000
30–44	31.3	42.0	21.9	4.8	0.0	5,416,000	22.7	49.0	21.4	6.9	0.0	5,613,000
45–64	20.1	57.6	8.3	13.2	0.8	7,254,000	13.8	59.6	6.4	16.6	3.6	7,493,000
65/65+	3.0	69.0	4.1	11.9	12.0	5,165,000	0.7	47.1	3.2	13.9	35.1	6,176,000
All 16+	**30.9**	**45.5**	**13.1**	**8.1**	**2.4**	**22,575,000**	**22.5**	**44.5**	**12.8**	**11.0**	**9.2**	**23,969,000**

Sep/Div'd = Separated/Divorced. Those who are separated, divorced or widowed and also cohabiting are included under "cohabiting"

Source: *Population Trends* No 115, National Statistics, Table 1.5 and www.gad.gov.uk/news/marital_status_projections_1996-based.html

The numbers on **Page 4.8** are graphed in **Figures 4.9.1–4**, showing the trends in marital status by age and by gender between 1996 and 2021. The percentage of single people will increase across all adult ages, except those aged 65 and over. They increase most sharply among those aged 30 to 44 and 45 to 64. This increase is partly due to the numbers of lone parents, mostly lone mothers, which these single figures include.

Figures 4.9.1 and **4.9.2** show the varying proportions of married people in the English and Welsh population. These percentages are decreasing, again except for those aged 65 and over. The proportion of married men aged 30 to 44 in 1996 was 62%; by 2021 it is set to become 42%, a very great decline. Among women the drop is similar, from 69% to 49%. Among those aged 45 to 64, the drop of married men falls from 78% in 1996 to 58% by 2021, although among women of this age, the drop is less severe – from 75% to 60%. The major period of these changes is between the years 2001 and 2011, that is, the decade in which we are currently living.

Figures 4.9.3 and **4.9.4** graph the proportions who are cohabiting. It should be noted that the percentages shown as separated/divorced or widowed on **Page 4.8** are lower than they might be as cohabiting people in these categories are included among those shown as "cohabiting". The proportions who are cohabiting increase between 1996 and 2021 across all ages, including those aged 65 or over. The greatest increase takes place between those aged 30 to 44, where the proportion of men cohabiting rises from 12% in 1996 to 22% by 2021, and of women from 10% to 21%.

Figure 4.9.5 shows that the decline in marriage (from 55% of the adult population in 1996 to 45% by 2021) is due to the increasing numbers who are single (never married) and those who are cohabiting. The single include lone parents, the very large majority of whom are lone mothers. The proportions of those who are divorced or widowed but also cohabiting are again included within the cohabiting percentage.

The challenge for the church is to find ways of welcoming and including lone parents, other single people and those who are cohabiting within their family. Larger churches are often able to do this more easily than smaller churches as more of such people are likely to attend and thus be able to form a fellowship group.

Figure 4.9.6 shows a large disparity between churchgoers and the general population. The church has a greater proportion of married people and widowed (because the church has many more older people pro rata) and fewer single, separated, divorced or cohabiting people. Most of the single people in the church will not be cohabiting, unlike many in the general population. These differences are likely to increase with time not diminish if changes do not take place.

Table 4.9 is quite different to the above, and gives the proportion of Christian people marrying someone from their own denomination. This information is not available in the UK, so the data comes from Australia. The proportion marrying someone of their own denomination was overall two-thirds, or 67%, in 1991, a percentage which dropped to 61% by 2001. The

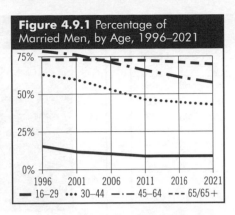

Figure 4.9.1 Percentage of Married Men, by Age, 1996–2021

— 16–29 ••• 30–44 –•– 45–64 – – – 65/65+

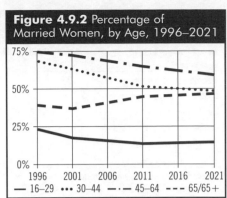

Figure 4.9.2 Percentage of Married Women, by Age, 1996–2021

— 16–29 ••• 30–44 –•– 45–64 – – – 65/65+

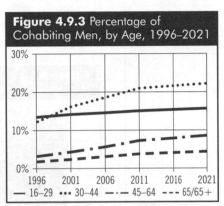

Figure 4.9.3 Percentage of Cohabiting Men, by Age, 1996–2021

— 16–29 ••• 30–44 –•– 45–64 – – – 65/65+

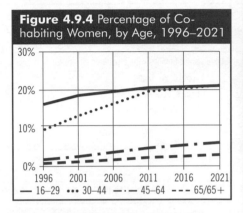

Figure 4.9.4 Percentage of Cohabiting Women, by Age, 1996–2021

— 16–29 ••• 30–44 –•– 45–64 – – – 65/65+

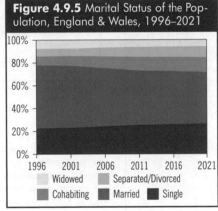

Figure 4.9.5 Marital Status of the Population, England & Wales, 1996–2021

Widowed   Separated/Divorced   Cohabiting   Married   Single

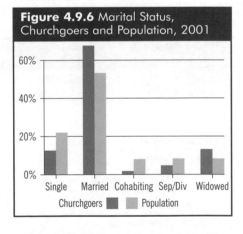

Figure 4.9.6 Marital Status, Churchgoers and Population, 2001

Single   Married   Cohabiting   Sep/Div   Widowed

Churchgoers   Population

Uniting Church, Lutherans and Salvation Army dropped more than 6% in this period, while the Orthodox Church increased their percentage.

In a 2004 American survey, 27% said they would not date someone not in their denomination, 36% said that they were concerned to find someone from the same denomination but would date someone else, and 37% said that religion was not a factor taken into account.

Sources: Marital Status projections for England and Wales, News release by Government Actuary's Dept, www.gad.gov.uk/news/marital_status_projections; Christian figures compiled from 6,594 people including 1,910 Anglican churchgoers in the 2003 Cost of Conscience survey, published in *The Mind of Anglicans,* Christian Research; 939 churchgoers in a private 2003 survey about Methodist care services undertaken by Christian Research; 2,656 churchgoers across three Deanery Strategic Reviews undertaken for the Diocese of Rochester by Christian Research between 1999 and 2002; and 1,089 churchgoers across all denominations in a private survey about Bible Reading undertaken by Christian Research in 2003.

Table 4.9 Percentage Marrying within Same Denomination, Australia

Denomination	Affiliation (1991 Census)	1991 %	2001 %
Orthodox	470,818	87	93
Pentecostal	150,665	89	87
Seventh-Day Adventist	48,341	80	75
Churches of Christ	78,039	73	70
Baptist	279,920	67	65
Catholic	4,590,478	68	62
Anglican	4,018,770	65	60
Uniting Church	1,387,646	64	56
Lutheran	250,844	59	50
Salvation Army	71,984	59	50
Presbyterian & Reformed	732,227	46	40
TOTAL Christian	**12,079,732**	**67**	**61**

Sources: Pointers, Christian Research Association, Australia, June 2004, Volume 14, Number 2, Page 12 [2001 figures], *Australian Social Trends* 1994, www.abs.gov.au/Aussstats/abs [1991 figures]; *Religion Watch,* June 2004, Volume 19, Number 8, Page 5.

Table 4.10.1
Family Composition in Great Britain, 1986–2010

Type of family with head aged under 60	1986 %	1988 %	1992 %	1996 %	2001 %	2010E %
Married-couple families[1]	83	79	74	67	62	49
Cohabiting-couple families[1]	5	8	9	11	13	18
Lone-parent families[2]	12	13	17	22	25	33
Couple families with no children:						
Married couples	22	22	21	20	19	17
Cohabiting couples	3	5	6	7	8	11
Couple families with dependent children:						
Married couples	49	46	42	37	34	24
Cohabiting couples	2	3	3	4	5	7
Couple families with only non-dependent children:						
Married couples	11	11	11	10	9	8
Cohabiting couples	0.3	0.3	0.3	0.3	0.2	0.2
Lone parent families with dependent children:						
Lone single mothers	2	3	5	7	10	14
Lone separated mothers	2	2	3	4	4	6
Lone divorced mothers	4	4	4	6	7	9
Lone widowed mothers	0.5	0.6	0.5	0.5	0.6	0.6
Lone fathers	0.8	0.8	1	2	1	1
Lone parent families with only non-dependent children						
	3	3	3	3	3	3
All families[1]: Sample size (=100%)	5,003	4,974	4,899	8,210	7,146	n/a

[1] With or without children [2] With either dependent children, non-dependent children, or both E = Estimate
Source: *General Household Survey* for relevant years

Table 4.10.2
Household Composition in Great Britain, 1961–2011

Type of household	1961 %	1971 %	1981 %	1991 %	2001 %	2011E %
One-person households	12	18	22	27	31	36
Married couple households	74	70	65	59	56	50
Lone-parent households	6	7	9	10	9	11
Other types of household	8	5	4	4	4	3
One-person households:						
Under pensionable age	4	6	8	11	13	15
Over pensionable age	8	12	14	16	18	21
Married couple households with:						
No children	26	27	26	26	29	28
1–2 dependent children[1]	30	26	25	20	18	14
3+ dependent children[1]	8	9	6	5	4	3
Non-dependent children only	10	8	8	8	6	5
Lone parent households with:						
Dependent children[1]	2	3	5	6	7	9
Non-dependent children only	4	4	4	4	2	2
Other types of household:						
Two or more unrelated adults	5	4	3	3	3	2
Two or more families	3	1	1	1	1	1
Number of households[2] (=100%)	16.2	18.2	19.5	22.4	24.5	26.4

[1] May also include some non-dependent children [2] In millions E = Estimate
Source: *General Household Survey* for relevant years.

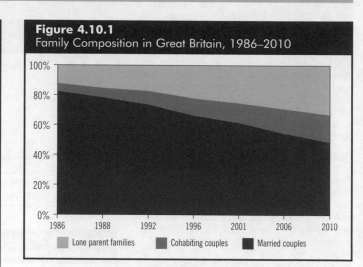

Figure 4.10.1
Family Composition in Great Britain, 1986–2010

Lone parent families | Cohabiting couples | Married couples

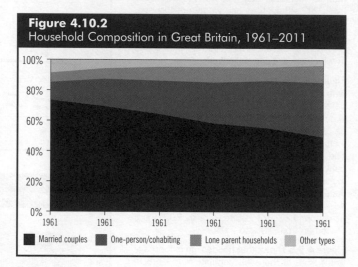

Figure 4.10.2
Household Composition in Great Britain, 1961–2011

Married couples | One-person/cohabiting | Lone parent households | Other types

Tables 4.10.1 and **4.10.2** show the make-up of families and households respectively, with a forecast to 2010 or 2011. The overall figures at the top of each Table are the basis for **Figures 4.10.1** and **4.10.2**. Both these charts show the smaller proportions of married people who make up either families or households, with increasing proportions of cohabiting couples (counted as one-person households officially) and lone parent families. In household terms the latter are only about a tenth of the total, but in family terms they will make up a third of all families by 2010.

It is therefore crucial that churches make both cohabitees and lone parents as welcome as they can as more and more people are choosing to live in this way, and some of these will be, or will become, churchgoers.

These changes mean that a decreasing number of children are being raised within the traditional British set up, that is, children living together with both their natural parents under the same roof. 41% of children live in a non-traditional family, made up of 2.7 million children living in lone parent households (57%), 1.3 million children living in households with cohabiting parents (28%), that is, their parents are not formally married, and 726,000 children living in step families with a parent who has re-married to a new partner (15%).

The number of children under 16 in 2002 in Britain with divorced parents was 149,335. This can be "very traumatic since two thirds of fathers never see their children within two years of divorce, often causing long-term problems. Overall, children of divorced parents do worse in school, in work and in their own marriages".

Sources: Sociology Update 2004, Martyn Denscombe, Olympus Books UK, 2004, Page 29; article "Women under 30 lead the rush to divorce lawyers" by Sarah Womack, *Daily Telegraph*, 29th August, 2003.

UK Society

Sources: Government statistics, specialist studies, Daily Newspapers, Census of Population, personal correspondence, *UK Christian Handbook* 2004/2005 edition, *Social Trends* No 34 2004 edition, Government Actuary's Department, magazines and books

Table 5.2.1 A-level Examination Results: Religious Studies, 2000–2004

A-Level Grade	Boys 2000 %	Boys 2003 %	Boys 2004 %	Girls 2000 %	Girls 2003 %	Girls 2004 %	Total 1995 %	Total 2000 %	Total 2003 %	Total 2004 %
A	17	24	25	16	23	25	13	16	23	25
B	24	27	29	22	30	31	18	23	29	31
C	22	25	24	24	25	24	23	23	25	24
D	18	14	14	19	15	14	20	19	15	14
E	9	7	6	11	5	5	14	10	6	5
N/U	10	3	2	8	2	1	12	9	2	1
TOTAL (=100%)	2,294	3,589	4,137	6,884	9,082	10,281	8,924	9,178	12,671	14,418
% RS is of total	0.6	1.0	1.2	1.6	2.2	2.5	1.2	1.2	1.7	1.9

Source: The Times 15th August 1996, The Daily Telegraph 17th August 2000, 19th August 2004

Table 5.2.2 A-level Examination Results: All Subjects, 2000–2004

A-Level Grade	Boys 2000 %	Boys 2003 %	Boys 2004 %	Girls 2000 %	Girls 2003 %	Girls 2004 %	Total 1995 %	Total 2000 %	Total 2003 %	Total 2004 %
A	17	20	21	18	23	24	16	18	22	22
B	18	21	22	20	24	25	17	19	23	23
C	21	22	23	22	23	24	19	21	23	23
D	19	19	18	18	17	16	18	19	18	18
E	13	12	11	12	9	8	14	12	10	10
N/U	12	6	5	10	4	3	16	11	4	4
TOTAL (=100%)	354,553	345,682	352,635	417,256	404,855	413,612	725,992	771,809	750,537	766,247

Source: The Times 15th August 1996, The Daily Telegraph 17th August 2000, 19th August 2004

Table 5.2.3 GCSE Examination Results: Religious Studies, 2000–2004

GCSE Grade	Boys 2000 %	Boys 2003 %	Boys 2004 %	Girls 2000 %	Girls 2003 %	Girls 2004 %	Total 1995 %	Total 2000 %	Total 2003 %	Total 2004 %
A*	4	6	6	10	11	12	3	8	9	10
A	10	12	15	16	19	20	12	13	16	18
B	15	18	18	20	21	21	20	18	20	20
C	19	19	19	20	19	18	21	19	19	18
D	16	15	14	13	12	12	15	14	13	13
E	13	11	11	9	8	8	12	11	10	9
F	10	8	8	6	5	5	9	8	6	6
G	7	6	6	3	3	2	5	5	4	3
U	6	5	4	3	2	2	3	4	3	3
TOTAL (=100%)	47,542	56,001	59,717	68,692	76,303	81,320	108,055	116,234	132,304	141,037
% RS is of total	1.8	2.0	2.1	2.5	2.6	2.7	2.2	2.1	2.3	2.4

Source: The Times 22nd August 1996, The Daily Telegraph 24th August 2000, 26th August 2004

Table 5.2.4 GCSE Examination Results: All Subjects, 2000–2004

GCSE Grade	Boys 2000 %	Boys 2003 %	Boys 2004 %	Girls 2000 %	Girls 2003 %	Girls 2004 %	Total 1995 %	Total 2000 %	Total 2003 %	Total 2004 %
A*	4	4	5	6	6	7	3	5	5	6
A	9	10	10	13	13	13	10	11	12	12
B	16	16	16	18	19	18	18	17	17	17
C	23	23	24	24	24	25	22	24	24	25
D	20	19	18	17	17	16	19	18	18	17
E	14	13	12	11	10	10	14	13	12	11
F	8	8	8	6	6	6	9	7	7	7
G	4	4	4	3	3	3	4	3	3	3
U	2	3	3	2	2	2	1	2	2	2
TOTAL (=100%)	2,708,887	2,833,611	2,891,646	2,773,033	2,899,876	2,983,727	4,971,667	5,481,920	5,733,487	5,875,373

Source: The Times 22nd August 1996, The Daily Telegraph 24th August 2000, 26th August 2004

Tables **5.2.1** and **5.2.3** respectively give the percentage of children getting each grade in their Religious Studies A-Level and GCSE examinations. It is clear that the proportion getting higher grades has dramatically risen between 1995 and 2004, with double the percentage getting As at A-Level (of both genders), a rate of increase not seen across subjects generally (**Table 5.2.2**). **Figures 5.2.1** and **5.2.2** illustrate the percentages in the total columns of **Tables 5.2.1** and **5.2.3**.

It is an identical story for those taking Religious Studies at GCSE, with a rate of increase in the higher grades not seen overall (**Table 5.2.4**). However the boys have shown the greater increase in A and A* between 2000 and 2004.

The percentage of children taking Religious Studies has also increased significantly between 2000 and 2004, proportionately in A-Level more among boys (80%) than girls (49%) and in GCSE (boys 26%, girls 18%). The number of children taking RS at GCSE in 2004, 141,000, is almost 4 times the number of children aged 16 going to church in the UK in 2004, estimated at 38,700. It may be presumed that not all attending church at this age will necessarily take RS at GCSE, though perhaps the large majority will. Even so, this shows a huge level of interest in Religious Studies by children which is not reflected in church attendance.

See also **Page 7.11** for highest qualifications.

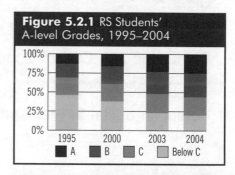

Figure 5.2.1 RS Students' A-level Grades, 1995–2004

Legend: A ■ B ■ C ■ Below C

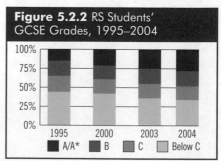

Figure 5.2.2 RS Students' GCSE Grades, 1995–2004

Legend: A/A* ■ B ■ C ■ Below C

Table 5.2.5 Number of Schools, Pupils and Teachers, England, 1985–2010

	Schools Nrsry	Primary	2ndary	Indpnd	Special	TOTAL	Pupils Nrsry	Primary	2ndary	Indpnd	Special	TOTAL	Teachers Nrsry	Primary	2ndary	Indpnd	Special	TOTAL
1985	563	19,734	4,382	2,311	1,529	**28,519**	49,850	3,747,850	3,525,770	501,420	116,280	**7,941,170**	1,570	164,430	218,610	44,520	16,850	**445,980**
1990	566	19,162	3,976	2,283	1,398	**27,385**	51,820	3,984,870	2,862,620	539,510	99,290	**7,538,110**	1,610	175,600	187,650	50,200	16,400	**431,460**
1995	553	18,551	3,614	2,259	1,577	**26,554**	52,770	4,312,200	2,992,860	533,420	103,430	**7,994,680**	1,580	181,910	181,450	53,060	16,920	**434,920**
2000	516	18,158	3,550	2,202	1,492	**25,918**	46,460	4,435,350	3,181,810	549,650	105,050	**8,318,320**	1,500	183,760	185,430	57,200	23,210	**451,100**
2004	470	17,762	3,409	2,328	1,574	**25,543**	39,090	4,252,540	3,324,450	585,760	104,800	**8,306,640**	1,460	181,230	195,240	63,590	27,460	**468,980**
2010E	460	17,104	3,030	2,258	1,571	**24,423**	39,730	4,620,300	3,140,350	597,950	100,170	**8,498,500**	1,440	190,880	202,890	67,930	28,920	**492,060**

Primary and Secondary Schools include Middle Schools as deemed; Special Schools include Pupil Referral Units (from 1995); Independent Schools include City Technology Colleges (from 1990).
Nrsry = Nursery, 2ndary = Secondary, Indpnd = Independent, E = Estimate. *Source: Statistics of Education: Schools in England, DfSS, 2004 edition.*

Christian Schools

Table 5.3.1 gives details of the various religious schools for 2004. The percentages under each line show that the Church of England has a higher percentage of schools, Primary or Secondary, than pupils, which means they will tend to have slightly smaller classes than other schools, as the proportion of teachers is about the same as pupils.

Keeping the Faith

The questions asked about religion in the Scottish 2001 Census, unlike England, included a question on "religion of upbringing". **Table 5.3.2** tabulates the proportions now in one grouping who were brought up in another. If one ignores the 9% who did not answer both questions, then the remaining 91% of the Scottish population (4.6 million) break down as shown in the Table.

The Table may be read in this way. 95% of those currently in the Church of Scotland (top left hand corner) were brought up in the Church of Scotland, 1% were brought up as Roman Catholics (next cell down), 2% in other Christian denominations, 0% in other religions, and 2% with no religion. In other words, 3% have "switched" from other Christian denominations to the Church of Scotland, nobody brought up in other religions has switched, but 2% with no religion initially are now Church of Scotland. Exactly the same proportions occur for the Catholics. The other Christian groups in Scotland however now include 12% brought up in the Church of Scotland, 2% as Catholics and 5% who had no religion.

Three-quarters, 73% of those now with a religion other than Christianity were brought up in that religion, but 18% (= 8% + 4% + 6%) now in other religions were brought up with a Christian background, twice the percentage now belonging to other religions who had no initial religion. Does a "faith culture" at home make it more likely that that person will continue with some kind of "faith" base even if in a different religion?

A quarter, 26%, of those who now have no religion were brought up in a Church of Scotland home, a much higher rate of "defection" than the 6% who were formally Roman Catholic or 7% other Christian. Three-fifths, 61%, of those brought up with no religious background still have no religious background.

The percentage brought up in a Christian household now belonging to those of other religions, or those brought up in other religions now in the Christian family are only 0.4% of the population. While there have been very few "conversions" in either direction, there are 7 times more of these going from Christianity than coming to Christianity.

Figure 5.3 graphs the data in **Table 5.3.4** combined for gender, showing partners in previous three months.

Table 5.3.1
Church Schools, 2004

	CofE	Roman Catholic	Methodist	Other Cian	Jewish	Muslim	Sikh	Other religions	No religious character	TOTAL
Maintained Primary Schools										
Schools	4,482	1,723	26	50	28	2	1	1	11,449	**17,762**
% of total	*25.2*	*9.7*	*0.1*	*0.3*		*All 0.2*			*64.5*	*100.0*
Pupils	762,990	396,450	4,470	9,380	8,270	430	200	100	2,930,250	**4,112,540**
% of total	*18.6*	*9.6*	*0.1*	*0.2*		*All 0.2*			*71.3*	*100.0*
Teachers	34,140	17,000	200	410	380	20	4	10	129,070	**181,234**
% of total	*18.9*	*9.4*	*0.1*	*0.2*		*All 0.2*			*71.2*	*100.0*
Maintained Secondary Schools										
Schools	199	352	0	30	5	2	1	1	2,819	**3,409**
% of total	*5.8*	*10.3*	*0.0*	*0.9*		*All 0.3*			*82.7*	*100.0*
Pupils	164,260	321,150	0	27,090	5,000	710	430	290	2,805,780	**3,324,710**
% of total	*4.9*	*9.7*	*0.0*	*0.8*		*All 0.2*			*84.4*	*100.0*
Teachers	9,500	19,170	0	1,590	310	40	20	10	164,610	**195,250**
% of total	*4.9*	*9.8*	*0.0*	*0.8*		*All 0.2*			*84.3*	*100.0*

Other Cian (= Christian) includes schools of mixed denominations. Includes Middle Schools as deemed
Source: Statistics of Education: Schools in England, DfSS, 2004 edition

Table 5.3.2
Current Religion (2001) and Religion of Upbringing in Scotland

	Current religion in Scotland					
	Church of Scotland	Roman Catholic	Other Christian	Other Religions	None	Overall
Religion of upbringing	%	%	%	%	%	%
Church of Scotland	95	2	12	8	26	52
Roman Catholic	1	95	2	4	6	19
Other Christian	2	1	81	6	7	9
Other Religions	0	0	0	73	0	1
None	2	2	5	9	61	19
Base (=100%)	2.07 mn	0.78 mn	0.33 mn	0.09 mn	1.34 mn	4.61 mn

Source: Scottish Census of Population, 2001

Table 5.3.3
Calls to ChildLine, by Cause, 2003

Cause	Males	Females	Total
Bullying	5,333	16,533	21,866
Divorce/family issues	3,081	12,983	16,064
Physical abuse	4,025	9,625	13,650
Concern for others	1,179	8,551	9,730
Facts of life	1,974	7,056	9,030
Sexual abuse	2,184	6,356	8,540
Emotional or physical health	1,314	6,030	7,344
Pregnancy	317	5,677	5,994
Problems with friends	524	4,389	4,913
Partner/relationships	745	3,657	4,402
Runaway/homelessness	1,167	2,326	3,493
Risk/neglect/emotional abuse	543	1,998	2,541
Sexuality	1,042	981	2,023
School problem	476	1,458	1,934
All other concerns	2,263	5,959	8,222
TOTAL for year	**26,167**	**93,579**	**119,746**

Source: ChildLine, quoted in Social Trends, No 34, 2004 edition, National Statistics, Table 8.18

Table 5.3.4 Number of Opposite Sex Partners in Previous Three Months, by Sex and Age, 1999–2001

	Males			Females		
Age	None %	One %	2/2+ %	None %	One %	2/2+ %
16–17	61	28	11	56	38	6
18–19	33	47	20	25	64	11
20–24	24	58	18	17	74	9
25–34	15	76	9	11	85	4
35–44	14	81	5	14	83	3
Av'ge	20	70	10	17	78	5

Source: National Survey of Sexual Attitudes and Lifestyle 2000, and others, quoted in Social Trends, No 34, 2004 edition, National Statistics, Table 7.22

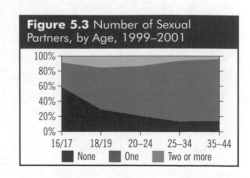

Figure 5.3 Number of Sexual Partners, by Age, 1999–2001

Table 5.4
Date of Easter Sunday by year, 1700–2299

11/04/1700	29/03/1750	13/04/1800	31/03/1850	15/04/1900	9/04/1950	23/04/2000	10/04/2050	28/03/2100	12/04/2150	6/04/2200	21/04/2250
27/03/1701	11/04/1751	5/04/1801	20/04/1851	7/04/1901	25/03/1951	15/04/2001	2/04/2051	17/04/2101	4/04/2151	19/04/2201	13/04/2251
16/04/1702	2/04/1752	18/04/1802	11/04/1852	3/03/1902	13/04/1952	31/03/2002	21/04/2052	9/04/2102	23/04/2152	11/04/2202	28/03/2252
8/04/1703	22/04/1753	10/04/1803	27/03/1853	12/04/1903	5/04/1953	20/04/2003	6/04/2053	25/03/2103	15/04/2153	3/04/2203	17/04/2253
23/03/1704	14/04/1754	1/04/1804	16/04/1854	3/04/1904	18/04/1954	11/04/2004	29/03/2054	16/04/2104	31/03/2154	22/04/2204	9/04/2254
12/04/1705	30/03/1755	14/04/1805	8/04/1855	23/04/1905	10/04/1955	27/03/2005	18/04/2055	5/04/2105	20/04/2155	7/04/2205	25/03/2255
4/04/1706	18/04/1756	6/04/1806	23/03/1856	15/04/1906	1/04/1956	16/04/2006	2/04/2056	18/04/2106	11/04/2156	30/03/2206	13/04/2256
24/04/1707	10/04/1757	29/03/1807	12/04/1857	31/03/1907	21/04/1957	8/04/2007	22/04/2057	10/04/2107	27/03/2157	19/04/2207	5/04/2257
8/04/1708	26/03/1758	17/04/1808	4/04/1858	19/04/1908	6/04/1958	23/03/2008	14/04/2058	1/04/2108	16/04/2158	3/04/2208	25/04/2258
31/03/1709	15/04/1759	2/04/1809	24/04/1859	11/04/1909	29/03/1959	12/04/2009	3/03/2059	21/04/2109	8/04/2159	26/03/2209	10/04/2259
20/04/1710	6/04/1760	22/04/1810	8/04/1860	27/03/1910	17/04/1960	4/04/2010	18/04/2060	6/04/2110	23/03/2160	15/04/2210	1/04/2260
5/04/1711	22/03/1761	14/04/1811	31/03/1861	16/04/1911	2/04/1961	24/04/2011	10/04/2061	29/03/2111	12/04/2161	31/03/2211	21/04/2261
27/03/1712	11/04/1762	29/03/1812	20/04/1862	7/04/1912	22/04/1962	8/04/2012	26/03/2062	17/04/2112	4/04/2162	19/04/2212	6/04/2262
16/04/1713	3/04/1763	18/04/1813	5/04/1863	23/03/1913	14/04/1963	31/03/2013	15/04/2063	2/04/2113	24/04/2163	11/04/2213	29/03/2263
1/04/1714	22/04/1764	10/04/1814	27/03/1864	12/04/1914	29/03/1964	20/04/2014	6/04/2064	22/04/2114	8/04/2164	27/03/2214	17/04/2264
21/04/1715	7/04/1765	26/03/1815	16/04/1865	4/04/1915	18/04/1965	5/04/2015	29/03/2065	14/04/2115	31/03/2165	16/04/2215	2/04/2265
12/04/1716	30/03/1766	14/04/1816	1/04/1866	23/04/1916	10/04/1966	27/03/2016	11/04/2066	29/03/2116	20/04/2166	7/04/2216	25/03/2266
28/03/1717	19/04/1767	6/04/1817	21/04/1867	8/04/1917	26/03/1967	16/04/2017	3/04/2067	18/04/2117	5/04/2167	30/03/2217	14/04/2267
17/04/1718	3/04/1768	22/03/1818	12/04/1868	31/03/1918	14/04/1968	1/04/2018	22/04/2068	10/04/2118	27/03/2168	12/04/2218	5/04/2268
9/04/1719	26/03/1769	11/04/1819	28/03/1869	20/04/1919	6/04/1969	21/04/2019	14/04/2069	26/03/2119	16/04/2169	4/04/2219	18/04/2269
31/03/1720	15/04/1770	2/04/1820	17/04/1870	4/04/1920	29/03/1970	12/04/2020	3/03/2070	14/04/2120	1/04/2170	23/04/2220	10/04/2270
13/04/1721	31/03/1771	22/04/1821	9/04/1871	27/03/1921	11/04/1971	4/04/2021	19/04/2071	6/04/2121	12/04/2171	15/04/2221	2/04/2271
5/04/1722	19/04/1772	7/04/1822	31/03/1872	16/04/1922	2/04/1972	17/04/2022	10/04/2072	29/03/2122	12/04/2172	31/03/2222	21/04/2272
28/03/1723	11/04/1773	3/03/1823	13/04/1873	1/04/1923	22/04/1973	9/04/2023	26/03/2073	11/04/2123	4/04/2173	20/04/2223	6/04/2273
16/04/1724	3/04/1774	18/04/1824	5/04/1874	20/04/1924	14/04/1974	31/03/2024	15/04/2074	2/04/2124	17/04/2174	11/04/2224	29/03/2274
1/04/1725	16/04/1775	3/04/1825	28/03/1875	12/04/1925	03/03/1975	20/04/2025	7/04/2075	22/04/2125	9/04/2175	27/03/2225	18/04/2275
21/04/1726	7/04/1776	26/03/1826	16/04/1876	4/04/1926	18/04/1976	5/04/2026	19/04/2076	14/04/2126	31/03/2176	16/04/2226	2/04/2276
13/04/1727	30/03/1777	15/04/1827	1/04/1877	17/04/1927	10/04/1977	28/03/2027	11/04/2077	3/03/2127	20/04/2177	8/04/2227	22/04/2277
28/03/1728	19/04/1778	6/04/1828	21/04/1878	8/04/1928	26/03/1978	16/04/2028	3/04/2078	18/04/2128	5/04/2178	23/03/2228	14/04/2278
17/04/1729	4/04/1779	19/04/1829	13/04/1879	31/03/1929	15/04/1979	1/04/2029	23/04/2079	1/04/2129	28/03/2179	12/04/2229	30/03/2279
9/04/1730	26/03/1780	11/04/1830	28/03/1880	2/04/1930	6/04/1980	21/04/2030	7/04/2080	26/03/2130	16/04/2180	4/04/2230	18/04/2280
25/03/1731	15/04/1781	3/04/1831	17/04/1881	5/04/1931	19/04/1981	13/04/2031	3/03/2081	15/04/2131	1/04/2181	24/04/2231	10/04/2281
13/04/1732	31/03/1782	22/04/1832	9/04/1882	27/03/1932	11/04/1982	28/03/2032	19/04/2082	6/04/2132	21/04/2182	8/04/2232	26/03/2282
5/04/1733	20/04/1783	7/04/1833	25/03/1883	16/04/1933	3/04/1983	17/04/2033	4/04/2083	19/04/2133	13/04/2183	31/03/2233	15/04/2283
25/04/1734	11/04/1784	3/03/1834	13/04/1884	1/04/1934	22/04/1984	9/04/2034	26/03/2084	11/04/2134	28/03/2184	2/04/2234	6/04/2284
10/04/1735	27/03/1785	19/04/1835	5/04/1885	21/04/1935	7/04/1985	25/03/2035	15/04/2085	3/04/2135	17/04/2185	5/04/2235	22/03/2285
1/04/1736	16/04/1786	3/04/1836	25/04/1886	12/04/1936	3/03/1986	13/04/2036	31/03/2086	22/04/2136	9/04/2186	27/03/2236	11/04/2286
21/04/1737	8/04/1787	26/03/1837	10/04/1887	28/03/1937	19/04/1987	5/04/2037	20/04/2087	7/04/2137	25/03/2187	16/04/2237	3/04/2287
6/04/1738	23/03/1788	15/04/1838	2/04/1888	17/04/1938	3/04/1988	25/04/2038	11/04/2088	3/03/2138	13/04/2188	1/04/2238	22/04/2288
29/03/1739	12/04/1789	31/03/1839	21/04/1889	9/04/1939	26/03/1989	10/04/2039	3/04/2089	19/04/2139	5/04/2189	21/04/2239	7/04/2289
17/04/1740	4/04/1790	19/04/1840	6/04/1890	24/03/1940	15/04/1990	1/04/2040	16/04/2090	3/04/2140	25/04/2190	12/04/2240	3/03/2290
2/04/1741	24/04/1791	11/04/1841	29/03/1891	13/04/1941	31/03/1991	21/04/2041	8/04/2091	26/03/2141	10/04/2191	4/04/2241	19/04/2291
25/03/1742	8/04/1792	27/03/1842	17/04/1892	5/04/1942	19/04/1992	6/04/2042	3/03/2092	15/04/2142	1/04/2192	17/04/2242	10/04/2292
14/04/1743	31/03/1793	16/04/1843	2/04/1893	25/04/1943	11/04/1993	29/03/2043	12/04/2093	31/03/2143	21/04/2193	9/04/2243	26/03/2293
5/04/1744	20/04/1794	7/04/1844	25/03/1894	9/04/1944	3/04/1994	17/04/2044	4/04/2094	19/04/2144	6/04/2194	31/03/2244	15/04/2294
18/04/1745	5/04/1795	23/03/1845	14/04/1895	1/04/1945	16/04/1995	9/04/2045	24/04/2095	11/04/2145	29/03/2195	13/04/2245	7/04/2295
10/04/1746	27/03/1796	12/04/1846	5/04/1896	21/04/1946	7/04/1996	25/03/2046	15/04/2096	3/04/2146	17/04/2196	5/04/2246	19/04/2296
2/04/1747	16/04/1797	4/04/1847	18/04/1897	6/04/1947	3/03/1997	14/04/2047	31/03/2097	16/04/2147	9/04/2197	28/03/2247	11/04/2297
14/04/1748	8/04/1798	23/04/1848	10/04/1898	28/03/1948	12/04/1998	5/04/2048	20/04/2098	7/04/2148	25/04/2198	16/04/2248	3/04/2298
6/04/1749	24/03/1799	8/04/1849	2/04/1899	17/04/1949	4/04/1999	18/04/2049	12/04/2099	30/03/2149	14/04/2199	1/04/2249	16/04/2299

Source: Rev Paul Rayner at prayner@globalnet.co.uk, correspondence of March 2004

5

Figure 5.5.1 Christian Organisations, 1982–2040

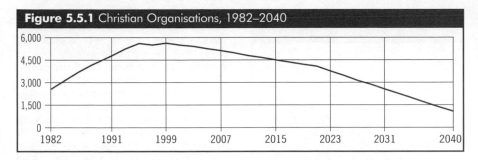

Figure 5.5.2 When Christian organisations started, 1995–2003

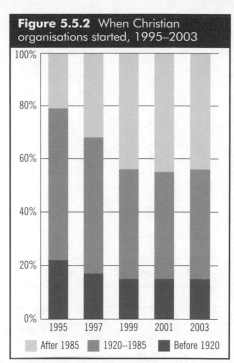

After 1985   1920–1985   Before 1920

Figure 5.5.1 shows the rapid growth in the number of Christian agencies in the 1980s and early 1990s, reflecting something of the energy and entrepreneurial spirit among many in the church in those years. In the late 1990s, the number of organisations held steady, but since the start of the new century, numbers have declined, something which is forecast to continue at least for the next decade.

The rate of decline is likely to be slow initially, partly because the market being served is only declining slowly, and partly because many Christian agencies have creative resources likely to be put to good use. Eventually, however, the decrease of the basic market, and its ageing, is bound to have an impact on products and activities, and the number of agencies serving these needs will reduce accordingly. Hence the sharper drop after 2020 rather than before.

Figure 5.5.2 indicates that it is by and large not the oldest organisations which are closing, but those started between 1920 and 1985, and, in many cases, between 1960 and 1985. Did the founder find it difficult to find a suitable successor? **Figure 5.5.2** also suggests the stability of agencies since 1999.

Table 5.5 totals the frequency with which Easter falls in the large Table given on **Page 5.4** across each of the 18th to 23rd centuries. These frequencies are then graphed in total in **Figure 5.5.3**. They show that there are some dates on which Easter tends to fall more frequently than others: March 25th, March 31st, April 5th, April 11th and April 16th, dates all 5 or 6 days apart.

This variation is in part because of the way our calendar is constructed, with leap years every 4 years except in the years ending in 00, unless the first two digits are divisible by four. Thus 2000 was a leap year, but 2100 will not be. On the other hand, 1700 *was* a leap year as it preceded the alteration of the calendar in September 1752.

Rev Paul Rayner, from whom these figures come, points out that while the first day of Lent falls on February 29th (when Easter is on April 11th) 7 times out of 26 (statistically normal), Ash Wednesday (when Easter is on April 15th) falls on February 29th only once out of 21.

Figure 5.5.3
Frequency of the Date of Easter Sunday, 1700–2299

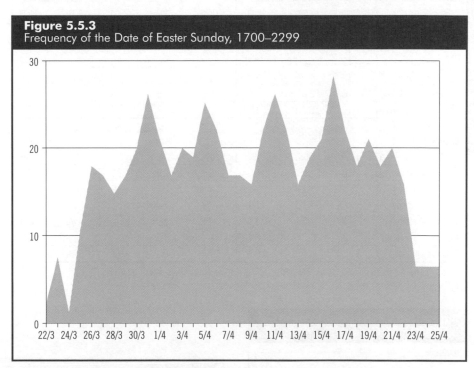

5

Table 5.5
Frequency with which Easter Sunday Falls on Each Day, by Century

Century	MARCH										APRIL																								
	22	23	24	25	26	27	28	29	30	31	1	2	3	4	5	6	7	8	9	10	11	12	13	14	15	16	17	18	19	20	21	22	23	24	25
18th	1	2	1	2	3	4	3	2	3	5	3	3	3	3	5	3	2	5	2	3	5	3	3	3	3	6	3	2	3	3	3	2	0	2	1
19th	1	2	0	2	3	3	3	3	2	4	4	4	3	2	5	4	3	3	2	4	4	3	4	4	2	4	4	4	3	2	3	3	1	1	1
20th	0	1	1	1	3	3	2	3	4	4	4	2	4	4	3	4	4	2	3	3	4	5	2	3	4	4	4	3	4	3	3	3	2	0	1
21st	0	1	0	2	3	2	2	3	4	5	3	2	3	4	4	3	2	3	3	4	4	4	2	3	5	4	3	3	3	5	4	2	2	2	1
22nd	0	1	0	2	3	2	3	4	3	4	4	2	3	3	4	4	2	2	4	4	4	4	2	4	3	5	5	3	3	3	3	3	1	1	2
23rd	1	1	0	2	3	3	2	2	4	4	3	3	4	3	4	4	4	2	2	4	5	3	3	2	4	5	3	3	5	2	4	3	1	1	1
TOTAL	**3**	**8**	**2**	**11**	**18**	**17**	**15**	**17**	**20**	**26**	**21**	**16**	**20**	**19**	**25**	**22**	**17**	**17**	**16**	**22**	**26**	**22**	**16**	**19**	**21**	**28**	**22**	**18**	**21**	**18**	**20**	**16**	**7**	**7**	**7**

Sources: *UK Christian Handbook, 2004/2005*, edited Heather Wraight, Christian Research, London, 2004, Table 1; Rev Paul Rayner at prayner@globalnet.co.uk

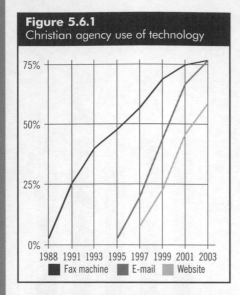

Figure 5.6.1
Christian agency use of technology

- Fax machine
- E-mail
- Website

(Years: 1988 1991 1993 1995 1997 1999 2001 2003; Y-axis: 0%, 25%, 50%, 75%)

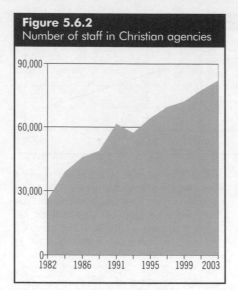

Figure 5.6.2
Number of staff in Christian agencies

(Years: 1982 1986 1991 1995 1999 2003; Y-axis: 0, 30,000, 60,000, 90,000)

Figure 5.6.1 shows the speed at which Christian agencies have taken advantage of the latest technology. The desire to be as efficient and professional as possible is clearly seen. At the same time the number of staff employed in Christian organisations has steadily increased, with the exception of the recession in the early 1990s, as **Figure 5.6.2** indicates. In part this is a natural consequence of new agencies being started, but the average number of full-time employees employed by agencies employing at least one person has increased from 14 in 1982 to 19 twenty years later. At the same time the percentage staffed entirely by volunteers has decreased from 23% in 1982 to 19% in 2003. The trend in both charts is upward.

Information for **Tables 5.6.1–3** and **Figure 5.6.3** comes from the *UK Christian Handbook* 2004/2005 Edition, published by Christian Research.

Table 5.6.1
Christian accommodation by size and type

Accommodation	Conference Centres, Guest Houses and Hotels			Retreat Houses			Sheltered Accommodation	
	1999	2001	2003	1999	2001	2003	2001	2003
Average capacity	54	59	68	27	29	34	25	27
% in single rooms	18	17	16	48	49	36	n/a	n/a
% in double rooms	42	44	45	37	36	55	n/a	n/a
% in larger rooms	42	39	39	15	15	9	n/a	n/a
Average in Day Room	110	107[3]	104	56	36	58	–	–
Total number listed	268	242	218	123	111	107	29	26

Accommodation	Hostels[1]			Residential Homes for the Elderly			Disadvantaged	
	1999	2001	2003	1999	2001	2003	2001	2003
Average capacity	44	57	66	23	26	36	25	16
% in single rooms	71	74	74	48	56	89	n/a	n/a
% in double rooms	16	15	15	9	34	} 11	n/a	n/a
% in larger rooms	13	11	11	43[2]	10		n/a	n/a
Average in Day Room	87	76	84	–	33	–	–	–
Total number listed	153	168	153	174	182	173	29	40

[1]Includes Hostels for Holiday events, Social Welfare Hostels and Hostels for Young People and Students
[2]Figure shows percentage of 'other' accommodation as opposed to larger rooms   [3]Revised figure

Table 5.6.2 Size of Conference Centres, Guest Houses and Hotels, 2003

Number of rooms	Number
Under 10	2
10 to 19	24
20 to 29	29
30 to 39	25
40 to 49	25
50 to 59	17
60 to 69	11
70 to 79	11
80 to 89	8
90 to 99	9
100 to 109	11
110 to 119	6
120 to 129	6
130 to 139	4
150	3
200 to 299	7
400 or over	2
TOTAL	**200**

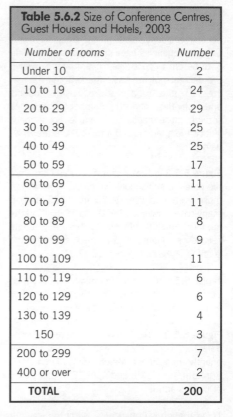

Figure 5.6.3 Places and Students at Theological Colleges, 1993–2003

(Y-axis: 0, 2,500, 5,000, 7,500, 10,000; Years: 1993 1995 1997 1999 2001 2003)

- Places
- Students

Table 5.6.3
Places, Students and Fees at Theological Colleges and Bible Schools, 1993–2003

Year	Number Total	Number Reply-ing %	Residential student places Male	F'male	Mixed	Total	Total number of students Male	F'male	Total	Places taken %	Tuition & Accommodation Fees Average cost (£)	Annual increase %	Average length of course (years)
1993	96	97	1,914	1,310	4,113	7,337	3,500[1]	2,300[1]	5,800[1]	79	3,560	+6	2.8
1995	93	94	2,053	1,352	4,004	7,409	3,650[1]	2,450[1]	6,100[1]	82	3,750	+3	2.6
1997	91	92	2,300	1,903	3,442	7,645	3,750	2,500	6,250	82	3,990	+6	2.4
1999	96	94	2,671	1,968	3,209	7,848	4,450	2,700	7,150	91	4,150	+4	2.5
2001	101	85	2,556	1,920	3,483	7,959	4,400	3,000	7,400	93	4,940	+9	2.5
2003	104	94	2,282	1,440	4,674	8,396	4,460	3,120	7,580	90	5,360	+4	2.4

[1]Estimate

Table 5.7.1 Church Activities which Proved Best for Encouraging People to Start Attending Church

% churches with group	Type of group	Average attendance
65	Parents and toddlers	30
64	The elderly	32
38	Those getting married	14
31	Those desiring baptism of their child	20
26	Young adults	21
17	Those requiring counselling	15
16	The bereaved	17

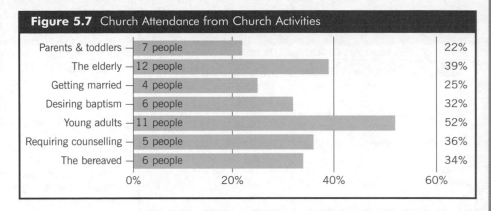

Figure 5.7 Church Attendance from Church Activities

Parents & toddlers	7 people	22%
The elderly	12 people	39%
Getting married	4 people	25%
Desiring baptism	6 people	32%
Young adults	11 people	52%
Requiring counselling	5 people	36%
The bereaved	6 people	34%

Nearly 4,000 churches were approached in 2002 in a survey undertaken on behalf of The Salvation Army explicitly to ascertain what were the key reasons why churches grew. A large number of factors were statistically evaluated, broken down by the growth or decline variable, some results of which were published in *Religious Trends* No 4, Pages 5.2 and 5.3, and in a 2004 booklet *Leadership, Vision and Growing Churches*.

Churches are involved in many kinds of social and spiritual activities. The top 7 which proved best for attracting new people are given in **Table 5.7.1**, which gives the percentage which have a particular activity and their average attendance. Some churches engage in more specialist activity (to the disabled, single parents, immigrants, etc.). All such activities, both those in the Table and more specialised ones, can be a gateway through which some people start attending church. It is essential that churches should be involved in such work – if they don't replace those who leave or die the church's future is very limited.

The percentage of those who started attending church per church in the past year as a result of attending certain activities is shown in **Figure 5.7**, with the actual number indicated. The activities are listed in the same order as given in **Table 5.7.1** for convenience, but their effectiveness is not the same for each activity. While the bar chart shows their effectiveness, programmes like these do not, on the whole, relate to whether a church is growing or declining, but to its size (a larger church runs more programmes). While such activities are important in adding people to the church, broadly these but replace those who die or leave. They are essential for "people flow" but do not register differently between growing and declining congregations. This was an unexpected and surprising finding in the survey.

Some of that analysis is extended here. **Table 5.7.2** shows the range of income received by churches in 1900, 1995 and 2000 by denomination. The overall totals were illustrated in *Religious Trends* No 4, Figure 5.2.1, showing that between 1990 and 1995 overall church income increased at the rate of inflation, from an average of £36,300 to £41,100, but between 1995 and 2000 it increased at double the rate of inflation, from £41,000 to £57,000.

Table 5.7.2
Church Income 1990–2000, by Denomination

Denomination	Year	Under £10,000 %	£10,000 –£19,999 %	£20,000 –£29,999 %	£30,000 –£49,999 %	£50,000 –£99,999 %	£100,000 or over %	Average income £
Anglican	1990	19	20	20	18	17	6	40,000
	1995	15	14	19	23	20	9	43,400
	2000	7	16	11	23	27	16	63,300
Baptist	1990	17	25	17	23	14	4	36,300
	1995	16	12	20	22	24	6	42,100
	2000	9	9	13	26	27	16	60,000
R Catholic	1990	4	35	15	15	27	4	43,700
	1995	7	28	14	10	31	10	49,100
	2000	3	18	20	12	29	18	60,100
Independent	1990	39	20	18	14	7	2	24,400
	1995	30	17	16	19	16	2	29,100
	2000	24	11	17	22	17	9	41,800
Methodist	1990	43	21	17	13	6	0	20,200
	1995	34	18	16	14	17	1	27,200
	2000	28	18	11	22	14	7	36,500
New	1990	10	18	15	25	22	10	51,900
	1995	10	8	4	38	24	16	58,000
	2000	7	4	4	19	35	31	87,200[1]
Pentecostal	1990	27	11	19	16	14	13	47,700
	1995	19	22	10	15	17	17	49,500
	2000	7	13	20	13	25	22	70,800
URC	1990	19	31	16	15	19	0	31,600
	1995	7	45	13	13	16	6	35,900
	2000	8	30	15	27	13	7	37,800
Smaller Denominations	1990	31	21	14	20	7	7	33,900
	1995	25	18	15	21	12	9	37,700
	2000	25	16	11	22	13	13	41,200[2]
Overall	**1990**	**24**	**17**	**19**	**19**	**15**	**6**	**36,300**
	1995	**18**	**17**	**16**	**22**	**20**	**7**	**41,100**
	2000	**12**	**14**	**12**	**22**	**24**	**16**	**57,000**

Based on the following number of churches (=100%): Anglicans 443; Methodists 152; Baptists 141; Roman Catholics 46; Independent churches 92; New Churches 62; Pentecostals 51; United Reformed 59; Smaller denominations 64. Note that all except the first three are small (though random) samples.
[1] Excluding 4 churches with incomes in excess of £500,000. [2] Excluding one church with an income of £800,000 in 2000.

This increase in the second half of the 1990s in the most wealthy churches corresponds to the finding that larger churches tend to be the growing churches.

Table 5.7.2 shows however that these overall numbers vary considerably by denomination. The Anglicans, Baptists and Catholics are within 10% of the overall 2000 figure, but the Independents, Methodists, URC and Smaller Denominations are on average only about two-thirds of the overall average. The Pentecostals and the New Churches are, on the other hand, considerably above the average; both these denominations teach tithing of income paid through the local church.

5

Table 5.8.1
Characteristics of Older People

Group	The younger old	The Third Age	The active frail	The inactive frail
Age	55 to 64	65 to 74	75 to 84	85 and older
Activity	Still employed	Retired	Enjoying being a grandparent	Confined to home
Sufficiency	Earning salary	Travelling with Saga	Loss of spouse	Increasing dependency
Church Life	In leadership	Supporting role	May need help to get there	Only attend on special occasions
Sense of belonging to a church	43%	34%	28%	19%

Older people are here defined as those generally 65 or older, although **Table 5.8.1** does describe some of the characteristics of the "younger old", aged 55 to 64. The proportion of those 65 and over increases from 16% of the population in 2001 to 25% by 2041 (**Table 4.3**) and to 27% by 2071 (**Table 4.2.1**). In actual numbers those 65 and over increase from 9.4 million in 2001 to 16.7 million by 2041.

In 2001, 12% or 1.1 million of these older people were active churchgoers, and by 2041 it is estimated that the number will decline to 0.6 million or 4% of those 65 and over. Even among the oldest people, the practice of churchgoing will have dropped off considerably, if present trends continue. In 2001, those over 65 were a quarter, 25%, of churchgoers, but by 2041, they will have become nearly two thirds, 65%, of all churchgoers (**Table 12.9.2**). Both these percentages are much higher than the population figures given in the previous paragraph.

Figure 5.8.1
Older People and Size of Church

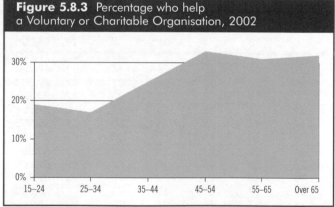

Source: *Bible Reading Today*, private research for Grow With the Bible by Christian Research, April 2004 Report.

Figure 5.8.2
Bible Version Read by Age-group

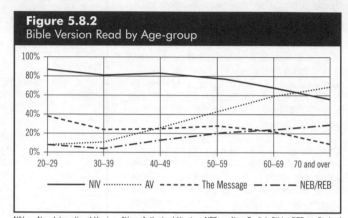

NIV = New International Version; AV = Authorised Version; NEB = New English Bible; REB = Revised English Bible.

Figures 5.8.1 and **2** come from a private survey on Bible Reading undertaken by Christian Research, and reproduced with permission. **Figure 5.8.1** shows that smaller churches (of all denominations) are more likely to have a greater proportion of older people than larger churches, something which the Christian Brethren also found (see **Figure 9.3.2**).

Figure 5.8.2 shows that of the 4 versions whose readership varied significantly by age, it was the Authorised Version (AV) which was read more by older people.

Figure 5.8.3 Percentage who help a Voluntary or Charitable Organisation, 2002

Source: From *The Responsibility Gap*, published by the Salvation Army, 2004 of a survey by the Henley Centre "Planning for Consumer Change 2002", Page 74.

Figure 5.8.3 comes from a different survey and shows the percentage who help a voluntary or charitable organisation including a church or school. These percentages endorse the comment in **Table 5.8.1** who take a "supporting role" when in their Third Age. A number of churches with older people in their congregation have seen growth when their Third Agers have invited their friends and neighbours to church.

Table 5.8.2 highlights the increasing proportion of older people who live alone, the more so the older they get. The declining marriage proportion is because one partner dies.

The number of people 85 and over in the UK in 1991 was 873,000, 1.5% of the total population. This had increased to 1,104,000 by 2003 (1.9%) and is expected to become 1,802,000 (2.8%) by 2021 and 2,479,000 (3.8%) by 2031. The proportion of men in these figures is, respectively, 24%, 28%, 38% and 39%. (*Population Trends*, No 120, Summer 2005, Page 16.)

Table 5.8.2 Living Arrangements for People Aged 65 and over, England and Wales, 2001

Arrangement	Males			Females		
	65–74 %	75–84 %	85/85+ %	65–74 %	75–84 %	85/85+ %
Married couple family	74	63	40	55	30	8
Cohabiting couple	2	2	1	2	1	0
Lone parent family	2	2	4	5	6	7
Living with others[1]	3	4	6	4	6	8
Living alone	18	26	37	33	52	54
Living in communal establishment	1	3	12	1	5	23
Base (millions) (=100%)	2.05	1.17	0.28	2.32	1.77	0.73

[1] Not in family unit Source: *Social Trends* No 34, 2004 edition, National Statistics, Table A.5.

Age of appointment

At the end of March 2003, there were 38 Diocesan Bishops in post, 66 Suffragans, 40 Deans and 121 Archdeacons, a total of 265, 3% of all the clergy. One Suffragan Bishop was appointed when he was 37 and another when 61, but half were appointed between the ages of 47 and 51. Half the Diocesan Bishops, many of whom were Suffragan Bishops first, were appointed when between 50 and 54; the youngest was 44, and two were appointed when 58. Half the Deans were appointed when they were between 48 and 53, and again the youngest (3 this time) were appointed at 44, and the eldest at 63. The youngest Archdeacon was appointed when 43 and the oldest when 65; half were appointed between 46 and 52. The overall average age of appointment is 52 for Archdeacons and 51 collectively for the others. This information is shown in more detail in **Figure 5.9.1**.

Present age, and length in post

How old they were in 2003 is shown in **Figure 5.9.2,** and how long they had been in post in **Figure 5.9.3**. As clergy need not retire until they are 70, few are retiring in the immediate future, unless they take early retirement. There have been many changes in the last few years, however; as a consequence the average experience in one of these posts was about 6 years in 2003. There were then 2 Suffragan Bishops and 1 Dean who had been in post for 18 years, and 4 Archdeacons who had been in post as long or longer.

Church of England leadership structure

Table 5.9 shows how the number of Archdeacons and Suffragan Bishops are distributed across the 43 Dioceses of the Church of England. Each Diocese has just one Diocesan Bishop, but he may have either none or up to 5 Suffragan Bishops, and between 1 and 6 Archdeacons. The most common combination, for 16 or nearly two-fifths, of the Dioceses is for there to be 1 Diocesan, 1 Suffragan and 2 Archdeacons.

Archdeaconries

If every person in England is in someone's Archdeaconry, then this works out at an average of 440,000 people per Archdeaconry. This however varies as follows:
- 28% Under 250,000
- 40% Between 250,000 and 499,000
- 27% Between 500,000 and 749,000
- 3% Between 750,000 and 1,000,000, with
- 2% Over a million people.

The average Archdeaconry is 525 square miles or 136,000 hectares in area. Each is divided into an average of 6 Deaneries, each of which in turn has an average of 22 worship centres, with about 13 full-time clergy, augmented by unpaid or part-time clergy, and by retired clergy still pastorally active. There are an average of 110 parishes in each Archdeaconry, but this figure varies widely.

Source: John Smallwood CBE

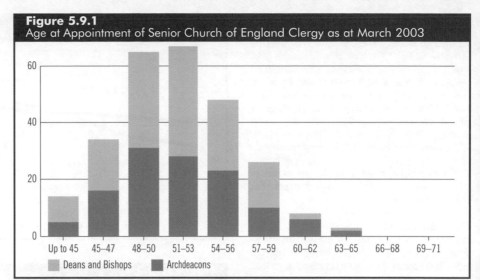

Figure 5.9.1
Age at Appointment of Senior Church of England Clergy as at March 2003

Average: Deans and Bishops 51 years, Archdeacons 52 years

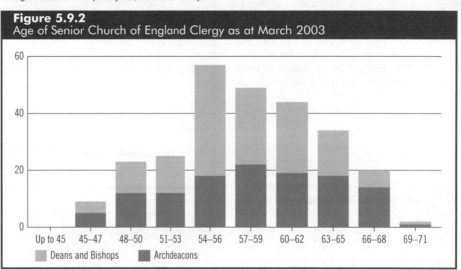

Figure 5.9.2
Age of Senior Church of England Clergy as at March 2003

Average: Deans and Bishops 57 years, Archdeacons 58 years

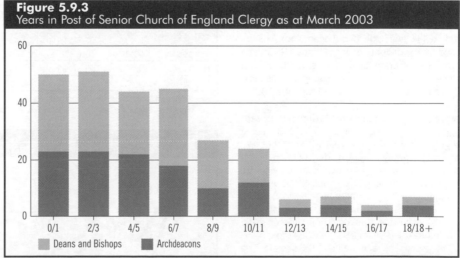

Figure 5.9.3
Years in Post of Senior Church of England Clergy as at March 2003

Average: Deans and Bishops 5.6 years, Archdeacons 5.9 years

Table 5.9
Number of Church of England Suffragan Bishops and Archdeacons, per Diocese

Number of Suffragans	None			One			Two			Three			Five
Number of Archdeacons	1	2	3	1	2	3	2	3	4	3	4	6	6
Number of Dioceses	1	2	1	1	16	5	5	3	2	3	2	1	1

Source: UK Christian Handbook, 2004/2005 edition, edited Heather Wraight, Christian Research, London, 2004

The General Household Survey is a long established government survey interviewing some 13,000 households every year, with an average response rate of 72%. One of its questions asks which of a number of items the household owns. As **Figure 5.10.1** makes clear, some are regarded as well nigh indispensable – a television (in 99% of households in 2001), a freezer (94%), central heating (92%) and a washing machine (92%). Not quite three-quarters, 72%, own a car (with 28% owning more than one), and half, 50%, have a computer at home. The ownership of more than one car increases 11% when the age of the oldest dependent child reaches 18!

Figure 5.10.2 graphs the way that the Retail Price Index has increased since it was first measured in June 1947 (which is based at 100.0). Since then prices have gone up 25-fold, so that £1 today had the purchasing power of just 4p then. The rate of change in the graph gives the indication of when prices especially jumped, such as with the oil crisis in the mid-70s, and the recession in the early 90s. Since then the graph increases in a virtually straight line, showing that the rate of increase has been much more steady. **Table 5.10.1** shows the increases in 5 year intervals since 1948. The average annual rate of increase between 1948 and 2003 is +5.7%; in the 5 years ending 2003 it has been +2.2%.

A Composite Price Index exists going back to 1750. In the 200 years since then prices have sometimes fallen for a decade or more, such as at the start of the 19th century during the Napoleonic Wars, then 1876 to 1891, and in the 1920s and early 1930s with the general depression.

Figure 5.10.3 shows how the colours of cars on the road have changed in the 50 years since 1954. In the mid-50s black cars were popular, and during the 1970s yellow cars boomed during the hippie era. In the Thatcherite 1980s red, white and blue cars became the colours used by the majority of cars. Since 1996 there has been a dramatic rise in silver cars, and since 2000 black cars are making a comeback. Green cars boomed in the 1960s and the 1990s.

Average speeds on trunk roads during the morning rush-hour was 50mph in 2003, being slightly more on motorways (56 mph), but less on single carriageway A roads (37 mph). Off-peak the average speed was 55mph, and 51 mph in the evening rush hour. In 1995 the average morning rush-hour speed was 53mph, off-peak 55mph, and evening rush-hour 55mph, showing that rush-hour speeds have slowed in the 8 years 1995–2003, though off-peak speeds have remained the same. The motto is simple: don't travel in the rush-hour!

Sources: *Living in Britain*, Alison Walker et al, Results from the 2001 General Household Survey, The Stationery Office, 2002, Table 4.19; *Census 2001: National Report for England and Wales*, National Statistics, 2004, Table T01, Page 46; *Horizons*, National Statistics, Issue 29, June 2004, Page 17. Car colour data from *The Sunday Times*, 19th September, 2004, Innovation Page 5. Speed data from *Transport Statistics Bulletin*, Traffic Speeds on English Trunk Roads, 2003, National Statistics, Table 12.

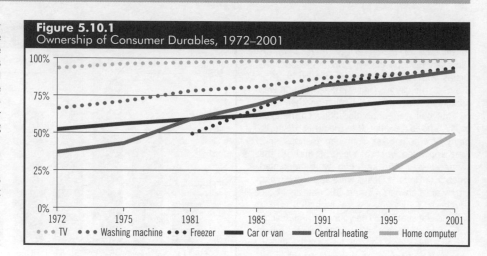

Figure 5.10.1
Ownership of Consumer Durables, 1972–2001

Legend: • • • TV   • • • Washing machine   • • • Freezer   — Car or van   — Central heating   — Home computer

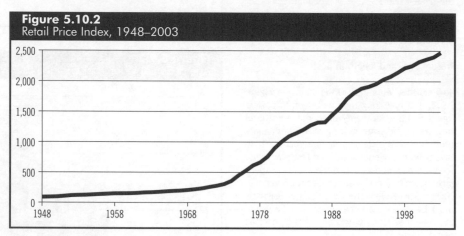

Figure 5.10.2
Retail Price Index, 1948–2003

Table 5.10.1
Rate of Increase of Retail Price Index

1948–53	1953–58	1958–63	1963–68	1968–73	1973–78	1978–83	1983–88	1988–93	1993–98	1998–03
+30%	+19%	+12%	+21%	+43%	+111%	+70%	+26%	+32%	+16%	+11%

Source: Retail Prices Index (RPI) all items, Consumer Prices and General Inflation Division, Office for National Statistics, Table RP02, June 2004

Table 5.10.2
Forecast Rate of Price and Earnings Increases

Increases in...	2000–10	2010–20	2020–30	2030–40	2040–50	2050–60	2060–70
Prices	+20.2%	+20.1%	+19.5%	+20.7%	+19.8%	+18.3%	+17.4%
Earnings	+20.4%	+22.7%	+24.5%	+28.6%	+29.9%	+29.4%	+29.6%

Source: Future contribution rates for the National Insurance Fund, assuming basic retirement pension is increased in line with prices or earnings, Government Actuary's Department, Introductory Booklet, Case Study, Page 7, www.gad.gov.uk

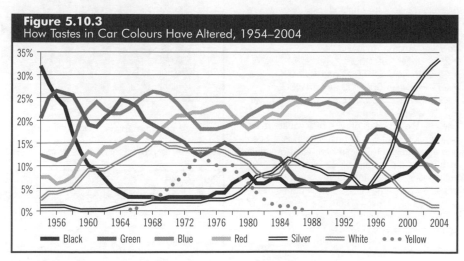

Figure 5.10.3
How Tastes in Car Colours Have Altered, 1954–2004

Legend: — Black   — Green   — Blue   — Red   — Silver   — White   • • • Yellow

Adults aged 15 to 49 were just over half, 52%, of the world's population in 2001. This is the group however which is perhaps most susceptible to AIDS or HIV, and the frightening statistic is that over 1% (1.16%) of them are infected. That means more than 37 million people.

The World Health Organisation (through UNAIDS) divides the world into 10 regions for purposes of analysing the AIDS trends. The incidence of AIDS in these regions is given in **Table 5.11.1**.

Table 5.11.1 shows that the world divides into four areas with respect to AIDS. The worst hit areas by far are sub-Saharan Africa and the Caribbean, with high percentages. After these areas come the American and Asian continents where the rate is on average 0.52%, or one person in every 190. Western Europe, North Africa and the Middle East have a rate half that amount, so that in these areas AIDS affects one person in every 380. East Asia and Oceania are half that rate again, affecting there one person in every 830.

So when in the Caribbean AIDS affects one person in every 42 and one in every 11 in sub-Saharan Africa the immensity of the problem can be seen. Transmitted in these countries mainly heterosexually, husband infects wife and vice versa, leaving thousands upon thousands of children not just orphans but having gone through the traumatic experience in many cases of watching their parents die of a terrible disease.

Table 5.11.1 also shows an implicit problem. Which takes priority – the areas where there are the most people affected (India has 3.8 million with AIDS, part of the 5.4 million in S & SE Asia), or those places where the rate is highest and thus spreading more and more rapidly (like South Africa where the percentage with AIDS is 20% and there are 24 million 15-49 year olds)? This is a very difficult problem, as the answer is probably BOTH!

This dilemma may be seen in **Table 5.11.2** which focusses on the 10 countries in Africa where the AIDS rate is highest. Three of the 4 countries with the highest rates of HIV (over 30%) have less than 400,000 15 to 49 year olds in their population. The two countries with most sufferers, South Africa and Kenya are 7th and 9th respectively.

Dr Bernard, who directs the Aids Feedback office in Geneva, has developed a series of "prevalence chains" to aid understanding of the complexities of this dilemma. The help needed, however it is understood, is huge. The problem eats at the living heart of African community life today, and if not careful will kill it for tomorrow, and what place then the Christian faith held by so many?

Source: Work/Reference Manuals and other material from Dr Bernard, Director of Epidemiology in Human Reproduction, Aids Feedback, Liaison for UN and NG organisations, 22, Avenue Riant-Parc, 1209 Geneva, Switzerland.

Table 5.11.1
Numbers with AIDS, World, 2001

Region	15–49 pop (millions)	Number with AIDS	% with HIV/AIDS
Sub-Saharan Africa	291.3	26,000,000	8.93
Caribbean	17.2	400,000	2.33
North America	161.4	940,000	0.58
Latin America	262.2	1,400,000	0.53
S & SE Asia	1,031.5	5,400,000	0.52
Eastern Europe and Central Asia	209.0	1,000,000	0.48
Western Europe	200.3	540,000	0.27
North Africa and Middle East	180.5	460,000	0.25
East Asia and Pacific	833.1	970,000	0.12
Australia/New Zealand	11.8	14,000	0.12
WORLD TOTAL	**3,198.3**	**37,124,000**	**1.16**

Table 5.11.2
African Countries with AIDS, 2001

Region	15–49 pop (millions)	Number with AIDS	% with HIV/AIDS
Botswana	0.9	347,000	38.8
Zimbabwe	6.4	2,160,000	33.7
Swaziland	0.6	187,000	33.4
Lesotho	1.2	370,000	31.0
Namibia	0.9	214,000	22.5
Zambia	5.1	1,095,000	21.5
South Africa	23.7	4,764,000	20.1
Malawi	6.1	925,000	15.2
Kenya	16.6	2,485,000	15.0
Mozambique	10.9	1,415,000	13.0
Rest of Africa	218.9	12,038,000	5.5
AFRICAN TOTAL	**291.3**	**26,000,000**	**8.9**

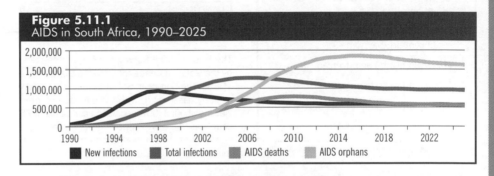

Figure 5.11.1
AIDS in South Africa, 1990–2025

Legend: New infections, Total infections, AIDS deaths, AIDS orphans

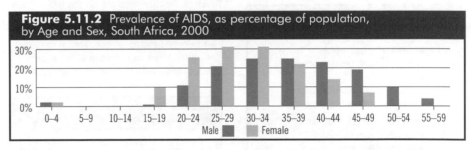

Figure 5.11.2 Prevalence of AIDS, as percentage of population, by Age and Sex, South Africa, 2000

Legend: Male, Female

5

Table 5.11.3 and **Figures 5.11.1** and 2 explore the AIDS situation in one country, South Africa, for which more detailed analysis is available. **Table 5.11.3** dramatically shows the impact of AIDS on life-span, with deaths from AIDS rapidly increasing, and overtaking deaths from other causes in 2003.

Figure 5.11.2 shows the incidence of AIDS by age. Most children born with AIDS mercifully die while they are very young, so that AIDS among those aged 5 to 14 is very rare. However, once puberty is passed, AIDS among teenage girls is high, and continues higher among females than males until the mid-30s, after which dominance may be seen in males. The impact this has on family life is huge, as the enormous number of AIDS orphans, shown in **Figure 5.11.1**, makes clear. These AIDS orphans form the vast majority of orphans in South Africa in the 21st century.

Source: Conference presentation given by Rob Dorrington, Director of the Centre for Actuarial Research, and immediate past Convenor of the ASSA AIDS Committee, South Africa, 2000.

Table 5.11.3
South African Mortality, 1990–2010

Year	1990	2000	2010
Probability of 15-year old dying before reaching age 60	30%	47%	79%
Life expectancy at birth, in years	62	53	41

Source: ASSA AIDS Modelling, Rob Dorrington, Centre for Actuarial Research, 2000

See also **Page 7.11** for further graphs.

A comprehensive manual on HIV/AIDS is the 2004 edition of *The Truth about AIDS* by Dr Patrick Dixon. Available through www.acet-international.org/publications

Table 5.12.1 If the World was a Village of 100 people, then:

57 would be from Asia
21 would be from Europe
 8 would be from Africa
14 would be from elsewhere

52 would be women
48 would be men

48 would be urban dwellers
52 would be rural dwellers

70 would have coloured skin
30 would have white skin

67 would be non-Christian
33 would be Christian

89 would be heterosexual
11 would be homosexual

 6 would own 75% of village's wealth, all from the USA

80 would have a simple and uncomfortable home

70 would not be able to read

50 would live in famine

 1 would have a university degree

 1 would own a computer

Source: Newsletter, Above Bar Church, Southampton, April 2004

Table 5.12.2 Self-perceived Religiousness by Religion, UK, 2002

Religion	Not at all %	1 %	2 %	3 %	4 %	5 %	6 %	7 %	8 %	Very 9 religious %	Av'ge score
Other Christian	0	0	8	11	0	8	8	14	19	5	27	7.0
Roman Catholic	2	1	2	6	10	20	12	22	13	7	5	6.1
Protestant	2	2	5	8	7	21	16	16	13	5	5	5.8
Eastern religions	0	6	0	3	9	21	9	12	19	3	18	6.5
Islam	0	5	3	6	3	19	6	33	11	8	6	6.2

Av'ge = Average

Table 5.12.3 Frequency of Attendance, by Religion, UK, 2002

Religion	Every day %	More than once a week %	Once a week %	At least once a month %	Only on special holy days %	Less often %	Never %	Average visits per year
Other Christian	3	30	19	5	8	13	22	54
Roman Catholic	2	6	35	11	13	15	18	35
Protestant	1	6	12	10	19	22	30	19
Eastern religions	6	12	6	24	37	12	3	44
Islam	11	3	22	8	19	20	17	57

The British Social Survey has been undertaken by the National Centre for Social Research since 1983. The European Social Survey is a biennial study based on it, with the intention of interviewing about 1,000 people in each of up to 22 countries across Europe. Its website is www.naticent02.uuhost.uk.uu.net. Its first round was in 2002.

Seven of the questions are on the topic of religion, two asking if a person belongs to any religion, and, if so, which, and two are if they have ever belonged to any religion, and, if so, which. The other three questions are for a person's sense of their religiousness on a score of 0 to 10, their frequency of attendance and how often they pray. Answers for first of these for the 1,009 UK respondents are given in **Table 5.12.2**, and show that most religious people on average score themselves between 6 and 7, whatever their religion.

Table 5.12.3 gives the frequency of visiting the appropriate place of worship. As is common with such interviews, the answers given of intention or memory are considerably greater than the percentage attendance when actually counted. This has been verified in both English and American counts of worshippers, and will presumably be true for other religions also.

Table 5.12.4 If all the World's Christians were reduced to 100, then:

28 would be from Europe
24 would be from Latin America
18 would be from Africa
17 would be from Asia/Oceania
14 would be from North America

42 would be Roman Catholic
19 would be Independent
11 would be Orthodox
 4 would be Anglican
24 would be other denominations

32 would be Evangelical, and mostly in growing churches

30 would listen to Christian radio or TV

78 would have the complete Bible in their language

0.3 would be Christian workers (including ministers), 8% of which would be cross-cultural mission workers

Source: Global Connections handout in May 2004 Conference

Table 5.12.5 Gender Differences in Religious Belief in Britain

Females	Believe in...	Males
84%	God	67%
9%	no God	16%
76%	a soul	58%
72%	sin	66%
69%	heaven	50%
57%	life after death	39%
42%	the devil	32%
35%	hell	27%

Source: Hearing Men's Voices, Roy McCloughry, Hodder & Stoughton, 1999, Page 67, quoting 1990 MORI poll by E Jacobs and R Worcester

How Smaller Churches Grow

A 2003 survey of 109 growing smaller churches in the middle United States had these characteristics in common:

1) The pastor and members were involved in community activities
2) They were located in towns of 2,500 people or more
3) They were fewer than 10 miles from a Wal-Mart (=ASDA) store
4) The population was in transition
5) They were pastored by younger pastors
6) The church was "very friendly", not just friendly
7) The church was open to new methods
8) Evangelism was a number one priority
9) The atmosphere of the church was open and safe for newcomers
10) The church had multiple children's ministries
11) Mentoring activities were available for newcomers
12) A high percentage of members was involved in ministry
13) Evangelism was the strongest skill of the pastor
14) Guests were welcomed and treated as though they were members
15) The church had written plans and goals

Source: The McIntosh Church Growth Network newsletter, quoted on *Christianity Today* website www.christianity today.com accessed 9th September 2003

Books
and Christian Bookshops

6

Sources: *The Bookseller*, J Whitaker, *UK Christian Handbook* 2004/2005 edition and previous editions, and various articles.

Table 6.2.1 Turnover and Titles by Size of Christian Bookshops, 2003

Total titles	Small shops (under 1,000 sq ft) Turnover							Large shops (1,000 sq ft or over) Turnover						
	Under £10,000	£10,000–£30,000	£30,001–£75,000	£75,001–£150,000	Over £150,000	Not stated	TOTAL	Under £30,000	£30,000–£75,000	£75,001–£150,000	£150,001–£300,000	Over £300,000	Not stated	TOTAL
Less than 1,000	2	4	4	3	2	42	**57**	—	—	—	—	2	2	**4**
1,000 - 3,000	1	9	34	17	12	59	**132**	—	1	4	5	3	12	**25**
3,001 - 5,000	—	3	8	16	15	41	**83**	1	—	1	3	19	11	**35**
5,001 - 7,500	—	1	1	2	1	15	**20**	—	—	—	1	5	7	**13**
More than 7,500	—	1	—	3	5	29	**38**	—	—	—	—	15	32	**47**
Not stated	—	1	1	1	—	4	**7**	—	—	—	1	1	3	**5**
TOTAL	**3**	**19**	**48**	**42**	**35**	**190**	**337**	**1**	**1**	**5**	**10**	**45**	**67**	**129**
Average titles	1,200	2,700	2,300	3,400	3,900	3,600	**3,300**	4,000	2,000	2,400	3,100	5,600	6,100	**5,500**

Table 6.2.2 Number of Titles held by Christian Bookshops, 1993–2003

Total titles	Small Bookshops						Large Bookshops						All Bookshops					
	1993 %	1995 %	1997 %	1999 %	2001 %	2003 %	1993 %	1995 %	1997 %	1999 %	2001 %	2003 %	1993 %	1995 %	1997 %	1999 %	2001 %	2003 %
Less than 1,000	19	17	26	14	14	17	3	4	5	3	3	3	15	15	22	12	14	13
1,000–3,000	48	48	37	47	34	39	18	20	20	16	12	19	42	42	34	40	29	34
3,001–5,000	18	20	20	22	26	25	26	24	31	29	22	27	20	20	22	24	23	25
5,001–7,500	6	5	6	6	13	6	7	8	6	10	20	10	6	5	6	7	14	7
Over 7,500	5	6	8	8	10	11	41	39	35	39	38	37	13	13	12	14	16	18
Not stated	4	4	3	3	3	2	5	5	3	3	5	4	4	5	4	3	4	3
TOTAL	**429**	**429**	**448**	**395**	**366**	**337**	**115**	**114**	**97**	**111**	**116**	**129**	**578**	**579**	**550**	**530**	**528**	**466**
Average titles	1,500	2,900	3,000	3,000	3,600	3,300	6,800	6,000	5,800	5,600	5,800	5,500	2,600	3,600	3,400	3,600	4,000	3,900

Table 6.2.3
Average Turnover of Christian Bookshops, 1993–2003

	1993	1995	1997	1999	2001	2003
Small bookshops[1]	£46,500	£74,900	£92,400	£95,500	£102,700	£101,400
Large bookshops[2]	£152,100	£168,100	£238,200	£221,000	£294,000	£371,600
All bookshops	£68,800	£94,500	£118,800	£123,000	£148,700	£176,200

[1] Area under 1,000 sq ft   [2] Area 1,000 sq ft or over

Table 6.2.4
Books Published

Year	Total Books	Religious	Occult
1998	104,634	4,379	637
1999	110,155	4,595	655
2000	116,415	4,466	695
2001	119,001	4,229	697
2002	125,390	4,641	789
2003	130,200	4,530	800
2005[1]	138,000	4,580	870
2010[1]	161,000	4,690	1,060

[1] Estimate   Source: *Bookseller*, J Whitaker

Figure 6.2.1
Average Turnover of Christian Bookshops, 1993–2003

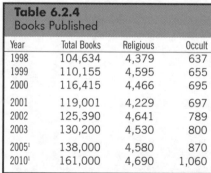

Figure 6.2.2 Average Number of Titles held by Christian Bookshops, 1993–2003

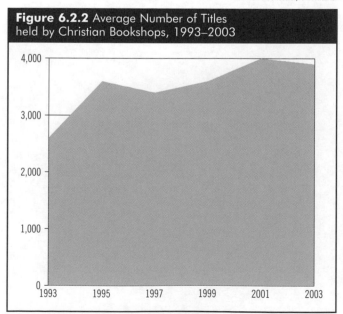

Source: *UK Christian Handbook,* 1994/95, 1996/97, 1998/99, 2000/01, 2002/03 and 2004/05 editions, Christian Research, London.

Source: *UK Christian Handbook,* 1994/95, 1996/97, 1998/99, 2000/01, 2002/03 and 2004/05 editions, Christian Research, London.

Christian Newspapers and periodicals

It is clear from both **Table 6.3.1** and **Figure 6.3.1** that circulation numbers of many Christian newspapers and periodicals have declined between 1988 and 2003. Of the 12 listed in the Table, the average decline of the first nine has been −53% over this period, though if the growth of the last three is added in, this becomes a net decline of −44%, or an average of 3.8% per year. This is faster than the decline in attendance or membership shown in **Table 12.13**.

On the other hand, these 12 have all survived for the 15 years covered. A number of other Christian magazines have not. Some have gone through renewal and transformation (like *Redemption*) and are now called a different name.

Table 6.3.2 gives the results of a survey which shows that clergy spend much less time in reading for pleasure than those in other professions. However, the Bishop of Oxford, the Rt Rev Richard Harries, pointed out that there is a very thin line for clergy in reading for pleasure and reading for work, study or devotion.

Table 6.3.4 shows that of all the various London radio stations, Premier Radio (the only specifically Christian station in this list) has, on average, been listened to second only to LBC News for the 5 years 1999 to 2003. While the Table shows a steadily decreasing proportion of the audience listening to these programmes, the proportion listening to Premier has risen from 12% of the total in 1999 to 21% in 2003. Of a total potential media reach audience of 30 million a day, Premier's daily average in 2003 was just under 180,000 people.

The peak time for listening to radio is early in the morning, over breakfast, as shown in **Figure 6.3.2**. However radio listening is more important than watching the TV until 3.30pm, the crossover point, although until 7.00pm, the TV is a secondary activity not a main activity.

In the evening of 26th February, 2004, BBC 2 broadcast a programme *What the World Thinks of God*, based on 10,000 interviews across 10 countries: India, Indonesia, Israel, Lebanon, Mexico, Nigeria, Russia, South Korea, UK and the USA. Some of the answers are given in **Table 6.3.3**.

Table 6.3.1
Circulation of Selected Largest Christian Newspapers and Periodicals

Title	1988	1993	1997	2003	% change 1988–2003
Weekly					
The War Cry	115,000	90,000	80,000	74,000	−36
The Universe	125,000	108,000	100,000	55,000	−56
Church Times	44,800	40,600	38,000	35,000	−22
Methodist Recorder	28,800	26,000	25,000	25,000	−13
Catholic Herald	30,000	30,000	26,000[1]	22,000	−27
Monthly					
The Sign	350,000	182,150	100,000	61,000	−83
Challenge	88,000	80,900	71,900[1]	60,000	−32
News Special	75,330	66,900[1]	50,000	50,000	−34
Life and Work	125,000	81,000	72,100[1]	45,569	−64
Redemption/Joy Magazine	8,000	7,000	6,000	30,000	+275
Bi-monthly or Quarterly					
Share It!	49,000[1]	50,000	55,000	55,000	+12
Idea	15,000	48,000	55,000	43,000	+187

[1] Estimate

Table 6.3.2 Average Time Spent Reading for Pleasure in a Week, 2004

Profession	Time
Accountants	5 hrs 15 mins
Secretaries	4 hrs 59 mins
Politicians	4 hrs 58 mins
Journalists	4 hrs 57 mins
Taxi drivers	4 hrs 56 mins
Lawyers	4 hrs 33 mins
Clergy	2 hrs 40 mins

Source: Report in *Church Times*, 19th March, 2004, of a survey undertaken by Book Marketing Ltd. Sample 700.

Table 6.3.3 'Yes' Answers Given in BBC programme *What the World Thinks of God*

Question	% UK
Do you believe in God, a higher power or spirituality?	84
Do you believe in God or a higher power?	67
Do you find it hard to believe because of suffering?	52
Did God create the Universe?	52
Have you always believed in God?	46
Does the encouragement to believe come from outside the family?	29
Would you die for God?	19

Sources: As given under Tables 6.3.2 and 6.3.4, and Page 11 of the paper "The way we live now" by James Holden, BBC and Graeme Griffiths, TNS (Paper 13) presented by the Market Research Society March 2004, the data shown coming from the BBC Daily Life data. Personal observation of BBC2 programme.

Table 6.3.4
Average Hours per Listener for 10 Greater London Radio Station Audiences, 4th Quarter, 1999–2003

Station	1999	2000	2001	2002	2003	Av'ge
LBC News 1152	15.1	15.9	14.3	12.6	5.6	12.7
Premier Radio AM	9.5	9.6	8.7	10.1	15.9	10.8
Capital FM 95.8	8.4	9.4	8.6	8.0	7.5	8.4
Magic 105.4	9.3	8.6	8.3	7.9	7.3	8.3
Heart FM 106.2	6.5	7.6	8.5	7.4	8.2	7.6
XFM 104.9	5.8	7.4	6.5	7.7	6.5	6.8
Capital Gold 1548	6.4	5.6	6.0	5.6	4.7	5.7
BBC London 94.9	5.7	4.9	5.3	5.8	6.0	5.5
Jazz FM 102.2	6.3	5.7	3.9	5.4	5.0	5.3
LBC 97.3	4.0	3.8	4.7	4.5	9.6	5.3
TOTAL hours	77.0	78.5	74.8	75.0	76.3	76.4
% share	35.5	33.1	32.4	31.1	27.3	31.9

Source: RAJAR – Radio Joint Audience Research report, J Peter Wilson, Christian Broadcasting Council, peter@dayoneradio.co.uk
Av'ge = Average

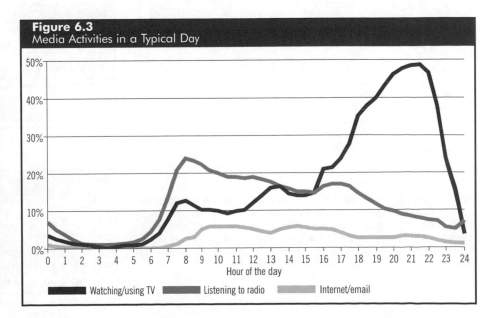

Figure 6.3
Media Activities in a Typical Day

Legend: Watching/using TV — Listening to radio — Internet/email

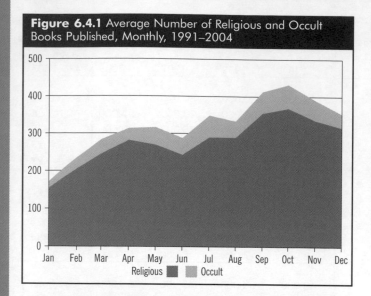

Figure 6.4.1 Average Number of Religious and Occult Books Published, Monthly, 1991–2004

Religious ■ Occult ■

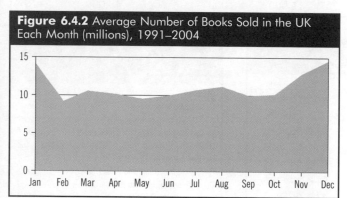

Figure 6.4.2 Average Number of Books Sold in the UK Each Month (millions), 1991–2004

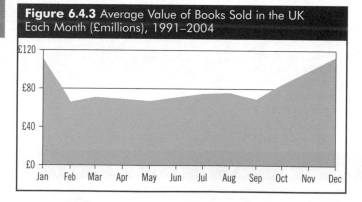

Figure 6.4.3 Average Value of Books Sold in the UK Each Month (£millions), 1991–2004

Table 6.4.1
Religious Books Published by Month, 1991–2004

Year	Jan	Feb	Mar	Apr	May	Jun	Jul	Aug	Sep	Oct	Nov	Dec	Total
1991	79	215	221	232	186	171	180	223	184	228	319	258	**2,496**
1992	115	283	172	164	241	232	252	202	297	282	232	226	**2,698**
1993	79	236	259	221	227	205	191	200	253	305	275	243	**2,694**
1994	156	221	199	337	245	273	271	265	419	273	340	375	**3,374**
1995	183	340	320	375	236	357	203	416	756	406	387	428	**4,407**
1996	192	264	306	377	335	284	430	298	311	413	588	345	**4,143**
1997	196	231	306	411	447	242	373	289	481	509	320	301	**4,106**
1998	188	156	321	312	386	385	397	324	454	523	350	403	**4,199**
1999	164	166	273	440	242	195	438	264	326	541	469	569	**4,087**
2000	275	223	251	308	257	325	359	230	251	149	172	337	**3,137**
2001	83	116	173	152	164	209	148	353	415	436	398	256	**2,903**
2002	116	173	298	218	394	155	313	334	256	261	233	149	**2,900**
2003	124	160	170	160	242	191	295	364	214	459	283	234	**2,896**
2004	193	92	154	231	169	183	203	187	304	413	382	334	**2,845**
Avge	**153**	**205**	**245**	**281**	**269**	**243**	**290**	**282**	**351**	**371**	**339**	**318**	**3,384**

Source: The Bookseller, lists of books each week. Not every religious book published actually is listed. The total is purely the sum of the previous columns, not the number actually published.

Table 6.4.2
Occult Books Published by Month, 1991–2004

Year	Jan	Feb	Mar	Apr	May	Jun	Jul	Aug	Sep	Oct	Nov	Dec	Total
1991	12	21	54	18	31	51	37	40	49	29	82	12	**436**
1992	23	30	23	18	48	64	68	47	41	59	35	24	**480**
1993	16	43	22	22	36	55	28	63	32	45	42	33	**437**
1994	17	40	12	35	28	53	93	43	61	40	37	49	**508**
1995	17	31	32	37	21	65	45	29	75	70	33	57	**512**
1996	12	30	55	43	58	27	77	58	36	67	64	34	**561**
1997	18	43	39	46	61	33	41	52	51	113	38	37	**572**
1998	19	23	37	60	47	51	83	40	77	95	70	43	**645**
1999	25	25	53	31	65	48	58	33	45	113	117	61	**674**
2000	35	36	49	43	31	44	59	29	83	41	33	56	**539**
2001	7	7	34	36	90	33	43	35	90	54	70	39	**538**
2002	21	55	63	22	54	38	43	54	49	37	53	14	**503**
2003	20	24	13	21	75	33	88	56	66	66	41	22	**525**
2004	15	10	41	17	19	22	52	25	121	76	41	54	**493**
Avge	**18**	**30**	**38**	**32**	**47**	**44**	**58**	**44**	**63**	**65**	**54**	**38**	**531**

Source: The Bookseller, lists of books each week. Not every occult book published actually is listed. The total is purely the sum of the previous columns, not the number actually published.

Table 6.4.3 Number of Books Sold in the UK (millions) each month, 2001–2004

Year	Jan	Feb	Mar	Apr	May	Jun	Jul	Aug	Sep	Oct	Nov	Dec	Total
2001	n/a	n/a	n/a	n/a	7.75	10.13	9.19	11.30	8.85	8.80	13.27	13.88	**83.17**
2002	14.15	8.93	11.43	8.31	10.41	8.56	9.53	12.08	11.08	9.41	13.71	16.10	**133.70**
2003	16.26	9.50	9.77	9.99	10.96	10.48	10.90	10.35	9.99	12.26	11.56	13.69	**135.71**
2004	12.15	9.21	10.54	12.12	9.19	10.42	13.16	10.85	10.44	12.56	11.74	12.46	**134.84**
Avge	**14.19**	**9.21**	**10.58**	**10.14**	**9.58**	**9.90**	**10.70**	**11.14**	**10.09**	**10.76**	**12.57**	**14.04**	**132.90**

Source: The Bookseller, sales of books each week.

Table 6.4.4 Value of Books Sold in the UK (£millions) each month, 2001–2004

Year	Jan	Feb	Mar	Apr	May	Jun	Jul	Aug	Sep	Oct	Nov	Dec	Total
2001	n/a	n/a	n/a	n/a	56.69	73.75	63.80	77.71	66.05	70.92	105.65	116.84	**631.41**
2002	113.71	65.32	79.55	56.63	72.87	58.16	64.25	79.16	67.09	72.87	106.59	121.30	**957.50**
2003	130.72	66.56	64.23	67.42	76.46	77.61	80.24	70.95	74.44	97.54	91.00	113.82	**1,010.99**
2004	88.08	65.82	69.24	83.36	63.50	73.82	92.04	74.42	74.07	99.37	92.10	101.88	**977.70**
Avge	**110.84**	**65.90**	**71.01**	**69.14**	**67.38**	**70.84**	**75.08**	**75.56**	**70.41**	**85.17**	**98.84**	**113.46**	**973.63**

Source: The Bookseller, value of books sold each week.

The number of religious books published per month, as seen in **Table 6.4.1** and **Figure 6.4.1**, peaks in April because of Easter, but then rises steadily towards an annual peak in September and October ready for the Christmas market, though the number published in November and December is still higher than any earlier part of the year.

Occult books, given in **Table 6.4.2**, follow a similar trend except for Easter.

The number of general books sold each week (not just religious books) is given in **Table 6.4.3** and **Figure 6.4.2**. There are peaks for the January sales, Easter and August holidays, and the Christmas period. The value of such books is given in **Table 6.4.4** and **Figure 6.4.3**. The graphs in **Figures 6.4.2** and **6.4.3** are virtually identical, suggesting that the average price of books is much the same throughout the year.

Recent Research Reports

This section of *Religious Trends* records recent, past (and in a few cases known forthcoming) research on Christian topics. The entries are listed alphabetically by author, and the address from which the book or report may be obtained is given underneath each entry. Where there is more than one entry from a particular author, the address is given under the first entry only.

The number after each name in the Subject Index on Page 7.13 is the sequential number of the papers for a particular author. Thus Barna (2) is the second of the papers listed by George Barna.

For a list of **Doctoral Dissertations on Mission**, 1992–2001 by author and by subject, see *International Bulletin of Missionary Research*, Vol. 27, No. 3, July 2003, available through the Overseas Ministries Study Centre in New Haven, Connecticut, United States, www.OMSC.org

For a list of **African Old Testament Dissertations**, see *Old Testament Research for Africa: A Critical Analysis and Annotated Bibliography of African Old Testament Dissertations*, 1967–2000, by Knut Holter, published by Peter Lang, New York, 2002, 152 pages, £35.

Sources: Individual authors

Archbishops' Council (1)
Formation for Ministry within a Learning Church.
Hind Report of a working party set up by the Archbishops' Council on the structure and funding of ordination training.
Church House Bookshop, Great Smith Street, London SW1P 3BN
Published 2003; 196 pages; Publisher Church House Bookshop; Price £12.50

Archbishops' Council (2)
Review of Clergy Terms of Service.
Report of the first phase of the work of the review of Clergy Terms of Service Working Group.
Published 2001; 118 pages;
Publisher Church House Bookshop; Price £6

Archbishops' Council (3)
Church Statistics for 2002.
Published 2004;
Publisher Church House Bookshop

Archdeacons of the Diocese of Chelmsford
Review of Church Buildings in the Diocese of Chelmsford.
Free download www.chelmsford.anglican.org/churchbuildings/
Published 2003 mailto: acolchester@chelmsford.anglican.org

Aspinall Peter
Should a Question on "Religion" be asked in the 2001 British Census?
A Public Policy Case in favour.
Published 2000; Social, Policy and Administration, Vol.34, No 5, pp 584–600;
Publisher Blackwell Publishing Ltd

Bartholomew Richard
Community and Consumerism:
The case of Christian publishing.
Email rbarthy@yahoo.co.uk
Published 2004;
PhD Thesis, University of London (SOAS)

Bamford Keith
Examining attitudes to and experience of evangelism in order to formulate an evangelism policy for a Methodist Circuit, with reference to the demon 'acedia' (sloth).
Cliff College, Calver, Hope Valley, Nr Sheffield S32 3XG
Published 2003; 20,000 words;
MA in Evangelism studies; Price £30

Baptist Union of Great Britain (1)
Church Life Profile 2001.
Denominational results for the Baptist Union.
Baptist Union Department for Research & Training in Mission;
Email mission@baptist.org.uk
Published 2003;
Publisher Churches Information for Mission

Baptist Union of Great Britain (2)
Small Churches Project. Findings from various forms of research including Annual Returns statistics, focus groups and questionnaires.
Published 2004; 32 pages

Bees John
Connections Between Ecumenism and Mission: with particular reference to developments in Nailsea, North Somerset.
Cliff College, Calver, Hope Valley, Nr Sheffield S32 3XG
Published 2002; 20,000 words;
MA in Evangelism studies; Price £30

Belcher Harriet
& S Waterman, B Kosmin, K Thomson
A Portrait of Jews in London and the South-east: a community study.
Institute for Jewish Policy Research, 79 Wimpole Street, London W1G 9RY
Published 2002; 70 pages; Publisher Institute for Jewish Policy Research;
Report No 4; Price £10

Bellamy John & A Black, K Castle, P Hughes, P Kaldor
Why People Don't Go to Church.
Based on the 1998 Australian Community Survey.
205 Halifax Street, Adelaide, South Australia 5000
Published 2003; Publisher Openbook

Benson Paddy & John Roberts
Counting Sheep: Attendance Patterns and Pastoral Strategy.
Grove Pastoral Series Number P92.
Grove Books Limited, Ridley Hall Road, Cambridge CB3 9HU;
www.grovebooks.co.uk
Published 2003

Bhattacharyya Gargi
Minority Ethnic Attainment and Participation in Education and Training: the Evidence.
Published 2003; Research topic paper RTP01-03; Publisher Department for Education and Skills

Bing Rev Alan
Reflections on Renewal.
A sabbatical study of three contrasting sources of renewal, The Iona Community, New Wine and Taizé.
15 Ford Park Crescent, Ulverston, Cumbria LA12 7TR
Published 2003/4; 10,000 words;
Sabbatical report

Birnie Jacqueline
The response of Barrow-in-Furness to the death of Diana, Princess of Wales: a modern myth or the birth of new means of mission?
Cliff College, Calver, Hope Valley, Nr Sheffield S32 3XG
Published 2002; 20,000 words;
MA in Evangelism studies; Price £30

Bishop Gary
Journeys into a Postmodern Church.
Cliff College, Calver, Hope Valley, Nr Sheffield S32 3XG
Published 2004; 20,000 words;
MA in Evangelism studies; Price £30

Board for Church in Society
Cohabitation: A Christian Reflection.
A report by a working party of the Board for Church in Society.
BCS, Trinity House, 4 Chapel Court, London SE1 1HW
Published 2003; 122 pages; Publisher The Diocese of Southwark; Price £7

Bong Ah Loi
Church Growth amongst Protestant Churches in Miri.
Cliff College, Calver, Hope Valley, Nr Sheffield S32 3XG
Published 2003; 20,000 words;
MA in Evangelism studies; Price £30

Booker B B & M Fearn, L J Francis
The Personality Profile of Artists.
The Welsh National Centre for Religious Education, University of Wales, Bangor, Meirion, Normal Site, Bangor, Gwynedd LL57 2PX
Published 2001;
Irish Journal of Psychology, Vol 22, No 3–4

Bourke Rosamund
& L J Francis, Dr M Robbins
Locating Cattell's Personality Factors within Eysenck's Dimensional Model of Personality: a study among adolescents.
Published 2004; North American Journal of Psychology, Vol 6, No 1, pp 167-173

Bowers Rev Jacky
Let's get rid of Ecumenism!
Suggests thinking relationally rather than structurally about how local churches work together; get rid of the word not the concept.
5 Charleston Rd, Eastbourne BN21 1SE or email J.A.Bowers@btinternet.com
Published 2003; 21 pages

Brierley Dr Peter and H Wraight (1)
MHA Group: Strategy for the future.
A report of the 2003 survey.
Christian Research, 4 Footscray Road, Eltham, London SE9 2TZ
Published 2003; 38 pages

Brierley Dr Peter and H Wraight (2)
Bible Reading.
Survey into Bible reading habits and use of study aids amongst churchgoers.
Published 2004; 59 pages

Brierley Dr Peter (3)
Child Protection Survey. A study by the CCPAS across 750 congregations.
Published 2003; 66 pages

Brierley Dr Peter (4)
Churches, Children and Child Protection. Key findings from the 2003 survey by the CCPAS.
Published 2003; 16 pages; Price £0.50

Brierley Dr Peter (5)
USPG. A report of the research of USPG image.
Published 2003; 49 pages

Brierley Dr Peter (6)
What do Archdeacons do? Bishops, Archdeacons and Rural Deans looking at the role of Archdeacons.
Published 2003; 49 pages

Brierley Dr Peter & H Wraight (7)
Leadership, Vision and Growing Churches. Key findings based on the 2002 survey commissioned by the Salvation Army.
Published 2003; 24 pages; Price £1

Brierley Dr Peter (8)
Mind of Anglicans.
Key findings from the 2002 survey undertaken for Cost of Conscience.
Published 2003; 16 pages; Price £0.50

Brierley Dr Peter (9)
Implicit Religion:
72% Christian, 8% Attendance.
The gap between the Civil Census and church attendance.
Published 2003; 17 pages;
Leaders Briefing No 20; Price £4

Brierley Dr Peter (10)
Evangelicals in the World of the 21st Century. The current situation numerically. Written for the 2004 Lausanne Forum.
Published 2004; 21 pages;
Leaders Briefing No 21; Price £5

Brierley Dr Peter (11)
Alpha Initiative.
Numbers attending Alpha 2002
Published 2003; 34 pages

Brierley Dr Peter (12)
Alpha International 2002 & 2003.
Numbers attending Alpha Worldwide.
Published 2004; 24 pages

Buchanan Rt Rev Colin
Mission in South-East London; follow up on 2003.
Focuses particularly but not exclusively on the Woolwich area and shows a slow but steady growth.
Communications and Resources, Diocese of Southwark, Trinity House, 4 Chapel Court, Borough High Street, London SE1 1HW
Published 2004

Buck Steve
Twelve Steps to Recovery: Pathway to peace for the postmodern world.
Cliff College, Calver, Hope Valley, Nr Sheffield S32 3XG
Published 2003; 20,000 words;
MA in Evangelism studies; Price £30

Buckley Anthony
The Issue of Loneliness in Full-time Stipendiary Anglican Clergy.
Looking at three issues: person, context and vocation.
4 Cornwallis Ave, Folkestone CT19 5JA or email antmon64@hotmail.com
Published 2004; MA Dissertation

Cardy Donald
Survey of Church Members, Diocese of Chelmsford.
Email dfcardy@tiscali.co.uk
Published 2003

Chambers Paul
A New Monasticism:
Hope of the Western Church.
Cliff College, Calver, Hope Valley, Nr Sheffield S32 3XG
Published 2003; 20,000 words;
MA in Evangelism studies; Price £30

Chan Dr C K
The UK Christian Churches' Welfare Services.
Division of Social Work, Nottingham Trent University, Burton Street, Nottingham NG1 4BU
Published 2004

Charity Finance
Mergers and Collaboration,
Charities Survey.
Charity Finance, 3 Rectory Grove,
London SW4 0DX
or email info@charityfinance.co.uk
Published 2004

Charter Alan
Church and the Secularized Child.
Cliff College, Calver, Hope Valley,
Nr Sheffield S32 3XG
Published 2003; 20,000 words;
MA in Evangelism studies; Price £30

Church of Scotland
The Stained Glass Ceiling:
Gender Attitude Project.
Church of Scotland, 121 George
Street, Edinburgh EH2 4YN
Published 2001

Churches Regional Commission
for Yorkshire and the Humber.
Angels and Advocates: Church Social
Action in Yorkshire and the Humber
20 New Market Street, Leeds LS1 6DG
Published 2002; 78 pages; Price £5

Collinson Hilary
Training for Learning and Serving
(TLS) is an educational process that
encourages and equips people to engage
in theological reflection which is
sustained over time.
Cliff College, Calver, Hope Valley,
Nr Sheffield S32 3XG
Published 2003; 20,000 words;
MA in Training & Theological Reflection in
Church & Community; Price £30

Conradie Lynita
I was a stranger and you did not
welcome me. The Church's mission to
homosexual people as a marginalised
group in Namibia.
Cliff College, Calver, Hope Valley,
Nr Sheffield S32 3XG
Published 2002; 20,000 words;
MA in Evangelism studies; Price £30

Cooper Paul
The Decline in Churchgoing in
England in the 19th and 20th
centuries: the Exclusivity
Dimension.
The Coach House, 18 Sandford House,
Wareham, Dorset BH20 7DH
Published 2001; MA Thesis

Cooper Trevor (1)
The Care of Church of England
Church Buildings.
38 Roseberry Avenue, New Malden,
Surrey KT3 4JS
Published 2003

Cooper Trevor (2)
How do we keep our parish Churches?
Published 2004

Couchman-Boor Julie
Towards developing a model of
consultancy for training and
development officers working
within the training and
development function of Tearfund.
Cliff College, Calver, Hope Valley,
Nr Sheffield S32 3XG
Published 2002; 20,000 words;
MA in Consultancy, Mission & Ministry
studies; Price £30

Cracknell Paul
The Art of Connecting.
Cliff College, Calver, Hope Valley,
Nr Sheffield S32 3XG
Published 2003; 20,000 words;
MA in Evangelism studies; Price £30

Craig Charlotte
& L J Francis, J Bailey, Dr M Robbins (1)
Psychological types in Church
in Wales congregations.
The Welsh National Centre for
Religious Education, University of
Wales, Bangor Meirion, Normal Site
Bangor, Gwynedd LL57 2PX
Published 2003; The Psychologist in Wales,
Vol 15, pp 18-21

Craig Charlotte
& L J Francis, Dr M Robbins (2)
Psychological Type and Sex
Differences among church leaders
in the United Kingdom.
Published 2004; Journal of Beliefs and
Values, Vol 25, pp 3-13

Crossland John
The use of Cathedrals for Evangelism.
Cliff College, Calver, Hope Valley,
Nr Sheffield S32 3XG
Published 2002; 20,000 words;
MA in Evangelism studies; Price £30

Crossley John
Leadership and Church Growth:
an analysis and a critique of responses
to the book *'Leading your Church to*
Growth' by C P Wagner.
Cliff College, Calver, Hope Valley,
Nr Sheffield S32 3XG
Published 2002; 20,000 words;
MA in Evangelism studies; Price £30

Dalpra C
Addicted to Planting (Encounters
on the Edge 17): Can we learn from
Alcoholics Anonymous 12 step model
of recovery as we seek models for
emerging church in the 21st century?
The Sheffield Centre, Church Army's
Research Unit, 50 Cavendish Street,
Sheffield S3 7RZ
Published 2003; 28 pages;
Publisher Church Army; Price £4

Dandelion Dr P
The Nature of Quaker Believing,
and its consequences for the
longevity of the group.
CARFAX Publishing, Rankine Road,
Basingstoke RG24 8PR
Published 2004; 4,500 words; Journal of
Contemporary Religion, pp 219-300

DAWN
Christianity in Finland in the 21st
century. Finnish DAWN Report.
Email heikki.lassila@kolumbus.fi or
pekka@sahimaa.pp.fi
Published 2002

Devine J P
Faith in England's North West.
A survey of every individual place of
worship of all faiths throughout the
region.
Churches' Officer for NW,
North West Development Agency,
Renaissance House, Box 37,
Centre Park, Warrington WA1 1XB
Published 2003; 95 pages;
Publisher North West Development Agency

Duursma K J
Living Stones: Community Survey in
the Old Town area of Eastbourne.
Order via Email
livingstones@ukonline.co.uk
Published 2003

Edwards Helen
An evaluation of the role
of Cliff College Evangelists
from 1990 to the present day,
leading to an essential development
of the role for the future.
Cliff College, Calver, Hope Valley,
Nr Sheffield S32 3XG
Published 2003; 20,000 words;
MA in Evangelism studies; Price £30

Erwich Dr R
Missional Churches; identical global
"plants" or locally grown "flowers"?
Christian A Schwarz's "Natural
Church Development" revisited.
Order via Email dr.r.erwich@planet.nl
Published 2003

Fearn Joanne
Diocese of Durham.
Can the training and ministry of the
Methodist Local Preacher and the
Church of England Reader be more
effective and useful to the mission of
the Church in the North-East of
England if it is done together?
Cliff College, Calver, Hope Valley,
Nr Sheffield S32 3XG
Published 2003; 20,000 words; MA in
Evangelism studies; Price £30

Fearn M & L J Francis (1)
From A-level to higher education:
Student perceptions of teaching and
learning in theology and religious
studies.
The Welsh National Centre for
Religious Education, University of
Wales, Bangor, Meirion, Normal Site,
Bangor, Gwynedd LL57 2PX
Published 2004; Discourse, Vol 3, No 2, pp
58-91

Fearn M, C A Lewis & L J Francis (2)
Religion and personality
among religious studies students:
a replication.
Published 2003; Psychological Reports, Vol
93; pp 819-822

Ferrer Simon
The Church on Ynys Môn Part one:
A pilot study based on map evidence.
Caelan, Drury Lane Leeswood,
Mold, Flintshire CH7 4SJ
Published 2004; 64 Pages

Fickus Joseph
Transformational Prayer Survey:
Stories and surveys from Africa and
Asia.
Order via Email John.robb@wvi.org
Published 2003

Fillingham Richard
Church for the doubting generation:
Christian ministry among adults in a
sceptical world.
Cliff College, Calver, Hope Valley,
Nr Sheffield S32 3XG
Published 2002; 20,000 words;
MA in Evangelism studies; Price £30

Francis Rev Prof Leslie (1)
Research of Dr John Payne.
An article describing this research
which assembled psychological type
profiles from male clergy in the
Church in Wales.
The Welsh National Centre for
Religious Education, University of
Wales, Bangor, Meirion, Normal Site,
Bangor, Gwynedd LL57 2PX
Published 2004; Church Times 2/1/04

Francis Rev Prof Leslie (2)
The Impact of Age, Personality and
Churchmanship on baptism policy
among Anglican clergy in Wales.
Published 2004;
Modern Believing, Vol 45, No 1, pp 20-32

Francis Rev Prof Leslie (3)
Recognizing and Educating
Religious Minorities in England and
Wales. Y Iram (ed)
Published 2003; Education of Minorities
and Peace Education in Pluralistic Societies,
Chapter 8; Publisher Praeger, Connecticut
and London

Francis Rev Prof Leslie (4)
Psychological Type and Biblical
Hermeneutics: SIFT method of
preaching.
Published 2003;
Rural Theology, Vol 1, pp 13-23

Francis Rev Prof Leslie (5)
Religion and Social Capital:
the flaw in the 2001 census in
England and Wales, in P. Avis (ed.)
Published 2003; Public Faith? The state of
religious belief and practice in Britain,
pp 45-64; Publisher SPCK, London

Francis Rev Prof Leslie (6)
A Socio-psychological profile of
young Anglicans in Wales: a study
in empirical theology in R.Rope (ed.)
Honouring the past and shaping the
Future: essays in honour of Gareth
Lloyd Jones.
Published 2003; pp 233-252; Publisher
Gracewing, Leominster

Francis Rev Prof Leslie (7)
Living without the clerical persona:
lie scale scores among male
Evangelical Clergy.
Published 2003; Research in the Social
Scientific Study of Religion, Vol 14, pp 103-
111

Francis Rev Prof Leslie (8)
Personality Theory
and Empirical Theology.
Published 2002; Journal of Empirical
Theology, Vol 15, No 1

Francis Rev Prof Leslie & R Bourke (9)
Personality and Religion: applying
Cattell's model among secondary
school pupils.
Published 2003; Current Psychology, Vol 22,
pp 125-137

Francis Rev Prof Leslie
& R Bourke, Dr M Robbins (10)
Quakerism: a faith for introverts ?
Published 2003; Pastoral Psychology,
Vol 51, pp 387-390

7

Francis Rev Prof Leslie
& Geraint Davies (11)
School Worship in the Primary School: a premature obituary?
Published 2002; Panorama: International Journal of Comparative Religion and Education and Values, Vol 14, No 1, pp 37-43

Francis Rev Prof Leslie
& B Duncan, C L Craig, G Luffman (12)
Type Patterns among Anglican Congregations in England.
Published 2004; Journal of Adult Theological Education, Vol 1, No 1, pp 66-77

Francis Rev Prof Leslie
& Trond Enger (13)
The Norwegian translation of the Francis Scale of Attitude toward Christianity.
Published 2002; Individual Differences Research, Vol 43, No 5

Francis Rev Prof Leslie
& M Fearn, B B Booker (14)
Artistic Creativity: Personality and the Diurnal Rhythm.
Published 2003; North American Journal of Psychology, Vol 5, No 1, pp 147-152

Francis Rev Prof Leslie J
& C J Jackson (15)
Eysenck's dimensional model of personality and religion: are religious people more neurotic?
Published 2003; Mental Health, Religion and Culture, Vol 6, pp 87-100

Francis Rev Prof Leslie & S H Jones, Dr M Robbins, C J Jackson (16)
The Personality profile of female Anglican clergy in Britain and Ireland: a study employing the Eyseck Personality Profiler.
Published 2003; Archiv für Religionspsychologie, Vol 25, pp 222-231

Francis Rev Prof Leslie
& P Kaldor, M Shelvin, A Lewis (17)
Assessing Emotional exhaustion among the Australian Clergy: internal reliability and construct validity of the Scale of Emotional Exhaustion in Ministry (SEEM).
Published 2004; Review of Religious Research, Vol 45, pp 269-277

Francis Rev Prof Leslie
& Yaacov Ktaz (18)
Religion and Happiness a study among Israeli female undergraduates.
Published 2002; Research in the Social and Scientific Study of Religion, Vol 13, pp 75-86

Francis Rev Prof Leslie
& C A Lewis, P Ng (19)
Assessing Attitude toward Christianity among Chinese speaking adolescents in Hong Kong: the Francis Scale.
Published 2002; North American Journal of Psychology, Vol 4, No 3

Francis Rev Prof Leslie
& C A Lewis, P Ng (20)
Psychological health and attitude toward Christianity among secondary school pupils in Hong Kong.
Published 2003; Journal of Psychology in Chinese Societies, Vol 4, pp 231-245

Francis Rev Prof Leslie
& Dr K Littler (21)
Staying Away: what keeps rural churches empty?
Published 2003; Implicit Religion, Vol 6, pp 161-169

Francis Rev Prof Leslie & J Payne (22)
The Payne Index Ministry Styles (PIMS): Ministry Styles and psychological type among male Anglican clergy in Wales.
Published 2002; Research in the Social Scientific Study of Religion, Vol 13, pp 125-141

Francis Rev Prof Leslie
& Dr M Robbins (23)
Belonging without Believing: a study in the social significance of Anglican identity and implicit religion among 13-15 year olds.
Published 2004; Implicit Religion, Vol 7, No 1, pp 37-54

Francis Rev Prof Leslie
& Dr M Robbins (24)
Christianity and dogmatism among undergraduate students.
Published 2003; Journal of Beliefs and Values, Vol 24, pp 89-95

Francis Rev Prof Leslie
& Dr M Robbins (25)
Personality and glossolalia: a study among male evangelical clergy.
Published 2003; Psychological Reports, Vol 51, pp 391-396

Francis Rev Prof Leslie
& Dr M Robbins (26)
Personality and the Practice of Ministry.
Published 2004; pp 28; Publisher Grove Books

Francis Rev Prof Leslie & Dr M Robbins, S Bhanot, R Santosh (27)
Measuring Attitudes: the Santosh-Francis Scale of Attitude towards Hinduism.
Published 2001; The Hindu Youth Research Project 2001, pp 41-51

Francis Rev Prof Leslie & Dr M Robbins, S Bhanot, R Santosh (28)
Mental Health and Religion among Hindu Young People.
Published 2001; The Hindu Youth Research Project 2001, pp 52-59

Francis Rev Prof Leslie
& Dr M Robbins, A Boxer, A Lewis, C McGuckin, C J McDaid (29)
Psychological type and attitude towards Christianity: a replication.
Published 2003; Psychological Reports, Vol 92, pp 89-90

Francis Rev Prof Leslie & Dr M Robbins, C A Lewis, C Quigley, C Wheeler (30)
Religiosity and general health among undergraduate students: a response to O'Connor, Cobb and O'Connor.
Published 2003; Personality and Individual Differences, Vol 37, 2004, pp 485-494

Francis Rev Prof Leslie
& Dr M Robbins, A White (31)
Correlation between religion and happiness: a replication.
Published 2003; Psychological Reports, Vol 92, pp 51-52

Francis Rev Prof Leslie
& G Smith, Dr M Robbins (32)
Establishment or Disestablishment: a survey among Church of England clergy.
Published 2002; Implicit Religion, Vol 5, No 2, pp 105-120

Francis Rev Prof Leslie
& E M Thomas (33)
Personoliaeth a chrefydd ymysg siaradwyr Cymraeg 9-11 mlwydd oed.
Published 2004; Welsh Journal of Education, Vol 12, No 2, pp 99-110

Francis Rev Prof Leslie
& E M Thomas (34)
The reliability and validity of the Francis Scale Attitude toward Christianity among Welsh-speaking 9 to 11 year olds.
Published 2003; The Psychologist in Wales, Vol 16, pp 9-14

Francis Rev Prof Leslie
& D W Turton (35)
Assessing ministerial job satisfaction: the reliability of the revised MJSS among male Anglican clergy.
Published 2002; Review of Religious Research, Vol 44, No 2, pp 169-172

Francis Rev Prof Leslie
& D W Turton (36)
Recognising & Understanding Burnout Among the Clergy: a perspective from Empirical Theology.
Published 2004; Building Bridges over Troubled Waters: Enhancing Pastoral Care and Guidance, Chapter 19, pp 307-331

Francis Rev Prof Leslie & Hans-Georg Ziebertz, C A Lewis, Panorama (37)
The Psychometric Properties of the Francis Scale of Attitude toward Christianity among German students.
Published 2002; International Journal of Comparative Religion and Values, Vol 14, No 1

Francis Rev Prof Leslie
& H G Ziebertz, C A Lewis (38)
The relationship between personality and religion among undergraduate students in Germany.
Published 2003; Archiv für Religionspsychologie, Vol 24, pp 121-127

Francis Rev Prof Leslie
& H G Ziebertz, C A Lewis (39)
The relationship between religion and happiness among German students.
Published 2003; Pastoral Psychology, Vol 51, pp 273-281

Fulljames P & L J Francis
Creationism among people in Kenya and Britain, in S. Coleman & L. Carlin (eds) The Cultures of Creationism: anti-evolutionism in English-speaking countries.
The Welsh National Centre for Religious Education, University of Wales, Bangor, Meirion, Normal Site, Bangor, Gwynedd LL57 2PX
Published 2004; pp 165-173; Publisher Ashgate, Aldershot

Gardiner Andrew
Effective Youth Leadership – the key to the church reaching and discipling today's teenagers.
Calver College, Calver, Hope Valley, Nr Sheffield S32 3XG
Published 2003; 20,000 words; MA in Evangelism studies; Price £30

Gascoyne Baz
The effectiveness of sports ministry through an evaluation of Ambassadors In Sports between 1992-2000.
Calver College, Calver, Hope Valley, Nr Sheffield S32 3XG
Published 2002; 20,000 words; MA in Evangelism studies; Price £30

Gelder Alison & P Escott
Profile of Youth Workers, from the 2001 Church Life Profile.
Email a.gelder@housingjustice.org.uk
Published 2003

Gerloff Rev Dr Roswith (1)
Africa as Laboratory of the World: The African Christian Diaspora in Europe as challenge to Mission and Ecumenical relations. Essay in book *Mission is Crossing Frontiers.*
39 West Park Road, Roundhay, Leeds LS8 2HA
Published 2003; 37 pages; Publisher Cluster Publications; Price £15 (for book)

Gerloff Rev Dr Roswith (2)
The African Diaspora in the Caribbean and Europe from pre-emancipation to the present day: History of Christianity in the Caribbean from 1780 to 2000 in relation to migration and African Diaspora in Europe.
Cambridge University Press, Humanities and Social Services, Shaftesbury Road, Cambridge CB2 2RU
Published 2004; 35 pages, Chapter 18, Vol 8; Publisher Cambridge History of Christianity

Greene Valerie
Where are they now? A research project conducted with young people who attended a church based group between 1975-2003 in rural Lincolnshire.
Calver College, Calver, Hope Valley, Nr Sheffield S32 3XG
Published 2003; 20,000 words; MA in Evangelism studies; Price £30

Gregory Ian
The Chair. An essential short guide to the conduct of meetings.
16 Grice Road, Hartshill, Stoke-on-Trent ST4 7PJ or Email ian@congist.fsnet.co.uk
Published 2004; 28 pages; Price £10 (with profits for the work of the Campaign for Courtesy)

Hall John
The Rise of the Youth Congregation and its missiological significance. Missiological study of three youth congregations describing their life and analyses their significance as missilogical phenomena.
26 Crane-Ley Road, Groby, Leics LE6 0FD
Published 2004; 458 pages; Thesis

Hall Richard
In a multi-cultural, multi-faith, society, where is the motivation for Christian Evangelism?
Calver College, Calver, Hope Valley, Nr Sheffield S32 3XG
Published 2003; 20,000 words; MA in Evangelism studies; Price £30

Hammond Mark
Evangelising Joseph: an exploration of the endeavour to share the Christian gospel with one autistic child.
Cliff College, Calver, Hope Valley, Nr Sheffield S32 3XG
Published 2002; 20,000 words; MA in Evangelism studies; Price £30

Handley Graham
Communities, neighbourhoods and Social Action: a case study of North West Baptist Churches.
University of Manchester, Oxford Road, Manchester M13 9PL
Published 2002; MA Thesis; University of Manchester, Dept of Geography

Hattam John
A Church for All Ages: One attempt to think about how to bring children into the heart of the church life. Sent in response to "Children and the Church".
12 Granville Terrace, Bingley, West Yorkshire BD16 4HW
Email johnandjoy@12granville. freeserve.co.uk
Published 2004

Hay Rob
Remap II. Follow up to WEA Missions Commissions 1994-1997 REMAP study on missionary attrition.
Generating Change, Redcliffe College, Wotton House, Gloucester GL1 3PT or email
rob.hay@generatingchange.co.uk
Published 2004

Hay Steve
Future of the church in rural NE Scotland with special reference to the Church of Scotland.
3A George Street, Banff AB45 1HS
Published 2003; 32 pages; Dissertation, University of Aberdeen

Heald Gordon
Annual Religious Survey of Affiliation and Practice.
Including perceptions of the role of local churches/chapels.
Published 2003;
Publisher Opinion Research, London

Henger Mr S
Syllabus on Islamics and Christian Witness among Muslims.
The courses described range on different levels and are suitable for a first introduction to raise awareness, a short course for pastors and evangelists, or for training mentors in an extended course. Vol 1 of Calabash Resources.
Life Challenge Africa, PO Box 23273, Calremont Cape Town 7735 Republic of South Africa or Email
LCA-south@lca.org.za
Published 2004; 60 Pages;
Publisher SIM-Life Challenge Africa

Hills Peter & L J Francis (1)
Discriminant validity of the Francis Scale of Attitude
towards Christianity with respect to religious orientation.
The Welsh National Centre for Religious Education, University of Wales, Bangor, Meirion, Normal Site, Bangor, Gwynedd LL57 2PX
Published 2003; Mental Health, Religion and Culture, Vol 6, pp 277-282

Hills Peter
& L J Francis, M Argle, C J Jackson (2)
Primary personality trait correlates of religious practice and orientation.
Published 2004; Personality and Individual Differences; Vol 36, pp 61-73

Hills Peter
& L J Francis, C J Rutledge (3)
The Factory Structure of a Measure of Burnout specific to Clergy, and its trial application with respect to some individual personal differences.
Published 2004; Review of Religious Research, Vol 46, No 1, pp 27-42

Hope Susan
Take nothing for the journey – mission as a matrix for spirituality.
Cliff College, Calver, Hope Valley, Nr Sheffield S32 3XG
Published 2003; 20,000 words; MA in Evangelism studies; Price £30

Hopkins B & G W Lings
Mission-Shaped Church:
The Inside and Outside View (Encounters on the Edge No 22): Examines the key issues at the heart of the 2004 Church of England report "Mission-Shaped Church".
The Sheffield Centre, Church Army's Research Unit, 50 Cavendish Street, Sheffield S3 7RZ
Published 2004; 32 Pages;
Publisher Church Army; Price £4

Horseman Penny
"Poetry or Scotland Yard" –
Assessing the use of Springboard's "Growing Healthy Churches" Process for Anglican Churches in the Colchester Episcopal Area.
Cliff College, Calver, Hope Valley, Nr Sheffield S32 3XG
Published 2003; 20,000 words; MA in Consultancy, Mission & Ministry Studies; Price £30

Hughes Philip
& S Bond, J Bellamy, A Black
Exploring What Australians Value.
Research Paper No 5 of Christian Research Associations and NCLS Research Australia.
www.openbook.com.au
Published 2003; Publisher Openbook

Hytînen Maarit
Contemporary Ethical Questions
and the Evangelical Lutheran Church of Finland.
The Research Institute, Box 239, FIN 33101 Tampere, Finland or Email
ktk@evl.fi
Published 2004;
Publication No 53, pp 88; Price €15

Irish Council of Churches
Annual Report of the Irish Council of Churches.
Irish Council of Churches, Inter-Church Centre, 48 Elmwood Ave, Belfast BT9 6AZ or at
www.irishchurches.org
Published 2003

Jackson Rev Bob
A Capital Idea:
Church growth in the Diocese of London, Causes and implications. A study of how and why the London Diocese has seen growth while others have not.
10 Paradise Lane, Pelsall, Walsall WS3 4NH
Published 2003

Jackson Chris J & L J Francis (1)
Are interactions in Gray's Reinforcement Sensitivity Theory proximal or distal in the prediction of religiosity: a test of the joint subsystems hypothesis.
The Welsh National Centre for Religious Centre for religious Education, University of Wales, Bangor, Meirion, Normal Site, Bangor, Gwynedd LL57 2PX
Published 2004; Personality and Individual Differences, Vol 36, pp 1197-1209

Jackson Chris J & L J Francis (2)
Primary Scale Structure of the Eysenck Personality Profiler (EPP).
Published 2004;
Current Psychology, Vol 22, No 4, 295-305

Jackson D
Research in Mission and Evangelism Project. Provides information about the work and progress of the Conference of European Churches Research in Mission and Evangelism project.
Email jackson@pmti.edi.hu
Published 2004; 8 pages; Publisher Conference of European Churches, Geneva; Briefing Paper No 1

Jeans Rev D B
Inside Out. Report of theology of mission and evangelism using Anglican reports, stories from practitioners and Church Army projects.
Wilson Carlisle College of Evangelism, 50 Cavendish Street, Sheffield S3 7RZ
Published 2004; 88 pages; Publisher SPCK for Church Army; Price £4

Job John
Jeremiah's Kings.
A study of Jeremiah's treatment of the monarchy with special reference to chapters 21-24.
Cliff College, Calver, Hope Valley, Nr Sheffield S32 3XG
Published 2003; 120,000 words; Doctor of Philosophy; Price £30

Jones S H & L J Francis
The pastoral care of the Anglican clergy: a matter of low self-esteem?
The Welsh National Centre for Religious Education, University of Wales, Bangor, Meirion, Normal Site, Bangor, Gwynedd LL57 2PX
Published 2003; Journal of Empirical Theology; Vol 16, No 1, pp 20-30

Jordan Stuart
Faithful and Effective: an exploration of strategy formulation in the Church from a Consultancy Perspective.
Cliff College, Calver, Hope Valley, Nr Sheffield S32 3XG
Published 2003; 20,000 words; MA in Consultancy, Mission & Ministry Studies; Price £30

Joseph Dr Stephen & S French
Religiosity ... happiness, purpose in life and self-actualisation.
Department of Psychology, University of Warwick, Coventry CV4 7AL
Published 1999; Mental Health, Religion and Culture, Vol 2, No 2

Joseph Rowntree Foundation
Crossroads after 50. Improving choices in work and retirement.
Joseph Rowntree Foundation, The Homestead, 40 Water Road, York YO30 6WP; or via www.jrf.org.uk
Published December 2003

Kalbheim B
& L J Francis, H G Ziebertz
Christlicher Glaube und Glück:
eine empirische studie zum zusammenhang von religiosität und glückserfahrungen.
The Welsh National Centre for Religious Education, University of Wales, Bangor, Meirion, Normal Site, Bangor, Gwynedd LL57 2PX
Published 2003; Archiv für Religions-psychologie, Vol 25, pp 42-61

Kay Rev Dr W K (1)
The Naked Parish Priest by S Louden and L J Francis. Review article of a major empirical study of Roman Catholic priests in the UK.
7 Croft Way, Everton, Doncaster DN19 5DL
Published 2004; 2,000 words; Journal of Beliefs and Values

Kay Rev Dr W K & Liz Kay (2)
Concepts of God:
the salience of gender and age. The paper argues that gender more than age may influence children's images of God.
Published 2004; 5,000 words; Journal of Empirical Theology

Kay Rev Dr W K, C Partridge (ed) (3)
Prosperity Spirituality.
In *Guide to New Religions, Sects and Alternative Spiritualities.*
Published 2004; Publisher Lion

Kay Rev Dr W K, C Partridge (ed) (4)
Jesus Fellowship (Jesus Army).
In *Guide to New Religions, Sects and Alternative Spiritualities.*
Published 2004; Publisher Lion

Kay Rev Dr W K, R Pope (ed) (5)
British Assemblies of God:
a sketch of 20th century missions. In *Honouring and shaping the past.*
Published 2003; pp 194-212;
Publisher Gracewing, Leominster

7

Kay Rev Dr W K
& A Walker, K Aune (eds) (6)
Revival: empirical aspects.
In On Revival: a critical examination.
Published 2003; pp 185-204;
Publisher Paternoster, Carlisle

Kendall Susan (1)
The Bread of life.
A poetic adventure exploring Genesis
through to Revelation.
27 Anne Street, Biggleswade,
Bedfordshire SG18 ODD
Published 2000; 128 pages; Christian
poetry; Publisher Proprint; Price £2.50

Kendall Susan (2)
The Hem of His Garment.
A celebration of Susan's faith which
she hopes will bless others.
Published 1999; 78 pages; Christian poetry;
Publisher Proprint; Price £2.50

Kendall Susan (3)
My Sister and the Angel.
A children's book with a Christian
theme. All the pictures were drawn
by children. This book is dedicated to
Gillian Faulkner who went to be with
the angels on the 7th May 1971,
aged 4.
Published 2002; 36 pages; Christian poetry;
Publisher Proprint; Price £2.50

Kenny Andrew
The beliefs and practices of koinonia,
John the Baptist:
an Ulster Protestant's journey of
understanding.
Cliff College, Calver, Hope Valley, Nr
Sheffield S32 3XG
Published 2003; 20,000 words;
MA in Evangelism studies; Price £30

Keston Institute
Religious Trends in Russia.
A paper in English giving a guide to
the research method and overview of
one denomination study and an area
study. (Volume I covers the Orthodox
and Roman Catholic Church; Volume
II covers the Protestant churches and
sectarians such as Christian Scientists
and Mormons)
Keston Institute,
38 St Aldgate's, Oxford OX1 1BN
Published 2004; Price £5

Kinder Lancer
The rural Methodist Chapel:
have we a future? A research project
aimed to investigate the future
viability of a number of Methodist
Chapels in the Chipping Norton and
Stow Methodist Circuit.
Cliff College, Calver, Hope Valley,
Nr Sheffield S32 3XG
Published 2003; 20,000 words;
MA in Evangelism studies; Price £30

Kivi Kaja
The attraction of the Orthodox Church
in England.
Cliff College, Calver, Hope Valley,
Nr Sheffield S32 3XG
Published 2003; 20,000 words;
MA in Evangelism studies; Price £30

Lattimer Bill & H Wraight
CRA Members Research.
Research across CRA Members
Christian Research, 4 Footscray Road,
Eltham, London SE9 2TZ
Published 2004; 48 pages

Lear Nick
Living it Large? Today's Young People.
Baptist Union Research Department,
Baptist House, PO Box 44, 129
Broadway, Didcot OX11 8RT; or Email
mission@baptist.org
Published 2003

Lewis A & L J Francis
Evaluer l'attitude d'étudiantes
françaises à l'égard du Christianisme:
l'Échelle de Francis.
The Welsh National Centre for
Religious Education, University of
Wales, Bangor, Meirion, Normal Site,
Bangor, Gwynedd LL57 2PX
Published 2003; Sciences Pastorals, Vol 22,
pp 179-190

Lewis Christopher & L J Francis (1)
Reliability and Validity of a Welsh
Translation of a short scale of
attitude towards Christianity to 8 to
15 year olds.
Published 2002; Irish Journal of Psychology,
Vol 23, Nos 1/2

Lewis Christopher
& L J Francis, T Enger (2)
Reliability and Validity of Norwegian
Translation of a short scale of
attitude towards Christianity.
Published 2003; Individual Differences
Research, Vol 1, No 3

Lewis Christopher
& L J Francis, T Enger (3)
Personality, Prayer and Church
Attendance among a sample of 11 to
18 year olds in Norway.
Published 2004; Mental Health, Religion
and Culture, Vol 7, No 3, pp 269-274

Lewis Christopher
& L J Francis, Shirley Kerr (4)
Reliability and Validity of a Short
Scale of Attitude toward Christianity
among 12-19 years old in South
Africa.
Published 2002; IFE PsychologIA, Vol 11, No
1

Lewis Christopher
& L J Francis, P Ng (5)
Reliability and Validity of a Chinese
Translation of a Short Scale of
Attitude toward Christianity.
Published 2003; Journal of Personality and
Clinical Studies, Vol 19, No 2, pp 195-200

Lewis Sarah
Beyond Belief? Faith at work in the
Community. A Report about faith
based regeneration activities.
South East England Faith Forum,
The Observatory, Brunel,
Chatham, Kent ME4 4NT
Published 2004; 28 pages;
Publisher South East England Faith Forum

Lings G W (1)
New Canterbury Tales
(Encounters on the Edge No 7):
The growth development of the first
Network Churches, that started in
the Canterbury Diocese.
The Sheffield Centre,
Church Army's Research Unit,
50 Cavendish Street, Sheffield S3 7RZ
Published 2000; 28 pages;
Publisher Church Army; Price £4

Lings G W (2)
Thame or Wild?
(Encounters on the Edge No 8):
Lessons from St Mary Thame, an
Oxfordshire town church which
trebled its membership and created
congregations by belief in diversity.
Published 2000; 28 pages;
Publisher Church Army; Price £4

Lings G W (3)
Leading Lights
– who can lead new churches?
(Encounters on the Edge No 9):
An examination of the issues
surrounding part time and solely lay
leadership of church plants.
Published 2001; 28 pages;
Publisher Church Army; Price £4

Lings G W (4)
Hard graft?
(Encounters on the Edge No 10):
An Examination of the issues
involved in revitalising existing
churches. How do you incorporate
the old elements with the new?
Published 2001; 28 pages;
Publisher Church Army; Price £4

Lings G W (5)
Never on a Sunday?
(Encounters on the Edge No 11):
As Sunday in Britain changes, what
can midweek churches offer children
and young families?
Published 2001; 28 pages;
Publisher Church Army; Price £4

Lings G W (6)
The Enigma of Alternative Worship
(Encounters on the Edge No 12):
What is Alternative Worship? Is it
creative or subversive? Why does it
live uncomfortably with the label
stuck on it by others?
Published 2002; 28 pages;
Publisher Church Army; Price £4

Lings G W (7)
Encountering Exile
(Encounters on the Edge No 13):
What can we learn from "Exile" in
the scriptures as we face the decline
of the church in the West?
Published 2002; 28 pages;
Publisher Church Army; Price £4

Lings G W (8)
The Eden Puzzle
(Encounters on the Edge No 14):
Can the church make a difference to
communities living in the inner city?
An examination of the Eden Projects
in Manchester.
Published 2002; 28 pages;
Publisher Church Army; Price £4

Lings G W (9)
Dynasty or Diversity?
– the HTB family of churches
(Encounters on the Edge No 15):
As one of the most well known
churches in the UK, how diverse and
transferable is Holy Trinity Brompton's
model of planting?
Published 2002; 28 pages;
Publisher Church Army; Price £4

Lings G W (10)
Mass Planting
– learning from Catholic evangelism
(Encounters on the Edge No 16):
A Story, inspired by Anglo-Catholic
instincts for evangelistic Eucharist,
that started in an ASDA supermarket.
Published 2002; 28 pages;
Publisher Church Army; Price £4

Lings G W (11)
Stepping Stones
(Encounters on the Edge No 18):
Cross cultural mission, planting on
deprived housing estates.
Published 2003; 28 pages;
Publisher Church Army; Price £4

Lings G W (12)
Net Gains
(Encounters on the Edge No 19):
Examines further examples of
Churches for networks of people,
as opposed to neighbourhoods, and
lessons for future development.
Published 2003; 28 pages;
Publisher Church Army; Price £4

Lings G W (13)
Soft Cell
(Encounters on the Edge No 20):
Growing a cell church along the
congregational model because cell is
caught not taught.
Published 2003; 28 pages;
Publisher Church Army; Price £4

Lings G W (14)
Reading the Signs
(Encounters on the Edge No 21):
How do we begin to connect teenagers
who have never been to church and
how can such work develop?
Published 2004; 28 pages;
Publisher Church Army; Price £4

Littler Keith & L J Francis (1)
What rural churches say
to non-churchgoers.
The Welsh National Centre for
Religious Education, University of
Wales, Bangor Meirion, Normal Site,
Bangor, Gwynedd LL57 2PX
Published 2003; Rural Theology, Vol 1; pp
57-62

Littler Keith
& L J Francis, Hugh Thomas (2)
The admission of children to
communion before confirmation:
a survey among Church in Wales clerics.
Published 2002; The Interdisciplinary
Journal of Pastoral Studies, Vol 139

Locke-Wheaton Margaret
Evangelism through Holy
Communion: a critical exploration
from a Methodist perspective.
Cliff College, Calver, Hope Valley,
Nr Sheffield S32 3XG
Published 2003; 20,000 words;
MA in Evangelism studies; Price £30

Louden S H & L J Francis
The Naked Parish Priest:
What priests really think they're doing.
The Welsh National Centre for Religious Education, University of Wales, Bangor, Meirion, Normal Site, Bangor, Gwynedd LL57 2PX
Published 2003; pp viii + 232;
Publisher Continuum, London

Love Anette
Effective Preaching.
Cliff College, Calver, Hope Valley, Nr Sheffield, S32 3XG
Published 2002; 20,000 words;
MA in Evangelism studies; Price £30

Loxley Ian
An Investigation into why people have left The Salvation Army
in the UK over the last 10 years in comparison with why people left other churches, leading to the formation of policies to prevent losses, support leavers and, when appropriate, encourage people to return.
Cliff College, Calver, Hope Valley, Nr Sheffield S32 3XG
Published 2002; 20,000 words;
MA in Evangelism studies; Price £30

Lucas Richard
The values and spirituality of the boys at Merchiston Castle School.
Cliff College, Calver, Hope Valley, Nr Sheffield S32 3XG
Published 2002; 20,000 words;
MA in Evangelism studies; Price £30

McAlpine Robert
The role of the External Consultant/Facilitator
in the Development of the Missional Congregation.
Regional Adviser in Mission & Evangelism, National Mission Regional Office, Church of Scotland, 10 Seton Place, Kirkcaldy, Fife KY2 6UX
Published 2003

McCartney Dr Hilary
Church Membership in the Presbyterian Church of Ireland, 1990-2003
23 Ballyhome Road, Coleraine, N. Ireland BT52 2LU
Published 2004; 6 pages;
Christian Research Leaders Briefing No 19

McCombe Drew
Can there be a church called the Salvation Army in the 21st century without soldiers?
Cliff College, Calver, Hope Valley, Nr Sheffield S32 3XG
Published 2002; 20,000 words;
MA in Evangelism studies; Price £30

McMullen Mrs C E
Right Reverend Women? Women Bishops in the Church of England.
114 Brown Edge Road, Buxton, Derby SK17 7AB
Published 2004; 20 pages;
Sabbatical Report

Mackrell-Hey Langley
Is God a magician, a gambler or a designer?
Creationism, theistic evolution or intelligent design: which way forward?
Cliff College, Calver, Hope Valley, Nr Sheffield S32 3XG
Published 2002; 20,000 words;
MA in Evangelism studies; Price £30

Mead Jonathan
The Relationship between Ignatian Spirituality and Mission.
Cliff College, Calver, Hope Valley, Nr Sheffield S32 3XG
Published 2003; 20,000 words;
MA in Evangelism studies; Price £30

Midrash-Creed (1)
Spiritual Discernment and Apostasy.
Reflections and responses on the downfall of Gentile Christianity. Papers looking at the causes and consequences of apostasy and ways Christians can respond to this problem.
www.geocities.com/midrashcreed
Published 2003;
Publisher Yes-Now Publications;
Download free but please see disclaimer

Midrash-Creed (2)
The Agony of Anglicanism:
Why Rowan? Mumbling in the Dark. Papers looking at the significance of Rowan Williams' appointment to be Archbishop of Canterbury; also provides an intriguing criticism of his poetry.
www.geocities.com/midrashcreed
Published 2003;
Publisher Yes-Now Publications;
Download free but please see disclaimer

Mitchell Peter W
2001 Census:
Religion by LA Nationality.
Main emphasis is on proportion stating "no religion" and how this varies by LA County within GB. One section looks especially at SW England.
Order via Email
p.w.mitchell@tesco.net
Published 2004; 2 pages plus appendix

Morton Gordon
Is the Methodist Circuit an effective tool for mission?
Cliff College, Calver, Hope Valley, Nr Sheffield S32 3XG
Published 2002, 20,000 words,
MA in Evangelism studies; Price £30

Moynagh Rev Dr M (1)
emergingchurch.intro
An overview of Emerging church and its significance, theological rationale and implications for local church denominations.
Available from Christian bookshops.
Published 2004; 256 pages;
Publisher Monarch; Price £7.99

Moynagh Rev Dr M (2)
The State of the Countryside, 2020.
The future of the countryside with four scenarios.
www.countryside.gov.uk
Published 2003; 40 pages;
Publisher Countryside Agency

Moynagh Rev Dr M
& Richard Worsley (3)
The Opportunity of a Lifetime:
Reshaping Retirement.
A look at the future of work and retirement in later life.
Published 2004; 172 pages;
Publisher Tomorrow Project with the Chartered Institute of Personnel and Development; Price £20

Moynagh Rev Dr M
& Richard Worsley (4)
Tomorrow's Workplace – Fulfilment or Stress?
Looking at the place, organisation and values of paid work in tomorrow's Britain.
Published 2001; 228 pages;
Publisher Tomorrow Project; Price £16

Newton Leslie
Why are people choosing to join Emmanuel Methodist Church, Barnsley?
Cliff College, Calver, Hope Valley, Nr Sheffield S32 3XG
Published 2003; 20,000 words;
MA in Evangelism studies; Price £30

Northwest Development Agency
Faith in England's Northwest: the contribution made by faith communities to civil society in the region.
Report of survey of places of worship in the NW Region.
Mgr John Devine, Churches Officer for the Northwest, c/o Northwest Development Agency, PO Box 37, Renaissance House, Centre Park, Warrington WA1 1XB
Published 2003; 95 pages;
Publisher Northwest Development Agency

Okill Clive
Job's Ashes:
a study in evangelising the bereaved.
Cliff College, Calver, Hope Valley, Nr Sheffield S32 3XG
Published 2002; 20,000 words;
MA in Evangelism studies; Price £30

Olayisade Femi Ade
Black Immigrant Churches in the Republic of Ireland.
Inter Church Centre, 48 Elmwood Avenue, Belfast BT9 6AZ
Published 2002; 15 pages

Page Stewart
Rediscovering the YMCA:
Action research programme.
2 Windmill Rise, Kingston-upon-Thames, Surrey KT2 7TU
Published 2003

Passey Don & C Rogers, J Machell, G McHugh, D Allaway
The Motivational Effect of ICT on Pupils.
DfES Publications, PO Box 5050, Sherwood Park, Annesleym, Nottingham NG15 0DJ
Published 2004; Publisher DfES

Pawlak Zbigniew
Life Transformation – evangelism in a secular society.
Can nominal Muslims of Central Asia enter the Kingdom of God without becoming Christian?
Cliff College, Calver, Hope Valley, Nr Sheffield S32 3XG
Published 2002; 20,000 words;
MA in Evangelism studies; Price £30

Pearce Jenny J, Mary Williams & Cristina Galvin
It's someone taking a part of you:
A study of young women and sexual exploitation.
National Children's Bureau for the Joseph Rowntree Foundation, 8 Wakley Street, London EC17 7QE
Published 2002; 90 pages; Price £14.95

Pereira M C
Factors effective/influential in church growth in Anglican churches in England from 1995-2004.
Survey of 20 churches that have grown to identify growth factors. Comparisons with recent church growth literature. Survey of 200 church members.
5 Canon Mohan Close, Southgate, London or Email melvyn02@yahoo.co.uk
Published 2004; 10,000 words;
BA Hons Theological and Pastoral Studies Undergraduate Dissertation

Phelps Andrew
Report of FIEC Churches Consultation Autumn 2003.
Survey of FIEC churches to reassess their position and future needs.
6 Berkeley Mews, Sandringham Court, Burnham, Slough SL1 6JD
Published 2003; 28 pages

Phillips Peter
The Prologue of the Fourth Gospel:
An Exploration into the meaning of a Text.
Cliff College, Calver, Hope Valley, Nr Sheffield S32 3XG
Published 2003; 120,000 words;
Doctor of Philosophy; Price £30

Pillinger Peter
Do English Cell Churches grow?
An investigation on how a 'new way of being church' is developing in England from a Methodist perspective.
Cliff College, Calver, Hope Valley, Nr Sheffield S32 3XG
Published 2002; 20,000 words;
MA in Evangelism studies; Price £30

Pimlott Jo
Integration and Incarnation:
the extent to which creative training methodologies engender deep learning.
Cliff College, Calver, Hope Valley, Nr Sheffield S32 3XG
Published 2003; 20,000 words;
MA in Training & Theological Reflection in Church & Community; Price £30

7

Povey Martin
A critical analysis of the way forward
for the 21st century Church,
with particular reference to recent
trends in evangelism and historical
models of the Church.
Cliff College, Calver, Hope Valley,
Nr Sheffield S32 3XG
Published 2002; 20,000 words;
MA in Evangelism studies; Price £30

Price Phillip
Touching the Ends of the Earth: The
Story of Medical Service Ministries.
MSM, PO Box 133, Ware SG12 7WJ
Published 2003; Price £9.99 + p&p

Prill Thorsten
Evangelism in the German Landes-
kirchen after the Liepzig Synod 1999.
Cliff College, Calver, Hope Valley,
Nr Sheffield S32 3XG
Published 2003; 15,000 words;
Postgraduate Diploma in Renewal &
Mission Studies; Price £30

Pursehouse Julian
The Missiological significance of
the spiritual themes in Harry Potter
amongst a sample group of seven
people drawn from the Peterborough
Methodist Circuit
Cliff College, Calver, Hope Valley,
Nr Sheffield S32 3XG
Published 2003; 20,000 words;
MA in Evangelism studies; Price £30

Ramsden Sarah
The Presbyter as Vision Bearer:
enabling the evangelistic ministry of
the whole people of God.
Cliff College, Calver, Hope Valley,
Nr Sheffield S32 3XG
Published 2002; 20,000 words;
MA in Evangelism studies; Price £30

Randall Dick
Impact of the Elliot Wave Theory
and its potential for the Church.
Order via Email Randall.dick@wcg.org
Published 2004

Ravat Riaz
Embracing the Present,
Planning the Future:
social action by the faith
communities of Leicester.
Leicester Faiths Regeneration Project,
c/o Diocese of Leicester,
St Martins East, Leicester LE1 5FX
Published 2004; 66 pages; Publisher
Leicester Faiths Regenerations Project;
Price £4.99

Reasbeck Colin
The growth of the Gospel
among the Iban people of Sarawak.
Cliff College, Calver, Hope Valley,
Nr Sheffield S32 3XG
Published 2002; 20,000 words;
MA in Evangelism studies; Price £30

Rees Adele
Is building self-esteem in
young people evangelism?
Cliff College, Calver, Hope Valley,
Nr Sheffield S32 3XG
Published 2002; 20,000 words;
MA in Evangelism studies; Price £30

Reid Ruth
The Peniel Model of Retention of
Young People for the Church of
tomorrow.
49 Coxtie Green Road, Brentwood,
Essex CM14 5PS
To be published 2005

Richards Carole
Learning in Cells.
An evaluation of the learning
environment of cell groups within a
Salvation Army Corps that is
transitioning to Cell Church.
Cliff College, Calver, Hope Valley,
Nr Sheffield S32 3XG
Published 2003; 20,000 words;
MA in Training & Theological Reflection in
Church & Community; Price £30

Robbins Dr Mandy
& P Babington, L J Francis (1)
Personal prayer and school-related
attitudes among 8 to 11 year olds.
The Welsh National Centre for
Religious Education, University of
Bangor, Meirion, Normal Site, Bangor,
Gwynedd LL57 2PX
Published 2003; Journal of Beliefs and
Values, Vol 24, pp 245-248

Robbins Dr Mandy
& P Babington, L J Francis (2)
Correlations between attitude
toward Christianity, Prayer and
Church Attendance among 9 to 11
year olds.
Published 2004; Psychological Reports, Vol
94, pp 305-306

Robbins Dr Mandy
& L J Francis, A Bradford (3)
Reliability and construct validity for
Scale of Rejection of Christianity.
Published 2003; Psychological Reports, Vol
92, pp 65-66

Robbins Dr Mandy
& L J Francis, E Elliott (4)
Attitudes towards education
for global citizenship among
trainee teachers.
Published 2003; Research in Education, Vol
69, pp 93-98

Robbins Dr Mandy
& L J Francis, N Williams (5)
Reliability of the Francis Scale of
Attitude toward Christianity among
8 year olds.
Published 2003; Psychological Reports,
Vol 92, pp 104

Roberts John
An analysis of the sociological,
theological and political influence
of DUP Paisleyism –
Free Presbyterian Paisleyism within
a Northern Ireland culture.
Cliff College, Calver, Hope Valley,
Nr Sheffield S32 3XG
Published 2002; 20,000 words;
MA in Evangelism studies; Price £30

Roberts Mike
The HIS World Orchestra:
understanding the power of music
in evangelism.
Cliff College, Calver, Hope Valley,
Nr Sheffield S32 3XG
Published 2002; 20,000 words;
MA in Evangelism studies; Price £30

Ronsvalle John & Sylvia
The State of Church Giving Through
2001: An analysis of 41 Protestant
denominations in the US.
Via www.emptytomb.org
Published 2002; 146 pages

Roof Wade-Clark
Spiritual Seeking in the United
States: Report on a panel study.
University of California-Santa Barbara,
Santa Barbara, CA93106, USA
Published 2000; Arch. De Sc. Soc. des Rel,
January-March; pp 49-66

Roper Mark
An investigation into the practice
of exorcism by Methodist Presbyters
in the active work within the Bristol
District of the Methodist Church.
Cliff College, Calver, Hope Valley,
Nr Sheffield S32 3XG
Published 2003; 20,000 words;
MA in Evangelism studies; Price £30

Rusama Jaakko
Ecumenical Growth in Finland.
The Research Institute of the Evangel-
ical Lutheran Church of Finland,
Box 239, FIN 33101 Tampere, Finland
or Email ktk@evl.fi
Published 2003;
Publication No 52; 84 pages; Price €7

Sahin Abdullah & L J Francis
Assessing Attitude toward Islam
among Muslim Adolescents:
The psychometric properties of the
Sahin-Francis scale.
The Welsh National Centre for
Religious Education, University of
Wales, Bangor, Meirion, Normal Site,
Bangor, Gwynedd LL57 2PX
Published 2002; Muslim Education Quarterly,
Vol 19, No 4, pp 35-47

Salter Colin
Khartoum International Church:
Obstacles and opportunities facing
the church on its mission in Sudan.
Cliff College, Calver, Hope Valley,
Nr Sheffield S32 3XG
Published 2002; 20,000 words;
MA in Evangelism studies; Price £30

Salvation Army & M Vickers
The Responsibility Gap.
A Report by the Henley Centre
exploring emerging trends in British
society.
The Salvation Army, 101 Newington
Causeway, London SE1 6BN or Email
er@salvationarmy.org.uk
Published 2004; 104 pages

Sauer Dr Christof
Reaching the unreached Sudan belt:
Guinness, Kumm and the Sudan-
Pionier-Mission.
This research in mission history
describes the vision of reaching the
Sudan-Belt in Africa of Irish visionary
Grattan Guinness, the origins of
pioneer missionary Karl Kumm and
the start of the German based SPM
PO Box 535, 7407 Edgemead,
Republic of South Africa, or Email
csauer@metroweb.co.zamailto:Csauer
@metroweb.co.za
To be published 2005; 382 pages;
DTh Missiology, University of South Africa

Sellwood Andrew
Leading the Worthing Area Team
Ministry Churches through the fires
of change.
An insight into the dynamics of a
newly formed teamed ministry,
ministerial deployment and mission
potential of churches with several
declining memberships.
Cliff College, Calver, Hope Valley,
Nr Sheffield S32 3XG
Published 2002; 20,000 words;
MA in Evangelism studies; Price £30

Sharp Marian
Is a caravan, as a mobile unit, an
effective tool for the Christian
mission in the 21st century?
Cliff College, Calver, Hope Valley,
Nr Sheffield S32 3XG
Published 2003; 20,000 words;
MA in Evangelism studies; Price £30

Smith Guy & L J Francis, M Robbins
Who wants establishment?
A comparison of clerical and lay
opinion in the Church of England.
The Welsh National Centre for
Religious Centre for Religious
Education, University of Wales,
Bangor, Meirion, Normal Site, Bangor,
Gwynedd LL57 2PX
Published 2003; Journal of Beliefs and
Values, Vol 24, pp 349-365

Spencer Nick
Beyond Belief?
Barriers and Bridges to Faith Today
LICC, St Peter's,
Vere Street, London W1G 0DQ
Published 2003; Price £5.50

Spriggs Steven
Characteristics of Evangelical
Leadership Succession:
A review of the limited material on
this topic. Part of a PhD thesis
Email stevespriggs@joshgen.org
Published 2004

Strange Alan
What do you Think They are Doing?
Consideration of two streams of
leadership understanding in the
church, covenanted relationships and
leadership function.
17 Essex Street, Norwich NR2 2BL
Published 2003

Street Sian
R.S.V.P.
Are invitations a foreign language
for the Church?
Cliff College, Calver, Hope Valley,
Nr Sheffield S32 3XG
Published 2002; 20,000 words;
MA in Evangelism studies; Price £30

Stringer Howard
Help! One of our churches is
growing! Why is it the only one?
Factors responsible for growth and
decline within a Methodist setting.
Cliff College, Calver, Hope Valley,
Nr Sheffield S32 3XG
Published 2002; 20,000 words;
MA in Evangelism studies; Price £30

Sutton Liz & A Cebulla, S Middleton
Marriage in the 21st Century:
An exploration of married people's perceptions of the attitudes and behaviours that helped marriages to last rather than end in a separation or divorce.
Care for the Family, Garth House, Leon Avenue, Cardiff CF15 7RG
Published 2003; 33 pages; Research Report; Publisher Care for the Family; Price £12.95

Swinton Prof J
Why are we here?
Report on a two year qualitative research project exploring the spiritual needs of people with learning disabilities.
The Foundation for People with Learning Disabilities, 83 Victoria Street, London SW1 0HW
Published 2004; 67 pages; Publisher Foundation for People with Learning Disabilities, London

The Tomorrow Project
Learning from the Future:
scenarios for post-16 learning.
Learning & Skills Research Centre
Email mfletcher@ldsa.org.uk
Published 2004; 82 pages; Publisher Tomorrow Project with the Learning and Skills Development Agency

Tyers Philip
Engaging with the Religion of those who do not habitually attend public worship.
St Matthew's Vicarage, 20 Fishwick View, Preston PR1 4YA
Published 2004; Report presented at Implicit Religion Study Day

Vesey Nicolas
Audit of Social Action Projects run by Churches and Christian Organisations in Norwich.
St Luke with St Augustine, 61 Aylsham Road, Norwich NR3 2HF
Published 2003; 82 pages

Voas David
Intermarriage and the Demography of Secularisation.
The Cathie Marsh Centre for Census and Survey Research, University of Manchester, Dover Street Building, Manchester M13 9PL
Published 2003; The British Journal of Sociology, Vol 54, No 1, pp 83-108

Warren Yvonne & Kevin Mayhew
The Cracked Pot: the state of today's Anglican parish clergy.
The Church Times Bookshop, Alphonsus House, Chawton, Hants GU34 3HQ
Published 2003; Publisher Church Times Bookshop; Price £14.40

Welliver Dotsey
& Northcutt Minnette
Mission Handbook 2004-2006, US and Canadian Protestant Ministries Overseas.
www.missionhandbookonline.com
Published 2004; 552 pages; Price $49.95 + p&tp

Williams Tricia
The Bible and Developing Faith:
a critical study of the role of the Bible in helping young Christians grow in faith, with special reference to 11-14 year olds and Scripture Union Bible resources.
Email triciaw@scriptureunion.org.uk
Published 2004; MA in Practical and Contextual Theology

Willans Rev J
Church Survey UK.
The Vicarage, Clayhill Road, Leigh, Reigate RH2 8PD or Email margaret.elkin@dswark.org.uk
Published 2005

Wild Steven
Communicating the Gospel through the Television Broadcasting Media.
A critical examination of the nature of this work and ways and means of developing Christian television creatively.
Cliff College, Calver, Hope Valley, Nr Sheffield S32 3XG
Published 2002; 20,000 words; MA in Evangelism studies; Price £30

Wolf Andreas
Church Planting Dynamics in European Nations.
Order via Email andreas@dawneurope.net
Published 2004; Publisher DAWN Europe

Woodman Paul
City Gate Church.
City Gate Church, PO 237, Southampton SO16 3TD
Published 2004

Woolever Dr Cynthia
& Deborah Bruce (1)
A Field Guide to US Congregations: Who goes where and why.
Book describing congregational life in the US based on results of US Congregational Life Survey of more than 2,000 congregations and over 300,000 worshippers.
Westminster John Knox Press, 100 Witherspoon Street, Louisville, KY 20402 USA or www.wjkacademic.com/
Published 2002; 85 pages; Price $14.99; Publisher Westminster John Knox Press, Kentucky

Woolever Dr Cynthia
& Deborah Bruce (2)
Beyond the Ordinary: 10 strengths of US Congregations.
This book provides an intricate look at vitality and health in congregations; helping them to begin to determine where and when change can begin.
Published 2004; 146 pages; Price $14.99; Publisher Westminster John Knox Press, Kentucky

Woolever Dr Cynthia
& Deborah Bruce (3)
Fastest Growing Presbyterian Churches.
Booklet describing results of fast growing Presbyterian congregations that participated in the US Congregational Life Survey.
www.uscongregations.org/Growing_Presbyterian_Churches.pdf or Research Services, Presbyterian Church (USA), 100 Witherspoon Street, Louisville, KY 20402 USA
Published 2004; 21 pages; Price $5 or free download; Publisher Research Services, Presbyterian Church (USA)

Wordsworth Rev
The Story so Far.
Report on analysis of Mission Action Planning in the Diocese of York and describes the process of developing Diocesan strategies using mission action plans provided by 75% of parishes.
12 Muncastergate, York YO31 9LA
Published 2003; 44 pages; Publisher Diocese of York; Price £2

Wraight Heather (1)
Men and the Church.
A sequel to Eve's Glue, this research report explores the attitudes and values of male churchgoers.
Christian Research, Vision Building, 4 Footscray Road, Eltham, London SE9 2TZ
Published 2003; 22 pages; Leaders Briefing No 18; Price £4

Wraight Heather (2)
Neighbourhood Survey of parts of Sidcup.
A survey of nearly 150 homes showing what a church can learn from such a survey.
Published 2003; 22 pages; Price £4

Yon Herbie
Short term ministry in the Salvation Army as paradigm shift: a Consultant's perspective.
Cliff College, Calver, Hope Valley, Nr Sheffield S32 3XG
Published 2003; 20,000 words; MA in Consultancy, Mission & Ministry Studies; Price £30

Yon Tricia
Can an 'activist movement develop and nurture reflective practitioners?
An exploration of the development of reflective practice in Salvation Army Ministry.
Cliff College, Calver, Hope Valley, Nr Sheffield S32 3XG
Published 2003; 20,000 words; MA in Consultancy, Mission & Ministry Studies; Price £30

7

7

Table 7.11 Highest Qualification of Population of Working Age[2]

Highest Qualification	1998 %	2002 %
Degree or equivalent	13	15[1]
Higher education below degree	8	10[1]
GCE A Level or equivalent	23	19
GCSE grades A*–C or equivalent	23	22
Other qualifications	15	19
No qualifications	18	15
All people of working age	29.9mn	25.8mn

[1] Estimate [2] Men aged 16–64 and women aged 16–59

Source: Labour Force Survey, National Statistics, 1999 quoted in *North East in Figures*, Martin Smith, Table 5.1; 2002 quoted in *Minority Ethnic Attainment*, DfSS, Research Topic Paper RTP01–03, 2003, Page 26

See **Page 5.2** for other information on qualifications.

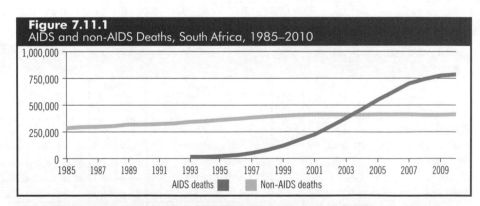

Figure 7.11.1
AIDS and non-AIDS Deaths, South Africa, 1985–2010

AIDS deaths   Non-AIDS deaths

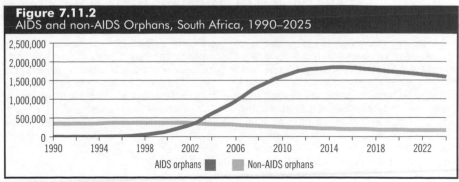

Figure 7.11.2
AIDS and non-AIDS Orphans, South Africa, 1990–2025

AIDS orphans   Non-AIDS orphans

See **Page 5.11** for more detail.

Table 7.12.1
Religion by Environment, England, 2001

Environment		Population 2001	91–01 %	Churchgoers 1989	1998	89–98 %	% of pop 1989 %	1998 %	C'ian %	Budd %	Hindu %	Jew %	Mus %	Sikh %	Other %	None %	n/a %
Rural Amenity	A	3,012,662	+5.8	336,000	249,900	−26	11.8	8.3	78.5	0.2	0.1	0.1	0.2	0	0.3	13.5	7.1
Coalfields	B	3,845,622	−2.0	339,200	233,700	−31	8.6	5.9	79.7	0.1	0.2	0	1.1	0.2	0.1	11.2	7.4
Coast and Country Resorts	C	3,858,752	+3.3	415,100	320,500	−23	11.4	83	74.6	0.3	0.2	0.4	0.5	0	0.4	15.6	8.0
New and Developing Areas	D	3,765,683	+6.4	300,300	248,700	−17	8.6	6.7	69.6	0.3	1.3	0.2	3.1	1.2	0.3	164	7.6
Education Centres & Outer London	E	3,789,712	+5.0	373,800	354,900	−5	10.5	9.3	56.3	0.8	6.0	2.7	7.8	2.0	0.6	15.3	8.5
Established Manufacturing Fringe	F	2,775,171	+2.6	227,900	171,900	−25	8.4	62	78.7	0.1	0.2	0	0.7	0.3	0.2	12.5	7.3
Growth Areas	G	6,759,943	+6.5	569,000	464,800	−18	8.9	6.9	75.7	0.2	0.5	0.2	0.7	0.3	0.3	15.1	7.0
Ports & Industry	I	3,055,014	−5.0	325,500	243,300	−25	10.2	7.6	73.2	0.3	0.4	0.5	3.1	0.3	0.2	13.9	8.1
Inner London	L	2,300,685	+7.2	200,200	192,300	−4	9.6	8.4	54.3	1.0	1.9	1.8	12.5	0.5	0.4	18.0	9.6
Manufacturing Centres	M	5,097,265	−1.1	523,700	356,000	−32	10.2	6.8	65.7	0.2	2.2	0.1	9.3	2.2	0.2	12.4	7.7
Most Prosperous	P	2,111,323	+3.3	231,100	204,800	−11	11.4	9.6	75.1	0.3	0.6	0.4	1.0	0.2	0.3	15.2	6.9
Remoter Rural	R	2,027,959	+7.6	209,300	158,700	−24	11.3	8.0	78.5	0.2	0.1	0.1	0.2	0	0.3	13.1	7.5
Established Service Centres	S	2,835,720	−0.5	305,100	218,100	−28	10.9	7.5	69.9	0.3	0.4	0.4	1.6	0.5	0.3	18.3	8.3
Mixed Urban	U	4,116,370	+2.4	386,600	297,100	−23	9.6	7.2	74.6	0.2	0.6	0.8	1.2	0.4	0.2	14.7	7.3
Total		49,351,881	+2.9	4,742,800	3,714,700	−22	9.9	7.6	71.7	0.3	1.1	0.5	3.1	0.7	0.3	14.6	7.7

C'ian = Christian Budd = Buddhist Mus = Muslim n/a = not answered

Table 7.12.2
Religion by Environment, Wales, 2001

Environment		Population 2001	91–01 %	C'ian %	Budd %	Hindu %	Jew %	Mus %	Sikh %	Other %	None %	n/a %
Rural Amenity	A	84,885	+5.8	74.7	0.2	0.2	0	0.1	0.1	0.2	16.7	7.8
Coalfields	B	1,370,360	−1.2	69.7	0.1	0.1	0	0.6	0.1	0.2	20.9	8.3
Coast and Country Resorts	C	673,306	+1.5	76.1	0.2	0.1	0.1	0.2	0	0.3	15.3	7.7
Established Manufacturing Fringe	F	148,594	+4.6	79.2	0.1	0.1	0.1	0.1	0	0.1	12.9	7.4
Remoter Rural	R	201,295	+8.6	73.3	0.3	0.2	0.1	0.2	0	0.4	17.7	7.8
Established Service Centres	S	305,353	+2.8	66.9	0.3	0.8	0.3	3.7	0.3	0.3	18.8	8.6
Mixed Urban	U	119,292	+1.0	73.0	0.2	0.2	0.1	0.4	0.1	0.2	18.6	7.2
Total		2,903,085	+1.1	71.9	0.2	0.2	0.1	0.7	0.1	0.2	18.5	8.1

C'ian = Christian Budd = Buddhist Mus = Muslim n/a = not answered. Churchgoing figures for Wales are unavailable, never having been published by Unitary Authority.

Table 7.12.3
Religion by Environment, Scotland, 2001

Environment		Population 2001	91–01 %	Churchgoers 1994	2002	94–02 %	% of pop 1994 %	2002 %	CofS %	RC %	OCian %	Budd %	Hindu %	Jew %	Mus %	Sikh %	Other %	None %	n/a %
New and Developing Areas	D	239,655	+4.4	21,400	17,440	−19	9.5	7.2	42.8	13.7	5.3	0.1	0.1	0	0.5	0	0.4	32.0	5.1
Education Centres	E	660,749	+0.2	69,690	56,850	−18	10.6	8.6	35.9	9.1	8.2	0.3	0.3	0.2	1.3	0.2	1.2	38.4	4.9
Ports & Industry	I	2,496,012	−3.2	370,940	306,460	−17	14.4	12.2	39.9	22.5	5.0	0.1	0.1	0.1	1.1	0.2	0.4	24.4	6.2
Remoter Rural	R	1,291,741	+0.3	173,430	144,900	−16	13.1	10.9	49.9	6.7	10.0	0.1	0	0	0.1	0	0.5	27.9	4.8
Mixed Urban	U	373,854	−1.0	55,660	44,480	−19	14.6	11.9	44.3	16.7	6.3	0.1	0.2	0.9	0.9	0.4	0.5	25.1	4.6
Total		5,062,110	−1.3	691,120	570,130	−18	13.5	11.2	42.4	15.9	6.8	0.1	0.1	0.1	0.9	0.1	0.5	27.6	5.5

CofS = Church of Scotland RC = Roman Catholic OCian = Other Christian Budd = Buddhist Mus = Muslim n/a = not answered

National Statistics publishes many journals. One of these is *Health Statistics Quarterly,* and in Issue No 7, Autumn 2000, a map was included which gave an environmental classification for each Local or Unitary Authority District for England, Wales and Scotland. The letter after each environment on this page was used to identify the classification for each Local Authority in the Church Attendance Tables in Section 12 of *Religious Trends* No 3. As a consequence of this classification it was possible to identify Church Attendance for each environment (Table 12.42 in No. 3). The same classification for each Local or Unitary Authority has been extended to the data on religion from the 2001 Population Census for each Authority given in Section 4 of *Religious Trends* No 4. This information, summarised for each environment, is shown in the Tables on this page.

8

Institutional Church Statistics

See notes and definitions on Page 0.6

Sources: Individual denominations, previous editions of *Religious Trends* and private surveys.

Table 8.2.1
TOTAL Anglican Churches[4]

	Membership	Churches	Ministers
2000	1,663,848	18,600	10,735
2001	1,653,296	18,598	10,702
2002	1,492,410	18,593	10,514
2003	1,524,875	18,546	10,655
2005	1,542,613	18,460	10,406
2010	1,397,311	18,299	9,404
2020	1,141,605	16,670	7,923

Table 8.2.2
Church of England

	Electoral Roll[5]	Churches	Clergy SC[6]	NSC[7]&CH[8]
2000	1,377,000	16,222	9,538	3,341
2001	1,372,000	16,220	9,487	3,075
2002	1,210,000	16,202	9,303	3,250
2003[1]	1,235,000	16,180	9,404	3,493
2005[1]	1,259,000	16,095	9,208	3,585
2010[1]	1,132,000	15,920	8,350	4,000
2020[1]	906,000	14,295	7,060	4,500

Table 8.2.3
Church in Wales

	Easter Communicants	Churches	Ministers
2000	83,400	1,511	648
2001	80,900	1,510	653
2002	75,000	1,511	646
2003	74,500	1,470	637
2005[3]	70,533	1,462[9]	580[10]
2010[3]	59,316	1,454[9]	426[10]
2020[3]	44,015	1,446[9]	215[1]

Table 8.2.4
Scottish Episcopal Church

	Membership	Churches	Ministers
2000[1]	48,270	310	167
2001[1]	46,930	310	158
2002	45,077	309	149
2003	44,280	313	185
2005[1]	41,700	308	177
2010[1]	35,500	304	145
2020[1]	24,000	295	126

Table 8.2.5 Church of Ireland
(Northern Ireland)

	Membership[11]	Churches	Ministers
2000	151,400[2]	445	290
2001	149,500[2]	440	300
2002	158,000[2]	440	300
2003	166,500	439	309
2005[1]	166,300	438	315
2010[1]	164,200	428	320
2020[1]	160,000	410	320

Table 8.2.6
Free Church of England

	Membership	Churches	Ministers
2000	1,410	302	45
2001	1,400	302	45
2002[1]	1,375	302	45
2003[1]	1,350	302	45
2005[1]	1,310	292	44[2]
2010[1]	1,220	272	41
2020[1]	1,060	242	36

Table 8.2.7 Protestant Evangelical
Church of England[12]

	Membership	Churches	Ministers
2000	90	3	7
2001	90	3	7
2002	95	3	6
2003	90	3	6
2005[3]	90	3	6
2010[3]	110	4	8
2020[3]	130	5	10

Table 8.2.8 Anglian Apostolic
Episcopal Free Church[13]

	Electoral Roll[5]	Churches	Ministers SC[6]	NSC[7]
2000[2]	1,840	42	0	72
2001[2]	1,870	42	0	73
2002[2]	1,890	43	0	75
2003[1]	1,920	44	0	78
2005[2]	1,970	46	0	81
2010[1]	1,930	45	0	79
2020[1]	1,800	42	0	74

Table 8.2.9
Anglican Catholic Church UK[12]

	Membership	Churches	Ministers
2000[2]	85	7	5
2001[2]	110	9	7
2002[2]	135	11	9
2003[1]	150	12	10
2005[3]	200	13	11
2010[3]	400	20	15
2020[3]	600	22	20

Table 8.2.10
Traditional Anglican Church[14, 15, 16]

	Membership	Churches	Ministers
2000[1]	163	18	19
2001[1]	165	19	19
2002[1]	168	19	18
2003	170[1]	20	18
2005[1]	175	21	18
2010[1]	185	23	19
2020[1]	200	26	21

Table 8.2.11
Traditional Church of England[17]

	Membership	Churches	Ministers
2000	20	4	4
2001	26	5	5
2002	40	8	6
2003	55	12	8
2005[3]	65	13	9
2010[3]	80	16	10
2020[3]	100	17	15

Table 8.2.12
Continuing Church of England[18]

	Membership	Churches	Ministers
2000	120[1]	6	10
2001	125[1]	6	10
2002	130[1]	6	10
2003	140[1]	7[1]	9
2005	150[1]	7[1]	9[3]
2010	170[1]	8[1]	10[3]
2020	200	8	10

Table 8.2.13
Other Anglican Churches[19]

	Membership	Churches	Ministers
2000[1]	50	2	2
2001[1]	180	4[2]	11
2002[2]	500	11	18
2003[1]	720	16	24
2005	1,120	25	29
2010[1]	2,200	50	60
2020[1]	3,500	80	90

[1] Estimate
[2] Revised figure
[3] Church's own estimate
[4] Totals of Tables 8.2.2–8.2.13; Ministers are paid clergy only.
[5] Counted as 16 yrs old and above.
[6] SC = Stipendiary Clergy, that is, paid clergy/ministers.
[7] NSC = Non-Stipendiary Clergy, that is, unpaid clergy/ministers. See Table 8.6.3 for detail.
[8] CH = Chaplains.
[9] Based on average closures during the last 11 years.
[10] Based on approximate forecasts for the future by the Church in Wales.
[11] Taken as 58% of the adult community, estimated from decadal Population Censuses, which in 1995 was 278,400, actual in 2001 257,788, and estimated in 2003 at 287,000.
[12] Began in 1992.
[13] Incorporating the Anglican Orthodox Free Church.
[14] Began in 1996.

[15] The British Province of the worldwide Traditional Anglican Communion (established in 1991) has 12 provinces in North, Central and South America, Europe, India, Pakistan, Africa, Japan and Australia.
[16] The figures for 1996 are respectively 153, 15 and 20.
[17] Began in 1994.
[18] Also known as 'The Church of England (Continuing)', it includes the Wesley Synod (incorporating the St Thomas-à-Becket Episcopal Synod) which started in the UK in 1996, whose Head Office and sole UK church is in Canterbury, Kent, which in 2000 had 20 members and 3 ordained ministers, and 25 members in 2003. Worldwide there are 800 churches, 1,200 members but 100,000 in attendance. It is strong in Nigeria, and has 4 Bishops in the United States.
[19] Includes the Open Episcopal Church and the Anglican Independent Communion of Great Britain, the latter started by Rev Jonathan Blake in 1993. In 2003 the AIC had 18 churches in the UK, with 10 priests and 3 deacons, expecting the last to become 6 by 2005.

Table 8.3.1 Other Church of England Statistics

	Baptisms[2]	Confirmations	Marriages	Sunday Attendance		Easter		Christmas	
				Total	of which Children[3]	Communicants	All Age Attendance	Communicants	All Age Attendance
2000	161,110	36,469	60,700	1,058,000	180,000	1,163,100	1,626,300	1,366,000	2,851,600
2001	153,300	33,400	57,500[1]	1,041,000	173,000	1,134,900	1,593,100	1,228,000	2,608,000
2002	151,400	33,400	54,800	1,005,000	167,000	1,061,300	1,473,000	1,218,300	2,606,900
2003	144,300	31,800	56,100	1,017,000	164,000	1,077,900	1,504,200	1,199,900	2,652,800
2005[1]	134,000	28,900	51,500	974,600	152,000	994,000	1,379,000	1,075,000	2,580,000
2010[1]	108,000	21,900	43,300	895,000	125,000	829,000	1,136,000	821,000	2,486,000

[1] Estimate [2] Adult and infant [3] Aged 15 and under

Five maps on **Page 2.20** illustrate some of the data in **Table 8.3.2**. They show considerable disparity between Dioceses, often related to whether they are in a rural or urban area. The Church of England is generally stronger in rural areas than urban. See also **Table 8.6.3**.

Sources: Research & Statistics Dept., Archbishops' Council; *Church Statistics* 2000, 2001 and 2002, Church House Publishing, 2002, 2003 and 2004; *Religious Trends* No 3 2002/2003, Table 8.8.2.

Table 8.3.2
Other Church of England Statistics

Diocese	% of infants born baptised under 1 year of age 1992 %	1997 %	2002 %	Total Baptisms 2000	2002	***	Electoral Roll[2] 2001	2002	Number of Churches	Clergy	Recurring income £ million 2001	2002	Recurring expenditure £ million 2001	2002	Average giving per week of ER 2002[3]	No. of churches with USA 350 or more 2003
Bath & Wells	35.3	34.0	24.3	3,290	3,120	68.6	43,000	38,000	568	233	12.2	12.5	12.8	13.3	£5.28	4
Birmingham	16.3	12.7	9.5	3,070	2,840	63.4	19,500	18,200	195	186	9.1	9.4	9.6	10.4	£7.40	4
Blackburn	30.7	26.1	23.1	4,400	4,375	72.5	39,400	34,300	285	234	10.8	11.2	11.2	11.7	£5.04	4
Bradford	17.5	15.9	11.6	1,610	1,435	73.9	13,200	12,300	167	115	5.4	5.5	5.7	6.0	£7.30	1
Bristol	23.9	19.2	15.0	2,420	2,130	70.9	20,000	16,600	205	146	8.3	8.4	9.1	9.6	£7.98	4
Canterbury	32.2	28.0	23.3	3,020	3,365	60.9	22,700	21,000	329	161	9.0	9.2	9.3	9.9	£6.84	1
Carlisle	50.6	48.4	43.9	2,620	2,380	81.1	24,800	21,600	348	153	6.0	6.2	6.5	6.8	£4.79	1
Chelmsford	15.3	13.7	11.0	6,690	6,430	58.6	54,500	48,600	617	400	18.6	19.4	19.3	20.3	£6.14	4
Chester	33.3	28.5	22.2	5,940	5,070	70.8	53,400	45,700	373	265	13.9	14.6	14.9	15.4	£4.99	4
Chichester	30.3	25.9	19.5	4,780	4,465	64.5	60,600	51,800	516	331	16.8	17.8	17.3	18.5	£5.41	7
Coventry	22.5	21.1	17.3	2,380	2,145	68.5	18,100	16,300	243	143	7.7	7.7	7.7	7.9	£7.21	2
Derby	31.5	25.1	19.6	2,930	2,900	70.3	22,200	20,700	333	174	7.5	7.8	7.7	8.0	£5.78	1
Durham	34.9	31.0	24.9	5,290	4,685	79.8	27,700	24,000	295	219	8.2	8.3	8.1	8.5	£5.47	1
Ely	31.8	28.9	24.3	2,950	2,335	71.9	21,200	19,100	335	148	6.9	7.2	7.1	7.5	£6.07	5
Exeter	31.9	27.9	24.0	3,730	3,530	68.0	34,100	30,500	619	267	10.8	11.5	11.5	12.2	£5.94	3
Gloucester	34.5	32.3	26.6	2,640	2,450	67.3	27,200	23,600	397	147	8.2	8.5	8.7	9.6	£5.86	5
Guildford	31.2	27.4	22.1	3,710	3,505	66.2	32,700	29,500	218	189	14.5	15.4	15.3	16.5	£8.24	9
Hereford	49.5	45.8	37.6	1,350	1,490	73.2	19,800	18,100	425	105	4.7	5.0	4.8	4.9	£4.42	0
Leicester	20.0	17.2	14.0	2,320	2,130	67.6	17,200	17,000	327	164	7.4	7.7	7.2	7.5	£7.39	3
Lichfield	27.0	24.5	20.5	6,820	6,510	68.2	55,200	45,000	585	344	15.0	15.5	15.5	16.0	£5.25	2
Lincoln	46.0	45.7	34.6	5,000	4,295	75.7	30,900	27,800	645	204	7.1	8.0	7.4	8.1	£4.38	3
Liverpool	29.2	26.5	21.7	5,580	5,065	69.5	33,100	28,800	257	233	10.2	10.7	10.8	11.8	£5.50	5
London	10.3	8.1	6.0	5,760	5,660	54.6	64,600	59,600	479	524	42.0	47.2	45.8	51.6	£10.10	15
Manchester	23.9	20.1	16.4	5,670	5,480	71.4	40,500	34,500	356	286	12.5	12.4	12.3	13.0	£5.57	4
Newcastle	33.1	28.8	23.8	2,550	2,530	73.5	18,600	16,700	247	150	5.2	5.4	5.6	6.0	£5.28	2
Norwich	31.2	28.6	24.4	2,600	2,625	71.6	27,000	23,900	645	202	8.5	8.8	8.7	9.1	£5.84	4
Oxford	29.4	25.5	20.4	7,920	7,520	68.8	62,300	54,600	820	410	25.1	27.0	26.1	28.5	£7.92	12
Peterborough	23.6	21.7	18.2	2,490	2,455	68.8	19,800	18,000	379	154	7.6	7.9	7.6	8.0	£7.21	4
Portsmouth	24.2	23.3	20.0	2,210	2,095	68.7	20,500	17,500	173	112	5.7	6.0	5.9	6.2	£5.04	0
Ripon & Leeds	26.6	24.1	19.5	2,310	2,335	69.4	19,700	17,600	264	141	6.4	6.9	6.7	7.3	£6.11	3
Rochester	26.3	20.7	16.4	3,880	3,850	60.0	33,800	29,900	264	219	14.7	15.2	15.9	16.8	£7.09	7
St Albans	21.2	19.7	15.2	5,190	4,885	64.5	47,200	39,400	411	271	15.1	15.9	15.5	16.3	£6.20	3
St Edmds & Ipswich	29.8	25.3	20.7	2,010	1,945	64.8	26,400	24,100	475	162	7.4	7.8	7.4	8.1	£5.14	1
Salisbury	36.0	31.6	26.7	3,680	3,230	68.7	48,700	42,500	581	226	12.2	12.6	11.8	12.5	£5.02	5
Sheffield	27.9	26.2	20.7	4,090	3,665	71.2	22,000	18,600	222	185	7.6	8.0	8.4	9.0	£6.86	4
Sodor & Man	35.4	27.9	28.9	350	350	74.3	2,800	2,400	45	19	0.9	0.8	0.9	0.9	£5.35	0
Southwark	13.1	12.1	8.1	6,040	4,940	56.5	48,500	44,200	378	358	22.2	23.1	22.6	23.7	£7.43	4
Southwell & Nott'm	22.0	21.3	18.3	3,030	2,985	66.7	18,900	18,300	318	166	8.5	8.9	8.3	8.8	£7.87	2
Truro	34.4	30.1	26.1	1,740	1,680	71.4	17,900	16,900	315	126	4.6	4.9	4.9	5.1	£4.50	0
Wakefield	24.9	23.3	17.7	3,480	3,110	70.7	24,900	20,300	242	169	6.7	7.1	7.7	7.7	£5.41	0
Winchester	36.1	31.6	26.3	4,850	4,580	71.8	45,200	38,500	413	246	13.6	14.0	14.4	15.1	£5.70	10
Worcester	34.6	28.3	23.9	3,190	3,000	69.3	22,700	20,300	282	153	6.8	7.3	6.9	7.2	£5.41	5
York	37.8	32.9	27.9	5,548	5,230	75.3	40,300	35,000	611	245	11.3	11.6	12.1	12.4	£5.46	4
Europe	n/a	n/a	n/a	580	575	55.7	9,800	9,300	n/a	99	n/a	n/a	n/a	n/a	n/a	n/a
TOTAL	**26.0**	**22.8**	**18.1**	**161,708**	**151,400**	**68.2**	**1,372,600**	**1,210,000**	**16,202**	**9,194**	**462.7**	**486.6**	**483.1**	**513.8**	**£6.20**	**163**

[1] Estimate [2] Numbers are lower in 2002 as 2002 was the six-yearly revision year when everyone had to re-sign the Electoral Roll afresh. [3] Annual giving reflected in this column is *total* giving, not just towards the parish share.
Sources: Relevant issues of *Church Statistics*. Last column, private survey. *** % 2002 infants are of total. ER = Electoral Roll USA = Usual Sunday Attendance Nott'm = Nottingham

8

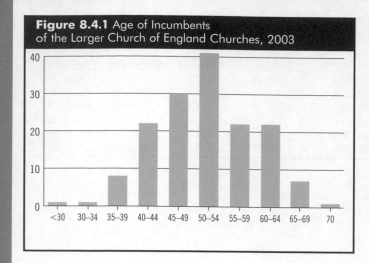

Figure 8.4.1 Age of Incumbents of the Larger Church of England Churches, 2003

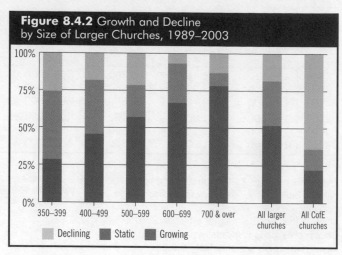

Figure 8.4.2 Growth and Decline by Size of Larger Churches, 1989–2003

There were at least 163 Church of England churches in 2003 which had an average Sunday congregation of 350 or more, adults and children. The Vicar or other Senior Minister in all cases, as far as is known, was male. His average age was 51, which is a year or two younger than the average incumbent (at the time of writing in the autumn of 2004, when 9 of these churches had interregnums). The actual spread of ages, shown in **Figure 8.4.1**, is a typical "bell-shape" except that there were fewer aged 55–59 than might have been normally expected.

The majority of these (90% or more) were evangelical churches, with most of the rest being Anglo-Catholic. They include some of the larger Reform churches, many New Wine churches, and doubtless other affiliations.

These 163 churches, 1% of the total number of Church of England churches, represented 6% of the total average congregation in 1989, which rose to 8% by 1998 and 11% by 2003, and is projected to become 14% by 2010. These percentages exclude churches which were larger than 350 prior to 2003 but, for whatever reason, were below that figure that year.

Over half, 52%, of these churches grew during the 1990s, more than double the rate for all Church of England churches, 22%. As **Table 8.4.1** shows, some of this growth was quite spectacular. Furthermore, the larger the church, the greater the likelihood of it being a growing one, as shown in **Figure 8.4.2**. Far fewer, just 18%, of these churches declined during the 1990s, against 64% of all Church of England churches.

Table 8.3.2 shows these larger churches are spread across all Dioceses, except five (Hereford, Portsmouth, Sodor & Man, Truro and Wakefield). **Table 8.4.2** lists the Dioceses with the largest numbers: 11 Dioceses, a quarter, account for 85, or half, 52%, of these churches.

The bottom part of the page turns to a different topic. Every week the Anglican newspapers give details of the numbers of clergy retiring or resigning, and **Table 8.4.3** lists the number of resignations (not normal retirements) per month

Table 8.4.1 Number of Larger Churches in 2003 by Previous Size

Size	1989 %	1998 %	2003 %
Under 300	20	13	0
300–349	9	11	0
350–399	14	16	34
400–499	18	23	20
500–599	18	13	13
600–699	9	8	13
700–999	8	10	11
1,000 or over	4	6	9
TOTAL	100	100	100

Table 8.4.2 Number of Larger Churches in 2003 by Diocese

Diocese	Number
London	15
Oxford	12
Winchester	10
Guildford	9
Chichester	7
Rochester	7
Ely	5
Gloucester	5
Liverpool	5
Salisbury	5
Worcester	5

Table 8.4.3 Resignations of Vicars, Curates and Chaplains, 2000–2003

Year	Jan	Feb	Mar	Apr	May	Jun	Jul	Aug	Sep	Oct	Nov	Dec	Total
2000	1/0/0	2/2/0	1/1/2	0/0/0	1/2/2	2/4/2	0/1/1	2/2/0	4/3/0	3/2/0	3/1/1	0/0/0	19/18/ 8
2001	2/0/1	1/3/2	0/1/0	3/1/2	2/4/2	2/3/2	0/0/0	4/3/2	2/1/0	2/3/2	5/4/0	2/2/2	25/25/15
2002	1/3/0	0/0/0	1/0/0	3/2/1	6/4/4	0/3/0	6/2/2	3/3/3	6/3/3	9/4/2	1/1/0	0/2/1	36/27/16
2003	5/2/1	3/3/1	1/2/1	2/3/0	2/0/0	1/2/1	2/4/0	4/6/1	3/11/3	7/3/3	1/1/1	4/1/2	35/38/14
Av'ge	4	4	3	4	7	6	5	8	10	10	5	4	**29/27/13**

V/A/C = The first figure refers to resignations of Vicars, the second to Assistant Curates and the third to Chaplains

Source: Notices of resignations and retirements in national Anglican newspapers Av'ge = Average per month, all groups

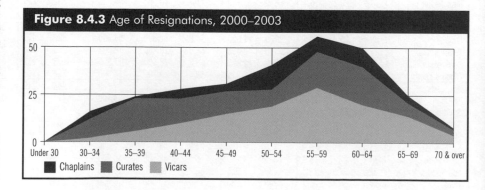

Figure 8.4.3 Age of Resignations, 2000–2003

for the four years 2000–2003 for Vicars, Curates and Chaplains. Some of these resignations will be because of coming to the end of a contract, retirement age or ill-health or such like reasons. The average number of such resignations per year across these three groups was respectively 29, 27 and 13, a total of 69.

Figure 8.4.3 shows the numbers leaving in each age-group for Vicars, Curates and Chaplains. Resignations peak during the ages of 55 and 64, and additionally for Curates between the ages of 35 and 44, when perhaps they realise this is not the job they are most suited for.

Table 8.5.1
TOTAL Catholic Churches[4]

	Mass Attendance	Churches	Priests
2000	1,771,121	4,741	6,926
2001	1,741,677	4,730	6,756
2002	1,809,736	4,727	6,505
2003	1,730,323	4,731	6,379
2005	1,681,519	4,705	6,103
2010	1,529,525	4,647	5,498
2020	1,275,590	4,442	4,257

Table 8.5.2
Roman Catholic Church in England

	Mass Attendance[5]	Churches[6]	Priests
2000	973,000	3,359	5,145
2001	954,132	3,351	4,996[2]
2002	1,034,200[7]	3,362	4,776
2003[1]	965,000	3,360	4,680
2005[2]	938,000	3,340	4,450
2010[1]	840,000	3,300	4,000
2020[1]	657,000	3,150	3,000

Table 8.5.3
Roman Catholic Church in Wales

	Mass Attendance[5]	Churches[6]	Priests
2000	40,500	236	253
2001	39,500	231	255
2002	37,016	217	247
2003[1]	36,200	215	243
2005[1]	33,400	210	235
2010[1]	26,500	200	212
2020[1]	12,700	170	168

Table 8.5.4
Roman Catholic Church in Scotland

	Mass Attendance	Churches	Priests
2000	222,956	595	866
2001[1]	212,500	594	851
2002	202,110	594[8]	835
2003[1]	192,000	593	820
2005[1]	172,000	592	790
2010[1]	126,000	587	721
2020[1]	70,000	570	600

Table 8.5.5
Roman Catholic Church in N. Ireland[9]

	Mass Attendance	Churches	Priests
2000	521,000	470	554
2001[1]	522,000	471[2]	547
2002[1]	523,000	472[2]	540
2003[1]	523,500	473	530
2005[1]	524,000	473[2]	520
2010[1]	522,600	470	480
2020[1]	522,000	460	410

Table 8.5.6
Old Roman Catholic Church of GB[10]

	Mass Attendance	Churches	Priests
2000	50	4	10
2001	50	4	10
2002	55	4	10
2003	56	4	10
2005	59	3	9
2010[1]	65	3	9
2020[1]	60	3	8

Table 8.5.7
Croatian Catholic Church

	Mass Attendance	Churches	Priests
2000	160	1	1
2001	160	1	1
2002	160	1	1
2003	140	1	1
2005[3]	160	1	1
2010[3]	200	1	1
2020[3]	300	1	1

Table 8.5.8
Hungarian Catholic Church

	Mass Attendance	Churches	Priests
2000[2]	320	0	2
2001[2]	320	0	2
2002[2]	320	0	2
2003	320	0	2
2005[3]	300	0	2
2010[1]	280	0	2
2020[1]	250	0	2

Table 8.5.9
Lithuanian St Casimir Catholic Church

	Mass Attendance	Churches	Priests
2000[2]	150	1	1
2001[2]	180	1	1
2002[2]	200	1	1
2003	200	1	1
2005[3]	200	1	1
2010[3]	180	1	1
2020[3]	180	1	1

Table 8.5.10
Slovenian Roman Catholic Mission

	Community Figure	Churches	Priests
2000	95[2]	9	1
2001	95[2]	9	1
2002	95[2]	9	1
2003[1]	100	9	1
2005[1]	100	9	2
2010[1]	100	9	2
2020[1]	100	9	2

Table 8.5.11
Traditional Roman Catholic Church[11]

	Mass Attendance	Churches	Priests
2000	–	–	–
2001	–	–	–
2002	–	–	–
2003	107	12	4
2005[3]	250	18	6
2010[3]	700	24	9
2020[1]	1,000	30	12

Table 8.5.12
Ukrainian Catholic Churches

	Mass Attendance	Churches	Priests
2000	1,740	15	11
2001	1,640	18	11
2002	1,540	18	11
2003	2,000	18	12
2005[3]	2,500	18	12
2010[1]	3,000	18	12
2020[1]	3,500	18	10

Table 8.5.13
Other Roman Catholic Churches[12]

	Mass Attendance	Churches	Priests
2000	11,150	51	82
2001	11,100	50	81
2002	11,040	49	81
2003	10,700	45	75
2005	10,550	40	75
2010[1]	9,900	34	49
2020[1]	8,500	30	43

[1] Estimate
[2] Revised figure
[3] Church's own estimate
[4] Total of Tables 8.5.2–8.5.13
[5] As measured on the first Sunday in October each year.
[6] Taken as the full number of churches and other buildings open to the public for Mass.
[7] Catholic population 3,976,723 in 2001; 3,896,467 in 2002.
[8] In 491 parishes.
[9] The Northern Ireland proportion is based on the following percentages of the 4 Dioceses that straddle the border: 95% of Derry, 75% of Armagh, 60% of Clogher and 5% of Kilmore, plus 100% of the 2 Dioceses wholly within N. Ireland – Down and Connor & Dromore.
[10] The Old Catholic Church broke with Rome in 1724 over the question of who should appoint bishops, and in Germany and Austria in 1871 over papal infallibility. The churches are autonomous but joined together in the Treaty of Utrecht in 1889, regarding the Archbishop of Utrecht as Primate. There are churches in 2004 in Austria, the Czech Republic, Germany, the Netherlands, Poland, Slovakia, Switzerland, with a tiny congregation in Bosnia Herzegovina, a single congregation in Milan as well as the UK. Full communion with the Church of England was established in 1932 under the Bonn Agreement. (From letters in the *Church Times*).
[11] Began in 2003 as the Archdiocese of Our Lady of Victories. Previously known as the English Catholic Church they describe themselves as "traditional Roman Catholics who are unable to accept the modernist agenda (liturgical and spiritual) of the Second Vatican Council". Congregations in England, Scotland, East Bohemia and Warsaw. Many students attend.
[12] Total taken from Table 8.6.1.

Table 8.6.1 Other Roman Catholic Churches

Church	Mass Attendance					Churches					Priests				
	2000	2001	2002	2003	2005[1]	2000	2001	2002	2003	2005[1]	2000	2001	2002	2003	2005[1]
German Catholic Church	1,400	1,400	1,400	1,400	1,400	1	1	1	1	1	1	1	1	1	1
Independent Catholic Church[2]	550[1]	600[1]	640	300[1]	150	14[1]	14[1]	14	10[1]	5	26[1]	26[1]	26	20[1]	10
Latvian Catholic Church[3]	500	500	500	500	500	0	0	0	0	0	0	0	0	0	0
Other Catholic Churches[4]	8,700	8,600	8,500	8,500	8,500	36	35	34	34	34	55	54	54	54	54
TOTAL	11,150	11,100	11,040	10,700	10,550	51	50	49	45	40	82	81	81	75	65

[1] Estimate [2] The Independent Catholic Church was established in 1992, but is not in communion with Rome. Its future is uncertain since the death of their Primate, Archbishop John Simmons, in 2003. [3] The Church meets twice a year in London. [4] Including the Ecumenical Old Catholic Church (not in communion with Rome) meeting infrequently in the parish of St Anselm and St Aelred in South East London; the Society of St Pius X (SSPX); the Tridentine Institute of Our Lady of Walsingham (untraced since they left Walsingham in 1995 but are believed to still be active from a *Daily Telegraph* article 22nd July 1997 giving their numbers as 330 total celebrants of the Tridentine Mass in 5 churches; like SSPX they are not in communion with Rome and both are followers of Archbishop Lefebvre); and other Catholic Churches.

Table 8.6.2
Other Roman Catholic Statistics

Year	Infant baptisms			Confirmations, England & Wales	Adult Conversions, Great Britain	First Communions	Education, England & Wales		Marriages					
	England & Wales	Scotland	% of births				Schools	Pupils	England & Wales			Scotland	Northern Ireland
									Number	% all marriages	% of religious		
2000	64,032	9,360	11.2	37,800	4,960	61,500	2,398	920,643	11,312	4.2	11.6	1,858	2,770
2001	58,716	9,050	10.5	37,600	4,920	62,000	2,374	825,431	10,518	4.2	11.8	1,690	2,680
2002	59,096	7,510	10.3	37,040[1]	4,860[1]	62,500[1]	2,382	824,861	9,980	3.9	11.6	2,196[1]	2,600[1]
2003[1]	56,180[2]	8,320	9.6	36,300	4,810	63,000	2,369[2]	823,700	9,300	3.6	11.5	1,440	2,520
2005[1]	53,250	7,660	9.3	35,330	4,710	64,000	2,396	825,000	7,940	3.3	11.4	1,300	2,390
2010[1]	44,770	6,120	7.8	33,400	4,470	66,000	2,400	826,000	5,050	2.3	9.9	1,020	2,100

[1] Estimate [2] Actual

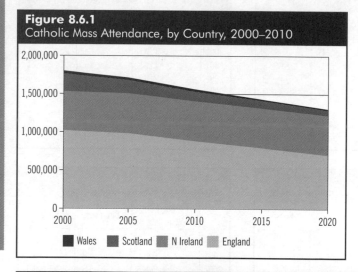

Figure 8.6.1
Catholic Mass Attendance, by Country, 2000–2010

Legend: ■ Wales ■ Scotland ■ N Ireland ■ England

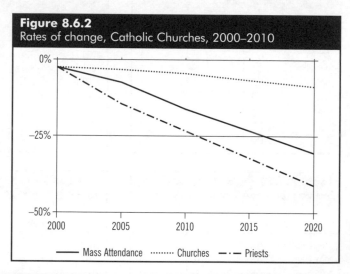

Figure 8.6.2
Rates of change, Catholic Churches, 2000–2010

Legend: —— Mass Attendance ······· Churches —·— Priests

Table 8.6.3 Total Church of England Clergy and Church Army Officers

	SC[2]	NSC	Chaps[4]	**Total**	CAO	RetdC
1990	11,072	1,300	1,000	**13,372**	560[1]	5,974
1995	10,260	1,900	1,100	**13,260**	500	6,745
1999	9,648	2,050[1]	1,250[1]	**12,948**	375[1]	7,531
2000	9,538	2,083	1,258	**12,879**	398	7,670[1]
2001	9,487	1,966	1,109	**12,562**	361	7,703
2002	9,303	2,091	1,159	**12,553**	244	7,931[3]
2003	9,404	2,277	1,216	**12,897**	370	8,095[5]
2005[1]	9,208	2,360	1,225	**12,793**	250	8,530

SC: Stipendiary Clergy **NSC:** Non-Stipendiary Clergy **Chaps:** Chaplains[3] **CAO:** Lay Workers and Church Army Officers **RetdC:** All retired Clergy

[1] Estimate [2] Total of senior church leaders, parochial and non-parochial stipendiary clergy. [3] Of whom 4,624 are pastorally active. [4] Armed Services, Prison, School, Higher Education, Hospital and other Chaplains, including 30 for deaf people, and 70 ordained staff in Theological and Bible Colleges and other Education Centres. [5] Of whom 4,466 are pastorally active.

Table 8.6.3 indicates a decline in the number of stipendiary clergy at an average rate of 1.4% per annum during the 1990s, a rate expected to reduce to 1.0% in the immediate years ahead. This is a much smaller rate than the decline in attendance – lay people are leaving the church faster than the clergy. The number of other leaders shown in this Table reflects the continued widespread ministry of the church.

Sources: Ministry Issues, Gordon Kuhrt, Church House Publishing, 2001; *UK Christian Handbook,* Christian Research, 1994/95 and 1996/97 editions, *Church Statistics,* 2000, 2001, 2002, Church House Publishing, 2002, 2003, 2004, *Church Times* 5th May 2000.

Table 8.7.1
Celibacy and Priesthood

| Statement | Canonical status | | Age | | | |
	Regular %	Secular %	<45 %	45–59 %	60/60+ %	Overall %
I believe a married man could validly be ordained priest	89	91	90	95	88	91
Chastity is essential for a Catholic priest	74	73	66	69	70	73
Most priests are faithful to their celibacy commitment	71	72	68	66	79	72
Celibacy should remain the norm for entry to priesthood	51	45	41	35	59	46
Catholic priests who marry should be re-admitted to ministry	45	45	45	57	35	45
The Catholic Church has too readily ordained married convert Anglican clergymen	29	33	43	35	24	32
If permitted, I would get married and stay in priestly ministry	12	20	18	24	12	18

Table 8.7.2
Fallen Priests

| Statement: A priest who... should be barred from ministry | Canonical status | | Age | | | |
	Regular %	Secular %	<45 %	45–59 %	60/60+ %	Overall %
Practises paedophilia	91	90	85	90	92	90
Practises homosexuality	72	63	47	61	79	65
Has had sex with a married woman	18	19	20	13	24	19
Has had sex with an unmarried woman	14	14	15	8	19	14
Becomes alcoholic	9	7	4	6	10	7

Table 8.7.3
Marriage, Sex and Death

| Statement | Canonical status | | Age | | | |
	Regular %	Secular %	<45 %	45–59 %	60/60+ %	Overall %
I support the Catholic Church's total ban on abortion	91	92	91	90	94	92
Direct euthanasia is morally unjustifiable	84	85	83	81	89	85
The divorced and remarried should be admitted to communion	47	49	50	59	39	49
The Catholic Church's teaching on divorce and remarriage should be liberalised	41	43	48	52	31	43
I support the Catholic Church's total ban on contraception	42	38	33	28	52	39
In the Catholic Church annulment is too easy	5	7	4	4	10	7

Table 8.7.4
Emotional Exhaustion

| Statement | Canonical status | | Age | | | |
	Regular %	Secular %	<45 %	45–59 %	60/60+ %	Overall %
I feel used up at the end of the day in parish ministry	30	38	40	39	32	36
I feel frustrated by my parish ministry	16	24	34	27	12	23
I feel emotionally drained by my parish ministry	16	20	26	20	14	19
I feel burned out from my parish ministry	14	14	15	17	11	14

Table 8.7.5
Personal Accomplishment through Parish Ministry

| Statement | Canonical status | | Age | | | |
	Regular %	Secular %	<45 %	45–59 %	60/60+ %	Overall %
I have accomplished many worthwhile things in my ministry	72	76	77	78	71	75
I am positively influencing people's lives through my ministry	76	70	76	71	68	71
I can easily understand how my parishioners feel about things	58	60	63	54	63	60
I deal very effectively with the problems of my parishioners	33	31	37	32	29	32

Published surveys of the Roman Catholic priesthood are relatively rare in the UK, so the book *The Naked Parish Priest: What priests really think they're doing* by Monsignor Stephen Louden (a former Vicar General to the British Army) and Professor Leslie Francis of the University of Wales, was especially welcome when published by Continuum, London in 2003. It gives the results of a 1996 study from a mailing to all 3,581 Catholic priests then serving in England and Wales; 1,482 or 42% replied.

Tables 8.7.1–5 give some of the results from this study. Altogether 22 topics were explored, and these Tables show what came from 5 of them. Those not given included training (4 questions), the theology and experience of priesthood (5 questions), Catholic institutions (2 questions), intercommunion, Church changes, ordination of women (49% in favour), depersonalisation and their future (1 question each).

Answers were analysed by the canonical status of priests, regular priests being those ordained by a Diocesan bishop and who would normally spend all their ministry within that Diocese, and secular priests being those ordained through one of the many Catholic Orders who may require them to serve in any part of the world. By and large there was little variation in the answers by status, as may be seen from the Tables. Those where the difference is at least 6% are the significant ones.

There was much more variation by age, however. All the answers in these Tables differed significantly. In some there is a progression in the percentage replies from young to old or from old to young, but in others the middle group (those aged 45 to 59) are quite different. It would seem as if this generation of priests, who would mostly be ordained in the 1960s or early 1970s, were more radical than those ordained earlier, perhaps because of the outcomes of Vatican II, an international Catholic Council of Bishops which concluded in 1964. Those coming after them tend in some respects to be more like the older priests!

Table 8.7.1 shows a large majority in favour of married priests, although three-quarters feel celibacy is important for Catholic priests.

Table 8.7.2 shows that a huge proportion of priests abhor the paedophile scandals which have hit the Catholic Church in various parts of the world in the last decade, but a majority of those under 45 do not think that homosexuality should debar a person from the priesthood.

Table 8.7.3 confirms high agreement with the Catholic ban on abortion by its leaders, and its opposition to euthanasia. A majority of priests 60 or over think that divorced and remarried people should be admitted to communion. A majority of those aged 45 to 59 consider that the Church's teaching on divorce and remarriage should be liberalised.

Helping priests overcome emotional exhaustion is of course very important, but the percentages in **Table 8.7.4** show that two-thirds of the priests do not feel "used up" at the end of their day and that three-quarters are not frustrated with their ministry.

This sense of enjoyment comes through the detail in **Table 8.7.5**. 91% of respondents said they gained "a lot of personal satisfaction from working with people" (a percentage which did not vary by age), and significant majorities feel they accomplish much, are positive influences, and understand where their parishioners are coming from. These have to be encouraging results when declining number of priests (**Tables 8.5.2** and **3**) is current experience.

8

Table 8.8.1
TOTAL Orthodox Churches[4, 12]

	Membership	Churches	Priests
2000	245,186	253	260
2001	252,428	259	269
2002	259,969	265	274
2003	262,443	273	287
2005	271,158	278	307
2010	276,240	293	311
2020	284,975	311	330

Table 8.8.2
EASTERN: Greek Orthodox[5, 12]

	Membership	Churches[6]	Priests[7]
2000	215,000	99	104[2]
2001[1]	220,000	105[2]	108[2]
2002[1]	225,000	111[2]	112[2]
2003	225,000[1]	111	116
2005[1]	230,000	111	122
2010[1]	230,000	115	122
2020[1]	230,000	120	125

Table 8.8.3 EASTERN: Russian
Orthodox: Pariarchate of Moscow[8]

	Membership	Churches	Priests
2000	2,620	35[2]	36[2]
2001	2,650[1]	35[2]	36[2]
2002	2,700[1]	35[2]	36[2]
2003	2,750[1]	35	36
2005	2,800[3]	35[1]	36
2010[1]	2,900	35	36
2020[1]	3,000	35	36

Table 8.8.4 EASTERN: Russian
Orthodox Church Outside Russia[9]

	Membership	Churches	Priests
2000	1,050	10	11
2001[1]	1,100	10	11
2002[1]	1,100	10	10
2003[1]	1,150	10	10
2005[3]	1,200	11	10
2010[1]	1,250	11	10
2020[1]	1,300	11	10

Table 8.8.5 EASTERN: Serbian Orthodox Church, Diocese of W. Europe

	Membership	Churches	Priests
2000	3,800	24[2]	11[2]
2001[1]	3,850	24[2]	11[2]
2002[1]	3,900	24[2]	11[2]
2003[1]	3,950	24	11
2005[1]	4,000	24	11
2010[1]	4,000	24	11
2020[1]	4,000	24	11

Table 8.8.6
EASTERN: Patriarchate of Antioch[10]

	Membership	Churches	Priests
2000	800	14	13
2001[1]	900	14	14
2002[1]	1,000	14	15
2003[1]	1,100	14	16
2005[1]	1,200	15	18
2010[1]	1,250	15	18
2020[1]	1,300	15	18

Table 8.8.7 EASTERN: Patriarchate
of Bulgaria, Diocese of W. Europe

	Membership	Churches	Priests
2000[3]	82	1	1
2001[1]	83	1	1
2002[1]	84	1	1
2003[1]	85	1	1
2005[1]	86	1	1
2010[1]	90	1	1
2020[1]	100	1	1

Table 8.8.8 EASTERN: Latvian Orthodox, Patriarchate of Constantinople

	Membership	Churches	Priests
2000[1]	160	1	1
2001[1]	150	1	1
2002	140	1	1
2003[1]	130	1	1
2005[1]	110	1	1
2010[1]	100	1	1
2020[1]	100	1	1

Table 8.8.9
EASTERN: Patriarchate of Romania

	Membership	Churches	Priests
2000	800	2	2
2001	900	2	2
2002	1,000	2	2
2003[1]	2,000	3	6
2005[3]	3,000	3	6
2010[1]	3,000	3	6
2020[1]	3,000	3	6

Table 8.8.10 EASTERN: Byelorussian
Orthodox, Patriarchate of Constantinople

	Membership	Churches	Priests
2000[1]	2,100	2[2]	2[2]
2001[1]	2,150	2[2]	2[2]
2002[1]	2,200	2	2
2003[1]	2,250	2	2
2005[1]	2,300	2	2
2010[1]	2,400	2	2
2020[1]	2,500	2	2

Table 8.8.11 EASTERN:
Ukrainian Autocephalous Patriarchate

	Membership	Churches	Priests
2000	1,150	12	7
2001	1,150	12	7
2002	1,130	12	7
2003	1,100	12	7
2005[1]	1,000	12	7
2010[1]	1,000	12	7
2020[1]	1,000	12	7

Figure 8.8 Membership of the
Orthodox Churches, 2000–2020

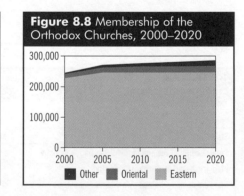

Other ■ Oriental ■ Eastern

[1] Estimate

[2] Revised figure

[3] Church's own estimate.

[4] Total of Tables 8.8.2–11 and Tables 8.9.1–9

[5] The Œcumenical Patriarchate of Constantinople, Diocese of Thyateira and Great Britain, an International Jurisdiction composed 99% of Greek and Cypriot members in the British Isles. Membership is taken as approximately two-thirds of the community.

[6] There are 4 monasteries not included in these figures.

[7] All male.

[8] Diocese of Sourozh. Revised figures taken from the *Orthodox Directory* of the Orthodox Fellowship of St John the Baptist, 2004.

[9] Diocese of Great Britain and Ireland; made up of Russian immigrant churches and the English Orthodox Deanery.

[10] The Patriarchate of Antioch is made up of the Antiochian Arab Orthodox Church and the British Orthodox Deanery.

[11] The nine Orthodox constituting the Eastern Churches (excluding the Latvian) were as given by Bishop Kallistos, Chair of the Orthodox Fellowship of St John the Baptist at the Orthodox Conference in Swanwick, August 2004. On this page "Churches" constitute both Parishes and Eucharistic Centres, the former holding the liturgy more than once a month, and the latter less frequently; the two groups are split almost evenly. "Priests" include Bishops (5 Greek, 2 Russian) and Deacons.

[12] All priests are unpaid, except two Greek Orthodox based in London. Bishops receive a stipend.

Table 8.9.1 ORIENTAL: Malankara Orthodox Syrian Church[3, 4]

	Membership	Churches	Priests
2000	110[2]	1[2]	1
2001	150[2]	1	1
2002	170[2]	1	1
2003	225	3	3
2005	250[2]	3	4
2010	450	5	5
2020	750	7	7

Table 8.9.2 ORIENTAL: Syrian Orthodox Church[3]

	Membership	Churches	Priests
2000	500[2]	2	2
2001	600[2]	2	2
2002	700[2]	2	2
2003	750	2	2
2005	800	2	2
2010	1,500	2	2
2020	3,000	2	3

Table 8.9.3 ORIENTAL: Coptic Orthodox Patriarchate[3, 5, 15]

	Members	Attendance	Congs	Priests
2000	494	815	5[1]	7
2001	510	865	5[1]	8
2002	530	900	5[1]	7
2003	532	907	5[1]	8
2005	550	920	7[1]	12
2010	700	1,000	10[1]	14
2020	1,000	1,400	12[1]	17

Table 8.9.4 ORIENTAL: British Orthodox Church[6]

	Membership	Churches	Priests[7]
2000	825	10	15
2001	835	11	15
2002	850	11	16
2003	865	11	15
2005[1]	900	12	18
2010[1]	975	13	18
2020[1]	1,125	15	21

Table 8.9.5 ORIENTAL: Armenian Orthodox Church[8]

	Membership	Churches	Priests
2000	10,090	3	4
2001	11,090	3	7
2002	12,100	3	6
2003	12,350	3	6
2005[3]	13,000	3	5
2010[1]	16,000	4	5
2020[1]	21,000	5	6

Table 8.9.6 ORIENTAL: Eritrean Orthodox Church[9]

	Membership	Churches	Priests
2000	250	2	1
2001	275	2	1
2002	300	2	1
2003	300	2	2
2005[3]	400	2	3
2010[1]	525	2	3
2020[1]	800	2	3

Table 8.9.7 OTHER: Orthodox Church in Wales

	Membership	Churches	Priests
2000	2,000	3	3
2001	2,000	3	3
2002	2,000	3	3
2003	2,000	3	3
2005[3]	2,000	3	3
2010[3]	2,100	5	5
2020[3]	2,500	8	8

Table 8.9.8 OTHER: Byelorussian Autocephalous Church

	Membership	Churches	Priests
2000	20	1	1
2001	20	1	1
2002	20	1	1
2003	14	1	1
2005[3]	7	0	1
2010[3]	0	0	0
2020[3]	0	0	0

Table 8.9.9 OTHER: Other Orthodox Churches[10]

	Membership	Churches	Priests
2000	3,335	26	38
2001	4,015	25	38
2002	5,045	25	40
2003	5,892	30	41
2005[1]	7,555	31	45
2010[1]	8,000	33	45
2020[1]	8,500	36	48

Table 8.9.10 Other Orthodox Churches

	Membership					Churches					Priests				
	2000	2001	2002	2003	2005[1]	2000	2001	2002	2003	2005[1]	2000	2001	2002	2003	2005[1]
Oriental: Ethiopian Orthodox Tewahido Church	300	250	250	250	250	3	2	2	2	2	5	4	4	4	4
Oriental: Coptic Orthodox Patriarchate, other Dioceses[11]	900	910	930	940	960	8	8	8	8	8	12	12	12	12	13
Other: Ukrainian Orthodox Church[12]	100	100	100	100	100	7	7	7	7	7	3	3	3	3	3
Other: Ancient Orthodox Church	130	130	130	132	135	2	2	2	2	2	1	1	1	1	1
Other: Assyrian Church of the East[13]	1,830	2,535	3,540	4,370	6,000	1	1	1	1	2	5	7	7	8	10
Other: Celtic Orthodox Church, British Eparchy[14]	75	90	95	100	110	5	5	5	10	10	12	11	13	13	14
TOTAL	3,335	4,015	5,045	5,892	7,555	26	25	25	30	31	38	38	40	41	45

8

[1] Estimate
[2] Revised figure
[3] Church's own estimate.
[4] Formerly listed as the Indian (Syrian) Church.
[5] Comprising the four Dioceses: a) Diocese of Birmingham; b) Diocese of Ireland, Scotland, North-East England and its affiliated territories; c) The British Orthodox Church which is listed separately; and d) the Churches directly under Pope Shenouda III. It includes one church in Co. Wicklow, Republic of Ireland.

[6] Part of the Coptic Orthodox Church, see Footnote 5.
[7] Includes full deacons.
[8] This is the longest established Orthodox Community in Britain.
[9] Began in 1996.
[10] As given in Table 8.8.10.
[11] Diocese of Birmingham (2 churches served by a bishop and 2 priests) and churches under Pope Shenouda III (6 churches and a theological college served by a bishop and 8 priests); see Footnote 5. Membership based on average size of other Oriental Orthodox churches, excluding the Armenians.

[12] The Patriarchate of Kiev in Great Britain and Ireland began in 1995, and is not in communion with any Orthodox Church.
[13] A Nestorian Church.
[14] All priests are unpaid.
[15] Full title: Coptic Orthodox Patriarchate: Diocese of Ireland, Scotland and North England.

Table 8.10.1
TOTAL Presbyterian Churches[4]

	Membership	Churches	Ministers
2000	992,880	5,140	2,638
2001	971,346	5,099	2,625
2002	948,140	5,036	2,589
2003	922,961	4,968	2,456
2005	876,970	4,827	2,386
2010	770,590	4,463	2,115
2020	576,310	4,073	1,636

Table 8.10.2
United Reformed Church[5]

	Membership[6]	Churches	Ministers
2000	92,787	1,753	750
2001[1]	90,314	1,745	749
2002[1]	87,732	1,719	742
2003[1]	84,963	1,698	660
2005[3]	79,950	1,660	620
2010[1]	68,000	1,560	490
2020[1]	46,200	1,390	250

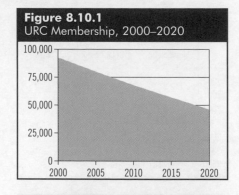

Figure 8.10.1
URC Membership, 2000–2020

Table 8.10.3
Presbyterian Church of Wales

	Membership	Churches	Ministers
2000	41,778	850	101
2001	39,805	832	97
2002	37,820	815	94
2003	36,100	775	84
2005[3]	32,600	700	78
2010[3]	25,200	540	58
2020[3]	15,000	450	40

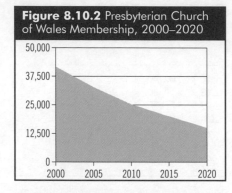

Figure 8.10.2 Presbyterian Church of Wales Membership, 2000–2020

Table 8.10.4 Evangelical Presbyterian Church in England and Wales

	Membership	Churches	Ministers
2000	170	7	6
2001[1]	185	8	6
2002[1]	200	8	6
2003[1]	220	8	6
2005[1]	240	8[2]	7[2]
2010[1]	300	8	7
2020[1]	400	8	7

Table 8.10.5
Church of Scotland[9]

	Membership	Churches	Ministers
2000	607,714	1,567	1,111
2001	590,824	1,555	1,100
2002	571,698	1,546	1,090
2003	553,248	1,546	1,052
2005[1]	517,000	1,530	1,020
2010[1]	432,800	1,495	928
2020[1]	275,700	1,426	757

Table 8.10.6
Free Church of Scotland

	Membership	Churches	Ministers
2000	13,600	181	77
2001	13,180[1]	176	77
2002[1]	12,760	172	73
2003[1]	12,150	167	77
2005[1]	11,500	162	82
2010[1]	9,500	160	82
2020[1]	6,000	155	80

Table 8.10.7
Free Church of Scotland (Continuing)[7]

	Membership	Churches	Ministers
2000	2,000	30	39
2001	2,002	30	39
2002[1]	2,000	32	39
2003	2,000	34	38
2005[3]	2,000	35	40
2010[1]	2,000	35	40
2020[1]	1,500	30	35

Table 8.10.8
Free Presbyterian Church of Scotland

	Membership	Churches	Ministers[8]
2000	4,100	51	15
2001	4,050	50	15
2002[3]	3,900	48	15
2003[3]	3,700	47	16
2005[1]	3,500	44	16
2010[1]	2,850	38	16
2020[1]	1,800	26	15

Table 8.10.9 Reformed Presbyterian Church of Scotland

	Membership	Churches	Ministers
2000	80	3	3
2001	75	3	3
2002	75	3	3
2003[1]	72	3	3
2005[3]	70	2	2
2010[1]	60	2	2
2020[1]	40	1	1

Table 8.10.10
United Free Church of Scotland

	Communicants	Churches	Ministers
2000	5,217	69	40
2001	5,117	68	38
2002	4,886	67	35
2003	4,618	66	33
2005[3]	4,120	63	29
2010[3]	3,100	55	23
2020[3]	2,000	40	18[1]

Table 8.10.11
Associated Presbyterian Churches

	Membership	Churches	Ministers
2000	1,200	20	10
2001	1,100	18	10
2002	1,000	16	8
2003	900	15	8
2005[3]	900	16	11
2010[3]	600	8	6
2020[1]	300	4	4

[1] Estimate
[2] Revised figure
[3] Church's own estimate
[4] Total of Tables 8.10.2–11 and 8.11.1–5.
[5] On the 1st of April 2000 the Congregational Union of Scotland merged with the URC. At the time of merger it had 5,588 members, 53 churches and 37 ministers.
[6] Figure is for communicant members only and excludes adherents.
[7] Separated from the Free Church of Scotland in Jan 2000.
[8] All male.
[9] See also Table 8.11.6.

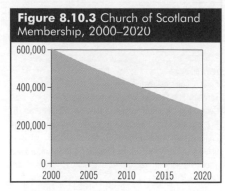

Figure 8.10.3 Church of Scotland Membership, 2000–2020

Table 8.11.1 Evangelical Presbyterian Church in Ireland

	Membership[4]	Churches	Ministers
2000	434	12	11
2001	430	12	11
2002	430	12[2]	10[2]
2003	440	12	10
2005[2]	440	12	10
2010[1]	450	12	10
2020[1]	470	12	10

Table 8.11.2 Free Presbyterian Church of Ulster

	Membership	Churches	Ministers
2000	16,200	75	70
2001	16,800	78	70
2002	17,100	78	72
2003[1]	16,000	78	75
2005[3]	15,000	78	75
2010[1]	14,000	78	70
2020[1]	11,000	78	55

Table 8.11.3 Non-subscribing Presbyterian Church of Ireland

	Membership	Churches[8]	Ministers
2000	3,561	34	14
2001	3,431	34	12
2002	3,529	33	12
2003[1]	3,550	33	13
2005[3]	3,600	33	14
2010[1]	3,630	33	14
2020[1]	3,700	33	14

Table 8.11.4 Presbyterian Church in Ireland (Northern Ireland)

	Community[5]	Membership[6]	Churches	Ministers
2000	347,557	202,000	452	365[2]
2001	348,742	202,000	454[2]	371[2]
2002	349,523	203,000	451[2]	363[2]
2003	350,305	203,000	450	354
2005[3]	351,868	204,000	447	355
2010[1]	355,775	206,000	400	340
2020[1]	362,362	210,000	380	320

Table 8.11.5 Reformed Presbyterian Church of Ireland

	Communicants[7]	Churches	Ministers
2000	2,039	36	26
2001	2,033	36	27
2002	2,010	36	27
2003	2,000	36	27
2005[3]	2,050	37	27
2010[3]	2,100	39	29
2020[3]	2,200	40	30

Table 8.11.6 Church of Scotland: Other Statistics

	The Guild[9]	Baptisms	
	Members	Adult	Infant
2000	42,939	540[2]	9,300[1]
2001	40,396	550[2]	9,170[1]
2002	38,802	540[1]	8,700[1]
2003	36,911	510[1]	8,100[1]
2005[1]	33,120	450	7,050[1]
2010[1]	24,300	310	4,900[1]

[1] Estimate
[2] Revised figure
[3] Church's own estimate
[4] Excludes adherents
[5] The Community figure is that given in the Northern Ireland Population Census. In 1971 the figure was 405,717; in 1981 339,818; in 1991 336,891, and in 2001 348,742. In 1991 the Presbyterian Church in Ireland was 20.95% of the population and in 2001 20.64% of the population. It is assumed that in 2011 the percentage will be 20.33% and in 2021 20.02%. The figures in 2010 and 2020 reflect these percentages of the population figures given in Table 4.3. The intermediate figures are taken pro rata to the decennial change.

[6] Active adult members taken as 58% of the Community figure.
[7] The number of *communicant* members which does not include adherents or covenant children.
[8] Including two in the Republic of Ireland.
[9] Also known as the Church of Scotland Guild since 1997, when it changed its name from the Women's Guild.

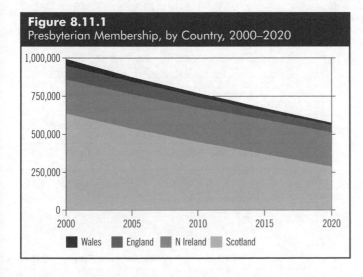

Figure 8.11.1 Presbyterian Membership, by Country, 2000–2020

Legend: ■ Wales ■ England ■ N Ireland ■ Scotland

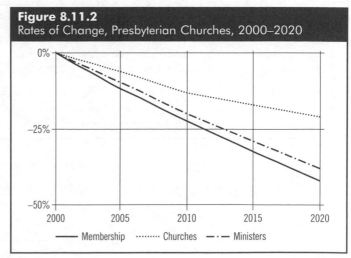

Figure 8.11.2 Rates of Change, Presbyterian Churches, 2000–2020

Legend: —— Membership ········ Churches — · — Ministers

Table 8.12.1
Size of Churches by Denomination — England 1989

Band: Size of Sunday congregation	Average size taken as	Church of England			Free Churches + Orthodox			Roman Catholic			Total: England		
		Churches %	No. of people	% of people*	Churches %	No. of people	% of people	Churches %	No. of people	% of people	Churches %	No. of people	% of people
1–10	5	3.2	2,620	0.2	1.7	1,565	0.1	1.0	191	0.0	2.0	4,376	0.1
11–25	12	15.0	29,471	2.3	6.9	15,243	0.9	1.0	459	0.0	9.4	45,173	1.0
26–50	30	23.4	114,938	9.1	22.7	125,372	7.3	1.0	1,147	0.1	20.8	241,457	5.5
51–100	55	25.1	226,029	17.9	27.1	274,401	16.0	1.6	3,365	0.2	23.8	503,795	11.6
101–150	110	14.9	268,353	21.2	21.3	431,346	25.2	7.0	29,445	2.2	17.2	729,144	16.8
151–200	165	9.6	259,348	20.5	11.2	340,217	19.8	12.8	80,763	5.9	10.8	680,328	15.7
201–300	220	6.8	244,940	19.3	4.5	182,259	10.6	14.3	120,303	8.8	6.9	547,502	12.6
301–400	330	1.5	81,046	6.4	2.4	145,807	8.5	13.7	172,883	12.7	3.2	399,736	9.2
401–500	440	0.3	21,612	1.7	1.2	97,205	5.7	10.4	174,986	12.8	1.7	293,803	6.8
500+	550	0.2	18,010	1.4	1.0	101,255	5.9	37.2	782,390	57.3	4.2	901,655	20.7
BASE (=100%) /TOTAL		16,373	1,266,367	100.0	18,410	1,714,670	100.0	3,824	1,365,932	100.0	38,607	4,346,969	100.0

Source: Prospects for the Nineties, Trends and Tables from the 1989 English Church Census, Peter Brierley, MARC Europe, London, 1991

Table 8.12.2
Size of Churches by Denomination — England 1998

Band: Size of Sunday congregation	Average size taken as	Church of England			Free Churches + Orthodox			Roman Catholic			Total: England		
		Churches %	No. of people	% of people*	Churches %	No. of people	% of people	Churches %	No. of people	% of people	Churches %	No. of people	% of people
1–10	5	7.8	6,350	0.6	3.0	2,650	0.2	1.0	189	0.0	4.8	9,189	0.2
11–25	12	21.7	42,398	4.3	13.7	29,041	1.7	2.1	950	0.1	18.0	72,389	2.0
26–50	30	25.4	124,061	12.7	18.5	98,041	5.8	6.7	7,580	0.7	19.7	229,682	6.2
51–100	55	23.6	211,328	21.6	27.8	270,098	15.9	9.7	20,118	2.0	24.0	501,544	13.5
101–150	110	11.0	197,000	20.1	13.9	270,098	15.9	10.8	44,799	4.3	11.1	511,897	13.8
151–200	165	4.6	123,572	12.6	9.1	265,240	15.6	12.4	77,155	7.5	7.1	465,967	12.5
201–300	220	3.5	125,364	12.8	7.0	272,041	16.0	14.5	120,295	11.6	6.6	517,700	13.9
301–400	330	1.5	80,593	8.2	3.9	227,349	13.4	11.0	136,887	13.2	3.4	444,829	12.0
401–500	440	0.6	42,982	4.4	2.0	155,452	9.2	7.5	124,443	12.0	1.9	322,877	8.7
500+	550	0.3	26,865	2.7	1.1	106,873	6.3	24.3	503,994	48.6	3.4	637,732	17.2
BASE (=100%) /TOTAL		16,281	980,513	100.0	17,665	1,696,883	100.0	3,771	1,036,410	100.0	37,717	3,713,806	100.0

Source: The Tide is Running Out, The Results of the 1998 English Church Attendance Survey, Peter Brierley, Christian Research, 2000

Table 8.12.3
Size of Churches by Denomination — England 2010

Band: Size of Sunday congregation	Average size taken as	Church of England			Free Churches + Orthodox			Roman Catholic			Total: England		
		Churches %	No. of people	% of people*	Churches %	No. of people	% of people	Churches %	No. of people	% of people	Churches %	No. of people	% of people
1–10	5	15.6	12,418	1.5	7.2	6,215	0.5	1.2	213	0.0	10.3	18,846	0.6
11–25	12	24.5	46,805	5.8	23.2	48,063	3.7	4.3	1,832	0.2	21.9	96,700	3.3
26–50	30	24.5	117,012	14.5	20.8	107,727	8.2	9.8	10,437	1.4	21.3	235,176	8.1
51–100	55	20.0	175,120	21.7	20.3	192,753	14.7	12.5	24,406	3.1	19.4	392,279	13.5
101–150	110	8.5	148,852	18.4	10.1	191,803	14.6	14.6	57,013	7.3	9.9	397,668	13.7
151–200	165	2.3	60,416	7.5	7.8	222,188	16.9	12.0	70,290	9.0	5.8	352,894	12.2
201–300	220	1.6	56,038	6.9	6.0	227,885	17.4	15.7	122,617	15.7	5.0	406,540	14.0
301–400	330	1.5	78,804	9.8	2.7	153,822	11.7	8.5	99,578	12.8	2.8	332,204	11.5
401–500	440	1.1	77,053	9.6	1.0	75,962	5.8	6.1	95,282	12.2	1.5	248,297	8.6
500+	550	0.4	35,024	4.3	0.9	85,457	6.5	15.3	298,733	38.3	2.1	419,214	14.5
BASE (=100%) /TOTAL		15,920	807,542	100.0	17,264	1,311,875	100.0	3,550	780,401	100.0	36,734	2,899,818	100.0

Source: Derived from the previous two tables

* Church of England figures are graphed in **Figure 12.13.2**

Table 8.12.4
Size of Churches by Denomination — Scotland 2002

Band: Size of Sunday congregation	Average size taken as	Church of Scotland			Smaller denominations			Roman Catholic			Total: Scotland		
		Churches %	No. of people	% of people	Churches %	No. of people	% of people	Churches %	No. of people	% of people	Churches %	No. of people	% of people
1–10	5	1.1	87	0.0	7.3	685	0.5	0.0	0	0.0	3.8	772	0.1
11–25	12	4.6	924	0.4	14.9	3,360	2.4	5.0	420	0.2	9.3	4,704	0.8
26–50	30	11.9	5,940	2.6	22.0	12,450	8.9	6.1	1,080	0.5	15.7	19,470	3.4
51–100	55	17.0	15,565	6.8	29.3	30,360	21.8	14.0	4,565	2.3	22.1	50,490	8.9
101–150	110	25.9	47,410	20.8	11.2	23,210	16.6	10.9	7,150	3.5	17.1	77,770	13.6
151–200	165	13.4	36,795	16.1	6.8	21,285	15.3	8.1	7,920	3.9	9.6	66,000	11.6
201–300	220	16.9	62,040	27.2	4.8	20,020	14.3	13.0	16,940	8.4	10.9	99,000	17.4
301–400	330	5.2	28,380	12.4	2.0	12,210	8.8	9.9	19,470	9.6	4.4	60,060	10.5
401–500	440	3.0	22,000	9.6	0.8	6,600	4.7	7.1	18,480	9.2	2.6	47,080	8.3
500+	550	1.0	9,350	4.1	0.9	9,350	6.7	25.9	126,085	62.4	4.5	144,785	25.4
BASE (=100%) /TOTAL		1,666	228,491	100.0	1,884	139,530	100.0	594	202,110	100.0	4,144	570,131	100.0

Source: Turning the Tide: The Challenge Ahead, The Results of the 2002 Scottish Church Census, Peter Brierley, Christian Research and the Church of Scotland, 2002

8

Free Church Statistics

See notes and definitions on Page 0.6

Sources: Individual denominations and previous editions of *Religious Trends*, private surveys and books

Table 9.2.1 Brethren Churches in Scotland by Size, 2002

Avge size	Band	Churches %	Number of attenders	% of attenders
5	1–10	4.8	51	0.3
12	11–25	16.7	421	2.3
30	26–50	19.4	1,222	6.7
55	51–100	28.1	3,246	17.8
110	101–150	8.9	2,056	11.3
165	151–200	6.0	2,079	11.4
220	201–300	10.2	4,712	25.9
330	301–400	4.5	3,119	17.2
440	401+	1.4	1,294	7.1
TOTAL (= 100%)		**210**	**18,200**	**100.0**

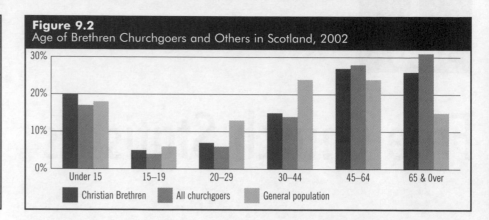

Figure 9.2
Age of Brethren Churchgoers and Others in Scotland, 2002

Legend: Christian Brethren — All churchgoers — General population

The third Scottish Church Census took place in 2002, and naturally the congregations approached included the Christian Brethren. The full results of the Census were broken down in seven groups of denominations, the Christian Brethren being included within the Independent group. Overall figures for the Independent group show that while they declined 6% between 1994 and 2002, they did not decline as much as the 18% for churchgoing in Scotland as a whole.

The Christian Brethren attendance however grew between 1994 and 2002, a fairly modest growth of 6% from 17,090 in 1994 to 18,200 in 2002. The Christian Brethren group in 2002 includes: 210 Assemblies of the Open Brethren; 9 Reunited Brethren Assemblies; and 43 Plymouth Brethren No 4 Assemblies. 97% of Scottish Christian Brethren Assemblies are Mainstream Evangelical.

Total Brethren **membership** in Scotland in 2002 was given as 16,926 in *Religious Trends* No 4, made up of 15,540 or 92% for the Open Brethren, and 1,386 or 8% for the other two groups combined. The average membership therefore is 74 and 27 respectively; the Open Brethren Assemblies are almost 3 times the size of the others. Christian Brethren church **attendance** averaged 87 per Assembly, but this number was distributed as shown in **Table 9.2.1**. This Table shows:

- Two-fifths, 41%, of Assemblies have under 50 in attendance most Sundays (averaging 20 each),
- A further two-fifths, 37%, have between 51 and 150 (averaging 68 each), and
- The remaining fifth, 22%, have over 150 (averaging 240 each).

It is the presence of this small number of much larger Assemblies, about 45, that is important. If trends elsewhere in Britain are true of these also, many are likely to be growing because of the range of activities they offer, as well as quality teaching. These churches are more likely to have a full-time worker leading them, and to have a clear vision of what they want to become.

Age of Attenders

The age of those attending Scottish Brethren Assemblies is shown in **Figure 9.2**, which

Table 9.2.2
Proportions Attending Brethren Assemblies by Age and Gender, 2002

Age group	Brethren Assemblies			All Scottish churchgoers			General population		
	Male %	Female %	Total %	Male %	Female %	Total %	Male %	Female %	Total %
Under 12	7	9	**16**	6	7	**13**	7	7	**14**
12–14	2	2	**4**	2	2	**4**	2	2	**4**
15–19	2	3	**5**	2	2	**4**	3	3	**6**
20–29	3	4	**7**	3	3	**6**	7	6	**13**
30–44	7	8	**15**	5	9	**14**	12	12	**24**
45–64	12	15	**27**	11	17	**28**	12	12	**24**
65/65+	11	15	**26**	11	20	**31**	6	9	**15**
All ages	**44**	**56**	**100**	**40**	**60**	**100**	**48**	**52**	**100**

shows that they are able to attract a slightly above average proportion of children. This might be one reason for their growth. Over two-fifths, 44%, of Brethren attenders are men compared with 40% among churchgoers as a whole, and 48% in the general population. The percentages behind **Figure 9.2** are given in **Table 9.2.2**, based on a total of 4,894 Brethren replies.

By comparison with the other Brethren in Scotland (who, as a group, replied poorly to the Census), the Open Brethren have a far smaller proportion of attenders over 65. In total, 61% of those attending the other Brethren groups were over 65; they had no-one attending aged 15 to 19; and only 11% were aged 20 to 44.

Leadership

The 2002 Census asked about the number and age of church leadership. Brethren Assemblies had on average 5 Elders, very close to other churches outside the Church of Scotland and Roman Catholic.

Brethren Assemblies had a slightly higher proportion of Elders under 65 compared to other Scottish churches, except that they had fewer under 35. This correlates with the fact that they are growing overall.

Substantial

The Christian Brethren are a substantial group of churchgoers in Scotland, almost as many in 2002 as the number of Baptists (18,200 to 24,800) and virtually identical to the numbers attending the Scottish Episcopal Church

(18,900). Like the Baptists, but unlike the Episcopals, the Brethren **have grown** over the last years of the 20th century.

One of their characteristics is that they have **an above average proportion of children** under 12, and a matching good proportion of those aged 30 to 44, of parental age. One important feature in their midweek youth work is the ability to attract those outside the church to their clubs. The Brethren also have a higher proportion of their children attending on Sunday than among Scottish churches generally.

Apart from the older group being parents, they are also more likely than their age-group in other denominations to be Elders in **leadership**. While there are many small Brethren Assemblies in Scotland, there are a small number of much more substantial ones. One of the key Brethren traits emerges from this brief analysis – their **commitment to the local church**. This is seen in their above average proportion attending twice every Sunday, and the higher numbers coming to a Bible Study each week.

Sources: Turning the Tide: The Challenge Ahead, and *Religious Trends* No 4, 2003/2004, both Christian Research, London, and special detailed denominational analyses.

The Christian Brethren Research Fellowship (CBRF), true to its name, undertook a number of surveys among the Open Brethren churches in Britain. The first of these was in 1966 with 75 churches (or Assemblies as the Brethren call their congregations), which was followed by a study of 249 churches in 1978. CBRF has now become Partnership, which has undertaken surveys in 1988 and 1998. The results of this latter study were published in 2003 by Paternoster under the title *Whatever happened to the Brethren?*, authored by researcher Graham Brown.

One key overall finding was that the Open Brethren churches appear to be moving into two broad groups – there are many fairly small churches which in the main are getting smaller, and there is a group of larger churches, fairly few in number, but which are growing. This experience, in general terms, is true of other denominations as well, such as the Church of England, for example.

The smaller churches "retain the basic approaches and style... characteristic of the Brethren movement for over a century", whereas the medium-size and larger churches "character and style has changed decisively over the period, while maintaining a commitment to certain key ecclesiological insights of the movement." A more detailed comparison of the features by size is given in **Table 9.3.1**.

How far did churches grow or decline in the 1990s? The answer varies by size, as shown in **Figure 9.3.1**. Half of the largest churches (70 or more) grew, whereas half (58%) of the middle-sized churches (between 30 and 70) remained stable, and two-thirds (68%) of the smallest churches (under 30) declined.

One feature in **Table 9.3.1** is the age of those attending. This is given in more detail in **Figure 9.3.2**. It is clear that the larger churches have more younger people, a feature common to larger churches. The average age of those attending these churches is 44, whereas it is 50 for those in medium sized churches and 57 for those in the smallest churches.

While size is a key feature of Brethren churches, basic numbers are also. The number of Open Brethren churches has reduced significantly between 1990 and 1998 as **Table 9.3.2** indicates. It will be seen that the numbers in Scotland are not the same as in **Table 9.2.1**; two different studies have yielded similar but not identical results.

It may also be seen from **Table 9.3.2** that although overall in Great Britain numbers of churches and attendance has dropped, the average size of church has increased in each country during the 1990s.

Source: Whatever happened to the Brethren?, Graham Brown, Partnership, Tiverton, Devon, and Paternoster Press, Carlisle, Cumbria, 2003.

Table 9.3.1
Open Brethren Churches by Size, 1998

Feature	Larger Churches (over 70 members)	Smaller Churches (under 30 members)
Average members/attenders	116	17
Change 1996–1998	Increase +5%	Decrease –3%
Key reason for change	Transfer growth	Death of members
Age profile	Close to GB population	Markedly skewed towards elderly
Conversions 1996–98	10	2
Baptisms 1996–98	8	1
Allows women to be audible in services?	Yes	No
Offers wide range of activities?	Yes	Tries but cannot resource
Centres Sunday worship around	A Sunday event	Breaking of Bread
Full- or part-time resident worker?	Yes (69%)	No, and none planned

Figure 9.3.1
Growth by Size of Brethren Churches, 1990–1998

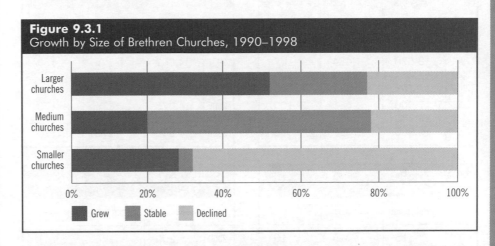

Legend: Grew | Stable | Declined

Figure 9.3.2
Age by Size of Brethren Churches, 1990–1998

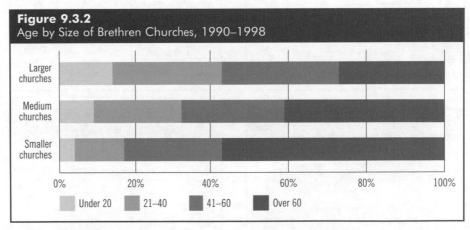

Legend: Under 20 | 21–40 | 41–60 | Over 60

Table 9.3.2
Churches and Attendance in Brethren Churches, 1990 and 1998

Year	England			Wales			Scotland			Great Britain		
	Churches	Attendance	Average	Churches	Attendance	Average	Churches	Attendance	Average	Churches	Attendance	Average
1990	977	48,850	50	102	3,978	39	277	16,066	58	1,356	68,894	51
1998	796	44,748	56	82	4,035	49	228	16,872	74	1,106	65,655	59
% change	–17	–8	+12	–20	+1	+26	–18	+5	+28	–18	–5	+16

9

Table 9.4.1
TOTAL Baptist Churches[4]

	Membership	Churches	Ministers
2000	206,416	3,475	2,714
2001	204,387	3,467	2,827
2002	202,872	3,433	2,871
2003	201,875	3,433	2,846
2005	199,171	3,512	2,906
2010	188,040	3,519	2,923
2020	170,750	3,491	2,919

Table 9.4.2
Baptist Union of Great Britain[5,8]

	Union Membership	Membership[6]	Churches	Ministers	Baptisms[6]	Children up to 12[7]	Young People (13–19)[7]
2000	142,636	135,759	2,122	1,773	4,087	105,749	35,594
2001	141,515	134,815	2,125	1,883	4,027	104,928	35,435
2002	141,300	134,631	2,107	1,925	4,318	96,295	34,755
2003[3]	141,000	134,290	2,110	1,925	4,120	92,380	34,380
2005[3]	139,200	132,575	2,200	2,000	4,070	83,550[1]	33,575[1]
2010[3]	132,100	125,810	2,250	2,050	3,860	62,890[1]	31,580[1]
2020[3]	121,000	115,240	2,300	2,100	3,535	25,000[1]	27,650[1]

Table 9.4.3
Baptist Union of Wales[9]

	Membership	Churches	Ministers
2000	19,228	494	109
2001	18,578	484	107
2002	17,774	473	106
2003	17,209	471	100
2005[3]	17,000	465	100
2010[1]	14,380	440	95
2020[1]	10,300	390	75

Table 9.4.4
Baptist Union of Scotland

	Membership[10]	Churches	Ministers
2000	14,384	176	158
2001	14,002	176	159
2002	13,991	174	170
2003	14,042	176	170
2005[3]	14,075	176	170
2010[3]	14,200	176	170
2020[3]	14,500	176	170

Table 9.4.5 Association of Baptist Churches in Ireland

	Membership[11]	Churches	Ministers
2000	7,969	109	85
2001	7,971	111	89
2002	7,576	111	87
2003	7,594	111	79
2005[1]	7,245	108	75
2010[1]	6,535	108	67
2020[1]	5,160	105	52

Table 9.4.6
Old Baptist Union

	Membership	Churches	Ministers
2000	515	15	10
2001	561	15	10
2002	605	15	10
2003	650	15	10
2005[3]	700	15	9
2010[3]	800	16	12
2020[3]	1,000	17	17

Table 9.4.7
Gospel Standard Strict Baptist

	Membership	Churches	Ministers
2000	5,200	126	141
2001	5,100	124	140
2002	5,000	122	138
2003	4,800	121	130
2005[3]	4,400	120	120
2010[1]	3,700	108	105
2020[1]	2,700	92	85

Table 9.4.8
Grace Baptist Churches[12]

	Membership[13]	Churches[14,15]	Ministers
2000[1]	7,061[2]	209[2]	190[2]
2001[1]	7,170[2]	209[2]	192
2002[1]	7,170[2]	208[2]	191
2003[1]	7,230	208	189
2005	7,340	208	191
2010[1]	7,600	208	191
2020[1]	8,150	208	200

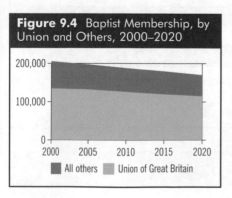

Figure 9.4 Baptist Membership, by Union and Others, 2000–2020

■ All others ■ Union of Great Britain

Table 9.4.9
Biblical Ministries Worldwide

	Membership	Churches	Ministers[16]
2000	100	3	8
2001	90	3	8
2002	75	3	5
2003	60	2	5
2005[1]	36	2	5
2010[1]	15	1	3
2020[1]	0	0	0

Table 9.4.10
Other Baptist Churches[17]

	Membership[18]	Churches	Ministers
2000	16,200	221	240
2001	16,100	220	239
2002	16,050	220	239
2003	16,000	219	238
2005[1]	15,800	218	236
2010[1]	15,000	212	230
2020[1]	13,700	203	220

[1] Estimate

[2] Revised figure

[3] Church's own estimate

[4] Total of Tables 9.4.2–9.4.10.

[5] The Baptist Union of Great Britain (BUGB) includes members in Wales and Scotland who are also members of the Baptist Unions of Wales or Scotland. The total "Union Membership" is given in the column with that heading while the column headed "Membership" gives the BUGB membership excluding the double-counting with the other Unions. It is this figure which is used for the membership totals.

[6] Estimates for 2003 onwards are pro rata to the BUGB figures given in "Union Membership" averaged across 2000–2002, producing 95.24% for members, and 2.92% for baptisms.

[7] Estimates for 2003 onwards estimated by dampened linear progression (or straight line fit).

[8] The figures also take into account a merger with the Independent Methodist Church in 2005, who had 92 churches and 2,195 mem-

bers in 2003 (see Table 9.8.6). For 4 years their churches will continue to be in membership with both denominations, after which, in 2009 they will have to choose between the two.

[9] Includes Baptist Union of Wales in England.

[10] Not including adherents, who would add another 50% to these figures.

[11] As the Baptist Union of Ireland includes the whole of Ireland, these figures are for the Northern Ireland proportion (taken as 94.4% of the Union Membership).

[12] Figures include the 3 Associations of Grace Baptist Churches: South East, East Anglia, and East Midlands; and a remnant of what used to be known as the Northern Fellowship; and the Grace Baptist Assembly.

[13] The Association of Grace Baptist Church East Anglia reported a falling number of baptised members, but an increasing number of attenders as follows: 1,366 members in 2002 (1,382 in 2000 and 1,377 in 2001) but attendance was 1,912 in 2002, 40% more. In 2003 the number of members had again fallen, to 1,343, but attendance was

2,015, 50% more. The Association of Grace Baptist Churches South East on the other hand had a rising membership: 1,893 in 2000, 1,932 in 2001, 1,936 in 2002 and 1,963 in 2003. The total figures are constructed from these two Associations assuming that the East Midlands figures are similar to those for the South East, likewise the combined total of the Northern Fellowship and Grace Baptist Assembly.

[14] Based on information from www.grace.org.uk for the South East and East Anglia Associations, though being identified either here or in the Directory is optional. These are grossed up as described in the previous footnote.

[15] Includes 3 churches in the Isle of Man and 2 in the Channel Islands. There are also 5 churches in Ireland not counted here.

[16] Full-time missionary workers.

[17] These figures include non-Baptist Union churches, some of which are or were listed in the Baptist Union of Great Britain (BUGB) Directory. All are estimated.

[18] Taken as pro rata to the BUGB 2000–2020.

Table 9.5.1
TOTAL Brethren Assemblies[4]

	Membership	Assembly Halls	Full-time Workers
2000	76,073	1,354	212
2001	75,187	1,341	210
2002	74,307	1,327	203
2003	73,532	1,314	203
2005	72,150	1,285	205
2010	68,485	1,199	215
2020	59,525	956	224

Table 9.5.2
Christian Brethren (Open)[13]

	Membership	Assembly Halls	Full-time Workers
2000	73,023[2]	1,198[2]	203[1]
2001	72,497[2]	1,188[2]	202[1]
2002	71,977[2]	1,177	196
2003	71,462	1,167	198[1]
2005[2]	70,500	1,145	200
2010[1]	67,100	1,075	210
2020[1]	58,800	890	220

Table 9.5.3 Church of God (International) Brethren[5]

	Membership	Assembly Halls	Full-time Workers
2000	300[6]	0	–
2001[1]	290	0	–
2002[1]	280	0	–
2003[1]	270	0	–
2005	250	0	–
2010[1]	210	0	–
2020[1]	150	0	–

Table 9.5.4
Plymouth Brethren[7,8]

	Membership	Assembly Halls	Full-time Workers
2000[1]	750[2]	50[2]	–
2001[1]	700[2]	49[2]	–
2002[1]	650[2]	48[2]	–
2003[3]	600	47	–
2005[3]	500	45	–
2010[1]	375	34	–
2020[1]	175	16	–

Table 9.5.5
Kelly Brethren[9]

	Membership	Assembly Halls	Full-time Workers
2000[1]	2,000[2]	106[2]	9
2001[1]	1,700[2]	104[2]	8
2002[1]	1,400[2]	102[2]	7
2003	1,200	100	5
2005[3]	900	95	5
2010[3]	800	90	5
2020[1]	400	50	4

Figure 9.5.1 Christian Brethren Membership, 2000–2020

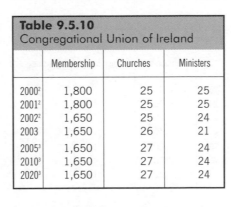

■ All others   ■ Open Brethren

Table 9.5.6
TOTAL Congregational Churches[10]

	Membership	Churches	Ministers
2000	57,742	1,021	322
2001	55,887	1,004	316
2002	53,431	992	312
2003	50,984	964	307
2005	46,900	922	298
2010	36,950	821	281
2020	18,450	634	248

Table 9.5.7
Congregational Federation

	Membership	Churches	Ministers
2000	11,432	312	78
2001	11,110	310	74
2002	10,883	313	73
2003	10,234	297	73
2005[1]	9,600	285	70
2010[1]	7,900	250	62
2020[1]	4,600	185	47

Table 9.5.8 Evangelical Fellowship of Congregational Churches

	Membership	Churches	Ministers
2000	5,400[1]	125	90
2001	5,300[1]	125	90
2002	5,200[1]	123	90
2003	5,000	124	90
2005[3]	4,750[1]	120	85
2010[3]	4,200[1]	120	85
2020[3]	3,000[1]	120	85

Table 9.5.9
Union of Welsh Independents[11]

	Membership[12]	Churches[12]	Ministers[12]
2000	34,885	514	119
2001	33,452	499	117
2002[1]	31,473	486	115
2003[1]	29,900	472	113
2005[1]	26,700	445	109
2010[1]	19,200	379	100
2020[1]	5,700	257	82

Table 9.5.10
Congregational Union of Ireland

	Membership	Churches	Ministers
2000[2]	1,800	25	25
2001[2]	1,800	25	25
2002[2]	1,650	25	24
2003	1,650	26	21
2005[3]	1,650	27	24
2010[3]	1,650	27	24
2020[3]	1,650	27	24

Figure 9.5.2 Congregational Churches Membership, 2000–2020

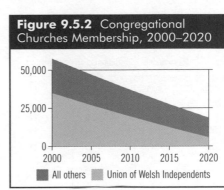

■ All others   ■ Union of Welsh Independents

9

---

[1] Estimate

[2] Revised figure

[3] Church's own estimate

[4] Total of Tables 9.5.2 to 9.5.5

[5] Since 1996 have closed all Assembly Halls and only rent one occasionally as needed. Used to include in Scotland the Church of God (Needed Truth) Assemblies and the Church of God (Green Pastures) or Vernalites.

[6] The "active" addresses out of a mailing list of 2,000. Outreach now undertaken by literature only (bi-monthly magazine *New Horizons*).

[7] Used to be called "Plymouth Brethren No 4", the "No 4" from a classification made in the American 1926 and 1936 Census of Religious Bodies. No 1 was the original American contingent. No 2 reflects the Open Brethren and the Church of God Brethren (an exclusive group of the Open Brethren). No 3 is the Tunbridge Wells Brethren, who were strong in the United States and Canada. No 4 reflects those Exclusive Brethren who initially followed the teachings of Raven and Taylor, who were strong in Australia and New Zealand as well as Great Britain, and were served by either the Bible and Gospel Trust, the Dunbar Trust, the Kingston Bible Trust or the Stone Publishing Trust. No 5 included some of the Kelly Brethren. Nos 3, 5, 6 and 7 include those following Lowe (formerly strong in Europe) and Stuart, but now united into the Reunited Brethren, and were strong in Egypt, Europe, India, South America and Zaire.

[8] Also incorporates the Renton Brethren, and the remainder of the Scottish Taylorites, the '59s and Shield's Road groups of Brethren.

[9] Incorporating the Glanton, Lowe, Reunited, Stuart, and Tunbridge Wells Brethren, of which there were 4 groups in the UK in 2003, served by Chapter Two. More details are in the footnotes on Page 254 of the 1996/1997 edition of the *UK Christian Handbook*.

[10] Total of Tables 9.5.7 to 9.5.10. The Scottish Congregational Church joined the United Reformed Church on the 1st April 2000; its figures are therefore included with the URC in Table 8.9.2.

[11] Or Welsh Congregational Union, or Annibynwyr.

[12] These figures exclude the following number of members from 45 associated churches with 10 pastors (assumed the same number to 2020), which are included however in Table 9.5.6: 4,225 in 2000 and 2005; 4,000 in 2010 and 3,500 in 2020.

[13] See Pages 9.2 and 9.3 for greater detail.

Table 9.6.1
TOTAL Independent Churches[4]

	Membership	Churches	Ministers
2000	180,418	3,184	1,258
2001	178,656	3,164	1,257
2002	176,012	3,126	1,248
2003	176,332	3,083	1,255
2005	171,993	3,015	1,255
2010	158,850	2,809	1,265
2020	140,535	2,369	1,287

Table 9.6.2
FIEC (Fellowship of Independent Evangelical Churches)

	Membership	Churches	Ministers
2000	29,937	463	336
2001	30,734	473	330
2002	31,224	464	324
2003	34,600	467	336
2005[3]	35,800	470	334
2010[3]	36,000	450	325
2020[1]	43,500	438	317

Table 9.6.3
UEC (Union of Evangelical Churches)

	Membership	Churches	Ministers
2000	409	19	24
2001	377	19	25
2002	412	19	26
2003	399	18	26
2005[3]	373	17	28
2010[3]	325	15	24
2020[3]	300	13	20

Table 9.6.4
Fellowship of Churches of Christ

	Membership	Churches	Ministers
2000	922	40	34
2001	1,011	40	34
2002	960	37	30
2003	950	36	26
2005[3]	980	37	28
2010[3]	1,050	42	36
2020[3]	1,210	50	48

Table 9.6.5
Non-Instrumental Churches of Christ[6]

	Membership	Churches	Ministers
2000	2,225	74	40
2001[1]	2,170	74	40
2002[1]	2,140	74	40
2003[1]	2,120	73	40
2005[1]	2,080	72	39
2010[1]	1,900	70	37
2020[1]	1,600	60	30

Table 9.6.6
CMA (Christian and Missionary Alliance)

	Membership	Churches	Ministers
2000[1]	350	7	4
2001[1]	350	7	4
2002	350	7	4
2003[1]	350	7	4
2005[1]	350	7	4
2010[1]	350	7	4
2020[1]	350	7	4

Table 9.6.7
Bruderhof Communities in the UK[7]

	Membership	Churches	Ministers
2000	500	2	7
2001	500	2	7
2002	500	2	7
2003	500	2	7
2005[3]	525	3	8
2010[1]	550	3	8
2020[1]	600	4	9

Table 9.6.8
London City Mission[8]

	Membership	Churches	Ministers
2000	950	28	28
2001[1]	950	28	28
2002[1]	900	28	28
2003[1]	900	28	28
2005[1]	800	28	28
2010[1]	700	27	27
2020[1]	500	25	25

Table 9.6.9
New Apostolic Church (UK)[9]

	Membership	Churches	Ministers
2000[1]	2,330	32	86
2001[1]	2,425	30	96
2002	2,538	29	107
2003[1]	2,567	28	109
2005[1]	2,625	28	113
2010[1]	2,950	28	133
2020[1]	3,750	30	180

Table 9.6.10
Universal Fellowship of Metropolitan Community Churches[10]

	Membership	Churches	Ministers
2000[1]	500	14	15
2001[1]	520	14	18
2002[1]	540	14	18
2003[1]	560	14	18
2005[1]	600	15	19
2010[1]	700	16	20
2020[1]	850	17	22

Table 9.6.11
Liberal Catholic Church; Province of GB and Ireland

	Membership	Churches	Ministers[11]
2000	1,000	11	21
2001	1,000	12	22
2002	1,100	12	21
2003	1,200	11	24
2005[3]	1,000	11	22
2010[3]	800	11	24
2020[3]	1,000	12	26

Table 9.6.12
Liberal Catholic Church (Grail Community)

	Membership	Churches[12]	Ministers[11]
2000	70	5	6
2001	70	5	6
2002	70	5	6
2003	70	5	6
2005[1]	80	5	6
2010[1]	90	5	6
2020[1]	100[13]	5	6

Table 9.6.13
Other Independent Churches[14]

	Membership	Churches	Ministers
2000	7,410	114	120
2001	7,475	115	121
2002	7,540	116	122
2003	7,600	116	122
2005	7,730	115	123
2010	8,000	115	125
2020	8,800	118	128

[1] Estimate
[2] Revised figure
[3] Church's own estimate
[4] Total of Tables 9.5.1, 9.5.6 and Tables 9.6.2 to 9.6.13.
[5] Includes adherents aged 16 and over.
[6] Includes groups called "Two by Two", "Cooneyites" and "People of the Way".
[7] The Community started in Germany in 1920, coming to England in 1937 to flee the Nazis. Choosing unity rather than internment of their German members, they then fled to Paraguay. They now have 7 communities in the US, 2 in the UK and 2 in Australia.
[8] These are preaching centres, whose attenders are encouraged to attend worship at other local churches.
[9] Emerged from the Catholic Apostolic Church in 1861. Their worldwide membership in 1990 was 6 million across 40,000 congregations in 170 countries.

[10] Part of the European & North Sea District which covers Scandinavia, Germany and the UK; one of 13 global district.
[11] All unpaid.
[12] These are "centres" not church buildings.
[13] They wrote "a modest growth is anticipated" after their 2003 figure.
[14] Other Independent Churches includes: (1) The Reformed Liberal Catholic Church which started on 23rd May 1999 breaking all ties with the Liberal Catholic Church; it affirms "Christ as Lord and Saviour in His death and resurrection in accordance with spiritual truth"; (2) The Catholic Apostolic Church; (3) The Gnostic Church of Sofia, an independent Trinitarian church in the Catholic tradition (previously included with "Other Churches"); (4) The Liberal Catholic Church (Theosophia Synod), another breakaway group from the Liberal Catholic Church (previously included with "Other Churches"); and (5) Other Independent Churches which are all estimated, with membership proportional to population.

The Independent Churches are made up of 4 broad strands: the Christian Brethren, the Congregational Churches (including the Union of Welsh Independents), the Fellowship of Independent Evangelical Churches (FIEC) and all the Others. **Figure 9.7.1** shows their respective strengths.

The Congregational Churches are declining fast in membership terms (an average decline of –5.5% per annum between 2000 and 2020); the Brethren are declining slowly (–1.2% per annum); the Others are growing slowly (+0.7% per annum), and the FIEC are growing rather faster (+1.9%) per annum. As a consequence of these changes the FIEC moves from being 17% of the British Independent sector in 2000 to 30% by 2020, if present trends continue.

In 2003 the FIEC surveyed its churches, and because of the increasing importance of the FIEC, this page summarises some of the findings of this survey.

Figure 9.7.1 Membership of the Main Groups of Independent Churches, 2000–2020

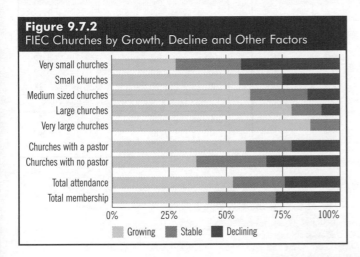

■ All others ■ FIEC ■ The Congregational Churches ■ The Christian Brethren

Figure 9.7.2
FIEC Churches by Growth, Decline and Other Factors

Very small churches
Small churches
Medium sized churches
Large churches
Very large churches

Churches with a pastor
Churches with no pastor

Total attendance
Total membership

0% 25% 50% 75% 100%

■ Growing ■ Stable ■ Declining

The Report shows that the larger the church the greater the likelihood of its growing. In this respect, FIEC match the experience of other churches, both within the Independent sector (like the Brethren, see **Figure 9.3.1**) and outside it (like the Anglican church, see **Figure 8.4.2**). More than four-fifths of the larger churches grew, against only 28% of the very small churches and 56% of the small churches. Overall in the five years 1998–2003, more than half of the FIEC churches had experienced growth in their Sunday morning service.

It is also apparent that attendance growth has outstripped membership growth, and that churches with a pastor are more likely to have grown than those without one.

Putting these trends together shows that FIEC churches are, on average, getting larger. **Table 9.6.2** shows that in 2000 the average membership of an FIEC church was 65 members; if present trends continue by 2010 this is likely to become 80, and by 2020 to be almost 100 members per church.

Almost two-thirds, 65%, of the churches said that effective evangelism was a key current challenge, and almost a third, 29%, backed this by specifying the need to have more young people or reaching the younger generation.

Two-fifths of the churches, 41%, the same proportion as nationally, had no meetings for young people at all, on Sunday or during the week, and one in six, 16%, had none for children (aged 4 to 11). Those that did have a meeting tended to meet both during the week and on Sundays (especially for children) unless the meeting was aimed specifically at those outside the church, as **Figure 9.7.3** indicates.

Figure 9.7.3
Activities for Younger People, Sunday and/or Weekday

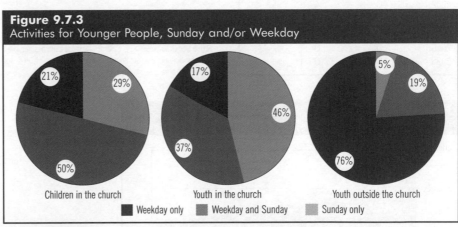

Children in the church   Youth in the church   Youth outside the church
■ Weekday only   ■ Weekday and Sunday   ■ Sunday only

Figure 9.7.4 FIEC Church Commitments: Average per Church, 1998–2003

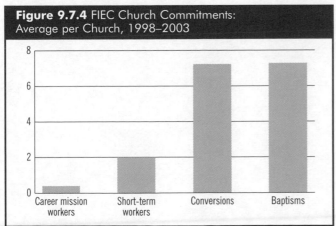

Career mission workers | Short-term workers | Conversions | Baptisms

One FIEC church in six, 18%, had sent someone abroad as a career mission worker in the period 1998–2003, half of whom (47%) had sent one person, a quarter (29%) had sent two, and the remainder more than two. The average was 2.4 for these churches, or 0.4 per church across the whole of the FIEC. However short-term workers averaged 2.0 per church.

While a fifth, 20%, of the churches had seen no conversions in the last 5 years, two-fifths, 37%, had seen between 1 and 5, 15% had seen between 6 and 9, 14% between 10 and 19, and 14% 20 or more, an average of 7 per church.

A fifth also, 22%, of the churches had seen no baptisms in the previous 5 years, but a third, 35%, had seen between 1 and 5, 13% had seen between 6 and 9, 19% between 10 and 19, and 11% 20 or more, an average also of 7 per church. These figures are illustrated in **Figure 9.7.4.**

Source: Report of FIEC Churches Consultation, Andrew Phelps, Autumn 2003, FIEC, May 2004, gensec@fiec.org.uk

9

Table 9.8.1
TOTAL Methodist Churches[4]

	Membership	Churches	Ministers
2000	353,562	6,552	2,452
2001	345,427	6,764	2,451
2002	336,155	6,537	2,345
2003	324,023	6,433	2,320
2005	303,973	6,139	2,186
2010	274,850	5,635	2,045
2020	221,620	4,785	1,797

Table 9.8.2
Methodist Church in Great Britain

	Membership	Churches	Ministers
2000	331,560	6,161	2,204
2001	323,821	6,378	2,204
2002	314,530	6,150	2,092
2003	302,440	6,048	2,079
2005[3]	284,300	5,850	2,040
2010[3]	255,000	5,350	1,903
2020[3]	200,000	4,500	1,655

Table 9.8.3
Methodist Church in Ireland[5]

	Membership	Community Roll[6]	Churches	Ministers
2000	16,191	42,118[2]	157	105
2001	16,101	41,815	157	105
2002	16,170	41,729	160	105
2003	16,069	40,788	160	103
2005[3]	16,000	40,500	158	100
2010[3]	15,800	40,000	155	95
2020[3]	15,500	39,000	155	90

Table 9.8.4
Wesleyan Reform Union

	Membership	Churches	Ministers
2000	2,146	112	16
2001	2,012	110	15
2002	2,003	109	17
2003	1,947	108	14
2005[1]	1,823	106	13
2010[1]	1,550	100	10
2020[1]	1,120	90	7

Table 9.8.5
Free Methodist Church in the UK

	Membership	Churches	Ministers
2000	892	20	20
2001	869	20	20
2002	928	22	30
2003	1,162	22	30
2005[3]	1,700	24	32
2010[3]	2,500	30	37
2020[3]	5,000	40	45

Table 9.8.6
Independent Methodist Church[7]

	Membership	Churches	Ministers[8]
2000	2,473	96	101
2001	2,354	94	102
2002	2,284	92	97
2003	2,195	92	91
See Footnote 8, Page 9.4 re merger with Baptist Union			
2005[3]	2,058	89	86
2010[3]	1,700	80	80
2020[1]	1,200	65	63

Table 9.8.7
Other Methodist Churches[9]

	Membership	Churches	Ministers
2000[1]	300	6	6
2001[1]	270	5	5
2002[1]	240	4	4
2003[1]	210	3	3
2005[1]	150	1	1
2010[1]	0	0	0
2020[1]	0	0	0

[1] Estimate
[2] Revised figure
[3] Church's own estimate
[4] Total of Tables 9.8.2–9.8.7.
[5] Figures are for Northern Ireland.
[6] Figures taken as 16 yrs old and over.
[7] See also Table 9.4.2; figures for 2005 and beyond are not included in the Methodist total figures as already included in Table 9.4.1.
[8] All unpaid.
[9] Since Methodist figures were first compiled in 1976 for what became the *UK Christian Handbook* allowance has been made for other Methodist churches, usually taken as 6 churches with 6 ministers with a total of 300 members. Evidence for these churches has failed to materialise and they are therefore assumed no longer to exist and are brought to zero as shown in this Table.

Figure 9.8
Methodist Church Membership, 2000–2020

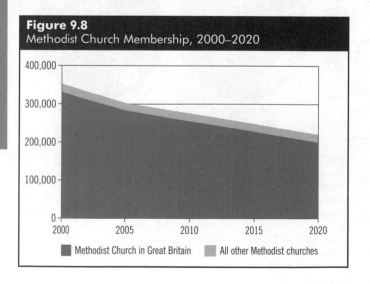

Legend: ■ Methodist Church in Great Britain   ■ All other Methodist churches

Table 9.9.1 — TOTAL New Churches[4]

	Attendance	Congregations	Leaders
2000	133,662	1,799	2,048
2001	137,219	1,836	2,089
2002	143,019	1,922	2,161
2003	147,698	1,972	2,241
2005	153,900	2,000	2,331
2010	163,290	2,112	2,494
2020	186,350	2,293	2,762

Table 9.9.2 — Abundant Life Ministries[6]

	Attendance	Congregations	Leaders
2000	700	1	3
2001	1,000[2]	1	5
2002	1,500[2]	2[2]	6
2003	2,000	2[1]	10[1]
2005[1]	2,500	3	12
2010[1]	3,000	5	15
2020[1]	4,000	8	20

Table 9.9.3 — Association of Vineyard Churches

	Attendance	Congregations	Leaders
2000	8,085	75	181
2001	8,895	77[2]	183
2002	9,700	80[2]	185
2003	10,000[1]	83	196[1]
2005[1]	11,600	89	204
2010[1]	14,000	97	217
2020[1]	19,000	111	238

Table 9.9.4 — Bristol Celebration

	Attendance	Congregations	Leaders
2000			
2001	As churches affiliated with		
2002	the Pioneer Partnership,		
2003	their numbers are included		
2005	within Table 9.10.6		
2010			
2020			

Table 9.9.5 — Christian Outreach Centre[7]

	Attendance	Congregations	Leaders
2000	1,050	14	26
2001	1,200	16	34
2002	1,530	21	48
2003	1,756	21	53[1]
2005[3]	2,000	22	63[1]
2010[3]	3,500	30	90
2020[3]	8,000	50	137

Table 9.9.6 — c.net (Cornerstone)

	Attendance	Congregations	Leaders
2000	5,100	41	49
2001	5,850	46	52
2002	6,000[2]	50[2]	60[2]
2003	6,250	52	65
2005[1]	6,750	61	78
2010[1]	8,000	76	102
2020[1]	10,000	108	157

Table 9.9.7 — Covenant Ministries/Together[8]

	Attendance	Congregations	Leaders
2000	2,964	13[9]	16
2001[1]	2,510	11	14
2002	1,940	10[9]	12
2003[1]	1,900	9	11
2005[1]	900	5	6
2010[1]	800	5	5
2020[1]	400	2	2

Table 9.9.8 — Ground Level

	Attendance	Congregations	Leaders
2000	2,908	26	64
2001[1]	4,000	41	70
2002	6,620	66	77
2003	6,700	67	79[1]
2005[1]	7,000	69	80
2010[1]	9,000	80	90
2020[1]	11,000	95	100

Table 9.9.9 — Ichthus Christian Fellowship[10, 11]

	Attendance	Congregations	Leaders
2000[2]	1,214	27	27
2001[2]	1,224	27	27
2002	1,248	27	27
2003	1,181	27	27
2005[1]	620	15	15
2010[1]	590	13	13
2020[1]	500	10	10

Table 9.9.10 — Ichthus Christian Fellowship[12]

	Attendance	Congregations	Leaders
2000[1]	2,444	12	47
2001[1]	2,605	12	49
2002[1]	2,766	18	52
2003[1]	2,620	18	52
2005[1]	2,300	16	45
2010[1]	1,750	16	45
2020[1]	1,150	10	25

Table 9.9.11 — Jesus Fellowship & Multiply Network

	Attendance	Congregations	Leaders
2000	3,975	48	149
2001	4,105	49	152
2002	4,240	50	154
2003	4,360	49	177
2005[3]	4,600	52	190
2010[3]	5,500	60	250
2020[3]	6,500	70	300

Table 9.9.12 — Kingdom Faith Church

	Attendance	Congregations	Leaders
2000	575[2]	6[2]	12
2001[1]	585[2]	6[2]	12
2002	600[2]	7[2]	13
2003	606	9	16
2005[1]	625[2]	9	16
2010[1]	650	9	16
2020[1]	700	9	16

9

[1] Estimate

[2] Revised figure

[3] Church's own estimate

[4] Total of Tables 9.9.2–9.9.12 and Tables 9.10.1–9.10.12

[5] Formerly called "House Churches".

[6] Till 1998 was part of Covenant Ministries.

[7] Also 30 Churches in the Ukraine, 1 in Slovenia, in France, 2 in Germany, 1 in Denmark and 2 in Bulgaria as of June 2004

[8] In 2004 Covenant Ministries International changed, with its member churches choosing to affiliate themselves with Lifelink International, Ministries Without Borders, or remaining with the reformed Together.

[9] Based on relevant editions of the Body Book.

[10] London based Ichthus Linked Churches only.

[11] There is a discontinuity between the figures for 2003 and 2005. In 2004 "all Ichthus congregations (were) released to choose how they wanted to move forward and with whom they would choose to associate as congregations" following the resignation of a number of senior leaders within the Ichthus London Leadership Team. Roger and Faith Forster continue to lead Ichthus Christian Fellowship, a movement known for its church planting, social action initiatives in central and south-east London, and for being the prime movers of March for Jesus. In addition to these London Linked churches and those given in Table 9.9.10, there were a further 130 congregations worldwide linked to Ichthus with 50 full-time mission workers in 2004. This information is taken from an article in Christianity + Renewal, June 2004.

[12] English Ichthus Linked Churches outside the London area, all estimated but based on respective editions of the Body Book. For 2005 and beyond it is assumed most of these congregations will continue, though will probably move to other networks. Since that linking cannot be known, their total numbers are estimated here.

Table 9.10.1
Kings Church, Aldershot[10]

	Attendance	Congregations	Leaders
2000	550	5	9
2001	550	5	8
2002	550	5	8
2003	550	5	8
2005[3]	1,000	5	8
2010[3]	1,500	5	8
2020[3]	2,000	5	8

Table 9.10.2
Lifeline Community Church

	Attendance	Congregations	Leaders
2000	310[2]	2	3
2001	270[2]	1[2]	2
2002	270	1[2]	2
2003[1]	270	1	2
2005[1]	300	1	2
2010[1]	300	1	2
2020[1]	300	1	2

Table 9.10.3
Lifelink International[11]

	Attendance	Congregations	Leaders
2000	1,359[4]	9[4]	17
2001	1,400	9	18
2002	1,450	9	20
2003	1,518	9[5]	22
2005[1]	1,630	10	25
2010[1]	1,800	11	28
2020[1]	2,000	12	32

Table 9.10.4
Ministries Without Borders[7,11]

	Attendance	Congregations	Leaders
2000[1]	2,230	8	18
2001[1]	2,420	10	22
2002[1]	2,600	12	26
2003[6]	2,782	15	32
2005[1]	3,000	17	37
2010[1]	3,300	19	40
2020[1]	3,700	24	50

Table 9.10.5
Newfrontiers

	Attendance	Congregations	Leaders
2000	20,750	141	359
2001	21,050	143	364
2002	22,225	174[1]	383
2003	24,000	206	390
2005	26,200	225	425
2010[1]	30,000	300	465
2020[1]	36,000	400	540

Table 9.10.6
Pioneer Partnership[9]

	Attendance	Congregations	Leaders
2000[4]	9,501	77	143
2001[1]	9,040	75	140
2002[1]	8,600	72	135
2003[8]	8,105	70	130
2005	7,200	66	120
2010	6,200	56	100
2020	5,300	48	80

Table 9.10.7
Plumbline Ministries

	Attendance	Congregations	Leaders
2000	690	8	17
2001	775	8	17
2002	950	7	20
2003	1,300	7	24
2005[3]	1,500	9	30
2010[1]	1,800	10	33
2020[1]	2,200	13	38

Table 9.10.8
Proclaimers International

	Attendance	Congregations	Leaders
2000	150	1	1
2001	150	1	1
2002	150	1	1
2003	160	1	1
2005[3]	350	1	3
2010[3]	700	1	5
2020[3]	1,500	1	12

Table 9.10.9
Rainbow Churches

	Attendance	Congregations	Leaders
2000	75	1	2
2001	80	1	1
2002	90	1	1
2003	90	1	1
2005[1]	105	1	1
2010[3]	150	1	1
2020[1]	300	1	1

Table 9.10.10
Salt & Light Ministries

	Attendance	Congregations	Leaders
2000	7,000	62	90
2001	6,200	64	93[2]
2002	5,400	66	96[2]
2003	5,700[1]	67	100
2005[3]	6,300[1]	69	105
2010[1]	6,700	73	114
2020[1]	7,000	79	130

Table 9.10.11
Other New Churches[12]

	Attendance	Congregations	Leaders
2000[1]	2,032	22	15
2001[1]	2,110	23	15
2002[1]	2,190	23	15
2003[1]	2,250	23	15
2005[1]	2,420	25	16
2010[1]	2,850	28	17
2020[1]	4,000	36	20

Table 9.10.12
Other Non-denominational Churches[13]

	Attendance	Congregations	Leaders
2000[1]	60,000	1,200	800
2001[1]	61,200	1,210	810
2002[1]	62,400	1,220	820
2003[1]	63,600	1,230	830
2005[1]	65,000	1,230	850
2010[1]	62,000	1,220	850
2020[1]	60,000	1,200	850

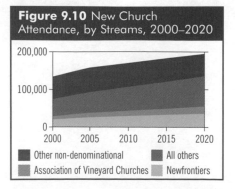

Figure 9.10 New Church Attendance, by Streams, 2000–2020

Legend: Other non-denominational; All others; Association of Vineyard Churches; Newfrontiers

[1] Estimate
[2] Revised figure
[3] Church's own estimate
[4] From the 8th edition of the *Body Book*.
[5] The Lifelink International website www.lifelink-international.org.uk/ Group indicates a further 7 linked churches.
[6] Number of churches taken from website www.ministrieswithoutborders.com/uk_churches, membership and leadership estimated from the 9th edition of the *Body Book*, Pioneer and Christian Research, 2003.
[7] Figures other than for 2003 taken pro rata to Lifelink International.
[8] Number of churches and attendance taken from the 10th edition of the *Body Book*, Pioneer and Christian Research, 2004.
[9] Also 5 International Partnership churches in Europe, and 5 International Associate churches: 2 in Europe, 2 in the United States

and 1 in Lesotho.
[10] Formerly Antioch Ministries
[11] See Footnote 8 on Page 9.9.
[12] Estimated from successive editions of the *Body Book*.
[13] These are all estimated figures of churches which follow New Church theology or practice but have not joined one of the various streams.

The tenth edition of the *Body Book* was published in 2004 giving details of 876 churches willing to be classified as charismatic. There were 89 fewer churches than in the previous edition two years ago, described in *Religious Trends* No 3, Page 5.16. The churches range in size from the 10 people who attend the Life Changing Ministries International Fellowship in Mold, Flintshire, Wales to the 2,250 at St Thomas Church, Crookes, Sheffield.

Overview

Total attendance for these 876 churches in 2004 (including estimates for the 10 which did not give figures) was 169,200 adults and children, an average of 189 each, a 15% increase on the 165 in 2000, suggesting many of those listed have grown in the last 4 years. The increase is the average of a 16% increase in adults and a 10% increase in children.

The large majority, 91%, of the churches are located in England, representing a sixth, 17%, of all the charismatic churches in England, but 31% of total attendance, indicating that while some of the smaller congregations are listed, generally it is the larger charismatic churches which are included.

Of the 169,200 attenders, 43,000 or 26% are children, down from the 27% in 2002, but much higher than the overall UK average of 19%. This points to one reason why larger charismatic churches are growing – they put a huge emphasis on their children's and youth work. With young people leaving the church in many places, this emphasis is of crucial importance, not just for the charismatic churches but for the future of the church generally.

Size of church

Table 9.11.1 and **Figure 9.11** shows the number of churches in different size bands for 2004 and 1988, the first year for which such figures can be compiled. The "median" figure is that size of church above which 50% of churches are larger and 50% of churches are smaller. It means that in 1988 half the churches had a total attendance of 91 or below.

As shown with other denominations in this edition of *Religious Trends*, **Figure 9.11** shows a general growth in the proportions of charismatic churches which are 400 or more strong, and a decline in the proportion with 100 or less. The proportion between 100 and 200 has not changed markedly between 1988 and 2004. This changing pattern is different from churches in the UK generally, where the proportion with under 100 in attendance has increased, and the proportion between 100 and 300 sharply decreased (as in **Figure 12.13.2**).

What makes churches grow? In two words – leadership and vision. Good teaching, a warm welcome, a wide range of youth work, involvement with the local community and many relevant activities all help, but nothing substitutes for quality, strategic, risk-taking leadership, and the vision which inspires such.

The different streams and denominations

Table 9.11.2 shows that across all groups of churches the percentage of children in the total congregation has gone down (in each case by 1%). This can only be because more adults than children are now attending. Does this signify that it is not just the non-charismatic churches which are experiencing problems in keeping children coming to church, even from those with churchgoing parents?

The average size of charismatic churches has increased some 15% between 2000 and 2004, whereas the common experience of most UK churches is one of decline. More than a quarter of the 2004 total attendance, 27%, of the New Church streams listed here is due to the strength of just one stream – Newfrontiers, almost half of whose churches have a Sunday attendance of 200 or more, whereas Pioneer specialises in smaller churches, only 8 of its churches being 200 or over.

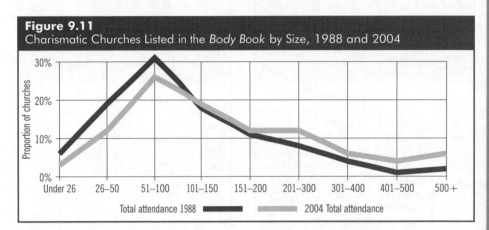

Figure 9.11
Charismatic Churches Listed in the *Body Book* by Size, 1988 and 2004

Total attendance 1988 ——— 2004 Total attendance ———

Table 9.11.1
Proportions of Charismatic Churches by Size, 1988 and 2004

Year	25 or under %	26–50 %	51–100 %	101–150 %	151–200 %	201–300 %	301–400 %	401–500 %	Over 500 %	Median
1988	6	19	31	18	11	8	4	1	2	91
2004	3	12	26	19	12	12	6	4	6	124

Table 9.11.2
Sunday Attendance and Number of Churches by Stream, 2000 and 2004

New Church Stream	Sunday Church Attendance TOTAL 2000	2004	% children 2000 %	2004 %	Average per church 2000	2004	Total churches 2000	2004
Barnabas	244	257	41	27	81	86	3	3
Bristol Celebration	2,264	1,380	30	30	755	460	3	3
Christian Growth International	440	521	24	25	147	130	3	4
Christian Outreach Centre	911	805	20	20	152	268	6	3
c.net (Cornerstone)	5,553	5,954	28	27	154	175	36	34
Covenant Ministries[1]	2,976	910	24	29	229	182	13	5
Ministries without Borders[2]	n/a	2,094	n/a	25	n/a	209	n/a	10
Ground Level	2,908	3,432	24	23	112	123	26	28
Ichthus	4,517	3,212	31	30	122	134	37	24
King's Church, Aldershot	1,169	1,837	31	30	106	167	11	11
Kingdom Faith Ministries	575	606	31	33	96	67	6	9
Lifelink International	1,359	1,518	30	34	151	169	9	9
Multiply Network	2,565	2,717	25	24	135	118	19	23
Newfrontiers	23,511	22,774	29	27	196	198	120	115
Partners in Harvest	1,450	1,150	21	27	483	383	3	3
Pioneer	9,501	8,105	29	28	123	116	77	70
Plumbline	1,068	1,158	23	23	119	165	9	7
Salt and Light	8,324	5,261	31	28	189	239	44	22
Vineyard Association	1,956	2,057	24	24	217	257	9	8
Others/Newly listed	12,925	20,144	34	26	89	183	145	110
TOTAL New Churches	84,216	85,892	28	27	145	171	579	501
Denominational Churches	69,277	66,496	25	24	203	236	342	282
Independent Churches	15,754	12,999	25	27	154	140	102	93
Grand TOTAL	169,247	165,387	27	26	165	189	1,023	876

[1] Including Together [2] Formerly part of Covenant Ministries

9

Table 9.12.1
TOTAL Pentecostal Churches[4]

	Membership	Congregations	Ministers
2000	226,413	2,348	3,356
2001	238,591	2,374	3,425
2002	258,257	2,395	3,511
2003	269,094	2,413	3,996
2005	288,183	2,570	4,419
2010	327,524	2,846	5,287
2020	405,800	3,249	6,691

Table 9.12.2
Apostolic Church

	Membership	Congregations	Ministers[5]
2000	5,302	110	88
2001	4,960	110	82
2002	4,909	103	82
2003	5,171	103	91
2005[3]	5,300	108	100
2010[1]	5,800	112	114
2020[1]	6,800	122	130

Table 9.12.3
Apostolic Faith Church

	Membership	Congregations	Ministers
2000[1]	330	4	7
2001[1]	354	4	7
2002[1]	378	5	8
2003[1]	400	5	9
2005[1]	440	5	10
2010[1]	510	6	11
2020[1]	650	8	15

Table 9.12.4
Assemblies of God

	Membership	Congregations	Ministers
2000	61,599	630	676
2001	62,862	628	648
2002	65,000	625	620
2003	65,000	638	1,008
2005[3]	68,000[1]	660	1,150
2010[3]	72,000[1]	685	1,400
2020[3]	79,000[1]	700	1,700

Table 9.12.5
Church of God of Prophecy

	Membership	Congregations	Ministers
2000	4,560	84	428
2001[1]	4,510	82	427
2002[1]	4,464	82	427
2003[1]	4,394	81	427
2005[3]	4,324	80	426
2010[1]	4,200	80	425
2020[1]	4,000	78	420

Table 9.12.6
Elim Pentecostal Church

	Membership	Congregations	Ministers
2000	51,020	490	595
2001	52,500	496	596[2]
2002	54,000	502	598[2]
2003	55,000	510	600
2005[3]	58,470	527	630
2010[1]	62,700	563	670
2020[1]	70,000	605	720

Table 9.12.7 Foursquare Gospel Church of Great Britain

	Membership	Congregations	Ministers
2000	810	13	9
2001	900	14	9
2002	1,000	15	11
2003	1,500	17	20
2005[3]	2,000	25	25
2010[3]	4,500	50	75
2020[3]	7,000	100	150

Table 9.12.8
Life-Changing Ministries[6]

	Membership	Congregations	Ministers
2000	120	5	3
2001	130	6	4
2002	140	6	5
2003	220	7	6
2005[3]	280	8	7
2010[3]	500	15	20
2020[1]	800	20	25

Table 9.12.9
New Testament Church of God

	Membership	Congregations	Ministers
2000	19,528	108	275
2001	19,915	118	275
2002	20,615	118	280
2003	21,440	118	290
2005[3]	22,512	120	302
2010[3]	28,137	125	320
2020[3]	42,197	135	370

Table 9.12.10
Peniel Church

	Membership	Congregations	Ministers
2000	700	1	9
2001	725	1	9
2002	750	1	9
2003	750	1	9
2005[1]	800	1	9
2010[1]	900	1	10
2020[1]	1,100	1	12

Table 9.12.11
Struthers Memorial Churches

	Membership	Congregations	Ministers
2000	438	15	15[1]
2001	458	15	15[1]
2002	421	15	15[1]
2003	484	13	13[1]
2005	579[3]	16[1]	16[1]
2010	700[3]	17[1]	17[1]
2020	856[3]	19[1]	19[1]

Table 9.12.12 United Pentecostal Church of Great Britain[8]

	Membership	Congregations	Ministers
2000[2]	2,200	35	40
2001[2]	2,280	36	42
2002[2]	2,360	38	43
2003	2,441	39	44
2005[3]	3,500	56	72
2010[3]	6,000	150	160
2020[3]	12,000	260	300

[1] Estimate
[2] Revised figure
[3] Church's own estimate
[4] Total of Tables 9.12.2 to 9.12.14 and Tables 9.16.1, 2 and 3.
[5] Including unpaid ministers of which there were 51 in 2000.
[6] Began in 1991.
[7] Ministers are unpaid; all are estimated.
[8] A Oneness Apostolic Church.
[9] All estimated; includes independent Pentecostal churches which are not African or Caribbean.
[10] From Table 9.13.

Table 9.12.13
Other Pentecostal Churches[9]

	Membership	Congregations	Ministers
2000[1]	500[2]	6	4
2001[1]	550[2]	6	4
2002[1]	600[2]	6	4
2003[1]	600	7	5
2005[1]	600	8	6
2010[1]	700	9	7
2020[1]	800	10	8

Table 9.12.14
TOTAL African and Caribbean[10]

	Membership	Congregations	Ministers
2000	42,063	462	656
2001	43,218	467	720
2002	45,703	480	769
2003	47,682	475	789
2005	53,222	526	899
2010[1]	60,282	562	1,065
2020[1]	73,337	625	1,400

There are many African and Caribbean Churches in the UK. On **Pages 9.13–17** they are separated into four groups:
1) African and Caribbean Churches with more than one congregation which are listed in **Table 9.13;**
2) Oneness Apostolic African and Caribbean Churches which are listed in **Table 9.17.3** (though the United Pentecostal Church in **Table 9.12.12** is also Oneness Apostolic);

3) Holiness Churches which are listed in **Table 9.17.4**; and
4) African and Caribbean Churches with just one congregation in 2003 (largely a new listing for *Religious Trends*) which are listed in **Tables 9.14** and **9.15.**

The first three groups have data shown for the years 2000, 2001, 2002, 2003 (estimated where necessary) and 2005 (always estimated).

The totals from these Tables are given respectively in **Tables 9.12.14, 9.17.1** and **9.17.2** where combined estimates for the years 2010 and 2020 are made. The totals for the last group are given in **Table 9.17.5** where all remaining data is estimated. These summary Tables are then included in the overall Total Pentecostal Table given in **Table 9.12.1.**

Table 9.13 Pentecostal Churches: African and Caribbean Churches

	Attendance					Congregations					Ministers				
	2000	2001	2002	2003	2005	2000	2001	2002	2003	2005	2000	2001	2002	2003	2005
Aladura International Church	750	750	750	800	850[3]	3	3	3	3	3[3]	0	0	0	0	1[3]
Assemblies of the World	120	135	160	200	235[3]	1	1	1	1[1]	2[3]	5	5	5	5	5[1]
Beneficial Veracious Christ Church	1,000	1,000	1,000	620	860[1]	6	6	6	3	3[3]	12	12	12	8	11[3]
Bethany Church of God Faith Temple	47	47	48	48	53[3]	2	2	2	2	2[3]	4	4	4	4	5[3]
Born Again Christ Healing Church	160	190[1]	225[1]	260	320[1]	2	2	2	2	2[3]	5	5	5	5	5[3]
Brethren in Christ Church UK	65	95[1]	123[1]	152	205[3]	1	2	3	3	4[3]	1	2	3	3	4[3]
Cherubim and Seraphim Church Council	5,000	5,200[2]	5,300[2]	5,400[1]	5,500[2]	30	32[1]	34[1]	35[1]	37[1]	22	24[1]	26[1]	27[1]	30[1]
Christ Apostolic Church Mount Bethel	800	650[2]	700[2]	400[1]	450[2]	10	8	8	4	4[2]	9	8	8	4[1]	4[1]
Christ Embassy	200[1]	500[1]	800[1]	1,500	1,860[3]	1[1]	2[1]	3[1]	5	14[3]	1[1]	2[1]	3[1]	5	14[3]
Church of God Ground of Truth	50	48[1]	46[1]	44[1]	40[1]	2	2[1]	2[1]	2[1]	2[1]	5	5[1]	5[1]	5[1]	5[1]
Church of God Reformation Movement	160	150[1]	145[1]	140[1]	120[1]	4	4[1]	4[1]	4[1]	4[1]	4	4[1]	4[1]	4[1]	4[1]
Church of the Lord (Brotherhood)	47	48[1]	49[1]	50	60[3]	2	2	2	2	3[3]	1	1	1	1	1[3]
Deeper Christian Life Ministry	1,000	1,000	1,100	1,300	1,500[3]	16	16	16	16	16[3]	17	17	17	17	17[3]
Full Gospel Revival Centre	150	160[2]	180[2]	260	310[3]	1[2]	1[2]	1[2]	1	1[3]	2	2	3[2]	3	3[3]
Gospel Faith Mission International	460	600[2]	760[2]	925	1,100[1]	4	4	4	4	4[1]	7	11[2]	15[2]	20	25[1]
Healing Church of God in Christ	60	59[1]	58[1]	57[1]	55[1]	2	2[1]	2[1]	2[1]	2[1]	3	3[1]	3[1]	3[1]	3[1]
The Latter-Rain Outpouring Revival	290	295[1]	300[1]	305[1]	315[1]	9	9[1]	9[1]	9[1]	9[1]	10	10[1]	10[1]	10[1]	10[1]
Miracle Church of God in Christ	81	85[2]	90[2]	130	250[3]	4	4[2]	3	3	4[3]	4	4[2]	4[2]	4	6[3]
New Covenant Church	1,350	1,500	1,650	1,700[1]	1,800[1]	20	22	23	24[1]	25[1]	34[4]	51[4]	57[4]	60[1]	70[1]
New Testament Assembly (Pentecostal)	2,200	2,200[1]	2,200[1]	2,200[1]	2,200[1]	16	16[1]	16[1]	16[1]	16[1]	45[1]	45[1]	45[1]	48[1]	50[2]
Pentecostal Assembly of Mount Calvary	50	55[2]	60[2]	65[1]	75[3]	4	4	4	4	5[3]	5	5	6[2]	7	8[3]
People's Christian Fellowship	120	120	120	130	200[3]	1	1	1	1	2[3]	2	2	2	2	2[3]
Progressive National Baptist Convention	1,375	1,375	1,375	1,375	1,800[3]	9[2]	10[1]	11[1]	12	12[3]	11	12[1]	13[1]	14	14[3]
Shiloh Pentecostal Church	500	500[2]	550[2]	600	700[3]	6	7[2]	7[2]	7	8[3]	6	7[2]	8[2]	8	8[3]
Triumphant Church of God in Christ	65	66[1]	67[1]	68[1]	70[1]	2[1]	2[1]	2[1]	2[1]	2[1]	4	4[1]	4[1]	4[1]	4[1]
Universal Prayer Ministries	800	850[1]	900[1]	925[1]	1,000[1]	3[1]	3[1]	3[1]	3[1]	3[1]	13	13[1]	14[1]	14[1]	15[1]
Vision International Ministries	500	200[2]	150[2]	70	90[3]	4	1[2]	1[2]	1	1[3]	7[2]	4[2]	3[2]	2	3[3]
Other Denominations[5]	11,652	11,972	12,660	13,208	14,744	111	113	116	115	127	131	144	154	158	180
Other African & Caribbean Churches[6]	13,011	13,368	14,137	14,750	16,460	184	186	191	189	209	286	314	335	344	392
TOTAL (Taken to Table 9.12.14)	**42,063**	**43,218**	**45,703**	**47,682**	**53,222**	**462**	**467**	**480**	**475**	**526**	**656**	**720**	**769**	**789**	**899**

[1] Estimate
[2] Revised figures.
[3] Church's own estimate
[4] Including 9 full-time ministers.
[5] Ten denominations were unable to provide complete information. These are cumulated together in this line; all figures are for 2003 unless otherwise stated. They are the Bethel United Church of Jesus Christ (Apostolic) which had 42 congregations with 6,000 members in 2002, Calvary Church of God in Christ with 4 congregations, Celestial Church of Christ with 35 congregations, Christ Apostolic Church of Great Britain with 11 congregations, Church of God World Fellowship with 7 congregations, Church of God World Mission with 3 congregations, Church of the Lord (Aladura) with 5 congregations, Forward in Faith Ministries International (the Zimbabwe Assemblies of God Africa Church in the UK), Holy Fire Revival Ministries with 2 congregations, and Liberty Ministries International with 2 congregations and 4 ministers.
[6] There are very large numbers of African and Caribbean churches, and it is not possible to count them all. Some known from previous editions of *Religious Trends* have not been traced for this edition. An attempt has been made to list many single congregations in **Tables 9.14** and **9.15** but inevitably this will not be complete. As an estimate for these missing churches, we have repeated here the figures in **Table 9.17.5** as the best likely estimate for these other churches, since this is based on an actual count. In effect we assume that there are as many churches *not* listed in **Tables 9.14** and **9.15** as are!

All the churches on these pages have, as far as is known, just one, single, congregation. Data is taken as, or estimated for, the year 2003.

The basic list of churches is taken from the *Black Majority Churches UK Directory 2003/2004*, African and Caribbean Evangelical Alliance and Churches Together in Britain and Ireland, 2003, but has been augmented from others known to Christian Research.

Table 9.14
Sole-Congregation African and Caribbean Pentecostal Churches

	Location	Began (UK)	Attendance	Ministers		Location	Began (UK)	Attendance	Ministers
Abundant Life Christian Fellowship	London	~	~	1[1]	Exousia Christian Fellowship	London	~	~	1
Abundant Life Christian Ministries	London	~	75	4	Faith Evangelistic Ministries	London	~	~	1
Action Chapel International					Faith Growth Christian Ministries	London	~	~	1
(Christian Action Faith Ministries)	London	~	75	1	Faith Miracle Centre	Chiswick	1999	125	4
Afro-Caribbean Apostolic Church of God	London	~	40[1]	1	Faith Restoration Outreach Ministry	Tottenham	~	40[1]	2
All Nations Christian Centre	London	~	75	2	Faith Tabernacle Church of God	London	~	~	1[1]
All Saints Pentecostal Assembly	London[1]	~	65	5	Faithful Ministries	Essex	~	~	1[1]
All Souls Trinity Church	London	~	75	2	Faithful International Christian Centre	London	1996	~	3
Alpha Apostolic Church	London	~	40[1]	2	First Born Church of the Living God	Birmingh'm	~	~	1
Anointed Saviour's Church International	London	~	~	1	Forever Word of God Ministries	London	2000	75	1
Anointed Word Ministries	London	~	~	1	Freedom's Ark	London	1993	~	1
Apostolic Life Ministry	London	1999	~	3	Full Gospel Pentecostal Church	London	~	~	1
Balm of Gilead Christian Ministries Intnl	Barking	~	~	1	Full Gospel Revival Centre	Nottingham	~	~	1
Baptist Pentecostal Church of God	Birmingh'm	1970	40[1]	1	Full Truth Gospel Fellowship	London	~	~	1
Bible Path Christian Ministries	London	1995	40[1]	3	Gethsemane Pentecostal Church	Croydon	1995	~	3
Bible Study Network Christian Centre	London	1996	75	4	Gilbert Deya Ministries	London	~	~	1[1]
Birmingham Victory United Centre	Birmingh'm	1999	75	2	Global Ministries for Christ	Middlesex	~	~	1
Bread of Life Christian Centre	Wembley	2000	40[1]	1	Global Revival Christian Centre	London[3]	2000	75	3
Bread of Life Ministries	London	1993	250	2	Global Vision Ministries	Slough	1998	75	10
Bread of Life Ministry, Hackney	London	~	~	1[1]	Glorious Christ Christian Ministries Intnl	London	~	40[1]	1
Brook of Life Ministries International	Hayes	~	~	1[1]	Glory House Ministries	London	1993	300	11
Built on the Rock International Ministries	London	1978	225	25	God is Able Ministries International	London	~	~	1[1]
Calvary Believers Ministry	London	1990	125	3	God is Grace Ministries	Croydon	~	~	1
Christ Above All Gospel Church	London	1990	250	3	God Worshippers Ministries	London	~	~	1[1]
Christ Disciple Faith Ministries	London	1997	75	1	God's Endtime Mission	London	~	~	1[1]
Christ Disciples Mission International	London	~	~	1[1]	God's Vineyard Church	Nottingham	~	~	1
Christ's Ambassador Mission	London	~	~	1	Good Samaritan Outreach Ministry	London	~	~	1
Christ King Pentecostal Church	Barking	2000	75	1	Gospel Light Church of God	London	~	~	1
Church of God Worldwide Mission	Reading	~	200	2	Gospel Tabernacle Assembly	London[1]	~	40[1]	1[1]
Church of the First Born	London[1]	~	~	1	Grace Centre Church International	London	~	40[1]	1
Church of Universal Prayer Fellowship	London	~	~	1	Grace Church	London	~	~	1
Citizenship in Christ Fellowship	London	~	~	1	Grace Impact Church	London	~	~	1
Communion Chapel	London	~	~	1	Grace Outreach Church	London	1995	225	6
Crown of Life International Ministries	Mitcham	2002	40[1]	1	Grace Temple Ministries International	London	~	~	1
Destiny House (New Hope International					Greater Grace Ministries	London	~	40[1]	1
Christian Centre)	London	1999	175	6	Guiding Light Pentecostal Church	London	~	~	1[1]
Divine Grace Ministries International	London	2000	~	3	Harmony Christian Ministries	London	~	~	1[1]
Divine Pentecostal Church	London	~	~	1	Harvest Chapel International	London	2001	75	1
Divine Redeemers Church	London	1986	40[1]	1	Harvest Christian Church International	London	2001	40[1]	1
Dominion Centre (Impartation Network)	Reading	2002	75	1	Harvestime Evangelistic Ministries	London	1999	75	5
Dynamic Gospel Ministries	London	1991	300	7	Harvestime Ministries	Chessington	~	~	1[1]
El Shaddai Christian Centre	London	1994	175	6	Heart 2 Heart Ministries	London	1998	100	2
Emmanuel Inspirational Church of God[2]	Croydon	~	~	2	Hephzibah Christian Centre	London	~	100	2
Emmanuel Pentecostal Faith Church of God	London	~	~	1	High Praises Christian Centre	London	~	~	1
Emmanuel Tabernacle	London	~	~	1[1]	Highland Church Tooting	London	1991	30	1
Evangelical Church of Yahweh	London	~	~	1[1]	Highway of Holiness	London	1995	75	1
Everlasting Grace Christian Ministries	London	~	~	1	His Divine Grace Ministries	London	2001	75	2

Intnl = International

[1] Estimate

[2] Branched off from the US-based Emmanuel Pentecostal Faith Church of God in 1993.

[3] Another church, subsequently notified, with a similar name which also began in London about the same time is the Global Impact Church by Jerome Obode.

Table 9.15
Sole-Congregation African and Caribbean Pentecostal Churches (continued)

	Location	Began (UK)	Attendance	Ministers		Location	Began (UK)	Attendance	Ministers
Holy Ghost Flame Ministries	London	1996	40[1]	1	Oracle Foundation	Enfield	~	~	1[1]
Hour of Visitation World Missions	London	~	~	1[1]	Path of Life Community Church	London	~	~	1[1]
House of El Shaddai International[2]	London	~	100	1	Pentecostal Evangelistic Outreach Ministries	Croydon	~	~	1
House of Judah Bible Church	Croydon	1995	75	2	Pentecostal Gospel International Centre	London	~	~	1
House of Prayer Assembly, Mt Olives	Milton				Pentecostal Holy Church International	London	~	~	1
	Keynes	~	~	1	Pentecostal Revival Church of Christ	London	~	229	1
House on the Rock -The London Lighthouse[3]	London	1997	250	1	Pentecostal Revival Fellowship	London	~	~	1
House on The Rock International Church	London	1995	175	7	People's Christian Fellowship	London	~	~	1
Immanuel Worldwide Evangelical Ministry	London	~	~	1	Petra Church	London	~	~	1
International Bible Temple	London	1998	~	1[1]	Pierres Vivantes Two	London	~	~	1
International Central Gospel Church	London	1996	125	1	Pillar of Prayer Christian Fellowship	Slough	~	~	1
International Charismatic Assembly of God	London	~	~	1[1]	Power Church	London	~	~	1
International Pentecostal Church of God	London	~	~	1[1]	Power House International Church	London	~	~	1
Jesus Christ of Nazareth International					Powerpoint	London	~	~	1
(Pentecostal)	London	1989	125	10	Praise Harvest Community Fellowship	London	~	~	1
Jesus Everlasting Foundation Ministry					Praise Revival Christian Church of God	London	1998	40[1]	1
International	London	~	~	1[1]	Prayer of Faith Ministries	London	~	75	1
Jesus International Outreach Ministries	London	~	40[1]	1	Ransom Church of God Universal Fellowship	London	~	120	5
Kenyan Back to God Fellowship	London	~	~	1[1]	Reconciliation Ministries International	Bewdley	~	~	2
Kingdom Vision Ministry	London	~	~	1[1]	Refuge Apostolic Church	Wolver-			
Kingsvine Church	London	~	40[1]	1		hampton		~	1
Latter Rain Gospel Ministries International	London	~	40[1]	1	Refuge Church of the Living God in Christ	London	~	~	1
Liberty International Fellowship	London	1997	~	1[1]	Restore International Christian Ministries	London	~	~	1
Life Glory Church	London	1995	40[1]	2	Rhema Community Church	London	~	~	1
Light and Life Full Gospel Fellowship	London	1981	175	2	Salem Church of Christ	London	~	75	4
Light of the World Gospel Hall	Bradford	1983	~	5	The Shepherd's Ministries	London	~	~	1
Living God International Bible Ministry	London	2000	175	1	Shiloh Church of God	London	~	~	1
Living Gospel International Ministries	London	1997	40[1]	1	Solid Rock Christian Centre	London	~	~	1
Living in Christ International Ministry Intnl	London	~	~	1[1]	Stanhope Gardens Church	London	~	~	1
Living Springs International Church	London	1989	175	1[1]	Stonebridge Community Fellowship	London	~	~	1
Living Waters Apostolic Church					Tabernacle of Praise Ministry	Croydon	~	~	1
of the Lord Jesus Christ	London	~	~	1[1]	Triumphant Global Ministries	London	~	~	1
Living Word International Church	London	2001	40[1]	1	True Christian Life International Church	London	2000	40[1]	2
Logos Revival Church	London	1991	1,000	2	True Vine Ministries	Croydon	~	~	1
Ministry of Faith Christian Centre	London	~	75	6	Understanding Ministries	Mitcham	~	~	1
Miracles Signs and Wonders Ministries	London	1995	275[1]	4	Universal Church of Christ	London	~	125	3
Mount Zion Ministries	Oxford	2002	75	3	Victory Pentecostal Church of God in Christ	Aylesbury	1960	15	1
New Birth Ministries	Reading	2003	40[1]	3	The Vineyard Pentecostal Church	London	1991	~	2
New Creation Gospel Church	London	~	75	2	Vision of Hope Assemblies	London	~	~	1
New Creation Ministries International	London	~	110	1	Wayside Christian Community Centre	London	~	~	1
New Hope Christian Ministries	London	~	~	2	We've Been Given Authority Ministries	Milton			
New Jerusalem Christian Centre	London	2000	40[1]	1	Worldwide	Keynes	~	~	1
New Life Holy Ghost Ministry	London	~	~	1[1]	White City Community Church	London	~	~	1
New Life Revival	London	1986	75	1	The Word Church	London	~	~	1
New Testament Christian Mission	London	~	~	1[1]	World Harvest Christian Centre	London	~	125	1
New Tidings	London	~	~	1[1]	Written Word Outreach Ministries	Southwick	~	~	1
New Wine Church	London	1993	1,200	9	**TOTAL** (Transferred to Table 9.17.5)	**189**	~	**14,750[4]**	**344**

Intnl = International

[1] Estimate

[2] Formerly a Shiloh Pentecostal Church.

[3] London branch of a Nigerian Church with 5,000 members in total.

[4] Grossed up on attendance when number of ministers was given, which it was for 228.

9

Table 9.16.1
Annual Congregational Decline, 1997

No. of years	Apostolic Church %	Assemblies of God %	Elim %	Church of God %	Overall %
None	82	71	67	70	**70**
1–5	17	22	22	25	**22**
6–10	0	3	6	5	**4**
11–20	0	3	3	0	**3**
Over 20	1	1	2	0	**1**
Base	100	401	367	48	**930**

Table 9.16.2
Number of Baptisms, 1996

No. of years	Apostolic Church %	Assemblies of God %	Elim %	Church of God %	Overall %
Under 5	80	50	48	67	**53**
5–9	12	20	22	16	**20**
10–19	4	18	15	13	**15**
20–29	4	6	9	4	**7**
Over 30	0	6	6	0	**5**
Average	5	10	10	6	**9**

Table 9.16.3
Age of Minister, 1997

Age in years	Apostolic Church %	Assemblies of God %	Elim %	Church of God %	Overall %
< 30	2	5	7	2	**5**
30–39	12	18	27	21	**21**
40–49	15	31	35	17	**30**
50–59	30	26	21	35	**25**
60–69	24	15	8	21	**14**
70/70+	17	5	2	4	**5**
Average	56	49	45	51	**49**

Table 9.16.4
Length of Time in Ministry, 1997

No. of years	Apostolic Church %	Assemblies of God %	Elim %	Church of God %	Overall %
Under 9	39	44	47	49	**45**
10–19	21	26	31	28	**28**
20–29	18	14	14	13	**14**
30–39	9	10	6	10	**8**
40/40+	13	6	2	0	**5**
Average	19	16	14	14	**15**

Table 9.16.5 Adult
Sunday Morning Attendance, 1996

No. of people	Apostolic Church %	Assemblies of God %	Elim %	Church of God %	Overall %
< 25	24	20	14	28	**18**
25–49	44	23	26	31	**27**
50–74	19	17	18	16	**18**
75–99	6	11	11	10	**10**
100–199	4	19	18	6	**17**
200–299	1.5	7	6	9	**6**
300/+	1.5	3	7	0	**4**
Average	51	89	100	66	**88**

Table 9.16.6
Weekly Take-home Pay, 1996

Pay	Apostolic Church %	Assemblies of God %	Elim %	Church of God %	Overall %
<£100	18	16	10	20	**14**
£100–149	31	13	11	14	**13**
£150–174	21	11	7	13	**11**
£175–199	6	9	8	3	**8**
£200–249	11	22	22	27	**21**
£250–299	4	13	22	6	**16**
£300/+	9	16	20	17	**17**
Average	£165	£205	£225	£195	**£210**

Table 9.16.7
Agreement with Various Statements, 1997

Statement I believe... OR Women should...	Apostolic Church %	Assemblies of God %	Elim %	Church of God %	Overall %
A minister who practices homosexuality should leave the ministry	96	99	98	100	**98**
The Church will be taken from the earth before the millennium	92	72	56	96	**69**
God made the world in six 24 hour days	67	70	56	65	**64**
The AV is the best version of the Bible for Christians to use	46	20	11	34	**20**
...exercise a preaching ministry	91	95	89	96	**92**
...have exactly the same opportunities as men	24	76	54	69	**61**
...not be in charge of a congregation	60	21	50	8	**36**
...wear head coverings in public worship	42	16	8	67	**18**

A very useful book, *Pentecostals in Britain*, was published (by Paternoster Press, Carlisle) in 2000. Written by Dr William Kay it gives the history of the Pentecostals, focussing especially on their origins and spread in the UK. It looks at the issues of spiritual gifts, healing, the Toronto Blessing, ethical issues and church growth. It also included the results of a detailed survey among the ministers of the four oldest UK Pentecostal denominations. Some of the findings of that study are given on this page.

Table 9.16.1 shows that a third, 30%, of Pentecostal congregations were experiencing decline in the late 1990s, about half the rate of other denominations. The Apostolic Church declined less but Elim rather more.

Table 9.16.2 gives the number of baptisms in 1996 and shows that both of the larger Pentecostal groups in this Table, the Assemblies of God and Elim, had about twice as many baptisms as the Apostolic Church and the Church of God; perhaps that's why they are larger!

Table 9.16.3 shows that the average age of a Pentecostal minister in 1997 was 49, slightly less for Elim ministers. The average is 4 years under the average in the 2002 survey reported in *Religious Trends* No 4 Table 5.2.2 and is younger than leaders in other denominations.

Table 9.16.4 gives the time Pentecostal ministers have been in the ministry. On average this is 15 years, which would mean that most begin their ministry in their 30s, that is, they would very likely have had some experience of life outside the full-time ministry before entering it.

Table 9.16.5 indicates the average size of the adult Sunday morning attendance. The 10th edition of the *Body Book* suggests that 24% of Pentecostal attendance is children, which would imply a congregation of 116 on an average Sunday morning. The 1998 English Church Attendance Survey found an average Pentecostal Sunday attendance of 102 (*The Tide is Running Out*, Christian Research, 2000, Table 11).

Table 9.16.6 looks at the weekly take-home pay of Pentecostal ministers. On average it is £210 a week, or £10,800 a year. If that has increased by the rate of inflation since 1996 it would be £12,800 in 2003, well below the average in the nation.

Table 9.16.7 shows the differences between these four Pentecostal denominations. They are quite different. While the Assemblies of God and Elim are similar in some beliefs they separate on others (whether women should be in charge of a congregation, for instance). These 8 statements are only a selection of those given in William Kay's book.

Table 9.17.1
TOTAL Oneness Apostolic Churches[11]

	Membership	Churches	Ministers
2000	22,431	148	193
2001	30,046	151	201
2002	41,950	153	232
2003	47,214	156	268
2005	49,436	165	299
2010[1]	57,220	174	380
2020[1]	70,800	190	560

Table 9.17.2
TOTAL Holiness Churches[12]

	Membership	Churches	Ministers
2000	1,801	53	72
2001	1,815	54	72
2002	1,830	55	73
2003	2,048	54	73
2005	2,260	56	76
2010[1]	2,550	59	80
2020[1]	3,100	66	89

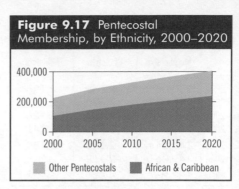

Figure 9.17 Pentecostal Membership, by Ethnicity, 2000–2020

Table 9.17.3 Pentecostal Churches: Oneness Apostolic Churches[14]

	Attendance					Congregations					Ministers				
	2000	2001	2002	2003	2005	2000	2001	2002	2003	2005	2000	2001	2002	2003	2005
Assembly of the First Born	2,650	2,700[1]	2,750[1]	2,800[1]	2,900[1]	21	21	22[2]	22[1]	22[1]	35	35[1]	36[1]	37[1]	40[1]
Bethany Fellowship of Great Britain	200[2]	200[2]	200[2]	200	250[3]	1[2]	1[2]	1[2]	1	1[3]	5[2]	5[2]	5[2]	5	7[3]
Bible Truth Church of God	220	220[1]	220[1]	220[1]	220[1]	4	4[1]	4[1]	4[1]	4[1]	5	5[1]	5[1]	5[1]	5[1]
Bibleway Churches UK[4]	1,000[1]	1,000[1]	1,000[1]	1,000[1]	1,000[1]	17[2]	17[2]	17[2]	17	17[3]	17[2]	17[2]	17[2]	17	17[3]
Christ Apostolic Church in Great Britain	3,700	3,800[1]	3,850[1]	4,000[1]	4,200[1]	23	24[1]	24[1]	25[1]	27[1]	20	21[1]	21[1]	22[1]	24[1]
Church of God in Christ Cong Ind	150	155[1]	160[1]	165[1]	170[1]	7	7[1]	7[1]	7[1]	7[1]	8	8[1]	8[1]	8[1]	8[1]
Church of J Christ of the Apostolic Faith	25	22[1]	20	18[1]	15[1]	1	1	1	1	1[1]	1	1[1]	2	2[1]	2[1]
Elijah Tabernacle	40	42[1]	44[1]	46[1]	50[1]	2	2[1]	2[1]	2[1]	2[1]	3	3[1]	3[1]	3[1]	3[1]
Greater Bibleway Church[5]	1,750	1,750[1]	1,750[1]	1,750[1]	1,750[1]	30	30[1]	30[1]	30[1]	30[1]	51	51[1]	51[1]	51[1]	51[1]
Hackney Pentecostal Apostolic Church	230	235[1]	240[1]	240[1]	250[1]	1	1[1]	1[1]	1[1]	1[1]	10	10[1]	10[1]	10[1]	10[1]
Mount Shiloh Utd Church of C Apostolic	300	300	406	450[1]	500[1]	5	5	4	4[1]	4[1]	4	4	4	4[1]	4[1]
Mount Zion Pentecostal Apostolic Church[6]	1,600	1,600[1]	1,590[2]	1,590	1,500[1]	15	15	15	15	15[3]	7	11	18	23	35[3]
United Church of God[7]	180	190	200	210[1]	220[1]	2	2[1]	2[1]	2[1]	2[1]	3	3[1]	3[1]	3[1]	3[1]
Universal Church of the Kingdom of God[8]	9,826[2]	17,082[2]	28,470[2]	33,343[2]	35,171[3]	8[2]	10[2]	12	14	20[3]	12[2]	14[2]	34[2]	61	71[1]
Other Churches[9]	560	750	1,050	1,182	1,240	11	11	11	11	12	12	13	15	17	19
TOTAL (Transferred to Table 9.17.1)	**22,431**	**30,046**	**41,950**	**47,214**	**49,436**	**148**	**151**	**153**	**156**	**165**	**193**	**201**	**232**	**268**	**299**

C = Christ; Cong = Congregational; Ind = Independent; J = Jesus; Utd = United

Table 9.17.4 Pentecostal Churches: Holiness Churches

	Attendance					Congregations					Ministers				
	2000	2001	2002	2003	2005	2000	2001	2002	2003	2005	2000	2001	2002	2003	2005
African Methodist Episcopal Church	200	200	200	400	600[3]	4	4	4	2	3[3]	4	4	4	3	3[3]
African Methodist Episcopal Zion Church	500	505[1]	510[1]	520[1]	530[1]	12	12[1]	12[1]	12[1]	12[1]	15	15[1]	15[1]	15[1]	15[1]
Cherubim & Seraphim Oke-Ayo Movement No 2 Ch'ch	150	160[1]	170[1]	180[1]	200[1]	8	9[1]	10[1]	11[1]	13[1]	8	9[1]	10[1]	11[1]	13[1]
Pentecostal Holiness Church	280	280[1]	280[1]	280[1]	280[1]	7	7[1]	7[1]	7[1]	7[1]	20	20[1]	20[1]	20[1]	20[1]
Pillar of Fire Church	25	35[2]	45	48[1]	50[3]	1	1	1	1	1[3]	3	2	2	2	2[3]
Wesleyan Holiness Church	496	485[1]	475[1]	470[1]	450[1]	17	17[1]	17[1]	17[1]	16[1]	17	17[1]	17[1]	17[1]	18[1]
Other Holiness Churches[10]	150	150	150	150	150	4	4	4	4	4	5	5	5	5	5
TOTAL (Transferred to Table 9.17.2)	**1,801**	**1,815**	**1,830**	**2,048**	**2,260**	**53**	**54**	**55**	**54**	**56**	**72**	**72**	**73**	**73**	**76**

Ch'ch = Church

Table 9.17.5
TOTAL Single Congregations

	Membership	Churches	Ministers
2000[1]	13,011	184	286
2001[1]	13,368	186	314
2002[1]	14,137	191	335
2003	14,750	189	344
2005[1]	16,460	209	392
2010[1]	20,825	238	533
2020[1]	33,360	310	773

[1] Estimate
[2] Revised figure
[3] Church's own estimate
[4] For details of the 17 Bibleway Churches in the UK see www.bible-waychurches.org.uk; there 50 churches and missions internationally.
[5] Or Bibleway Church of our Lord Jesus Christ.
[6] Attendance taken at one-tenth of that stated.
[7] All ministers are part-time.
[8] Begun in 1995, this church is linked to the Rainbow Theatre in London.
[9] Four denominations were unable to provide complete information. These are cumulated together in this line; all figures are for 2003 unless otherwise stated. They are the Church of Jesus Christ Apostolic with 7 congregations, Eagle's Nest Community Church with

300 members in 4 congregations with 6 ministers in 1995, First United Church of Jesus Christ with 2 congregations, and the Shiloh United Church of Christ Apostolic Worldwide with 2 congregations and 3 ministers in 2002.
[10] All estimated, but including Life for the World Christian Centre.
[11] Taken from Table 9.13.3.
[12] Taken from Table 9.13.4.
[13] Taken from Table 9.15. Years other than 2003 have been estimated pro rata to the totals in Table 9.11.14.
[14] These churches are more properly called Unitarian Pentecostal Churches, who baptise in the name of Jesus only. Some believe in three different expressions of the Godhead, and others conceive the functions of the Trinity as fulfilling three different roles, not being three different persons.

Table 9.18.1
TOTAL Other Denominations[4]

	Membership	Churches	Ministers
2000	140,066	2,158	2,150
2001	139,624	2,129	2,145
2002	140,044	2,131	2,126
2003	141,004	2,121	2,141
2005	144,844	2,129	2,150
2010	149,251	2,112	2,115
2020	156,016	2,207	2,041

Table 9.18.2
The Christian Community

	Membership	Churches	Ministers
2000	580	13	16
2001[2]	600	17	20
2002[2]	620	17	20
2003	700	17	20
2005[3]	1,000	17	20
2010[1]	1,360	20	24
2020[1]	2,300	27	32

Figure 9.18 Membership of Other Denominations, by Group, 2000–2020

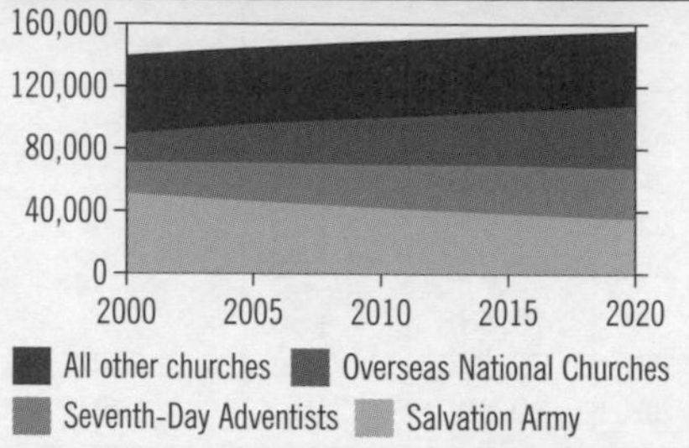

Legend: All other churches ▪ Overseas National Churches ▪ Seventh-Day Adventists ▪ Salvation Army

Table 9.18.3
Countess of Huntingdon's Connexion

	Membership	Churches	Ministers
2000	659[2]	23	20
2001	690[2]	23	19
2002	675[2]	23	18[1]
2003	690	23	16
2005[3]	700	20	16
2010[1]	750	19	15
2020[1]	850	18	14

Table 9.18.4
Emmanuel Holiness Church[5]

	Membership	Churches	Ministers
2000	300	4	5
2001	300	4	5
2002	300	4	5
2003			
2005	In 2002 the four churches and their ministers became independent charities, so there is now no Emmanuel Holiness Church as an affiliation of churches.		
2010			
2020			

Table 9.18.5
British Conference of Mennonites

	Membership[6]	Churches	Ministers
2000	30	1	1
2001	30[2]	1	1
2002	30[2]	1	1
2003	28	1	1
2005[1]	26	1	1
2010[1]	22	1	1
2020[1]	16	1	1

Table 9.18.6
Union of British Messianic Jews

	Membership	Churches	Ministers
2000	170	4	5
2001	172	4	6
2002	200	6	9
2003	250	7	10
2005[1]	300	8	11
2010[1]	500	10	15
2020[1]	1,000	16	20

Table 9.18.7 Moravian Church in Great Britain and Ireland[7]

	Membership[6]	Churches	Ministers
2000	1,864	35	19
2001	1,900	35	20
2002	1,800	35	20
2003	1,800	34	21[8]
2005[1]	1,740	33	19
2010[1]	1,620	32	18
2020[1]	1,400	30	17

Table 9.18.8
Church of the Nazarene[5]

	Membership North	Membership South	Churches North	Churches South	Ministers North	Ministers South
2000	1,848	2,184[2]	38	56[2]	35	57[2]
2001	1,859	2,061	37	55	36	57
2002	1,882	2,010	38	53	35	56
2003	1,880	1,748	38	53	38	58
2005[3]	2,000	1,620	42	48	40	56
2010[3]	2,200	1,400	50	43	42	57
2020[3]	2,500	1,150	55	38	50	50

Table 9.18.9
Religious Society of Friends (Quakers)

	Membership[9]	Churches	Ministers
2000	17,342	500	–
2001	16,243	487	–
2002	15,953	485	–
2003	15,775	484	–
2005[3]	14,500	482	–
2010[3]	13,800	481	–
2020[3]	8,200	480	–

Table 9.18.10
Salvation Army

	Membership[6]	Churches	Ministers
2000[2]	50,865	844	1,539
2001	49,704	823	1,534
2002	48,563	804	1,507
2003	47,972	776	1,496
2005[3]	46,000	735	1,450
2010[3]	42,000	650	1,350
2020[3]	35,000	625	1,150

Table 9.18.11
Seventh-Day Adventists

	Membership	Churches	Ministers
2000	20,637	241	163
2001	21,137	246	166
2002	21,864	251	174[2]
2003	23,129	256	181
2005[1]	25,000	266	194
2010[1]	27,600	280	210
2020[1]	32,300	300	245

Table 9.18.12
Mar Thoma Syrian Church UK

	Membership	Churches	Ministers
2000	800	2	4
2001	775[2]	2	3[2]
2002	750	2	2
2003	1,400	2	3
2005[3]	1,500	2	3
2010[3]	1,700	4	4
2020[3]	2,500	5	5

[1] Estimate
[2] Revised figure
[3] Church's own estimate
[4] Total of Tables 9.18.2–12 and Tables 9.20.1–3.
[5] A Holiness Church.
[6] Including adherents.
[7] Communicants are roughly double membership.
[8] Includes 1 lay pastor.
[9] Including children.

Table 9.19.1 Churches of Overseas Nationals (excluding Lutheran Churches)

	Attendance					Congregations					Ministers				
	2000	2001	2002	2003	2005	2000	2001	2002	2003	2005	2000	2001	2002	2003	2005
American Church in London	468	460	450	450	450[1]	1	1	1	1	1	2	2	2	2	2[1]
Asia Christian Fellowship (UK)[4,5]	5,000	5,500	6,500	7,000	10,000[3]	50	50	60	70	100[3]	50	50	60	70	100[3]
Chinese Churches in London	525[1]	547	558	605	660[3]	8	8	8	8	8[3]	10[1]	10	9	9	10[1]
Chinese Churches elsewhere in the UK	5,500[1]	5,600[1]	5,700[1]	5,800[1]	6,000[1]	63[1]	64[1]	65[1]	67[1]	69[1]	25[1]	25[1]	25[1]	27[1]	28[1]
Dutch Church	230	230	230	230[1]	230[1]	1	1	1	1[1]	1[1]	2	2	2	2[1]	2[1]
French Protestant Church in the UK[6]	300	259	230[1]	220[1]	200[1]	3	3	3	3[1]	3[1]	3	3	3	3[1]	3[1]
Greek Christian Fellowship	19	20[1]	21[1]	22[1]	24[1]	1	1[1]	1[1]	1[1]	1[1]	0	0[1]	0[1]	0[1]	0[1]
Hungarian Reformed Church[7]	55	55	55[2]	55	55[3]	2	2	2	2	2[3]	1	1	1	1	1[3]
International Presbyterian Church[8]	800	600	630	600	700[3]	9	8	8	8	9[3]	4[2]	4	3	4	6[3]
Iranian Christian Fellowship	120	120	120	150	200[3]	1	1[2]	1	1	2[3]	3	2[2]	2[2]	2	3[3]
Italian Pentecostal Church	150	150	150	185	200[1]	5	5	5	5	5[3]	5	5	5	5	5[3]
Japanese Churches[24]	65	80[1]	100[1]	120[1]	150[1]	2	3[1]	4[1]	5[1]	7[1]	5	5[1]	5[1]	5[1]	5[1]
Korean Churches	1,550[1]	1,600[1]	1,680[1]	1,750[1]	1,850[1]	22[1]	23[1]	24[1]	25[1]	26[1]	40[1]	41[1]	42[1]	44[1]	45[1]
Portuguese Churches (Bread of Life)	520	300	350	600[1]	1,000[3]	10	3	1	1[1]	1[3]	12	6	6	8[1]	10[3]
Spanish Evangelical Church	200[2]	250[2]	300[2]	250	500[3]	7	8	10	10[1]	13[1]	1[2]	1[2]	1	4	4[3]
Swahili Church	105	110	120	150	150[1]	1	1	1	1	1[3]	1	1	1	1	2[3]
Swiss Church in London[9]	150	150	150	150	200[3]	1	1	1	1	1[3]	1	1	1	1	1[3]
Swiss Evangelical Brotherhood	15	15	15	17	20[3]	1	1	1	1	1[3]	1	1	1	1	1[3]
Tamil Language Churches[10]	1,400	1,500[1]	1,600[1]	1,800	2,000[3]	24	26[1]	28[1]	30	32[3]	17	17[1]	16[2]	14	16[3]
Turkish Christian Fellowship[11]	3[2]	3[2]	3	3	5[3]	1	1	1	1	1[3]	0	0	0	0	0[3]
Other Language Groups[12]	850	855	855	885	900	17	16	16	16	15	9	9	9	10	10
TOTAL (Transferred to Table 9.20.2)	**18,025**	**18,404**	**19,817**	**21,042**	**25,494**	**230**	**227**	**242**	**258**	**301**	**192**	**186**	**194**	**213**	**254**

Table 9.19.2 Lutheran Churches[13]

	Active Members					Congregations					Ministers				
	2000	2001	2002	2003	2005	2000	2001	2002	2003	2005	2000	2001	2002	2003	2005
Danish Church and Seamen's Mission[14]	300[2]	300[2]	300[2]	300[1]	300[1]	2	2	2	2	2[3]	3	3	3	3	3[3]
Estonian Evangelical Lutheran Synod	550	530[1]	520[1]	510[1]	500[1]	5	5[1]	5[1]	5[1]	5[1]	3	3[1]	3[1]	3[1]	3[1]
Evangelical Lutheran Church of England	890[1]	895[1]	900[1]	900[1]	920[1]	13	13	13	14	14[3]	10[15]	10	10	11	12[3]
Finnish Church and Seamen's Mission[16]	480[1]	480[2]	480[2]	480	495[3]	1	1	1	1	1[3]	2	2	2	2	2[3]
German Evangelical Lutheran Synod	1,759	1,759[2]	1,759[2]	1,759	1,759[3]	22	22	22	22	22[3]	7	10[2]	10[2]	10	10[3]
Hungarian Lutheran Church[17]	100	100	100	100	100	1	1	1	1	1	2	2	2	2	2
Icelandic Lutheran Church in England[18]	180[2]	190[2]	200[2]	210	220[3]	1	1	1	1	1[3]	1	1	1	1	1[3]
Latvian Evangelical Lutheran Synod	1,915	1,895	1,875	1,850[1]	1,800[1]	8	8	8	8	8[3]	8	8	8	8	8[3]
Lutheran Church in Great Britain[19]	2,300	2,500	2,500	2,500[1]	2,600[3]	12	12	12[2]	12	12[3]	15	14[2]	14[2]	13[1]	12[3]
Norwegian Church & Seamen's Mission[20]	540	550	560	530[1]	500[3]	8[21]	8[2]	8[1]	8	8[3]	4	4	4[2]	4	4[3]
Polish Evangelical Church of the Augsburg Confession Abroad	2,700[1]	2,700[1]	2,700[1]	2,700[1]	2,700[1]	25[1]	25[1]	25[1]	25[1]	25[1]	4[1]	4[1]	4[1]	4[1]	4[1]
Swedish Lutheran Church[22]	7,065	7,797	7,765	7,326	7,500[1]	4	4	4	3	3[1]	4	4	4	3	3[1]
Other Lutheran Churches[23]	3,650	3,828	3,821	3,725	3,770	20	20	20	20	20	12	12	12	12	12
TOTAL (Transferred to Table 9.20.3)	**22,429**	**23,524**	**23,480**	**22,890**	**23,164**	**122**	**122**	**122**	**122**	**122**	**77**	**77**	**77**	**76**	**76**

9

[1] Estimate
[2] Revised figure
[3] Church's own estimate
[4] Includes Scottish Asian Christian Fellowship of 25 people in one church in 2002.
[5] Includes the Urdu and Swahili Churches; one Swahili Church is part of St Anne's Lutheran Church, London.
[6] Includes churches in London, Brighton and Canterbury; numbers are double actual attendance.
[7] Consisting of 1 church in London and 1 in Manchester.
[8] Including 5 Korean and 2 English congregations.
[9] In the 1980s the Swiss Reformed Church amalgamated with the Swiss Church in London.
[10] Including, from 2004, 3 Singhalese Language congregations in Ilford, Southall and Wembley, with a total attendance of 60 and no priest.
[11] Set up in 1994 and run by London City Mission.

[12] All estimated.
[13] Eleven churches are represented and co-ordinated by the Lutheran Council of Great Britain. These are all those listed in this Table except for the Evangelical Lutheran Church in England and Other Lutheran Churches.
[14] Has 1 church in London with 2 ministers and 1 in Hull with 1 female minister. Membership figures are estimated, and taken as a tenth of the community, as the church sees itself as a community rather than a congregation.
[15] Excluding in each year 2000–2005 the 5 emeritus ministers previously included.
[16] Active members taken as 3% of Finnish community of 16,000.
[17] Not previously included; all estimated.
[18] Active membership taken as 10% of the community; there is a monthly service at the German Church, Montpelier Place, London, and less frequent but regular services in Hull and Grimsby. Regular attendance in London is between 90–110 including 25 choir members; figures rise to about 300 for special services during the year.

[19] Includes Amharic, Chinese, English, Swahili and Tigrinya Lutherans.
[20] The average Sunday Mass is increasing by 2–3% pa according to their pastor. In 2003 there were 22,000 visitors to the church in London, 9,000 of whom were for services. The proportion of the Scottish community that regularly attend the church is 4%.
[21] In 2003 there were 5 churches in England, 2 in Scotland and 1 in Wales.
[22] Members are counted as the number of households on the address list which support the church financially; each household is assumed to contain three active members, including regular attenders and children.
[23] Includes the London Chinese Lutheran Church which began in 1994 with 50 ministers, 1 church and 1 minister. Originally these "other churches" were estimated by subtracting from the Lutheran Council figures those for the individual churches; they are all estimates and trended according to the overall total.
[24] Estimates provided by Hugh Trevor, a former missionary in Japan.

Table 9.20.1
The Worldwide Church of God

	Membership	Congregations	Ministers
2000	2,333	45	17
2001	2,225	46	15
2002	2,100	48	8
2003	1,700	50	8
2005[3]	1,800	52	10
2010[3]	2,000	55	12
2020[3]	2,500	60	15

Table 9.20.2
TOTAL Overseas National Churches

	Membership	Congregations	Ministers
2000	18,025	230	192
2001	18,404	227	186
2002	19,817	242	194
2003	21,042	258	213
2005	25,494	301	254
2010[1]	30,376	345	290
2020[1]	40,800	430	365

Table 9.20.3
TOTAL Lutheran Churches

	Membership	Congregations	Ministers
2000	22,429	122	77
2001	23,524	122	77
2002	23,480	122	77
2003	22,890	122	76
2005	23,164	122	76
2010[1]	23,923	122	77
2020[1]	25,500	122	77

Table 9.20.4 Ethnic Group by Religion, 2001

Ethnic Group	Christian %	Buddhist %	Hindu %	Jewish %	Muslim %	Sikh %	Other %	No Religion %	Not Stated %	Base (= 100%)
White: Total	**75.7**	**0.1**	**0.0**	**0.5**	**0.4**	**0.0**	**0.3**	**15.3**	**7.7**	**47,520,866**
British	75.9	0.1	0.0	0.5	0.1	0.0	0.3	15.5	7.6	45,533,741
Irish	85.5	0.2	0.0	0.2	0.1	0.0	0.3	6.3	7.4	641,804
Other White	62.7	0.3	0.1	2.4	8.6	0.0	0.6	15.9	9.4	1,345,321
Asian	**4.1**	**0.6**	**23.4**	**0.1**	**50.1**	**13.9**	**0.9**	**1.4**	**5.5**	**2,273,737**
Indian	4.9	0.2	45.0	0.1	12.7	29.1	1.7	1.7	4.6	1,036,807
Pakistani	1.1	0.0	0.1	0.1	92.0	0.0	0.0	0.5	6.2	714,826
Bangladeshi	0.5	0.1	0.6	0.1	92.5	0.0	0.0	0.4	5.8	280,830
Other Asian	13.4	4.9	26.8	0.3	37.3	6.2	0.9	3.4	6.8	241,274
Black or Black British	**71.1**	**0.1**	**0.3**	**0.1**	**9.3**	**0.1**	**0.4**	**7.5**	**11.1**	**1,139,577**
Black Caribbean	73.8	0.2	0.3	0.1	0.8	0.0	0.6	11.2	13.0	563,843
Black African	68.9	0.1	0.2	0.0	20.0	0.1	0.2	2.3	8.2	479,665
Other Black	66.6	0.2	0.4	0.1	6.0	0.1	0.6	12.1	13.9	96,069
Mixed	**52.5**	**0.7**	**0.9**	**0.5**	**9.7**	**0.4**	**0.6**	**23.2**	**11.5**	**661,034**
White & Black Caribbean	60.7	0.2	0.1	0.2	0.6	0.0	0.4	25.4	12.4	237,420
White and Asian	44.0	1.0	1.9	0.4	16.1	1.1	0.7	24.0	10.8	189,015
White and Black African	56.4	0.6	0.2	0.2	13.3	0.1	0.4	17.9	10.9	78,911
Other Mixed	48.2	1.2	1.2	1.1	14.1	0.3	0.9	21.7	11.3	155,688
Chinese or other ethnic group	**27.2**	**15.3**	**0.7**	**0.5**	**12.8**	**0.5**	**0.7**	**33.7**	**8.6**	**446,702**
Chinese	21.6	15.1	0.1	0.0	0.3	0.0	0.5	52.6	9.8	226,948
Other ethnic group	33.0	15.5	1.3	1.0	25.7	1.0	0.9	14.1	7.5	219,754
TOTAL All Groups	**71.7**	**0.3**	**1.1**	**0.5**	**3.0**	**0.6**	**0.3**	**14.8**	**7.7**	**52,041,916**

Not Stated = Religion not stated   *Source:* Population Census 2001: National Report for England and Wales Part 2, National Statistics, 2003, Table S104, Page 33.

Table 9.20.5 Religion by Ethnic Group, 2001

Ethnic Group	Christian %	Buddhist %	Hindu %	Jewish %	Muslim %	Sikh %	Other %	No Religion %	Not Stated %	All people %
White: Total	**96.4**	**38.8**	**1.3**	**96.8**	**11.6**	**2.1**	**78.4**	**94.5**	**90.9**	**91.3**
British	92.6	34.9	1.1	84.0	4.1	1.9	72.2	91.2	86.6	87.5
Irish	1.5	0.8	0.0	0.4	0.0	0.0	1.1	0.5	1.2	1.2
Other White	2.3	3.1	0.2	12.4	7.5	0.2	5.1	2.8	3.1	2.6
Asian	**0.2**	**9.6**	**96.6**	**0.7**	**73.6**	**96.2**	**13.7**	**0.4**	**3.1**	**4.4**
Indian	0.1	1.3	84.5	0.3	8.5	91.5	12.0	0.2	1.2	2.0
Pakistani	0.0	0.1	0.1	0.1	42.5	0.1	0.2	0.1	1.1	1.4
Bangladeshi	0.0	0.1	0.3	0.0	16.8	0.0	0.0	0.0	0.4	0.5
Other Asian	0.1	8.1	11.7	0.3	5.8	4.6	1.5	0.1	0.4	0.5
Black or Black British	**2.2**	**1.1**	**0.6**	**0.4**	**6.9**	**0.2**	**3.3**	**1.1**	**3.1**	**2.2**
Black Caribbean	1.1	0.7	0.3	0.2	0.3	0.1	2.2	0.8	1.8	1.1
Black African	0.9	0.3	0.2	0.1	6.2	0.1	0.7	0.1	1.0	0.9
Other Black	0.2	0.1	0.1	0.1	0.4	0.0	0.4	0.2	0.3	0.2
Mixed	**0.9**	**3.2**	**1.0**	**1.2**	**4.2**	**0.8**	**2.6**	**2.0**	**1.9**	**1.3**
White & Black Caribbean	0.4	0.3	0.0	0.1	0.1	0.0	0.6	0.8	0.7	0.5
White and Asian	0.2	1.3	0.6	0.3	2.0	0.6	0.9	0.6	0.5	0.4
White and Black African	0.1	0.3	0.0	0.1	0.7	0.0	0.2	0.2	0.2	0.1
Other Mixed	0.2	1.3	0.4	0.7	1.4	0.2	0.9	0.4	0.5	0.3
Chinese or other ethnic group	**0.3**	**47.3**	**0.5**	**0.9**	**3.7**	**0.7**	**2.0**	**2.0**	**1.0**	**0.8**
Chinese	0.1	23.7	0.0	0.0	0.1	0.0	0.7	1.6	0.6	0.4
Other ethnic group	0.2	23.6	0.5	0.9	3.6	0.7	1.3	0.4	0.4	0.4
Base (=100%) in millions	37.3	0.1	0.6	0.3	1.5	0.3	0.2	7.7	4.0	52.0

Not Stated = Religion not stated   *Source:* Population Census 2001: National Report for England and Wales Part 2, National Statistics, 2003, Table S104, Page 33.   [1] Estimate

10

Other Religions
and Non-Trinitarian Church Statistics

Sources: Individual religions and non-Trinitarian churches; special research by INFORM; previous editions of *Religious Trends;* 2001 Population Census; relevant websites and publications.

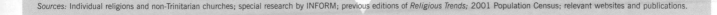

Table 10.2.1
TOTAL Non-Trinitarian Churches[4]

	Membership	Churches	Ministers
2000	539,968	3,298	14,034
2001	541,860	3,279	14,087
2002	545,396	3,257	14,008
2003	547,987	3,239	14,012
2005[1]	547,178	3,194	13,982
2010[1]	545,540	3,052	13,895
2020[1]	531,630	2,734	13,673

Table 10.2.2
Christadelphians

	Membership	Ecclesias	Ministers
2000[1]	18,400	292	–
2001[1]	18,200	291	–
2002[1]	18,000	290	–
2003[1]	17,900	288	–
2005[1]	17,600	285	–
2010[1]	16,000	271	–
2020[1]	12,000	233	–

Table 10.2.3
Church of Christ Scientist[5]

	Membership	Churches	Practitioners
2000	7,000	156	112
2001[1]	6,500	150	105
2002[1]	6,150	143	95
2003[1]	5,200	137[6]	80
2005[1]	4,200	125	65
2010[1]	2,500	100	38
2020[1]	900	64	15

Table 10.2.4
Church of God Sabbath-Keeping

	Membership	Churches	Ministers
2000	55	2	1
2001[1]	60	2	1
2002[1]	65	2	1
2003[1]	70	2	1
2005[1]	75	2	1
2010[1]	90	2	1
2020[1]	100	2	1

Table 10.2.5 Church of Jesus Christ of Latter-Day Saints (Mormons)[7]

	Membership[8]	Churches	Ministers[9]
2000	178,000	395	439
2001[1]	177,500	384	428
2002	176,998	373	417
2003[1]	176,500	362	406
2005[1]	175,000	345	389
2010[1]	169,000	295	339
2020[1]	152,000	220	264

Table 10.2.6
Community of Christ[10]

	Membership	Churches	Ministers
2000	1,303	21	157
2001[1]	1,270	21	157
2002[1]	1,230	21	158
2003[1]	1,200	21	160
2005[1]	1,100	21	162
2010[1]	840	18	153
2020[1]	450	10	117

Table 10.2.7
The Family[11]

	Membership	Churches	Ministers
2000	170	5	10
2001	170	5	10
2002	170	5	10
2003[1]	170	5	10
2005[1]	170	5	10
2010[1]	170	5	10
2020[1]	170	5	10

Table 10.2.8
International Churches of Christ[12]

	Membership	Churches	Ministers
2000	2,900	12	50
2001[1]	3,200	12	54
2002[1]	3,500	12	58
2003[1]	3,750	12	64
2005[1]	4,300	13	70
2010[1]	5,350	14	80
2020[1]	7,600	18	95

Table 10.2.9
Jehovah's Witnesses[20]

	Membership[13]	Churches	Ministers[14]
2000[2]	128,940	1,461	11,966
2001[3]	127,825	1,468	12,022
2002[3]	128,365	1,474	11,952
2003[3]	128,653	1,481	11,972
2005[1]	128,333	1,485	11,960
2010[1]	128,170	1,495	11,935
2020[1]	127,850	1,520	11,880

Table 10.2.10
The Lord's Witnesses[15]

	Membership	Churches	Ministers
2000	3	–	1
2001	9	–	1
2002	15	–	1
2003[1]	20	–	1
2005[1]	30	–	1
2010[1]	40	–	1
2020[1]	50	–	1

Table 10.2.11
Scientology, Church of[16]

	Membership[17]	Groups	Leaders[18]
2000[1]	144,400	15[2]	400[2]
2001[1]	150,000	15[2]	415[2]
2002[1]	155,000	15[2]	430[2]
2003[1]	160,000	15	440
2005[1]	165,000	15	450
2010[1]	180,000	15	490
2020[1]	200,000	15	540

Table 10.2.12
Spiritualists[19]

	Membership	Churches	Ministers
2000	36,315	520	260
2001	35,000	516	258
2002	34,000	512	256
2003	32,700	508	254
2005[1]	30,000	500	250
2010[1]	22,700	450	230
2020[1]	11,500	290	150

10

[1] Estimate
[2] Revised figure
[3] Church's own estimate
[4] Total of Tables 10.2.2–12 and Tables 10.3.1–4, 6 and 7.
[5] The Christian Science Church forbids the publication of membership numbers so the figures are all estimated. Members and churches are pro rata to practitioners, the majority of whom are women.
[6] Made up of 81 actual churches and 50 Societies, where services are also held, from the Church of Christ, Scientist website, accessed July 2004, and assumed to be 6 more a year earlier, in 2003.
[7] Also known as the LDS Church or Mormons. While the Church "firmly holds to a trinity of God, Christ and the Holy Spirit", it is included here because the book of Mormon is regarded as containing inspired writings which provide an added testimony to the divinity of Christ.
[8] Official figures are published every 2 years.
[9] Leaders are called Bishops, one per congregation. In 2002, there were 44 State Presidents (one each in charge of a Diocese), which are included in the total; a similar number has been added for each other year.
[10] Formerly the Re-organised Church of the Latter-day Saints.

[11] Previously called the Children of God which officially disbanded in 1978. The Family is Trinitarian but is included here because of the controversial outreach methods such as 'Flirty Fishing' that were encouraged by its founder, David Berg, who died in 1994. Worldwide in 2002 they had 8,048 Charter (full-time) members of 91 nationalities and 3,249 Fellow (part-time) members living in 1,045 homes, with 79,060 Active (congregational) members. See www.thefamilyeurope.org
[12] Formerly known as the London Church of Christ. Although Trinitarian the Church is included here because it teaches that salvation is only through their church, as well as through Christ.
[13] Membership is counted as the number of Witnesses who have submitted reports regarding their preaching activities.
[14] Jehovah's Witnesses do not have paid clergy; these figures represent the numbers of congregational elders.
[15] The Lord's Witnesses were established separately from the Jehovah's Witnesses in 1998. Their ministry is mainly via their website though they meet 3 times a week in Wapping mainly for research and Bible decoding purposes. Their first public meeting was held on March 21st 2000 at the Cumberland Hotel, London. Some 200 people were present. The first Lord's Witnesses were

"water" baptised later in 2000.
[16] Since 10th December 1996 Scientology (which handles the science of dianetics) has been officially recognised as a religion by the Home Office replacing its previous cult status. It is "a human potential group" founded by L Ron Hubbard in America in 1954; its UK headquarters are at Saint Hill Manor, East Grinstead.
[17] "Membership" is an estimate of the number who have taken a Scientology course.
[18] These are the elite "Sea Org" members, who have dedicated their lives to the movement.
[19] A summation of the figures of the Greater World Christian Spiritual Association (670 members in 1990 but with total attendance of 9,000), the Spiritual Association of Great Britain (15 congregations with 8,000 members in 1995, including 1 assembly in London with 65 mediums), and the Spiritualists National Union (formerly Federation) with 450 congregations and 26,000 members in 1995 (from World Christian Encyclopedia by Dr David Barrett, OUP, 2001). Using the trends given by Dr Barrett, the membership of the last two alone would be 32,920 in 2000.
[20] See also Tables 10.8.1 and 2.

Table 10.3.1
Swedenborgian New Church[4]

	Membership	Churches	Ministers
2000	1,292	28	15
2001	1,198	28[2]	13[2]
2002	1,148	28[2]	12[2]
2003	1,130	28	10[5]
2005[3]	1,000	24	11[5]
2010[3]	850	20	6
2020[3]	600	12	4

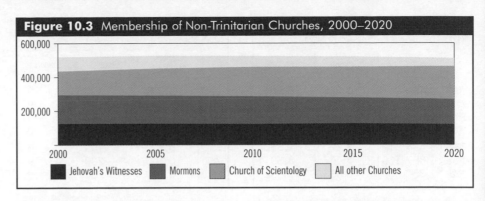

Figure 10.3 Membership of Non-Trinitarian Churches, 2000–2020

Legend: Jehovah's Witnesses · Mormons · Church of Scientology · All other Churches

Table 10.3.2
Theosophists[6]

	Membership	Churches	Ministers
2000[1]	2,000	51	–
2001[1]	1,950	50	–
2002[1]	1,900	49	–
2003[1]	1,850	48	–
2005[1]	1,800	45	–
2010[1]	1,500	40	–
2020[1]	750	30	–

Table 10.3.3
Unification Church[7]

	Membership	Churches	Ministers
2000[1]	1,000	17	27
2001[1]	1,100	17	27
2002[1]	1,200	17	27
2003[1]	1,200	17	27
2005[2]	1,200	17	27
2010[1]	1,000	17	27
2020[1]	500	10	15

Table 10.3.4
Unitarian and Free Christian Church[8]

	Membership	Churches	Ministers
2000	5,860	185	70
2001	5,550	182	70
2002[2]	5,329	178	65
2003	5,300	178	61
2005[3]	5,000	175	60
2010[3]	5,000	175	60
2020[3]	5,000	175	60

Table 10.3.5
Worldwide Church of God-originated Churches[16]

	Membership					Churches					Ministers				
	2000	2001	2002	2003	2005[1]	2000	2001	2002	2003	2005[1]	2000	2001	2002	2003	2005[1]
Churches of God UK[9]	2,000	2,000	2,000	2,000	2,000	15	15	15	15	15[2]	8	8	8	8	8[2]
Global Church of God[10]	40	40	40	40	40	4	4	4	4	4	1	1	1	1	1
Living Church of God[11]	60	60	60	60	60	6	6	6	6	6	6	6	6	6	6
Philadelphia Church of God[12]	30	28	26	24	20	3	3	3	3	3	3	3	3	3	3
United Church of God[13]	200	200	200	220	250	10	10	10	9	9	8	8	8	8	8
Total[14]	2,330	2,328	2,326	2,344	2,370	38	38	38	37	37	26	26	26	26	26

Table 10.3.6
Total of WCG-originated Churches

	Membership	Churches	Ministers
2000	2,330	38	26
2001	2,328	38	26
2002	2,326	38	26
2003	2,344	37	26
2005[1]	2,370	37	26
2010[1]	2,330	35	25
2020[1]	2,160	30	22

Table 10.3.7
Other Non-Trinitarian Churches[15]

	Membership	Churches	Ministers
2000	10,000	100	500
2001	10,000	100	500
2002	10,000	100	500
2003[1]	10,000	100	500
2005[1]	10,000	100	500
2010[1]	10,000	100	500
2020[1]	10,000	100	500

[1] Estimate

[2] Revised figure

[3] Church's own estimate

[4] Also known as the General Conference of the New Church. Although Trinitarian, it is included here because their members worship the Lord Jesus Christ as One God in whom is a trinity of Father, Son and Holy Spirit rather than the God in three persons of the traditional creeds.

[5] Includes one part-time minister.

[6] These figures cover the United Lodge of Theosophists (with 35 members in 1990) and the Theosophical Societies of England (with 1,500 members in 1990), Wales and Scotland, with estimates for N Ireland. They have no full time ministers. Numbers include the vegetarian Order of the Cross which had 30 congregations with perhaps 2,000 members in 1995 (Dr David Barrett, *World Christian Encyclopedia*, OUP, 2001).

[7] The full title is the Family Federation for World Peace and Unification (FFWPU), sometimes known as the "Moonies" after their founder, Rev S M Moon.

[8] The Unitarian Churches have strong links with the Non-subscribing Presbyterian Church of Ireland in which some of their members serve.

[9] Formerly known as the Church of God International, they re-formed in 1996 to become an association of independent local assemblies. These believe that the Holy Spirit is divine but not part of the Godhead. All figures are estimates.

[10] Began in 1995. All figures are estimated as they no longer make statistics available to the public. See website www.globalchurchof-god.co.uk

[11] Their leader, Roderick C Meredith, was originally an evangelist with the Worldwide Church of God. In 1995 he started the Global Church of God, which in 1998 split again with roughly 80% following Meredith as he started the Living Church of God. They have 2 churches in England, one in Wales, one in Scotland, one in Northern Ireland and one in Jersey. All other figures estimated. The website, www.truth.fateback.com, indicates they have 6,000 members worldwide.

[12] Began in 1994, and working in UK, Europe, the Middle East and north Africa. The figures are estimated, but, like some of the others in this Table, are based on conversations with representatives of the Worldwide Church of God (see Table 9.20.1).

[13] Began in 1996 with 150 members, 10 churches and 8 ministers, but later figures estimated. Website is www.ucg.org.uk

[14] These figures are carried into Table 10.3.6.

[15] Includes (1) the True Jesus Church who had 8 UK churches, and 4 Houses of Prayer (with congregations of between 15 and 30) in 2004; (2) The Way International, which in previous editions was listed separately, but now it is uncertain whether any members actually reside in the UK (see articles on sites www.pfo.org/close-way.htm and www.empirenet.com); (3) The General Church of the New Jerusalem with 2 churches with membership of 150 in 1995 according to Dr David Barrett (*World Christian Enclopedia*, OUP, 2001); (4) the Local Church Movement and (5) other groups. All figures are estimated.

[16] See also Table 10.8.3.

10

Table 10.4.1
TOTAL Other Religions & NRMs[4]

	Active Members	Groups	Leaders
2000	1,439,201	3,076	6,664
2001	1,479,857	3,102	6,885
2002	1,506,615	3,140	7,061
2003	1,538,079	3,188	7,343
2005	1,634,912	3,270	7,630
2010	1,887,150	3,467	8,391
2020	2,350,300	3,833	9,932

Table 10.4.2
Bahá'ís

	Active Members	Groups	Leaders[5]
2000[2]	5,900	190	9
2001[2]	6,000	190	9
2002[2]	6,000	190	9
2003	6,000	190	9
2005[3]	6,100	190	9
2010[3]	6,200	200	9
2020[3]	6,300	200	9

Table 10.4.3
Buddhists

	Active Members[6]	Groups	Priests
2000[1]	49,600	298[8]	955[2]
2001	50,605	302[1]	1,017[2]
2002[1]	51,600	306	1,078[2]
2003[7]	52,600	310	1,145
2005[1]	54,000	318	1,210[2]
2010[1]	58,400	332	1,260
2020[1]	65,300	355	1,350

Table 10.4.4
Buddhist Groups, 2003

	Active Members	Groups	Priests
Friends of the WBO[9]	21,000	64	670
New Kadampa Trad.[10]	3,700	42	40
ShinnyoEn[11]	300	3	5
Soka Gakkai Intnl[12]	5,000	3	50
Tibetan Buddhism[13]	18,000	555	180
Other groups[14]	4,600	143	300
TOTAL 2003	52,600	310	1,145

Figure 10.4.1
Main Buddhist Groups, UK, 2003

All other Buddhists 26%
Friends of the Western Buddhist Order 40%
Tibetan Buddhism 34%

Table 10.4.5
Hindus

	Active Members[15]	Groups[16]	Leaders
2000[1]	273,000	325[8]	160
2001	279,405	330	160
2002[1]	285,700	335	160
2003[1]	292,000	340	164
2005[1]	305,000	350	170
2010[1]	333,000	370	180
2020[1]	400,000	400	195

Table 10.4.6
ISKCON[17]

	Active Members	Core Groups	Full-time Leaders
2000[2]	9,000	50	135
2001[2]	9,000	50	140
2002[2]	9,500	55	145
2003	10,000[18]	56	150[1]
2005[1]	10,500	59	155
2010[1]	11,800	66	170
2020[1]	14,000	78	200

Table 10.4.7
Jains[19]

	Active Members	Groups	Leaders
2000[1]	15,000	16	–
2001[1]	15,000	16	–
2002[1]	15,000	16	–
2003[1]	16,000	17	–
2005[1]	17,000	18	–
2010[1]	19,000	20	–
2020[1]	22,000	22	–

Table 10.4.8
Jews

	Active Households	Synagogues	Rabbis and Ministers
2000	88,800	362	430
2001	87,790	362	430
2002	86,255	362	430
2003	86,000	365	433
2005[3]	86,000	365	435
2010[3]	85,500	365	435
2020[3]	85,100	366	436

Table 10.4.9
Muslims

	Active Members[20]	Registered Mosques[21]	Imams
2000[1]	768,238	612[22]	3,325
2001	795,563[23]	616	3,410
2002[2]	809,700	618	3,450
2003[1]	824,100	620	3,500
2005[1]	893,700	635	3,600
2010[1]	1,082,100	685	3,900
2020[1]	1,407,000	800	4,450

Figure 10.4.2
UK Muslims by Ethnicity, 2001

Pakistani	43%
Bangladeshi	17%
Indian	9%
Other Asian	13%
Black	6%
White British	4%
Irish/Other white	8%

Source: 2001 Population Census

[1] Estimate
[2] Revised figure
[3] Church's own estimate
[4] Totals of Tables 10.4.2,3; 10.4.5-9 and 10.5.1–6.
[5] There are no clergy or leaders in the position of personal leadership. These 9 people are the elected members of the National Spiritual Assembly's governing body whose size remains constant.
[6] In the 2001 Population Census 151,816 people in the UK said they were Buddhist. Our normal convention is to take half that community figure as an estimate for active membership as in *Religious Trends* No 4, but we have changed to a third of this number, reverting to the earlier estimates given in *Religious Trends* No 3, and closer to the 45,000 estimated in the website www.bbc.co.uk/schools/religion/buddhism (accessed September 2004). Other years are trended pro rata.
[7] These numbers are given in detail in Table 10.4.4, with the help of Inform. Numbers include 50 Buddhist monasteries and temples (so www.britainincanada.org accessed August 2004).

[8] *Religions in the UK*, Directory 2001–2003 lists all these Groups.
[9] WBO = Western Buddhist Order. Friends of the Western Buddhist Order was founded in 1967 by the English monk Sangharakshita (born Dennis Lingwood). He teaches a form of Mahayan Buddhism. Active Members, or Friends, are those on the mailing list, up from 6,000 in 1997. The 64 Groups include retreats, centres, businesses and charitable trusts as well as local groups; 7 are based in Scotland, 4 in Wales and 1 in N Ireland. Ordained leaders were 375 in 1997; in addition in 2003 there were a further 468 full-time workers.
[10] Trad = Tradition. The New Kadampa Tradition is a Mahayan school established in the UK in 1991 by Geshe Kelsang Gyatso, previously a monk in the Gelugpa School of Tibetan Buddhism. Its website www.kadampa.org lists 42 centres, including 2 each in Scotland and Wales (accessed September 2004). In 1991 there were a reported 3,000 followers in Great Britain, and Inform indicated there were 8,000 followers worldwide in 2001.
[11] ShinnyoEn claimed 100 followers in the UK in 1995; 2003 figures all estimated.
[12] Intnl = International. Soka Gakkai International broke away from the Nichiren Shoshu School of Buddhism in the 1990s. In 2001 there were 5,000 adherents

in the UK according to David Barrett's *The New Believers* (Cassell, 2002), and about 11.3 million worldwide, 10 million of whom are in Japan.
[13] The Office of Tibet indicated there were about 15,000 practitioners of Tibetan Buddhism in the UK in the early 1990s (*Religion Today*, Volume 8, Number 2, Spring 1993).
[14] All estimated but based in part on numbers in the *Buddhist Directory*.
[15] Active members taken as half the community, most of whom are Gujaratis or Punjabis from India or East Africa. Figures previously included adherents of the guru Sai Baba; these can now be found on Page 10.5 under Sri Sathya Sai Service Organisation. Figures exclude ISKCON given in Table 10.4.6.
[16] There are 150 Hindu Temples or Mandirs in the UK (www.ukvisas.gov.uk accessed September 2004).
[17] The International Society of Krishna Consciousness, also known as the Hare Krishna Movement, which began in 1969 in the UK with the opening of temple in London. Website: www.iskcon.org.uk
[18] Including some 4,200 patron members and 390 initiates in 1997.
[19] Active members taken as half the community.
[20] Including non-South Asians, and assumed to include approximately 8,000 members of the Ahmadiyya Movement, with 40 groups and up to 230 leaders.
[21] In addition to registered Mosques, Muslims meet in prayer rooms and other meeting places. In 1995 for example some 800 buildings were used, of which 200 were houses; in 2004 the website www.salaam.co.uk/mosques had a database of 1,550 mosques. The London Central Mosque is the largest with 5,000 in attendance at festivals.
[22] Including 584 mosques and meeting places in England and Wales in 1999, taken from *Religions in the UK* 2001.
[23] Active members taken as half the community figure of 1,591,126 Muslims in the UK, as given by the 2001 Population Census. Some believe this figure was too low; Professor Ceri Peach of Oxford puts the number of Muslims closer to 1.8 million and Dr Patrick Sookhdeo at 2.5 million. However in the absence of firm statistical evidence of a larger number the Census figure is used here for 2001. The "size of the UK Muslim population is slowly increasing as a result of migration of dependants, asylum and conversion" (Research and Documentation Dept., Muslim Council of Britain). Most UK Muslims observe the Sunni tradition.

10

Table 10.5.1
Satanists[4,5]

	Active Members	Groups	Leaders
2000[1]	750[2]	41	16
2001[6]	762[2]	42	17
2002[1]	770[2]	44	18
2003[1]	780	46	19
2005[1]	800	49	20
2010[1]	850	53	23
2020[1]	900	60	30

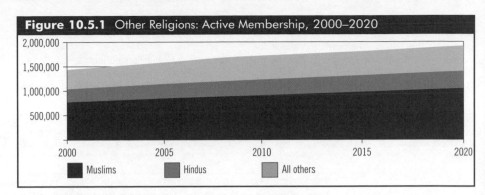

Figure 10.5.1 Other Religions: Active Membership, 2000–2020

Legend: Muslims · Hindus · All others

Table 10.5.2
Sikhs

	Active Members	Temples or Gurdwaras	Granthi
2000[1]	164,160	192	220
2001[8]	168,075	195	223
2002[1]	172,000	198	226
2003	176,000	201	229
2005[1]	184,000	208	235
2010[1]	200,000	220	249
2020[1]	230,000	241	272

Table 10.5.3
Zoroastrians

	Active Members[9]	Fire Temples[10]	Leaders
2000[1]	3,200	1	–
2001[1]	3,200	1	–
2002[1]	3,200	1	–
2003[1]	3,250	1	–
2005[1]	3,300	1	–
2010[1]	3,400	1	–
2020[1]	3,500	1	–

Table 10.5.4
Other Religions

	Active Members	Groups	Leaders
2000[2]	32,050	214	201
2001	33,250[11]	221	207
2002[2]	33,950	228	213
2003[1]	35,000	235	217
2005[2]	37,100	248	226
2010[1]	41,700	280	250
2020[1]	53,400	340	290

[1] Estimate
[2] Revised figure
[3] Church's own estimate
[4] Including members of the Temple of Set (about 60), Northern Order of the Prince, Society of the Dark Lily, Order of the Nine Angels and the Church of Satan (website: ChurchOfSatan.com).
[5] It is *not* true that "all witches are Satanists" (correspondence with the *Journal for the Academic Study of Magic*), nor that occultists, such as Wiccans, are Satanists either. A University of Newcastle survey suggested there were 50,000 witches in the UK in 2000 (*Church Times* article 7th July 2000), a number which appears too high and counts most Pagans as witches.
[6] Taken as half of the community, taken as the 1,525 who self-identified as Satanists in the 2001 Population Census. Previous editions have taken 10% of the estimated 4,000 in 2002 according to Vexen Crabtree (www.dpjs.co.uk).
[7] Not numbers enrolling.
[8] Active members taken as half the community of 336,149 recorded in the 2001 UK Population Census.
[9] In *Zoroastrians* (Routledge and Kegan Paul, 1976) Mary Boyce put the community in the UK at 3,000. An article by Harriot Crout-Tree in *Inter-Faith Network* on 17th February 1992 put it as 5,000 in 1990. A tribute to the rock musician Freddie Mercury in the *Independent* of 27th November 1991 put it that year at 6,000, an estimate given by Zal Sethna, the President of Zoroastrian Trust Funds. The 1997 edition of *Religions in the UK: A Multi-Faith Directory* gave a community figure of 5–10,000, concentrated in London and the North West. It has been assumed to be 6,000 in 1995, with active members taken as half that, with a slight growth in the 5 years to 2000.
[10] There are no Fire Temples in the UK, but the UK Headquarters in London is also a registered place of worship and marriage.
[11] Taken as half the community figure of 178,837 for "Other Religions" in the 2001 Population Census less the 2001 active membership for the Bahá'ís, Jains, Satanists, Zoroastrians and New Religious Movements. Other years spread pro rata to Table 10.8.3 in *Religious Trends* No 4.
[12] Taken from total of Table on Page 10.7, and spread across the years pro rata to Table 10.8.4 in *Religious Trends* No 4.
[13] Plotted in Figure 10.5.2.

Table 10.5.5
Minority Pagan and Occult Religious Affiliation, 2001 Population Census

Group	Number
Pagan	30,569
Wicca	7,227
Own Belief System	3,259
Druidism	1,657
Pantheism	1,603
New Age	906
Celtic Pagan	508
Animism	401
Heathen	278
Mysticism	158
Vodun	123
Occult	99
Ancestor Worship	98
Asatru	93
Santeri	21
Unspecified "other religion"	42,000
TOTAL 2001	**89,000**

Total excludes 32,404 Spiritualists included within Table 10.2.12 and 1,525 Satanists included within Table 10.5.1.

Table 10.5.6
New Religious Movements (NRMs)

	Active Members	Groups	Leaders
2000[2]	29,503	775	1,213
2001[2]	31,207	777	1,272
2002[2]	32,940	787	1,332
2004[12]	36,349	807	1,477
2005[2]	37,412	829	1,570
2010[1]	45,200	875	1,915
2020[1]	62,800	970	2,700

Table 10.5.7 Active Membership as Percentage of the UK Population[13]

	Non-Trinitarian Churches (Table 10.2.1) %	Other Religions (Table 10.4.1) %	Total Non-Christian %
2000	0.91	2.44	3.35
2005	0.91	2.73	3.64
2010	0.89	3.10	3.99
2020	0.84	3.72	4.56

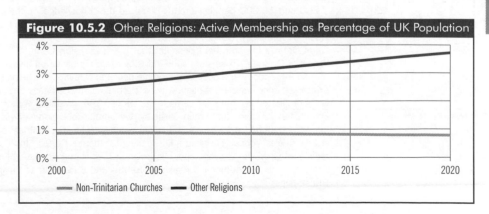

Figure 10.5.2 Other Religions: Active Membership as Percentage of UK Population

Legend: Non-Trinitarian Churches · Other Religions

10

We are grateful to Inform, London School of Economics, for their help in updating and expanding this Table. The primary criterion for inclusion in *Religious Trends* is that some statistical data about each New Religious Movement (NRM) is available, but it is impossible to make the meaning and comparability of the data given for each NRM identical.

Rather than have extended footnotes as in previous editions, a description of each NRM is embodied in the Table itself. Not all the descriptions given in previous editions of *Religious Trends* (Numbers 1 to 4) are repeated here, however. The total data, here estimated for the year 2004, is taken into **Table 10.5.6,** where the trends are taken from the totals given in **Table 10.10** in *Religious Trends* No 4.

Table 10.6
Some New Religious Movements, UK, 2004

Group	Notes	Active Members	Groups	Leaders
3HO	The Healthy, Happy, Holy Organization is made up of teachers and followers of Kundalini Yoga, as taught by Yogi Bahjan. Groups have been counted as the number of centres/classes run. Came to UK in early 1970s.	3,700[3]	74[2]	55[2]
11:11	Started in 1986. Followers believe that "11.11 is a cosmology and a map of [their] evolutionary journey from duality into Oneness" via the "Doorway" that opened on January 11th 1992 and is due to close on November 11th 2011. The founder, Solara, tours the world giving talks and sells 11.11 products under the company Star-borne Unlimited. There are no official meetings or membership figures, but have "Anchor Groups" that are formed around the times of Gate Activations, of which there will eventually be 11 at various worldwide locations. Website: www.nvisible.com	1,000[1]	10[1]	10[1]
Adidam	Formerly listed as Da Free John; began 1984. The official leader is their founder Adi Da. Members are organised into different guilds eg. educational, legal, finance etc, but membership and leadership of each is very fluid among and between these guilds. Combines teachings from Tibetan Buddhism, Hinduism and elements of Zen, est and Rajneesh. Places of worship are called Ashrams, of which there are 5 in England and 1 in Scotland. Leaders undertake pujas each day.	80	6	20
Aetherius Society	Claim to have about 8,000 people on their mailing list, with 700 "full members", who pay an annual fee and participate in 10 events a year. Website: www.aetherius.org	700	13	20[1]
Alternatives (Centre of New Age Movement)	Has one group in London, with 3 directors and 421 "friends" who make a direct financial contribution. Has a mailing list of just under 15,000. Is based at St James' Church, Piccadilly, London where they provide talks and lectures in Holistic Education.	421	1	3
Brahma Kumaris	Has been holding meditation courses in the UK since 1972. 30,000 attended these between 1972 and 1992, or 1,500 a year. Members are defined as regular attenders, 40 of whom are in Scotland and 20 are in Wales. One fifth are based in London. Website: www.db.bkwsu.com	1,500	60	100
Chrisemma	The full name is "The Chrisemma Foundation", founded by Chris Orchard and Emma Lea in November 1990. About 60 had tried their teachings by 1995; many were Sannyasins or Rajneesh members. Figures are for the "committed" who all live near Totnes in Devon.	60[1]	1[1]	4[1]
Creme, Benjamin	Creme is founder of a movement known as Share International who believe that the Maitreya, or the World Teacher, is yet to be revealed but is currently living in an Asian community somewhere in London. There is no organisation as such but its sphere of influence could be 10,000 people. Website: www.shareintl.org	400[1]	30[1]	24[1]
Da Free John	*See Adidam*			
Druid Network	Founded by Emma Restall Orr aka. Bobcat in late 2002, for the purpose of "inspiration and information". Although not an Order themselves, existing Orders can choose affiliation with the Network. They claim to be growing at an approximate rate of half a dozen per week. Have 12 groves (meetings) in England, 1 in Wales and 1 in Scotland. Website: www.druidnetwork.org	450	14	14[1]
Eckankar	There are no full-time workers, but each of the 27 local Directors has three helpers. Each major centre has a building, including Birmingham, London and Nottingham. 284 groups worldwide. Website: www.eckankar.org.uk	440[1]	17	115[1]
Elan Vital	The group renounced its Hindu connections when the old Divine Light Mission ceased operating in 1992; only the guru Maharaji continued as an instructor. Then between 7,000 and 10,000 people currently practiced the "Knowledge" in the UK, with 150 in training. In 2002 Elan Vital morphed again into the Prem Rawat Foundation, using satellite technology to promote its teachings.	3,000[2]	–	1
Falun Gong	Falun Dafa is the spiritual movement that practices Falun Gong, "The Practice of the Wheel of Dharma", 5 sets of health-inducing exercises based on ancient insights in the human mind, body and spirit that promote personal cultivation. The non-political, moral principles encourage practitioners to be truthful, compassionate and tolerant. Falun Gong originated in China and came to the UK in 1996. Website: www.falungong.org.uk	170[4]	28	6
Fellowship of Isis	Founded in 1976 in Huntingdon Castle by Rev Durdin Robertson with his wife and sister. In 1995 they had a following of 11,500 worldwide in 70 countries, being especially-strong in West Africa. They had a UK mailing list then of 5,000. In 2004, they have 2 registered Groves in England and 1 in Ireland, 3 registered Priories in England and 1 in Scotland, and an additional 3 registered Iseums and 8 Lyceums (training centres in the British Isles).	500[1]	7	15[2]

10

Table 10.7
Some New Religious Movements, UK, 2004

Group	Notes	Active Members	Groups	Leaders
Life Training	The program taught by the Kairos Foundation. Founded in 1979 Roy Whitten and Brad Brown. One leader is part-time.	400[1]	1[1]	4[1]
Mahakiri	Began in the UK in 1989 with 600 attending; a further 1,600 attended during the 1990s.	305	1[1]	4[1]
Mazdaznan Temple Association	American-based movement incorporating elements of Christianity, Islam and Zoroastrianism. Has no formal membership.	25[5]	2[1]	3[1]
Osho Movement	Refers to followers of the now deceased guru Osho aka. Bhagwan Shree Rajneesh (1931–1990). Group figures include both Meditation centres and Information centres. In Dorset a number of sannyasins live communally in the Osho Leela commune. The Osho Ko Hsuan School in Devon has approximately 50 pupils. Website: www.osho.com	1,000	18	30[1]
Outlook Training Organisation Ltd	Founded in 1988 by Pat Grove and Tony Wiseman; previously called "I am Grove". Was formerly called "Outlook Seminar Training" and in that name 7 courses were held in the UK in 1995; 5 will be in 2004. In 1995 there were 2,000 graduates, 65 people having done all 3 courses.	400[6]	2	3[1]
Pagan Federation	The 2001 Population Census gave the number of Pagans in Scotland as 1,930, England as 38,082, and Wales as 2,250. These figures include the Pagan paths of Wicca (7,227 people) and Druism (1,657) among others. Groups are called "moots". International membership in 2000 was 5,000; the quarterly *Pagan Dawn* has a readership of 10,000. See also Table 10.5.5. Website: www.paganfed.org	3,338[5]	121[2]	60[1]
Raelian Movement	Began in 1973. Raelians believe that the human race was created by aliens with cloning technology some 25,000 years ago. Membership statistics vary: 28,000 worldwide according to Belgian journalist Alain Allemand; 35,000 across 85 countries according to the Raelian flyer *Raelism*, atheistic religion of the year 2000; 40,000 according to the Raelian priest Yves Nawezi; 45,000 according to Rael himself; 55,000 in 84 countries according to article in *Cape Times*, South Africa, 5th July 2001; and 60,000 according to their website. The movement is notable for the work of Clonaid, their company that claimed to have produced the first cloned baby in December 2002. They are particularly strong in Belgium, Canada (Quebec), France, Italy, Japan and Switzerland.	4,380[7]	1	–
Sahaja Yoga	Founded in the early 1970s by Shri Mataji Nirmala Devi. Website: www.sahajayoga.org.uk	750[2]	51[2]	4[2]
School of Economic Science	Founded in 1938 by a small group of people including Leon MacLaren and his father Andrew. They do not claim to be a religion but rather a "new spiritual movement". Website: www.schooleconomicscience.org	2,500	52	2[1]
ShinnyoEn UK	Now included with Buddhist Groups in Table 10.4.4.			
Society of Inner Light	Founded by Dion Fortune in Glastonbury in 1924, the society claims to teach the development of "higher consciousness" through meditation and other techniques. Members have to complete an 18 month course. The society describes itself as a "Mystery School within the Western Esoteric Tradition". The headquarters are in London.	70	1[1]	12
Solara	See 11:11			
Sri Sathya Sai Service Organisation	Adherents of the guru Sai Baba in the UK, known by different names in different countries. Website: www.srisathyasai.org.uk	1,500[5]	64	20[1]
Subud	Founded in Indonesia in 1930s by Muhammed Subuh Sumohadiwidjojo (1901–1987), known as "Bapak". Promotes the principle of the worship of "God" known as *Susila Budhi Dharma*. Subud is an abbreviation of these 3 words: *susila* meaning humane behaviour that is in accordance with God's will; *budhi* being the inner power within human beings; and *dharma* meaning surrender in following God's will. The spiritual practice of *Subud* is known as *latihan*. Each group has a chairperson, a secretary and a treasurer. There are 8 administrative regions on the UK. Website: www.subud-britain.org	1,360[1]	70	210
Sukyo Mahikari	Began in Japan in 1959, and established in the UK in 1989 during which year about 600 attended. About 1,600 attended in the 1990s.			
Template Foundation	Previously known as Emin Foundation, Template Foundation is a Human Potential group which was founded by Raymond John Armin in London in the 1970s.	300	2[1]	2[1]
Transcendental Meditation (School of Meditation)	Based on Vedic Wisdom, this group was founded by Maharishi Mahesh Yogi in India in 1957. Has origins in the Hindu tradition but is now seen by many as part of the Human Potential Movement. They suggest that 160,000 people have learned Transcendental Meditation in Britain, through an introductory course of 90 minutes on 4 consecutive days, and 4,000 have completed the advanced Sidhi course. Websites: www.TM.org and www.t-m.org.uk	300 4,000[3]	5 80	1[1] 600
Other New Religious Movements		3,300	75	135
TOTAL (transferred to Table 10.5.6)		**36,349**	**807**	**1,477**

[1] Estimate
[2] Revised figure(s)
[3] Estimated members are those completing advanced course, and taken pro rata to Transcendental Meditation numbers.
[4] Voluntary practitioners.
[5] Membership taken as 10% of community or people involved.
[6] Membership taken as 10% of estimated total graduates in 2004.
[7] Membership taken as 10% of the average of the numbers cited.
[8] Taken at about 10% of total.

10

While Christian membership in the UK declines from 10% of the population in 2000 to an estimated 7% by 2020 (**Table 2.23.1**), that of the non-Christian religions increases 3% to 4% in the same period (**Table 10.5.7**). The consequence is not only that the trends are in opposite directions, but that the totality of active membership of religious bodies is decreasing over this period, as the Christian decline more than outweighs the non-Christian increase.

Both these trends are driven by main players in both groups. On the Christian side, it is the institutional churches which are declining not the Free Churches (**Table 2.22.1**), and among the institutional churches the Anglicans, Catholics and Presbyterians all see membership fall by the order of half a million over this 20 year period (**Tables 8.2.1, 8.5.1** and **8.9.1**), which in percentage terms are respectively –37%, –28% and –42%. On the non-Christian side, it is the Muslims, Hindus and Sikhs which are the main engines of growth, with increases of 36%, 28% and 30% respectively between 2000 and 2020.

It is therefore the changes taking place amongst the biggest groups (in both camps) which are determining the overall outcomes. The smaller groups, while in some cases seeing spectacular growth (or decline), cumulatively do not impact the overall outcomes significantly. It is the largest players that in this regard are the most important.

The changes taking place in these groups, –36% on the Christian side and +31% on the non-Christian side, are very similar in order of magnitude. It is not as though one particular group was making enormous gains or losses, but rather the larger denominations and religions are decreasing or increasing at roughly the same rate. A change of 34% over 20 years is equivalent to a change of 1.5% per annum, a relatively small rate of change which might not take too much to alter – a particularly important Christian event which drew many back to church, or a catastrophe (such as 9/11) which impeded the non-Christian growth. The outcomes, given as if present trends continue, are not necessarily certain.

Jehovah's Witnesses are in over 220 countries worldwide, virtually every country, as widespread as the Trinitarian Christian community. **Table 10.8.1** shows they are split 50%–50% between First World and Third World, unlike their Trinitarian companions who are more into the Third World than First (62% to 38% by 2010, **Table 1.2.2**).

Table 10.8.2 shows however that the average Memorial congregation is likely to be much higher in the Third World than the First (Peru, Angola, Venezuela, Democratic Republic of Congo and Zambia). It is in the Third World that enthusiasm may be seen, and which needs to be caught in the First World!

Table 8.10.3 shows the various changes which have taken the Worldwide Church of God from a cult to a mainline denomination, and the splits which have occurred along the way. See also **Tables 9.18.1** and **10.3.5**.

Table 10.8.1
Jehovah's Witnesses Worldwide, 2003

Continent	Number Baptised	Number of Congregations	Memorial Attendance
North America	64,665	28,296	4,953,004
Europe	46,247	19,784	2,819,095
Oceania	2,317	1,144	189,694
Latin America	64,927	17,463	3,464,844
Africa	61,544	19,125	3,395,102
Asia	17,581	9,695	1,167,454
Smaller countries	1,564	412	108,429
TOTAL 2003	**258,845**	**95,919**	**16,097,622**

Source: *The Watchtower*, 1st January 2004, Pages 18–21

Table 10.8.2
Countries with Largest Number of Jehovah's Witnesses, 2003

Country	Number of Congregations	Memorial Attendance	Average Attendance
United States	11,930	2,273,856	190
Mexico	10,968	1,738,387	160
Brazil	9,068	1,563,790	170
Dem Rep of Congo	2,943	722,387	245
Nigeria	4,606	585,163	125
Zambia	2,120	510,854	240
Philippines	3,450	435,318	125
Italy	3,029	428,982	140
Colombia	1,771	389,059	220
Japan	3,163	344,967	110
Venezuela	1,296	326,944	250
Argentina	1,735	290,256	165
Peru	916	288,021	315
Russia	1,246	282,350	225
Germany	2,175	281,149	130
Ukraine	1,333	270,505	205
Ghana	1,146	244,983	215
Poland	1,781	234,403	130
United Kingdom	1,481	217,961	145
Angola	735	208,038	285
All others	29,027	4,460,249	155
TOTAL 2003	**95,919**	**16,097,622**	**170**

Source: *The Watchtower*, 1st January 2004, Pages 18–21

Table 10.8.3
Worldwide Church of God, 1970–1998

Timeline of change		Splinter groups	
1986	Joseph Tkach becomes Pastor General	1970	Church of God (O'Brien)
1988	Members may seek medical help, observe birthdays, wear cosmetics	1978	Church of God International
1991	Revised teaching on new birth; divinity of Holy Spirit accepted	1985	Universal Church of God
1993	Doctrine of the Trinity accepted	1989	Philadelphia Church of God
1994	Church teaches true Christians are found in other denominations	1990	Twentieth Century Church of God
1994	Church teaches Christians are no longer under the Old Covenant laws	1991	Church of God (Philadelphia Era)
1995	Joseph Tkach dies; son succeeds him	1992	Global Church of God
1995	Members permitted to observe Christmas and Easter	1995	United Church of God
1996	Church apologises to members and others for its erroneous teachings	1996	Worldwide Church of God splits organisationally
1997	Worldwide Church of God joins American National Association of Evangelicals	1998	Living Church of God

Source: Website www.wordiq.com/definition accessed July 2004

11

Denominational Maps

Sources: *Regional Trends* and other Government publications

A Tribute to John Whitehorn

Picture courtesy *Inside Out*, CWM

The Christian world owes a large debt of gratitude to John Whitehorn. He studied languages at university and then trained in linguistics and phonetics at the School of Oriental and African Studies in London, before going as a missionary in 1951 to Taiwan (then known as Formosa). He spent 19 years co-ordinating the translation of the Bible into Paiwan, the language of a minority aboriginal tribe which lives in mountains in south Taiwan, living on farming as well as hunting, animal husbandry and creek fishing.

Behind this translation work was a man of intense detail, determined to get everything correct. "How do you translate the phrase 'I will give you the keys of the kingdom of heaven'", he asked, "when there are no keys in aboriginal society?" Early in his retirement he somehow learned of our endeavours at MARC Europe (as Christian Research was previously called) to draw maps of the boundaries of the various districts, dioceses, associations (or whatever their name may be) for the different denominations in the UK, and volunteered to draw them. He superimposed them upon an outline map showing the civil counties enabling one to determine very easily which geographical areas were covered (and to which secular statistics could be applied). These first appeared in the 1989/1990 edition of the *UK Christian Handbook.*

They were brilliant, a unique achievement, detail not previously captured, and were much appreciated by users of the *Handbook*, researchers, denominational planners and others. Very kindly he volunteered to keep them up-to-date, writing to denominational headquarters each time asking if there had been any changes. The research undertaken was meticulous, looking at large scale maps to determine just which side of a boundary a particular church went, and how a denominational boundary exactly related to the civil boundary. Woe betide us if in the setting of his maps the typesetter made a mistake! John would come back with his red pen to indicate absolutely precisely what change should be made!

He also drew some large scale maps of individual counties with virtually all the churches shown, maps which appeared in *Religious Trends* No 3, although one, for Northumberland, is shown in this volume on **Page 11.16** (having missed No 3), to show the kind of detail John excels at. The maps on the following pages, his final selection, all completely revised and redrawn, are included in this edition of *Religious Trends*, as his final offering of maps of this kind which are so useful for so many. We are hugely grateful for his persistence, his humility, his concern for accuracy, and his sheer professional skill to do this work over 15 years. Now in his 80s, John acts as Secretary to the Ecumenical Order of Ministry, and lives with his wife in Birmingham. Thank you, John, for your stirling work over the years; we are all immensely grateful for your devotion as a cartographer!

Church of England

Province of York
3 Blackburn
4 Bradford
7 Carlisle
9 Chester
13 Durham
22 Liverpool
24 Manchester
25 Newcastle
30 Ripon & Leeds
35 Sheffield
36 Sodor & Man
38 Southwell and Nottingham
40 Wakefield
43 York

Church of Ireland

Province of Armagh
1 Connor
2 Derry and Raphoe
3 Down and Dromore
4 Armagh
5 Clogher
6 Kilmore, Elphin and Ardagh
7 Tuam, Killala and Achonry

Province of Dublin
8 Meath and Kildare
9 Dublin and Glendalough
10 Cashel, Waterford, Lismore,
   Ossory, Ferns and Leighlin
11 Limerick, Ardfert, Aghadoe,
   Killaloe, Kilfenora, Clonfert,
   Kilmacduagh and Emly
12 Cork, Cloyne and Ross

Church in Wales

A St Asaph
B Bangor
D St Davids
L Llandaff
M Monmouth
S Swansea and Brecon

Scottish Episcopal Church
1 Aberdeen & Orkney
2 Argyll & the Isles
3 Brechin
4 Edinburgh
5 Glasgow & Galloway
6 Moray, Ross & Caithness
7 St Andrews, Dunkeld & Dunblane

Shetland Islands

— Provincial boundaries
— Diocesan boundaries

Church of England

Province of Canterbury
1 Bath and Wells
2 Birmingham
5 Bristol
6 Canterbury
8 Chelmsford
10 Chichester
11 Coventry
12 Derby
14 Ely
15 Exeter
16 Gloucester
17 Guildford
18 Hereford
19 Leicester
20 Lichfield
21 Lincoln
23 London
26 Norwich
27 Oxford
28 Peterborough
29 Portsmouth
31 Rochester
32 St Albans
33 St Edmondsbury & Ipswich
34 Salisbury
37 Southwark
39 Truro
41 Winchester
42 Worcester

39
Scilly Isles
0 Miles 4

41
Alderney   Jersey
Guernsey   Sark
0 Miles 8
Channel Islands

Isle of Man

Isle of Wight

0   MILES   50

11

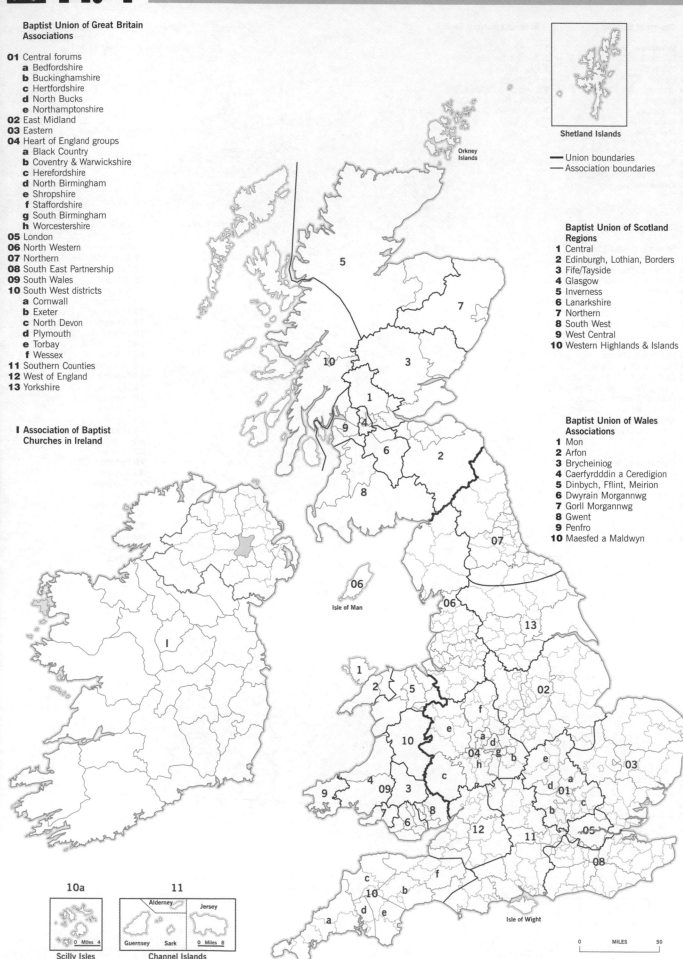

Baptist Union of Great Britain Associations

01 Central forums
  a Bedfordshire
  b Buckinghamshire
  c Hertfordshire
  d North Bucks
  e Northamptonshire
02 East Midland
03 Eastern
04 Heart of England groups
  a Black Country
  b Coventry & Warwickshire
  c Herefordshire
  d North Birmingham
  e Shropshire
  f Staffordshire
  g South Birmingham
  h Worcestershire
05 London
06 North Western
07 Northern
08 South East Partnership
09 South Wales
10 South West districts
  a Cornwall
  b Exeter
  c North Devon
  d Plymouth
  e Torbay
  f Wessex
11 Southern Counties
12 West of England
13 Yorkshire

I Association of Baptist Churches in Ireland

Baptist Union of Scotland Regions

1 Central
2 Edinburgh, Lothian, Borders
3 Fife/Tayside
4 Glasgow
5 Inverness
6 Lanarkshire
7 Northern
8 South West
9 West Central
10 Western Highlands & Islands

Baptist Union of Wales Associations

1 Mon
2 Arfon
3 Brycheiniog
4 Caerfyrdddin a Ceredigion
5 Dinbych, Fflint, Meirion
6 Dwyrain Morgannwg
7 Gorll Morgannwg
8 Gwent
9 Penfro
10 Maesfed a Maldwyn

Shetland Islands

—— Union boundaries
—— Association boundaries

Orkney Islands

Isle of Man

Scilly Isles

Channel Islands

Alderney
Jersey
Guernsey Sark

Isle of Wight

0 MILES 50

Scotland Provinces

St Andrews & Edinburgh
1 St Andrews & Edinburgh*
2 Aberdeen
3 Argyll & the Isles
4 Dunkeld
5 Galloway

Glasgow
6 Glasgow*
7 Motherwell
8 Paisley

Ireland Provinces

Province of Armagh
1 Armagh*
2 Ardagh & Clonmacnois
3 Clogher
4 Derry
5 Down & Connor
6 Dromore
7 Kilmore
8 Meath
9 Raphoe

Province of Dublin
10 Dublin*
11 Ferns
12 Kildare & Leighlin
13 Ossory

Province of Cashel
14 Cashel & Emly*
15 Cloyne
16 Cork & Ross
17 Kerry
18 Killaloe
19 Limerick
20 Waterford & Lismore

Province of Tuam
21 Tuam*
22 Achonry
23 Clonfert
24 Elphin
25 Galway
26 Killala

Shetland Islands

── Provincial boundaries
── Diocesan boundaries
 *Archdiocese

England & Wales Provinces

Liverpool
1 Hexham & Newcastle
2 Middlesbrough
3 Hallam
4 Leeds
5 Salford
6 Liverpool (inc Isle of Man)*
7 Lancaster

Westminster
8 Nottingham
9 East Anglia
10 Brentwood
11 Westminster*
12 Northampton

Southwark
13 Southwark*
14 Arundel & Brighton
15 Portsmouth (inc Channel Isles)
16 Plymouth (inc Scilly Isles)

Birmingham
17 Clifton
18 Birmingham*
19 Shrewsbury

Cardiff
20 Cardiff*
21 Menevia
22 Wrexham

Orkney Islands

Isle of Man

Scilly Isles

Alderney
Jersey
Guernsey Sark
Channel Islands

Isle of Wight

0 MILES 50

Areas

1 North West Area Districts
  a North Lancashire & Cumbria
  b Merseyside & South Lancashire
  c Derbyshire, High Peak
  d North Manchester
  e South Manchester
  f Lancashire, Oldham
2 North East
3 Wales
4 North West Midlands and North Wales
5 South West Midlands
6 East Midlands
7 Norfolk
8 Eastern
9 South West
10 South East
11 Central Southern
12 Congregational Federation
   in Scotland

Shetland Islands

Orkney Islands

Isle of Man

1a

2

12

1d 1f
1b 1e 1c

4

6

7

3

5

8

11

10

9

Isle of Wight

0   MILES   50

Alderney   Jersey

Guernsey   Sark   0   Miles   8

Channel Islands

0   Miles   4

Scilly Isles

11

Regions

1 Scotland
2 Wales & South West Midlands
3 Southern
4 North Midlands & North West
5 Metropolitan East
6 North East
7 Midland
8 London City
9 Ireland
10 Metropolitan West

(8 is a special region with no specific boundaries.)

Shetland Islands

Orkney Islands

Isle of Man

Isle of Wight

Scilly Isles

Channel Islands
Alderney
Jersey
Guernsey   Sark

11

11.8 Denominational Maps: Methodist Districts

Stationing Regions and their Districts

South East
1 London NE
2 London NW
3 London SW
4 London SE
14 East Anglia

Lancashire
6 Bolton and Rochdale
15 Isle of Man
18 Liverpool
19 Manchester & Stockport
21 North Lancashire

Wales/West Midlands
5 Birmingham
8 South Wales
11 Chester and Stoke
28 Wolverhampton & Shrewsbury
33 North Wales

East Midlands
17 Lincoln & Grimsby
22 Nottingham & Derby
23 Oxford & Leicester

North
9 Cumbria
13 Darlington
20 Newcastle upon Tyne
31 Scotland
32 Shetland

South West
7 Bristol
10 Channel Isles
12 Cornwall
24 Plymouth & Exeter
26 Southampton

Yorkshire
16 Leeds
25 Sheffield
27 West Yorkshire
29 York & Hull

Wales
30 Cymru (Welsh-speaking)
(stationed independently)

Ireland
1 Dublin
2 Midlands & Southern
3 Enniskillen & Sligo
4 Londonderry
5 North East
6 Belfast
7 Down
8 Portadown

Shetland Islands

—— Stationing Region boundaries
— District boundaries

Orkney Islands

Isle of Man

Isle of Wight

0   MILES   50

12
Scilly Isles
0 Miles 4

10
Alderney   Jersey
Guernsey   Sark
Channel Islands
0 Miles 8

Boundaries between General Meetings
are not recognised by the Britain
Yearly Meeting, but are included for
comparison with other denominations.

Britain Yearly Meeting

General Meetings
1 Bedfordshire
2 Berks and Oxon
3 Bristol and Somerset
4 Cumberland
5 Derbyshire, Lincolnshire and
  Nottinghamshire
6 Devon and Cornwall
7 Durham
8 Essex and Suffolk
9 Hampshire, Isle of Wight and
  Channel Islands
10 Kent
11 Lancashire and Cheshire
12 London and Middlesex
13 Norfolk, Cambridge and
   Huntingdon
14 Sussex and Surrey
15 Warwick, Leicester and Stafford
16 Western
17 Westmorland
18 Yorkshire

Scotland General Meeting

(Monthly Meetings)
19a North of Scotland
19b East of Scotland
19c South-East Scotland
19d West of Scotland

Ireland Yearly Meeting

Quarterly Meetings
1 Ulster
2 Leinster and Connaught
3 Munster

Shetland Islands

Scilly Isles

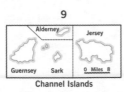

Channel Islands

Divisions
1 Anglia
2 Central North
3 Central South
4 East Midlands
5 East Scotland
6 Ireland
7 London Central
8 London North-East
9 London South-East
10 Northern
11 North Scotland
12 North-Western and Isle of Man
13 Southern inc Channel Islands
14 South and Mid Wales
15 South-Western
16 West Midlands
17 West Scotland
18 Yorkshire

Shetland Islands

Orkney Islands

Isle of Man

15
Scilly Isles

13
Alderney   Jersey
Guernsey Sark
Channel Islands

Isle of Wight

11

IM Irish Mission
SM Scottish Mission
WM Welsh Mission

North England Conference Regions
1N The North
2N The North West
3N Yorkshire & Humberside
4N East Midlands
5N West Midlands
6N South Midlands

South England Conference Areas
1S Devon & Cornwall
2S Somerset, North Somerset, Gloucestershire & Wiltshire
3S Hampshire & Dorset
4S Kent & Sussex
5S Berkshire, Buckinghamshire, Oxfordshire & Surrey
6S London
   a North
   b South
   c East
   d West
7S Bedfordshire. Hertfordshire & Buckinghamshire
8S Cambridgeshire, Essex, Suffolk & Norfolk

Shetland Islands

——— Conference/Mission boundaries
——— Region/Area boundaries

Orkney Islands

Isle of Man

Isle of Wight

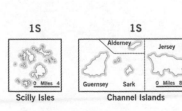

1S

Scilly Isles

1S

Alderney   Jersey

Guernsey   Sark

Channel Islands

0   MILES   50

Synods
1 Northern
2 North Western
3 Mersey (inc Isle of Man)
4 Yorkshire
5 East Midlands
6 West Midlands
7 Eastern
8 South Western
9 Wessex (inc Channel Islands)
10 Thames North
11 Southern
12 Wales Districts
  a North Wales
  b East Wales
  c South Wales
  d West Wales
  e Pembrokeshire
  f Mid Wales
  g Bridgend Area
13 Scotland

Shetland Islands

Orkney Islands

Isle of Man

Scilly Isles

Channel Islands
Alderney
Jersey
Guernsey
Sark

Isle of Wight

Regions
1 Scottish
2 Northern
3 North Western
4 Central Northern
5 West Midlands
6 East Midlands
7 Welsh
8 Central
9 Eastern
10 South Western
11 South Eastern

Shetland Islands

Orkney Islands

Isle of Man

10
Scilly Isles

11
Alderney   Jersey
Guernsey   Sark
Channel Islands

Isle of Wight

MILES

Figure 11.14.1
Union of Welsh Independents Associations

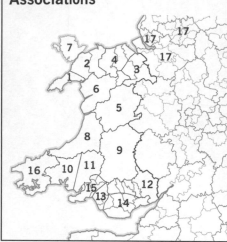

Union of Welsh Independents (Figure 11.14.1)

Associations
1 Cyfundeb Llyn ac Eifionydd
2 Gogledd Arfon
3 Dwyrain Dinbich a Fflint
4 Gorllewin Dinbich a Fflint
5 Maldwyn
6 Meirion
7 Mon
8 Aberteifi
9 Brycheiniog
10 Gorllewin Caerfyrddin
11 Dwyrain Caerfyrddin
12 Gogledd Morgannwg a Mynwy
13 Cynffig Nedd
14 Dwyrain Morgannwg
15 Gorllewin Morgannwg
16 Penfro
17 Lerpwl a'r Cylch
18 Llundain
   (not shown)

Church of Scotland
(Figure 11.15.1)

Presbyteries
1 Edinburgh
2 West Lothian
3 Lothian
4 Melrose and Peebles
5 Duns
6 Jedburgh
7 Annandale and Eskdale
8 Dumfries and Kirkcudbright
9 Wigtown and Stranraer
10 Ayr
11 Irvine and Kilmarnock
12 Ardrossan
13 Lanark
14 Greenock and Paisley
16 Glasgow
17 Hamilton
18 Dumbarton
19 Argyll
22 Falkirk
23 Stirling
24 Dunfermline
25 Kirkcaldy
26 St Andrews
27 Dunkeld and Meigle
28 Perth
29 Dundee
30 Angus
31 Aberdeen
32 Kincardine and Deeside
33 Gordon
34 Buchan
35 Moray
36 Abernethy
37 Inverness
38 Lochaber
39 Ross
40 Sutherland
41 Caithness
42 Lochcarron-Skye
43 Uist
44 Lewis
45 Orkney
46 Shetland (not shown)

Free Church of Scotland
(Figure 11.15.2)

Presbyteries

Southern Synod
1 Edinburgh & Perth
2 Glasgow & Argyll

Northern Synod
3 Inverness, Lochaber & Ross
4 Northern

Western Synod
5 Skye & Western Ross
6 Western Isles

Presbyterian Church in Ireland
(Figure 11.15.3)

Presbyteries
1 Ards
2 Armagh
3 Ballymena
4 Belfast North
5 Belfast South
6 Belfast East
7 Carrickfergus
8 Coleraine
9 Derry and Strabane
10 Donegal
11 Down
12 Dromore
13 Dublin and Munster
14 Foyle
15 Iveagh
16 Monaghan
17 Newry
18 Omagh
19 Route
20 Templepatrick
21 Tyrone

Presbyterian Church of Wales
(Figures 11.15.4 and 5)

Presbyteries
1 Aberteifi – De
2 Aberteifi – Gogledd
3 Arfon
4 Brecon, Radnor and Hereford
5 Caerfyrddin – De
6 Caerfyrddin – Gogledd
7 Cheshire, Flint and Denbigh*
8 Wrecsam
9 Dyffryn Clwyd
10 Dyffryn Conwy
11 Fflint
12 Glamorgan – East*
13 Glamorgan – West*
14 Lancashire and Cheshire*
15 Liverpool
16 Lleyn ac Eifionydd
17 Llundain
18 Manchester
19 Dwyrain Meirionydd
20 Garllewin Meirionydd
21 Mon
22 Montgomery & Shropshire*
23 Morgannwg – Dwyrain
24 Morgannwg – Gorllewin
25 Gwent
26 South Pembroke*
27 Penfro – Gogledd
28 Trefaldwyn Isaf
29 Trefaldwyn Uchaf
30 North Wales Coast*

* English-speaking presbyteries
  (15, 17 and 18 are not shown)

Figure 11.14.2 Distribution of all Church Buildings on Ynys Môn

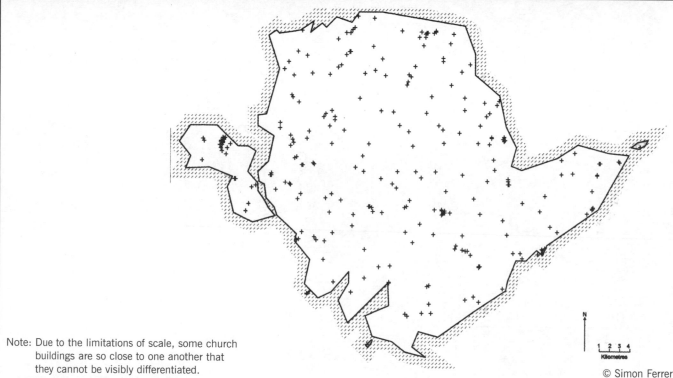

Note: Due to the limitations of scale, some church buildings are so close to one another that they cannot be visibly differentiated.

© Simon Ferrer

Figure 11.15.1
Church of Scotland
Presbyteries

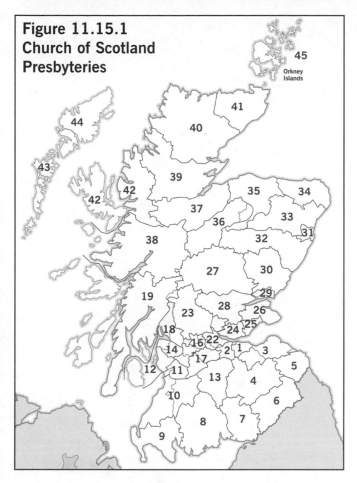

Figure 11.15.2
Free Church of Scotland
Presbyteries

— Synod boundaries
— Presbytery boundaries

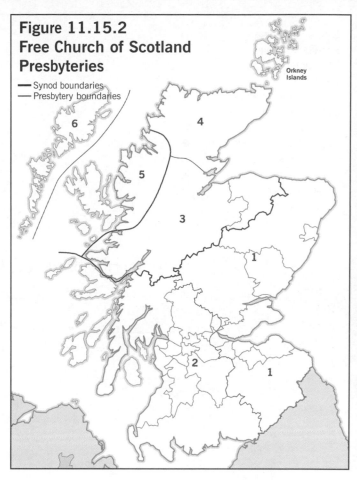

Figure 11.15.3
Presbyterian Church in Ireland
Presbyteries

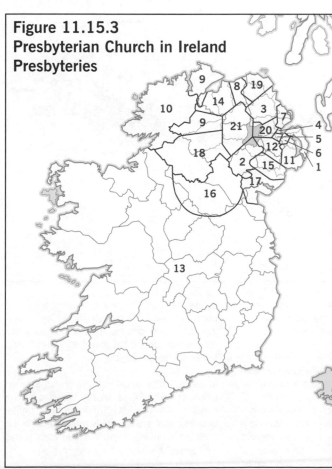

Figure 11.15.4
Presbyterian Church
of Wales Presbyteries
(Welsh-Speaking)

— Province boundaries
— Presbytery boundaries

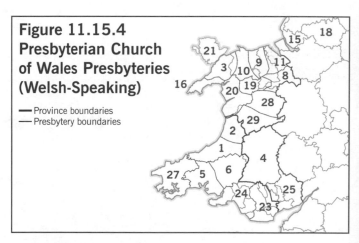

Figure 11.15.5
Presbyterian Church
of Wales Presbyteries
(English-Speaking)

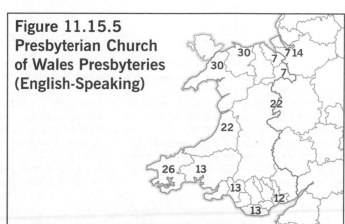

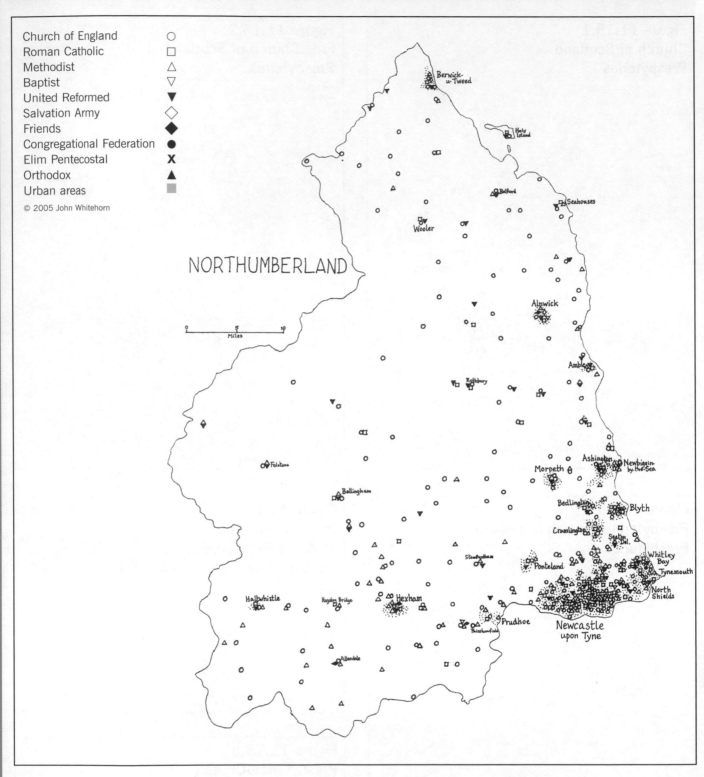

Church of England ○
Roman Catholic □
Methodist △
Baptist ▽
United Reformed ▼
Salvation Army ◇
Friends ◆
Congregational Federation ●
Elim Pentecostal ✕
Orthodox ▲
Urban areas ▪

© 2005 John Whitehorn

NORTHUMBERLAND

This map gives the detailed location of 473 churches, not all of which are open every week (and thus are not reflected in the usual totals for numbers of churches). All the churches for the 10 denominations given in the Key are shown, representing 97% of the Northumberland churches. The ones not indicated are some of the Independent Churches, the New Churches and others in the smaller denominations.

The huge dominance of the Church of England and Methodists in the rural areas is readily

observed. The United Reformed Church is also well represented, reflecting the fact that one of its constituent churches in 1972 was the Presbyterian Church of England. Northumberland, being close to Presbyterian Scotland, had many such Presbyterian churches which have continued under the union.

The Local Authority in which Newcastle is situated, Blyth Valley, had only 6.4% of its population in church on Sunday in 1998, whereas the rural areas of Tynedale (the west of Northumberland) and Alnwick (a band going

across the county north and south of the town) both had over 10% of their population, showing that rural communities are often more closely knit around the life of the church than those in urban contexts.

In 1998, Northumberland county had a population of 308,000, a county the size of the London Borough of Bromley, but, unlike Bromley, was seeing steady growth during the 1990s. With an overall 7.8% in church this was above the national average of 7.5%.

Church Trends to 2040

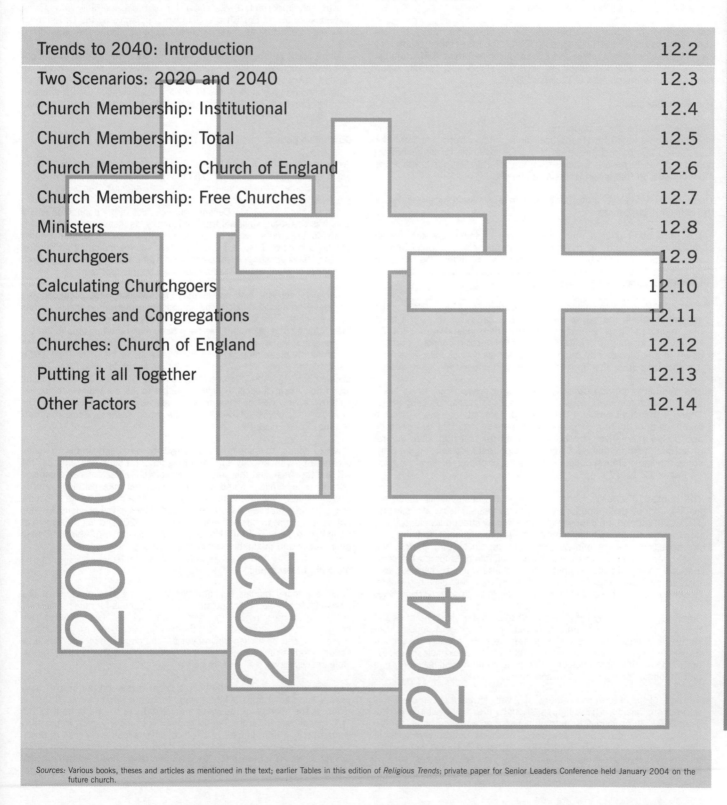

Sources: Various books, theses and articles as mentioned in the text; earlier Tables in this edition of *Religious Trends*; private paper for Senior Leaders Conference held January 2004 on the future church.

This section primarily looks at the church situation as it may have become by the year 2040. Why choose the year 2040? Many take a generation to be 18 years (see, for example, Table 5.6.1 in *Religious Trends* No.3). Two generations thus are 36 years, and 36 years on from 2004 when this piece is being penned, is 2040. It will be the generation of those who are under 30 today.

In his latest brilliant book, *The Church Invisible* (Zondervan, 2004), Nick Page describes the future of the church and takes as his *modus operandi* the year 2040. Even Arthur Clarke, the famous science fiction author, used to spanning millennia with ease, takes the year 2037 in his latest novel *Time's Eye* (Gollancz, 2004) because, he says, after that date "earth has run out of history to change." Whether that be true or not, the year 2040 seems a sensible place to settle.

The Government Actuary's Department is responsible for future UK population projections, but only goes to 2041 for its detailed country by country projections by gender and age (as given in Tables 4.3), although it does give broad UK projections to 2071 (Table 4.2.1). This again affirms the reasonableness of the year 2040.

The available data

Future projections are extrapolations of past and present data, usually based on some kind of mathematical model known to fit past data. The data has to be comprehensive, in this case, available for all denominations, and has to have a sufficient number of observations to make the model viable, in this case ideally for many years.

There are only five types of quantitative data available for use as far as the church is concerned:

• The number of *church members*. This is certainly available for all denominations, and, in most cases, for many years. Unfortunately almost every denomination defines "membership" differently, and while figures within a denomination are homogeneous, across all denominations the numbers are heterogeneous.

It is possible to ignore such differences as being small in relation to the general trends in the figures (which is true), and it is on such a basis that membership is projected forwards here (see **Pages 12.4–7**). However, and much more importantly, membership cannot be broken down in any further way, such as geographically, or by age or gender. It is this inability which limits the value of membership for forecasting.

• The number of *church buildings* or congregations. This also is available for all denominations and, again in most cases, for many years. There is the slight problem that a few denominations have no church buildings but counting congregations is usually regarded as a perfectly acceptable alternative. This allows then for the fact that, often in rural or ethnic minority areas, different denominations, with agreement, share the same church building. A forecast of church buildings is given on **Pages 12.11,12**.

• The number of *church leaders* or ministers/priests, which again are available for all denominations across many years. Historically, say pre-1970, virtually all the data would relate to only stipendiary clergy. Even now, some denominations only have full-time salaried staff in such positions, others have ministers who are unpaid by their church, and most churches have a mixture of both. Available data for most denominations do not differentiate between paid and unpaid. There is therefore a heterogeneity implicit in the figures for church leaders. Notwithstanding, a forecast of their numbers is given in detail on **Page 12.8**.

Since 1980, especially with the growth of both the black churches and the New Churches, non-stipendiary ministers have been appointed in some denominations in quite large numbers. It is easier to appoint unpaid leaders than paid: many black churches, for example, have several unpaid ministers, whereas white congregations will have only one paid minister as this is all they can afford.

• The size of the *church community,* as given, for example, in the 2001 Population Census. These figures, though, are only available for the year 2001, the previous time they were collected being 1851, far too long ago to be of use in forecasting! The 2001 figures were given in detail in *Religious Trends* No 4 (Pages 2.2 and 2.3), and will eventually be available broken down by all the key census variables, such as age, gender, occupation, education, marital status, housing, etc. It is however not available by denomination in England. Discussion of the

figures is given in this *Religious Trends* (No 5) on **Page 2.3**, but the data is such that it cannot be used for forecasting at the present time.

• The number of *church attenders*. This is available in theory for all denominations, but published data mostly groups the denominations together in 10 broad categories in England, 7 in Scotland and 6 in Wales. They are not available however for many years – just 3 in England (1979, 1989 and 1998) and Scotland (1984, 1994 and 2002) and 2 in Wales (1982 and 1995).

However the data can be broken down by age and gender, as well as geographically and by churchmanship (for recent years). It is the first two of these control variables, age and gender, which makes this data extremely important. These allow, for example, mortality information (published in the English and Scottish *Life Tables* by the Government Actuary Departments in each country) to be applied to the projections.

There are a number of caveats with this data which have to be considered, such as whether attend*ers* or attend*ances* are counted when there is more than one service on a Sunday, whether midweek attendance should be included, the frequency of attendance (and services in some churches), etc. Nevertheless the data is used for projecting ahead on **Pages 12.9,10**.

Qualitative data

While it is quantitative data which has to be used for extrapolation, there are a number of measures of "spirituality" or "religiosity" which are of interest. Some of these were published in *Religious Trends* No 3 and mostly show declining trends across the last half of the 20th century. On the other hand, the 2001 Census figure of 72% of the population which says it is Christian, suggests that Christianity, as measured by the quantitative data listed above, may not necessarily follow the numeric trends. The arguments on **Page 2.3** of this present volume indicate that this figure may be suggesting an inherent belief system which the behavioural, personnel or plant data (listed above) may be mis-representing.

Especially over the last half-century, sociologists have predicted the demise of organised religion, the so-called 'secularization thesis'. It has been especially associated with Emile Durkheim, the French 'father' of the sociology of religion, but has been particularly promulgated in the UK by, for example, Bryan Wilson of Oxford and Steve Bruce of Aberdeen. In an article "A bleak outlook is seen for religion" in the 25th April 1968 issue of the *New York Times*, the American sociologist Peter Berger claimed that by "the 21st century, religious believers are likely to be found only in small sects, huddled together to resist a worldwide secular culture", a view he has since recanted according to Reginald Bibby, the Canadian sociologist of religion in his book *Restless Gods* (Stottart, Toronto, 2002, Page 8).

It would appear that some kind of religiosity, spirituality, implicit religion or whatever will certainly survive during the 21st century in Europe, the UK and the West. But this volume of *Religious Trends* looks at 'organised religion' which means some kind of behavioural manifestation of faith, however infrequently it might be expressed. As a consequence it focusses on the quantitative measures described above, in the previous sections largely looking at trends between 2000 and 2020, and in this section at trends up to the year 2040. However, please note that in Table 12.3 both quantitative and qualitative data are shown together.

Method of forecasting

There are many models available for fitting data to some kind of line whose trajectory can be calculated ahead by various formulae. However, virtually all of these require much more data than we have available from church records, especially for the variable of greatest importance (because it can be broken down by age): church attendance. I have tried various models, including curvilinear regression, but they all give impossible answers even a few years hence.

The one which is consistently best is linear regression, although I have used a dampened form, which means that an estimate for say 2030 is taken as the average of the trend from 2000 and the trend from 2020. This means that if the decline (or growth) is especially great in the early years, the long-term impact is modified. This is frequently seen in practice when after a period of rapid change there is a much more stable period when consolidation takes place. Even so, the trends shown are bad enough! However, other methods are used when more appropriate.

Table 12.3 The UK Christian Scene in 2020 and 2040 (perhaps)

Factor	2020	2040
Christian community	The 72% of the 2001 Census fallen to about 50%	Now shrunk to perhaps 35%, and most of these elderly
Non-Christian religions (Table 12.14.1)	Perhaps 10% of the population (up from 6% in 2001)	Perhaps now 15% of the population
No religion	Perhaps 40% of the population (up from 22% in 2001)	Now about 50% of the population
Media	*Songs of Praise* discontinued Christian radio in London and other cities struggles	A booming cyberchurch? Christian radio ceased a decade ago (no viable audience or finance)
Church buildings (Table 12.7.1)	Some 2,000 rural churches closed	Virtually all rural and inner city churches closed
Church membership	Probably 7% of the population (down from 10% in 2000)	Now under 5% of the population, and almost all older people
Average congregation (Table 12.13)	Average is now 64 people (down from 95 in 2000)	Average is now 42 people (but 40% of the churches existing in 2000 gone)
Church attendance (Table 12.9.1)	Almost halved since 2000 when percentage was 7.6% in Great Britain; now 4.4%	More than halved since 2020; now 2.0%
Larger churches	50% of churchgoers go to 10% of churches (down from 18% in 1989, 15% in 1998 and 12% in 2010)	50% of churchgoers go to perhaps just 5% of churches
Attendance frequency	Sticks at about once a month; 10% of population attend at Christmas (down from 20% in 2000); Christmas increasingly secular	"Regulars" twice a month; Christmas no longer special – now called Winterval
Average age (Tables 12.9.1,2)	46% 65 or over (25% in 2000); average age 56 (was 43)	65% now 65 years or over; average age now 64
Churchmanship	Evangelicals dominate, but splits occurred 10 years ago	Churchmanship irrelevant – so are denominations
Weekday worship	Increased to a third of Sunday attendance (10% in 2000)	No significant change on 20 years ago (novelty worn off)
Ministers and leaders (Table 12.8)	Down to 32,000 from 35,000 in 2000	Fallen by twice as many in previous 20 years; now 26,000 but many part-time
Home worship	Became popular in some areas	No longer especially popular (not enough people)
Work worship	Weekly services held in work time or held locally at lunch-time; popular in urban areas	No longer especially popular (not enough people)
Ethnic churches (Tables 9.12.14, 9.20.2)	Still expanding, especially through immigrants	Many fewer, but some new churches being started!
Evangelism	Alpha Courses still occasionally held	Alpha Courses forgotten
Social action projects	Many church-run care and advice centres, mostly run by those in their Third Age, more by Free Churches than by Institutional Churches Some after-school clubs remain	Staffing inadequate for clubs, care and advice centres, so majority taken over by Government agencies
Black churches	Fail to win many white converts	Now as demoralised as white churches
Church Schools	Still popular though none have opened in last 5 years	Much less distinctive than they were; largely replaced by multi-faith schools
Church of England	In financial trouble; selling off assets to remain viable	Disestablished 10 or 15 years before
Occasional Offices	Funerals still an opportunity	Few church weddings, and very few infant baptisms
Christian lifestyle	Christian divorce as commonplace as non-Christian	Christian lifestyle no longer distinctively different, except in small sect-like groups which have retreated from society
Christian agencies (Figure 5.5.1)	Down to perhaps 75% of the 5,400 in 2003	Down to about 1,000, only 20% of the number 40 years ago

This Table is probably as depressing reading as one could envisage about UK church life in the years ahead. While very happy to revise statements which others judge should be made less extreme, the factors interlink in a number of ways, and so while the odd percentage can of course be changed, cumulatively the overall trends we can already see developing are not totally mistaken. I wish they were. The impact is clear: rapidly moving towards virtual wipe-out.

Is there therefore no hope? Behind the gloom are these unassailable, unshakeable, unchanging truths:
- 1) God is Sovereign;
- 2) The Lord Jesus is building His church and the devil's worst will never overcome it or obliterate it (even if many churches are closed); and
- 3) The Spirit's power in bringing people into the Kingdom is limitless and not subject to statistical forecasting!

Source: *The Future of the Church in the UK*, paper by Dr Peter Brierley for the Senior Leaders Conference, January 2004.

Table 12.4
Number of Church Members in the UK, 1980–2040

Year	CofE	Other Ang	Catholic	Presbyterian	Orthodox	Free Churches	TOTAL	
Source	*Table 8.2.2*	*T8.2.3–13*	*Table 8.5.1*	*Table 8.9.1*	*Table 8.7.1*	*6 Tables†*	*Table 2.23.1*	*% of pop*
1980	1,815,100	364,708	2,454,803	1,437,474	171,735	1,285,175	**7,528,995**	*13.4*
1985	1,551,000	344,943	2,281,340	1,322,047	179,301	1,268,968	**6,947,599**	*12.2*
1990	1,396,000	331,977	2,205,494	1,214,020	186,867	1,299,977	**6,634,335**	*11.5*
1995	1,468,000	317,033	1,921,486	1,098,763	200,826	1,297,618	**6,303,726**	*10.8*
2000	1,377,000	286,848	1,771,121	992,880	245,186	1,240,537	**5,913,572**	*10.0*
2005	1,259,000	283,613	1,681,519	876,970	271,158	1,262,064	**5,634,324**	*9.4*
2010	1,132,000	265,311	1,529,525	770,590	276,240	1,261,805	**5,235,471**	*8.6*
2015	1,019,000	250,458	1,402,558	673,450	280,607	1,271,438	**4,897,511**	*7.9*
2020	906,000	235,605	1,275,590	576,310	284,975	1,281,071	**4,559,551**	*7.2*
2025	916,000	218,783	1,120,243	467,386	293,961	1,222,560	**4,239,933**	*6.6*
2030	775,000	200,000	980,521	364,174	300,480	1,175,791	**3,795,966**	*5.9*
2035	650,000	179,201	840,798	260,962	306,999	1,121,162	**3,359,122**	*5.2*
2040	544,000	157,411	701,076	157,750	313,518	1,062,847	**2,936,602**	*4.5*
80–00	*−1.4%*	*−1.2%*	*−1.6%*	*−1.8%*	*+1.8%*	*−0.2%*	*−1.2%*	*+0.2%*
00–20	*−2.1%*	*−1.0%*	*−1.6%*	*−2.7%*	*+0.8%*	*+0.2%*	*−1.3%*	*+0.3%*
20–40	*−2.5%*	*−2.0%*	*−2.9%*	*−6.3%*	*+0.5%*	*−0.1%*	*−2.2%*	*+0.2%*

† Total of Tables 9.4.1, 9.6.1, 9.8.1, 9.9.1, 9.12.1 and 9.18.1 for 2000 to 2020   Pop = Population

Introduction

Church membership is a heterogenous collection of data since every denomination measures membership in different ways. Some churches, like the Roman Catholic and the Orthodox Churches, have no membership equivalent to the Protestant definition; we use Mass attendance in lieu (at their request). Church membership is not available by age or gender. However, membership is known for each of the 258 denominations in the UK and totals are available for each of the four constituent countries of the UK.

Table 12.4 repeats the total membership column in **Table 2.23.1** up to 2020, but breaks the figures down into the major constituent institutional groups. The figures for 1980 and 1985 have been taken from *Religious Trends* Nos 2 and 1 respectively; those for 1990 and 1995 have been taken from relevant Tables in *Religious Trends* No 4; the 2015 figure is the average of the 2010 and 2020 figures; and the extrapolations to 2040 are largely a dampened linear regression (by taking the average from the figures for 1990–2020 and 2005–2020). For the three growing denominations in the Free Church sector, growth in a five year period has been assumed to be at half the rate of growth in the previous five year period to allow for consolidation.

The percentages in the bottom three rows are the average annual rate of change respectively for each denomination between 1980 and 2000, 2000 and 2020 and between 2020 and 2040, the numbers in the final column referring to the general population.

Anglican extrapolations

See explanation on Page 12.6.

Catholic and Presbyterian extrapolations

Post-modern people dislike joining anything and this is as true of church membership as it is of book clubs, trade unions, or political parties. The only consistent exception is membership of environmental associations like the National Trust, the Royal Society for the Protection of Birds or the World Wildlife Fund for Nature, all of which have seen their membership grow considerably in the last 15 years. Likewise the Woodland Trust has seen its membership grow from 60,000 in 2000 to 130,000 in 2004.

The implication of lack of reasonable replacement numbers of new church members is that as the older people who are church members die off there is a rapid decline in numbers. This has been taken into account especially with the Roman Catholic and Presbyterian extrapolations.

The proportion of elderly people among Presbyterians, especially the Church of Scotland, is very high. **Table 12.30.6** in *Religious Trends* No 4 showed that 38% of churchgoers were 65 or over against 15% of the general population in 2002. This means that while many of these may be around between 2005 and 2020, most will have been "promoted to glory" (as the Salvation Army puts it) in the period 2020 to 2040, and the cohort of members coming after this group is simply much smaller. Thus numbers will fall dramatically as **Table 12.4** suggests.

The problem is not quite so great among the Catholics where in 1998 the proportion 65 or over was 22% against 16% in the English population (*The Tide is Running Out*, Christian Research, 2000, Page 117), so the rate of change between 2020 and 2040 is not such a

sharp increase over the 2000 to 2020 percentage as for the Presbyterians.

Orthodox extrapolation

The key component of the Orthodox figures is the estimated size of the membership of the Greek Orthodox Church. They formed 91% of total Orthodox membership in 1990 and 85% in 2005. This percentage is projected to decrease to 73% by 2040, largely by assuming that their membership remains at the same level in 2040 as it will be in 2005. There is much that is changing in the Orthodox community, but it is seen more in the numbers of priests, churches and attendances than in membership.

Population proportions

The final column in **Table 12.4** shows the percentage of total church membership of the population, using the population figures given in **Table 4.3**. If these trends prove true, then by 2040 the proportion of the UK population who are members of a church will have fallen below 5%.

Some say that the "critical mass" in a population of any group, church or otherwise, is when it forms 5% of the population. "Critical mass" is taken here to mean that number of people who, if they so put their mind to it, could wield sufficient influence on a nation to make their values be taken seriously.

The peak of church membership in the UK occurred in 1930 when there were 10.4 million church members; as a percentage of the adult population however the highest percentage, 33%, was before the First World War. Since 1960 the number of members has consistently declined, though whether this began in 1963 as Callum Brown suggests in his book *The Death of Christian Britain* (Routledge, London, 2001) is open to debate.

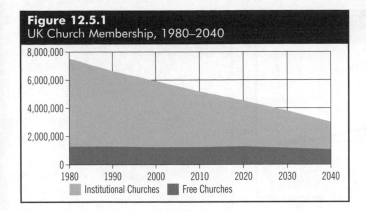

Figure 12.5.1
UK Church Membership, 1980–2040

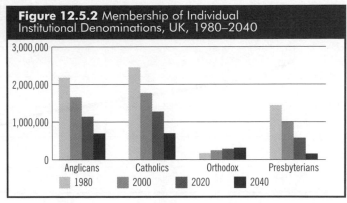

Figure 12.5.2 Membership of Individual Institutional Denominations, UK, 1980–2040

Tables 12.4 and **12.7** give the detail by denominational group of known figures from 1980 to 2005 (the latter requiring very little estimation), and the forecast figures from 2010 to 2040. The text on each page describes the broad methods used for these forecasts, and the individual figures are given in each Table, which, for convenience in subsequent reference, have not been rounded. They should not however be supposed to have that degree of accuracy implicit by not rounding the figures to the nearest thousand members.

The overall change in UK church membership is shown in **Figure 12.5.1**, where it is clear that the main reason for the decline is in the institutional churches. These churches have problems which the Free Churches often do not; some of these are indicated in **Table 12.6.2**. The Free Churches become an increasingly major component of the total, moving from being 17% of the total in 1980 to 35% of the total by 2040.

Figure 12.5.1 shows the decline in membership. It is easy to assume that because only three out of the ten denominational groups into which the data has been divided are growing (and these the smaller groups), this decline is inevitable. The figures are but extrapolations from the present, and assume that many of the present trends continue. **Figure 12.5.2** charts the numbers in **Table 12.4** in an analogous way to **Figure 12.7** of the numbers in **Table 12.7**.

Growth not decline

There is, however, another division of the data behind **Figure 12.5.1** which gives an important supplementary picture. It is shown in the detailed analyses in this volume that in several denominations larger churches are growing. This is true for the Anglicans (**Figure 8.4.2**), the Christian Brethren (**Figure 9.3.1**), the FIEC churches (**Figure 9.7.2**), and the charismatic New Churches (**Figure 9.11**), although "larger" in each case is relative to the particular denomination being considered. It is therefore very likely to be true for those denominations for which there is no special survey to report. The combined result of these studies suggests that the very large churches are growing, most likely more in attendance than membership.

As, however, overall church membership is reducing, this can only mean that the collective membership of smaller churches is declining. Such a trend is not unique among churches. It is happening among charities: the *UK Christian Handbook* shows that there are more larger and fewer smaller Christian agencies, with more income going to the very largest.

Churchmanship

There is also another way of looking at **Figure 12.5.1**. This is from a churchmanship perspective. **Figure 1.4.2** shows that the proportion of evangelicals is growing both in the First World and the developing world. It is also happening in the UK, among both institutional and Free Churches.

Other commentators

These projections may be used to evaluate the comments that various commentators make upon the obvious decline. "In 2031, if it has not by then merged with the Church of England, British Methodism will die and other denominations will be close behind," says Professor Steve Bruce in Chapter 4 "The Demise of Christianity in Britain" in *Predicting Religion* (edited by Grace Davie, Paul Heelas and Linda Woodhead, Ashgate, 2003). Steve Bruce goes on to say further:

- "The church form of religion cannot return. There will be no national revival of religious identity.
- "There will be steady drift from more conservative to more liberal positions.
- "The cultic religion of New Age spirituality ... will die out as it fails to recruit the next generation.
- "Total Christian church membership will be below 5%... in 2031. Perhaps 50% of funerals will be glossed with some sort of vaguely religious ceremony, but fewer than 10% of babies will be baptised or marriages celebrated in church. The proportion of people describing themselves as Christian will have fallen to below 20%."

However, the figures in **Table 12.4** do not support such an imminent death of Christianity, although they certainly show a steep decline. Nor is the evidence currently of a drift from conservatism to liberalism. Total Christian church membership is likely to be below 5% in 2040, but not 2031. The proportion of people describing themselves as Christian will certainly have fallen but not to only 20% by 2031, largely because the proportion of those over 40 now exceeds 20% and most of these will not have died by 2031. Steve Bruce's forecasts might well be true by 2061, however.

In the same book, *Predicting Religion,* Rob Hirst (Page 93) predicts "that by the year 2050 only 3–5% of the total population of Britain will be active church members." Helen Cameron (Page 118) says that by 2050 of those involved in church only "a quarter will be members", and that affiliation to the church will come through association with parachurch agencies, campaigning organisations or "participation in an informal small group". The numbers in **Table 12.4** concur with these more moderate forecasts.

Paul Cooper concludes his MA Thesis "The decline in churchgoing in England in the 19th and 20th centuries" (details of which are in Section 7) by saying that although "the demise of the straight-jacketed institutional church as we know it" is inevitable, "it does not mean the diminution of faith nor necessarily the disappearance altogether of what is now regarded as orthodoxy."

Figure 12.6.1
Church of England Electoral Roll, Revision Years 1978–2044

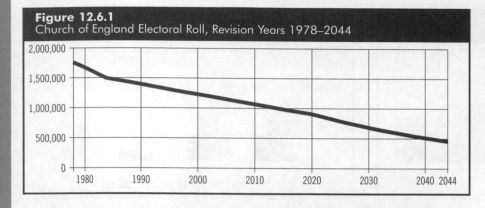

Figure 12.6.2
Church of England Electoral Roll Year by Year, 1978–2044

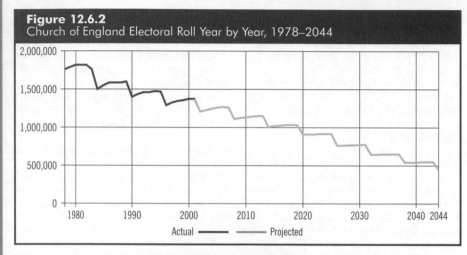

Actual ——— Projected

Table 12.6.2
Problems of Institutional Churches

1. They find it hard to change quickly and so cannot easily adapt to changes in society such as post-modernism.

2. They have local structures that are sometimes for centuries old, and which cannot therefore be altered easily.

3. Their buildings or other property may be legally registered in a way which makes it very difficult to alter them, sell them, or use them for other purposes.

4. If they are State churches their legal and financial responsibilities cannot be amended without lengthy discussions.

5. They are more likely to see themselves as guardians of the Christian heritage. This sometimes means leaders are more comfortable looking back to the past rather than forward to the future.

6. They are usually broader theologically than the non-institutional churches, and therefore are accountable to a wider range of people for any change.

7. Most have a hierarchical bureaucracy which can make it really hard to take clear and decisive decisions.

Table 12.6.3
Calculations for the Electoral Roll of the Church of England, 1978–2044

Year revised	Revision Year	Revision Year + 1	Revision Year + 2	Revision Year + 3	Revision Year + 4	Revision Year + 5
1978	1,761,000	1,791,000	1,815,100	*1,815,600*	1,814,000	1,760,600
1984	1,495,000	1,551,000	1,583,000	1,584,000	1,585,000	1,601,212
1990	1,396,000	1,437,400	1,459,000	1,467,000	1,475,000	1,468,000
1996	1,290,400	1,324,700	1,345,000	1,357,000	1,377,000	1,372,000
2002	1,206,000	*1,225,000*	*1,245,000*	*1,259,000*	*1,270,000*	*1,262,000*
2008	*1,109,000*	*1,126,000*	*1,132,000*	*1,144,000*	*1,154,000*	*1,147,000*
2014	*1,008,000*	*1,019,000*	*1,024,000*	*1,029,000*	*1,035,000*	*1,030,000*
2020	906,000	909,000	912,000	915,000	918,000	916,000
2026	765,000	768,000	770,000	772,000	775,000	773,000
2032	643,000	646,000	648,000	650,000	653,000	652,000
2038	540,000	542,000	544,000	546,000	548,000	546,000
2044	454,000					

All figures in italics are estimated

Table 12.6.1 Electoral Roll of the Church of England in Millions, Actual and Projected, 1978–2044

Actuals	
1978	1.76
1984	1.50
1990	1.40
1996	1.29
2002	1.21
Projections	
2008	1.11
2014	1.01
2020	0.91
2026	0.77
2032	0.64
2038	0.54
2044	0.45

Church of England extrapolations

The Electoral Roll, which is totally revised every 6 years, is used for Church of England membership, which in 2005 was 82% of the total of all UK Anglicans. As a consequence the numbers increase gradually during the 6 year period and then drop drastically in the sixth year (sometimes slightly in the fifth year). All the known Electoral Roll figures since 1978 are given in **Table 12.6.3**, displayed so that the change each year of the revision may be seen; these figures are then graphed in **Figure 12.6**. The 1996 revision-year figure was 87.9% of the 1995 figure, and the 2002 revision-year figure was also 87.9% of the 2001 figure. In the revision years 2008, 2014 and 2020, the figure has been taken as 87.9% of the year before. In 2026 and subsequently it is taken as between 83.5% and 82.8% by applying half the average mortality given in **Table 12.10** to allow for the ageing of the people on the Roll.

The intermediate figures have been calculated using similar proportional increases as actually occurred between 1978 and 2002, adjusted because these increases also are changing. Thus, for example, the 1985 figure of 1,551,000 is +3.75% over the 1984 revision-year figure of 1,495,000; the 1991 figure is +2.97% over the 1990 figure; the 1997 figure is +2.66% over 1996. The 2003 figure has been taken as +2.04% over 2002 as 2.04% is a straight line projection from the previous 3 increases. Similar methods have been used for other intermediate years. This creates some anomalies in **Table 12.4**, as, for example, the number of members in 2025 is higher than in 2020, despite an obvious decreasing trend in the Electoral Roll figures.

Table 12.7
Number of Church Members in the UK, 1980–2040

Year	Baptist	Independent	Methodist	New Church	Pentecostal	Others	TOTAL
Source	Table 9.4.1	Table 9.6.1	Table 9.8.1	Table 9.9.1	Table 9.12.1	Table 9.18.1	Table 12.4
1980	238,805	236,706	539,804	10,037	117,852	142,241	**1,285,175**
1985	243,221	232,531	482,600	36,606	134,446	139,564	**1,268,968**
1990	232,168	231,667	449,520	80,663	167,006	138,953	**1,299,977**
1995	224,229	210,406	402,746	108,811	208,631	142,795	**1,297,618**
2000	206,416	180,418	353,562	133,662	226,413	140,066	**1,240,537**
2005	199,171	171,993	303,973	153,900	288,183	144,844	**1,262,064**
2010	188,040	158,850	274,850	163,290	327,524	149,251	**1,261,805**
2015	179,395	149,693	248,235	174,820	366,662	152,633	**1,271,438**
2020	170,750	140,535	221,620	186,350	405,800	156,016	**1,281,071**
2025	158,783	117,700	168,223	192,495	427,458	157,901	**1,222,560**
2030	148,652	102,952	130,102	195,669	438,865	159,551	**1,175,791**
2035	138,520	88,203	91,981	197,282	444,721	160,455	**1,121,162**
2040	128,389	73,455	53,861	198,095	447,688	161,359	**1,062,847**
80–00	−0.7%	−1.3%	−2.1%	+13.8%	+3.3%	−0.1%	**−0.2%**
00–20	−0.9%	−1.2%	−2.3%	+1.7%	+3.0%	+0.5%	**+0.2%**
20–40	−1.4%	−3.2%	−6.8%	+0.3%	+0.5%	+0.2%	**−0.9%**

Figure 12.7
Membership of Individual Free Church Denominations, UK, 1980–2040

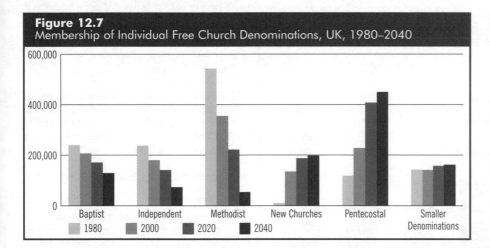

These are the various New Church streams whose figures are known or estimated, of which the largest are Newfrontiers and the Association of Vineyard Churches, and the remaining "non–denominational" churches. These latter churches have a worship pattern and lifestyle similar to or even patterned on New Church examples, but are not part of any New Church stream; they are often called names like "Anytown Christian Fellowship". Their overall numbers are loosely based on the 1989 English Church Census, but tracking them is extremely difficult, and their numbers of necessity are entirely estimated. While it may be true that the New Churches will continue to expand slowly, it is unlikely that these independent expressions of New Church philosophy will continue to do the same, when their independent counterparts are declining. As shown in **Table 9.10.12** it is suggested that they will peak and decline after 2005, something which will continue after 2020. Thus the total growth rate of New Churches between 2020–2040 reduces quite considerably from that seen in the first 20 years of the 21st century.

The Pentecostal churches have two broad groups: the largely white churches and the black majority churches. In 2000 the whites were 55% of the total, but by 2020 will become only 42% of the total, as the black churches are growing faster. However the rate of growth for the black group is expected to reduce in the years 2020 to 2040 since the high rate of expansion (anticipated by the churches themselves) in the years 2000 to 2020 can hardly continue without some period of consolidation. Thus while the white churches grew at an average rate of +1.6% per year between 2000 and 2020 and the black churches at +4.3% per annum, these are expected both to reduce between 2020 and 2040, allowing for that consolidation, though the black churches are likely to still grow faster than the white churches. This reduction means that the overall combined Pentecostal rate of growth between 2020 and 2040 is much less than between 2000 and 2020, as shown in **Table 12.7**.

The smaller denominations in the "other" category again consist of some which are growing, like the Seventh–Day Adventists, offset by those which are declining, like the Salvation Army (see **Tables 9.18.10** and **9.18.11**). These two denominations, however, are but two–fifths, 43%, of the total membership in 2020. The largest single group are the Overseas National Churches, **Table 9.20.2**, a further 26% of the overall total, again a composite group of churches, the largest of which (and growing) are the Asian and Chinese churches. Overall, in the period 2000 to 2040, there is estimated to be a small net increase in the membership of these smaller denominations.

Figure 12.7 shows these six denominations, using the figures of **Table 12.7**.

Table 12.7 breaks down the "Free churches" column in **Table 12.4** by the six component denominations, which are then extrapolated for a further 20 years. The Free Churches split into two groups, three denominations which are declining and three which are growing. The combined effect of these two movements is to keep total numbers almost stationary between 2005 and 2040.

Declining denominations

The Independent and Methodist churches are similar to the Presbyterians on **Page 12.4** in that they have a well-above-average proportion of elderly churchgoers, which, it is assumed, means a well-above-average proportion of elderly members.

In 1998, 29% of Independent attenders and 38% of Methodists were 65 or over against a general population figure of 16% and a general churchgoing percentage of 25%. Hence the period 2020 to 2040 is bound to see a greater rate of decline than the years 2000 to 2020,

as many of these members are "promoted to glory". This is shown by the higher percentages in the bottom two lines of **Table 12.7** for these denominations.

The same argument does not apply for the Baptists. The Baptist Union of Great Britain membership (as given in **Table 9.4.2**) was two-thirds, 66%, of total Baptist membership in 2000, is estimated to be 67% in 2020, and is assumed to remain at about this proportion in the years afterwards. Between 2000 and 2020 it declined at −0.8% per annum. The other third of Baptist membership, however, will decline faster between 2000 and 2020, at an average rate of −1.2% per annum. This also is assumed to continue between 2020 and 2040, and means that the overall rate of decline in this period is higher than between 2000 and 2020.

Growing denominations

The New Church total is given by two broad groups of churches, shown in **Figure 9.10**.

Table 12.8
Number of Ministers in the UK, 1980–2040

Year	Anglican	Catholic	Presbyterian	Baptist	Pentecostal	All others	TOTAL
Source	Table 8.2.1	Table 8.5.1	Table 8.9.1	Table 9.4.1	Table 9.12.1	Subtraction	Table 2.23.1
1980	12,472	9,004	3,633	2,414	2,279	5,892	35,694
1985	12,158	8,370	3,413	2,519	2,320	6,846	35,626
1990	12,374	7,798	3,121	2,592	2,360	7,313	35,558
1995	11,582	7,472	2,746	2,719	2,816	7,739	35,074
2000	10,735	6,926	2,638	2,714	3,356	8,168	34,537
2005	10,406	6,103	2,386	2,906	4,419	8,229	34,449
2010	9,404	5,498	2,115	2,923	5,287	8,230	33,457
2015	8,664	4,877	1,876	2,921	5,989	8,221	32,548
2020	7,923	4,257	1,636	2,919	6,691	8,213	31,639
2025	6,973	3,501	1,334	2,942	7,149	8,230	30,129
2030	6,102	2,822	1,068	2,941	7,568	8,169	28,670
2035	5,295	2,211	828	2,940	8,035	8,109	27,418
2040	4,542	1,552	608	2,939	8,456	8,048	26,145
80–00	–0.7%	–1.3%	–1.6%	+0.4%	+2.0%	+1.6%	–0.2%
00–20	–1.5%	–2.4%	–2.4%	+0.4%	+3.5%	0.0%	–0.4%
20–40	–2.7%	–4.9%	–4.8%	0.0%	+1.2%	–0.1%	–0.9%

Figure 12.8
Number of Ministers in the UK, 1980–2040

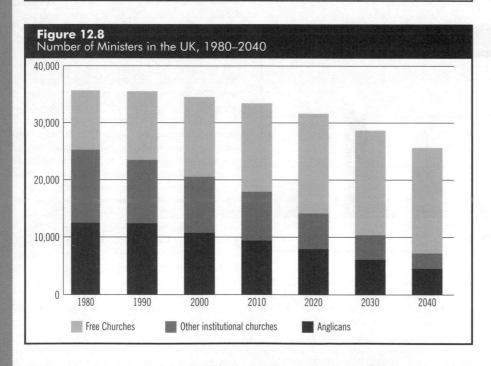

Free Churches Other institutional churches Anglicans

Retirement

One seventh, 14%, of all English clergy are due to retire in the years 2002 to 2007, a drop of nearly 2,000 clergy which is larger than the newcomers likely to join their ranks, although perhaps two-fifths, 38%, will carry on ministering (especially Roman Catholic priests). Ignoring resignations (for which see **Table 8.4.3**), assuming that numbers working after 65 are the same proportion as in 2002, and that new ministers continue to be ordained at the same rate as in 2002, but allowing for death, we get, after a complicated calculation, denomination by denomination, numbers which are reflected in **Table 12.8** and **Figure 12.8**.

The increasing importance of the Free Church ministerial force is easily seen in **Figure 12.8**. From being a third, 34%, of the total in 1990, they are nearly three-quarters, 72%, by 2040. This is partly because the number of Anglican clergy declines as the number of churches decreases (and perhaps dis-establishment occurs), and because of the marked decline in Roman Catholic priests. Another factor is the huge increase in Pentecostal ministers, the large majority of whom are part-timers in the black majority churches.

Churches v ministers

The number of ministers does not decrease at the same rate as the number of churches. On the above figures, the number of ministers was 72% of the number of churches in 1990, but will be 84% by 2040.

What we are seeing here are two conflicting trends:

• The huge decline of the institutional churches: The Church of England, the Roman Catholic Church and the Church of Scotland especially, and with that the number of ministers serving within them.

• The increase in church leadership in other ways, much of which will be part-time (and thus often needing more than one minister per congregation). This is already happening with a whole variety of other ministries such as the OLM (Ordained Local Ministry) and lay evangelists and other like leadership in the Church of England (see **Table 8.6.3**), which will probably spread and be copied in the other denominations.

• Thus we can expect to see many more churches closed in the next 40 years and while the overall number of ministers will reduce, the swing will be more to the independent churches (in the broadest sense of that term) rather than the institutional. This assumes that dramatic changes in the political sphere do not occur in the UK – there is no persecution of Christians, for example, as has happened in China, India or Indonesia, nor does Shariah Law come to the UK.

The number of ministers in the UK was just under 36,000 in 1980, a number expected to fall to just over 34,000 by 2005. Most of these are ordained, but the number includes denominations which do not ordain their leaders, having full- or part-time workers instead.

Female ministers

The proportion who are female is increasing, from 7.3% in 1992 to an estimated 11.9% in 2005, equivalent to an annual increase of +3.6%. In contrast the number of male ministers is decreasing, from 32,800 in 1992 to 30,200 by 2005, an annual decrease of –0.6%. Putting male and female together the annual decrease for the period 1992 to 2005 is –0.3%, that is, less than the rate of decline

in church buildings described on **Page 12.11**.

Age of ministers

The Church of England is the only denomination which regularly publishes the age of its stipendiary parochial clergy. In 1988 the average age was 47, in 1998 it was 50 (their official figures) and in 2002 it was 52 (from a large scale survey). Furthermore the average age of the clergy in 2002 in all the other denominations (from the same survey), except Baptists and New Churches, was as old or older than those in the Church of England! Across the various Scottish denominations in 2002, the average age of lay church leaders was 56 (52 for Baptists and Catholics) .

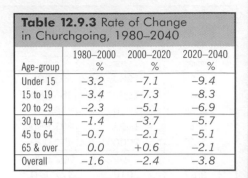

Table 12.9.1 Total Sunday Churchgoers in GB, 1980–2040

Year	TOTAL	% of pop	Average age
1980	6,022,000	11.0	37
1985	5,623,000	10.2	39
1990	5,370,000	9.6	40
1995	4,795,000	8.5	41
2000	4,380,000	7.6	43
2005	3,976,000	6.8	47
2010	3,529,000	6.0	51
2015	3,099,000	5.1	54
2020	2,684,000	4.4	56
2025	2,272,000	3.6	59
2030	1,890,000	3.0	61
2035	1,543,000	2.4	63
2040	1,246,000	2.0	64

Table 12.9.2 Proportions in each Age-Group, 1980–2040

Age-group	1980 %	2000 %	2020 %	2040 %
Under 15	26	19	7	2
15 to 19	8	5	2	1
20 to 29	10	9	5	3
30 to 44	16	17	13	9
45 to 64	21	25	27	20
65 and over	19	25	46	65
Base (=100%)	6.0m	4.4m	2.7m	1.2m

Table 12.9.3 Rate of Change in Churchgoing, 1980–2040

Age-group	1980–2000 %	2000–2020 %	2020–2040 %
Under 15	–3.2	–7.1	–9.4
15 to 19	–3.4	–7.3	–8.3
20 to 29	–2.3	–5.1	–6.9
30 to 44	–1.4	–3.7	–5.7
45 to 64	–0.7	–2.1	–5.1
65 & over	0.0	+0.6	–2.1
Overall	–1.6	–2.4	–3.8

The number of Sunday church attenders has been measured in England, Scotland and Wales but not yet in Northern Ireland. The figures on this page and the next, focusing on church attendance, are therefore confined to Great Britain, and not the UK as with church membership, churches and ministers on the previous or following pages.

Table 12.9.1 is taken from the more detailed **Table 12.10** which gives the numbers broken down by six age-groups. Here they are also rounded to the nearest thousand. In the 60 years covered by this Table, the number of churchgoers reduces by nearly four-fifths, 79%, equivalent to an average annual rate of decline of –2.6%.

The declining percentage of churchgoers in the population is obvious. It reduces from 11% in 1980 to 2% by 2040, as illustrated in **Figure 12.9.2**. It is clear that while going to church decreases sharply, it does not reduce to zero in this period. This is largely because there is a substantial body of churchgoers in 2005, a proportion of whom will still be alive in 2040. A projection of recent trends based only on total numbers would produce a starker result (under 1% of the population going to church by 2040), but the figures in **Table 12.9.1** are more reasonable, as once people have started going to church, the majority continue to do so.

Thus a considerable number of the fairly significant cohort of churchgoers aged 45 to 64 in 2010 will most likely still be going to church 20 or even 30 years later. It is the 20 years or

so after 2040 which will see a very drastic drop, if these trends continue, as the cohort behind is much smaller. It should be noted that against the decline in churchgoing the UK population increases from 56 million in 1980 to 65 million by 2040, as shown in **Table 4.3**, equivalent to an annual increase of +0.2%.

Table 12.9.2 gives the percentage of all churchgoers which are in each age-group for the years 1980, 2000, 2020 and 2040. In these 60 years, the proportion of churchgoers under 30 reduces from 44% of the total to just 6%, and the proportion who are 65 and over increases from 19% in 1980 to an incredible 65% by 2040. The consequence of this ageing of the churchgoing population is that their average age increases, as is given in the final column of **Table 12.9.1**. The detail of **Table 12.9.2**, given in **Table 12.10**, is graphed in **Figure 12.9.1**.

Table 12.9.3 analyses the figures in **Table 12.10** in another way. The average annual percentage rate of decline over the three 20 year periods

is given. The percentages increase as you move from left to right, that is, the situation between 2020 and 2040 is worse than that which existed between 1980 and 2000.

However, the rates of decline broadly speaking reduce the older the age-group, showing that the younger a person the greater the likelihood of their leaving church. This has already been noticed from the 1998 English Church Attendance Survey, reported in detail in *Religious Trends* No 3, but still a cause of great concern. Between 2000 and 2020 the number of people attending church aged 65 and over actually increased, so the percentage is positive.

These two changes are captured in **Figure 12.9.3**. The lower changes for the period 1980–2000 are reflected in the line at the top of the chart, with the line at the bottom reflecting the larger changes for the 2020–2040 period. At the same time the larger declines at younger ages are shown on the left, and the smaller declines at older ages on the right.

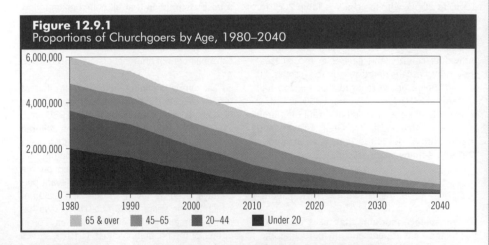

Figure 12.9.1
Proportions of Churchgoers by Age, 1980–2040

65 & over ■ 45–65 ■ 20–44 ■ Under 20

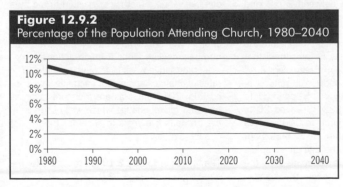

Figure 12.9.2
Percentage of the Population Attending Church, 1980–2040

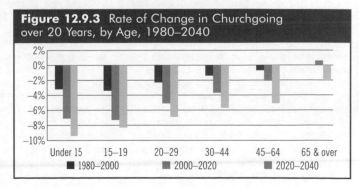

Figure 12.9.3 Rate of Change in Churchgoing over 20 Years, by Age, 1980–2040

Under 15 15–19 20–29 30–44 45–64 65 & over

■ 1980–2000 ■ 2000–2020 ■ 2020–2040

Table 12.10
Number of Churchgoers in Great Britain, by Age, 1980–2040

% of children in or joining	Mortality Year	0 Under 15	0.9975 15 to 19	0.9970 20 to 29	0.9919 30 to 44	0.9468 45 to 64	0.8443 65 & over	~ TOTAL
13.88	1980	1,553,220	470,310	634,080	988,140	1,256,270	1,119,580	**6,021,600**
13.04	1985	1,356,980	410,220	576,970	947,910	1,214,950	1,115,770	**5,622,800**
11.66	1990	1,238,330	361,530	534,920	920,880	1,194,140	1,119,970	**5,369,770**
9.12	1995	991,860	296,400	459,010	830,120	1,132,690	1,084,770	**4,794,850**
7.50	2000	807,090	236,090	396,720	747,240	1,083,330	1,109,410	**4,379,880**
5.89	2005	602,680	166,990	323,800	657,620	1,059,830	1,165,140	**3,976,060**
3.81	2010	377,770	115,170	238,550	574,170	1,021,380	1,201,670	**3,528,710**
1.92	2015	268,410	76,330	173,180	457,000	881,840	1,242,150	**3,098,910**
0.97	2020	185,660	52,210	139,940	353,380	712,930	1,239,830	**2,683,950**
0.49	2025	121,330	33,440	106,900	272,160	556,650	1,181,880	**2,272,360**
0.247	2030	75,250	20,320	80,820	206,050	427,980	1,079,160	**1,889,580**
0.125	2035	44,790	15,980	50,360	154,900	325,910	951,440	**1,543,380**
0.063	2040	25,890	9,300	33,420	109,990	251,120	816,350	**1,246,070**
	80–00	–3.2%	–3.4%	–2.3%	–1.4%	–0.7%	–0.1%	**–1.6%**
	00–20	–7.1%	–7.3%	–5.1%	–3.7%	–2.1%	+0.6%	**–2.4%**
	20–40	–9.4%	–8.3%	–6.9%	–5.7%	–5.1%	–2.1%	**–3.8%**

Table 12.10 shows the number of Sunday churchgoers in Great Britain in six age-groups from 1990 through to 2040. The numbers for the years 1990, 1995 and 2000 are taken from **Table 2.21.4**, which in turn are based on the actual counts of church attendance found from the English Church Censuses of 1979, 1989 and 1998, the Welsh Church Censuses of 1982 and 1995 and the Scottish Church Censuses of 1984, 1994 and 2002.

These Census counts have been "smoothed" into figures for the quinquennial years from 1980 to 2000, with forecasts in **Table 2.21** for the years 2005 and 2010 which have been carried over also into **Table 12.10**. Since these forecasts are based on 20 years data (and by individual country and gender in most cases) they may be considered reasonably robust. It should, however, be realised that the top half of **Table 12.10** for the years 1980 to 2010 represents the only detailed age data of church attendance that exists for Great Britain, and that the remainder of the Table is an extrapolation for as many years ahead!

In that extrapolation process several factors have been taken into account. These include:

1) The average mortality that takes place in a five year period of people in any particular age-group. Although the Scottish and English Life Tables are not identical, the mortality taken here is based on the English Life Table and shown in the line labelled "mortality" above the age-groups. This fraction represents the proportion of those who are alive at the beginning of any five year period and who may be expected to be so at the end. We have assumed that these fractions will continue until 2040, that is to say, the natural lengthening of life which is currently taking place (shown in **Table 4.6.3**) has not been taken into account. If it were it would mean a small extra number of churchgoers in 2040 aged 65 or over.

2) Actuarial calculations for Church of England clergy for pension purposes have shown that they may be expected to live about 5 years longer than those in the general population. It might be presumed that the same follows for churchgoers, given that they also are less likely to smoke or drink alcohol. A study of seventh-day Adventists in the United States in the 1980s showed that they also could be expected to live longer, again on average about 5 years, given their strict vegetarian diet. Similar studies of British churchgoers have not been undertaken, so far as is known, and it may be a false assumption that all churchgoers follow the example of Anglican clergy. A lower mortality for churchgoers has therefore not been incorporated; again if it were it would mean extra numbers of churchgoers aged 65 or over.

3) The numbers joining the church at different times. Despite the drastic drop in the number of children in church between 1980 and 2010, 76%, it is assumed that some children will still start attending church each year between 2010 and 2040. This number to some extent may be taken as based on the number in the population, and the relevant percentage used is given in the first column, which for the years 1980 to 2010 shows the actual percentage of children under 15 in church of the population under 15. It assumes a similar rate of decline between 2010 and 2040.

4) There is a natural relationship implicit in the Table. For example, it may be presumed that at least some of the 236,090 teenagers aged 15 to 19 in church in 2000 will still be in church in 2005 when they will be aged 21 to 25 and thus part of the 323,800 aged 20 to 29 shown as being in church in 2005. This kind of diagonal relationship exists throughout the Table, though where the age-group spans more than five years it is assumed that the numbers are evenly spread across that band.

5) There is also a vertical attrition in the Table. Thus, for example, some of the 396,720 people aged 20 to 29 in church in 2000 will still be in church five years later and thus part of the 323,800 shown for that age-group in 2005. They are there simply because they were aged 20 to 24 in 2000 and therefore will be 25 to 29 five years later. However during those five years some of them will have left the church, while others of that age-group will doubtless have joined. The trend in the number aged 20 to 29 between 1980 and 2000 is decreasing so it may be assumed that the number leaving exceeds the number joining.

6) Each number in the Table for years after 2010 is therefore made up of two components: (a) a proportion of a particular age-group who have grown five years older in the past five years and consequently moved into the next higher age-group, some of whom will have stayed in church, and (b) a proportion of a particular age-group who have stayed in the same age-group although they too will have grown five years older. Different rates of change have been calculated for each of these proportions for each age-group for each 5 year interval to give the numbers shown.

7) The rates of change have been calculated from the relevant rate of change over the previous five years, a method suggested to me by a Professor of Statistics. However (and this is a very important caveat) it is assumed that the church will not simply sit by and watch its numbers decline without much action to consider alternative ways of retaining people. The rates of changes applied for each five year period from 2010 onwards are therefore taken as *half* that rate of change which was observed in the previous five years to allow for the impact of such action.

The figures in **Table 12.10** are the basis for the details given on **Page 12.9**.

There were just over 48,000 churches or congregations in the UK in 2000, as may be seen in **Table 12.11**. This includes some 2,000 congregations meeting in schools, civic buildings or places other than a purpose-built building. While the number had declined by almost exactly 2,000 since 1980, it is set to decline by almost twice as many in the next 20 years, down to 44,000 in 2020. In the following 20 years, however, the decline is much more marked, reducing by a further 13,000 to just under 31,000 by 2040.

Catholic, Presbyterian and Methodist churches are projected to close at a faster rate between 2020 and 2040 than between 2000 and 2020. The Methodists close at a similar rapid rate as the Church of England. This is partly on the assumption that the Methodist and Church of England Covenant signed on 1st November 2003 leads to practical collaboration between churches at a local level, so that there is likely to be some rationalisation of their church buildings, probably before 2020.

Church of England churches

See comments on Page 12.12.

Opening Churches

Churches in new areas are being started by many denominations every year, sometimes with a new building, although the total has reduced from the heyday of the 1980s when nearly 3,000 new congregations began in that decade. Details are in **Table 12.12.2,** which shows that in round terms on average *each year*, a good number of new churches were opened, but a larger number were closed:

In the 1980s 290 started but 310 closed
In the early 1990s 230 started but 240 closed
In the late 1990s 110 started but 220 closed
In the 2000s 125 started but 270 closed
In the 2010s 90 started but 370 closed.

The openings are not evenly spread across the denominations, however. Very few of the new churches are Anglican or Catholic; they are mostly Pentecostal or New Church, although the Baptist Union hopes to see 140 new churches in the seven years to 2010 (some from amalgamation with the Independent Methodist Church) and a further 50 in the next decade. Almost half, 46% (405), of the churches expected to open between 2010 and 2020 are Pentecostal churches, a quarter, 25% (217), are New Churches (almost half of which are Newfrontiers), and 10% (85) are the expanding churches for various overseas nationals.

Nor are the closures evenly spread: almost a third, 31% (698), of the closures between 2003 and 2010 are Methodist, and almost a quarter, 23% (850) in the following decade. 260 Church of England churches are expected to close between 2003 and 2010 and a further 1,625 (44% or almost half of total closures) in

Table 12.11
Number of Churches in the UK, 1980–2040

Year	Anglican	Catholic	Presbyterian	Baptist	Methodist	All Others	TOTAL
Source	Table 8.2.1	Table 8.5.1	Table 8.9.1	Table 9.4.1	Table 9.8.1	Subtraction	Table 2.23.1
1980	19,399	4,507	5,920	3,457	8,419	8,529	**50,231**
1985	19,025	4,603	5,667	3,467	7,912	8,856	**49,530**
1990	18,830	4,700	5,489	3,583	7,537	9,182	**49,321**
1995	18,673	4,634	5,273	3,603	7,067	9,749	**48,999**
2000	18,600	4,741	5,140	3,475	6,552	9,751	**48,259**
2005	18,460	4,705	4,827	3,512	6,139	9,992	**47,635**
2010	18,299	4,647	4,463	3,519	5,635	10,172	**46,735**
2015	17,436	4,544	4,268	3,505	5,210	10,300	**45,263**
2020	16,670	4,442	4,073	3,491	4,785	10,429	**43,890**
2025	14,289	4,258	3,673	3,473	3,958	10,582	**40,233**
2030	12,044	4,050	3,297	3,457	3,189	10,768	**36,805**
2035	9,604	3,845	2,932	3,441	2,455	10,974	**33,251**
2040	7,214	3,643	2,576	3,426	1,750	11,186	**29,795**
80–00	−0.2%	+0.3%	−0.7%	0.0%	−1.2%	+0.7%	**−0.2%**
00–20	−0.5%	−0.3%	−1.2%	0.0%	−1.6%	+0.3%	**−0.5%**
20–40	−4.1%	−1.0%	−2.3%	−0.1%	−4.9%	+0.4%	**−1.9%**

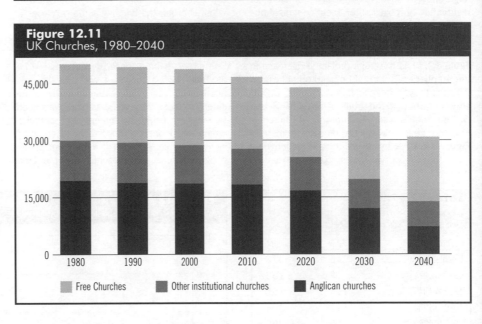

Figure 12.11
UK Churches, 1980–2040

Free Churches ■ Other institutional churches ■ Anglican churches

the following 10 years. Between 2003 and 2010 235 Presbyterian Church of Wales churches are expected to close, followed by 138 United Reformed Church and 126 Salvation Army. In the next decade the main losses are among the Brethren (collectively 243 churches), 150 Roman Catholic churches, 122 by the Union of Welsh Independents, and another 90 by the Presbyterian Church of Wales. It is presumably the smallest churches which are most likely to close or be closed; the Free Churches are able to close churches reasonably easily.

Projecting forwards

Assuming that church buildings will be kept open for as long as possible, then the number in the UK over the next four decades might be as shown in **Table 12.11**, which is illustrated in **Figure 12.11**. This represents a fairly small

rate of decline, −0.5% per year averaged over 2000 to 2020, increasing to −1.9% between 2020 and 2040. This means just over 50,000 churches in 1980 drop to just under 30,000 by 2040.

Table 12.12.1
Churches Started and Closed in the UK, All Denominations, 1980–2002

Period	Opened	Closed
1980 to 1989	2,863	3,105
1990 to 1994	1,178	1,215
1995 to 2002	897	1,792
2003 to 2010E	1,006	2,244
2011 to 2020E	882	3,727
TOTAL 1980–2020	6,826	12,083

E = Estimate

Church of England churches

The Church of England cannot close churches without fuss. It had 11,222 listed churches in 2003[1] out of the 14,915 churches whose listing was known. As may be seen from **Figure 12.12.1** these were distributed almost equally between Grade 1 (3,996), Grade II* (3,843), Grade II (3,383) and not listed (3,693). These listed churches will most likely remain as heritage sites or be developed for commercial or residential purposes after their congregations have gone.

The major reason for the overall decline in **Table 12.11** is the huge projected decrease in the number of Church of England churches. In 2000, it was responsible for over 8,200 churches in England built before 1500[2] and currently still in use. The number of Church of England churches still in use are shown in **Figure 12.12.2** by the century in which they were built.[3] Over two-thirds, 70%, of these old

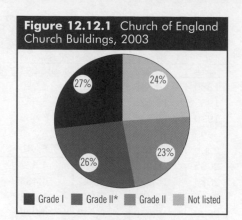

Figure 12.12.1 Church of England Church Buildings, 2003

- Grade I — 27%
- Grade II* — 26%
- Grade II — 23%
- Not listed — 24%

churches are in remote rural areas (our beautiful Gothic churches), with congregations which averaged 14 people in 1998 and are likely to be just 3 by 2010 if present trends continue (see **Table 2.24.5**). This cannot be sustainable in the long term, and hence in projecting forwards we assume 10% will no longer have a congregation by 2020, and thus not be used as a worship centre, and a further 75% by 2040, whether or not the building actually "closes".

Viability of churches

The reason behind these percentages is that, as **Table 12.10** shows, it will probably take another 20 years before the majority of the elderly in these congregations have passed on. However, it could be argued that churches which are financially unsustainable are more likely to be closed even if a remnant elderly congregation is still present. On the other

hand, recent history has shown that the local community often comes to the rescue when a village church is threatened with closure so viability per se may not be a good indicator.

Some churches, eager to prove their usefulness to the local community, have become weekday shops or post offices, or have had a cash point put into their thick walls, or a mobile mast in their tower. A few are already serving food midweek to tourists and passers-by in an attempt to become or remain financially viable.

Many of these churches will doubtless struggle on, with financial problems and difficulties with government legislation relating to disability, safety, etc. The implication of the figures is that the Church of England will no longer be taking ultimate responsibility for the financial support and upkeep of their churches. That reduction in support, perhaps beginning in earnest in the early 2020s, will almost certainly mean the closure of many churches in rural, city centre and council estate areas. Whether or not this is accompanied by "dis-establishment", is a totally separate matter.

[1] *How do we keep our Parish Churches?*, by Trevor Cooper, The Ecclesiological Society, 2004, Table F1, Page 67.
[2] *Religious Trends* No 2, 2000/2001, Christian Research and HarperCollinsReligious, London, 1999, Table 2.3.
[3] *Date of Foundation of Churches in England*, for English Heritage, Christian Research, March 1999.

Table 12.12.2
Redundant and New Church of England Churches, 1970–2002

Period	New	Redundant
Inherited[1]	0	370
1970 to 1974	112	169E
1975 to 1979	112	155
1980 to 1984	111	308
1985 to 1989	56	259
1990 to 1994	72	161
1995 to 1999	44	144
2000 to 2002	25	60
TOTAL 1970-2002	532	1,626
Average per year	16	38

E = Estimate   [1] The CCT inherited 370 existing redundant churches when it was formed as the Redundant Churches Fund in 1970.
Source: Church Commissioners Redundant Churches Committee, Report, 2002, as quoted in *How do we keep our Parish Churches?* by Trevor Cooper, The Ecclesiological Society, 2004

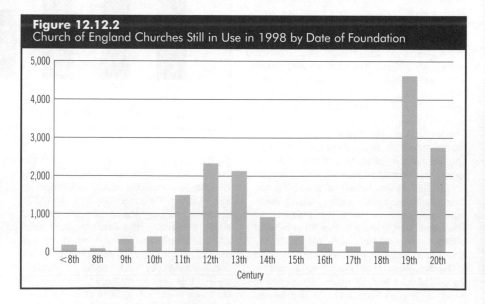

Figure 12.12.2
Church of England Churches Still in Use in 1998 by Date of Foundation

(Bar chart: Number of churches by century of foundation — <8th, 8th, 9th, 10th, 11th, 12th, 13th, 14th, 15th, 16th, 17th, 18th, 19th, 20th)

The Redundant Churches Committee report whose information is given in **Table 12.12.2** shows that on average over the last third of a century the Church of England has opened 16 churches per year, but made more than twice as many redundant, 38. The redundant churches are the concern of the Churches Conservation Trust (CCT), which estimated it would require grant income of £4.9 million per annum for each of the three years 2003-2005.

Just one sixth, £800,000, of this sum was for spending on newly made redundant churches, the majority of the remainder being spent on repair and maintenance of the churches in its care.

Over two-thirds, 70%, of this is received from the Government, which, however, did not pay the full amount requested, so the CCT actual grant totalled £4.2 million, which assuming

the same projected amount was used for newly redundant churches, means that on average existing redundant churches cost just over £2,000 per year.

If the number of churches in the Church of England which are forecast to close between 2020 and 2040, just over 8,000, then the cost could be more than £16 million per year at 2002 prices!

Table 12.13 repeats the totals of the Tables on the previous pages so that comparisons may be made more easily. The totals may also be used to derive various ratios, three of which are given in the last columns of **Table 12.13** which show the decreasing number of members per church, the decreasing number of churchgoers and the number of ministers per church. Between 1990 and 2005 the proportion of UK churches situated in Northern Ireland was 4.5%; the number of churches has been reduced by this percentage in calculating the number of churchgoers per church.

Figure 12.13.1 shows the varying rates of decline for the different factors in **Table 12.13**.

The key features that emerge from this study of future church statistics are:

1) The problems the institutional churches face are enormous, because there is rapid loss of attendance accompanied by a great fall in membership but not an accompanying fall in church closures. As a consequence financial pressure will be very great, and likely to affect the supply of ministerial candidates.

2) Church attendance reduces extremely quickly largely because the huge loss of young people in the 1990s has ongoing effects for later age-groups as years pass. No young people in the 1990s means very few 20 to 30 year olds 20 years later, so the assumed ongoing loss of young people, if true in reality, is extremely serious for the church's future.

3) The loss of younger people in turn leads to an increasing dominance of older people in the church. While some churches with an older congregation grow, the large majority do not. The image of an older church, the difficulty of remaining financially viable with fewer attenders in employment, and the problems of finding people to run the church activities and take leadership roles can all become very acute if younger people are absent.

4) The loss of people (attenders or members) is at a much more rapid rate than either ministers or church buildings as **Figure 12.13.1** demonstrates. This has implications for the morale of church leaders as well as likely financial pressures.

5) **Figure 12.13.2** shows the increasing importance of the larger Church of England churches, the data for which comes from **Tables 8.12.1–3**, something which is explored in more detail on **Page 8.4**. The same is also true of the Free Churches, although it is less true of the Roman Catholic churches.

6) The bottom three lines of **Table 12.13** indicate that the loss of any item will be heavier in the period 2000 to 2020 than it was in the 20 years prior to 2000. However, the loss in the 20 years after 2020 will be more extreme still. It is not only that the number of members, churches, etc are declining but also that they

are declining at an accelerating rate. That is what makes the situation so precarious and urgent.

It will be said, "It is easy to indicate the problem; what of the solution?" William van Dusen Wishard wrote, "The core of leadership is vision. Vision is seeing the potential purpose

hidden in the chaos of the moment, but which could bring to birth new possibilities for a person, a company or a nation." The impending chaos is described by these figures. What can be seen through the fog of that chaos and beyond its worse effects? That is vision; deciding what then to do is strategic leadership.

Table 12.13
Trends in UK Statistics, 1980–2040

Year	Church Members **UK** Table 12.4.1	% of pop	Churches Table 12.11	Ministers Table 12.8	Church attenders **GB** Table 12.9.1	% of pop	Members per church	Attenders per church	Members per minister
1980	7,528,995	13.4	50,231	35,694	6,022,000	11.0	150	125	211
1985	6,947,599	12.2	49,530	35,626	5,623,000	10.2	140	119	195
1990	6,634,335	11.5	49,321	35,558	5,370,000	9.6	135	114	187
1995	6,303,726	10.8	48,999	35,074	4,795,000	8.5	129	98	180
2000	5,913,572	10.0	48,259	34,537	4,380,000	7.6	123	95	171
2005	5,634,324	9.4	47,635	34,449	3,976,000	6.8	118	87	164
2010	5,235,471	8.6	46,735	33,457	3,529,000	6.0	111	79	155
2015	4,897,511	7.9	45,263	32,548	3,099,000	5.1	107	72	149
2020	4,559,551	7.2	43,890	31,639	2,684,000	4.4	103	64	143
2025	4,238,933	6.5	40,233	30,129	2,272,000	3.6	105	56	139
2030	3,795,966	5.9	36,805	28,670	1,890,000	3.0	103	51	132
2035	3,359,122	5.2	33,251	27,418	1,543,000	2.4	101	46	123
2040	2,936,602	4.5	29,795	26,145	1,246,000	2.0	99	42	115
80–00	−1.2%	~	−0.2%	−0.2%	−1.6%				
00–20	−1.3%	~	−0.5%	−0.4%	−2.4%				
20–40	−2.2%	~	−1.9%	−0.9%	−3.6%				

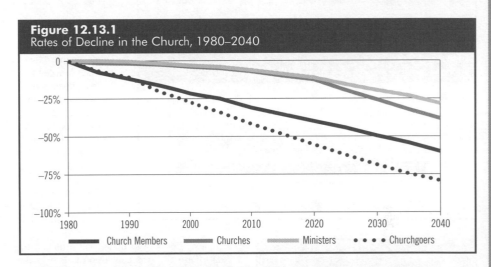

Figure 12.13.1
Rates of Decline in the Church, 1980–2040

Legend: Church Members ▬▬ Churches ▬▬ Ministers ▬▬ Churchgoers ●●●●

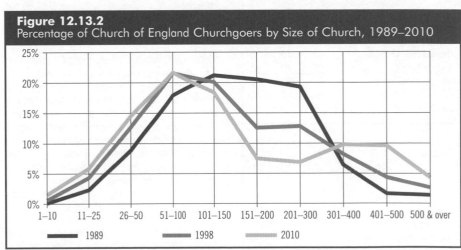

Figure 12.13.2
Percentage of Church of England Churchgoers by Size of Church, 1989–2010

Legend: ▬▬ 1989 ▬▬ 1998 ▬▬ 2010

Table 12.14.1
Trends in Active Membership of Other Religions, 1980–2040

Year	Non-Trinitarian	Muslims	Other Religions	TOTAL	
Source	Table 10.2.1	Table 10.4.9	Table 10.4.1 less Table 10.4.9	Table 10.5.7	% of pop.
1980	348,756	306,000	433,560	1,088,316	1.9
1985	401,657	434,979	463,875	1,300,511	2.3
1990	457,672	495,000	537,894	1,490,566	2.6
1995	517,888	631,619	620,749	1,770,256	3.0
2000	539,968	768,238	670,963	1,979,169	3.3
2005	547,178	893,700	741,212	2,182,090	3.6
2010	545,540	1,082,100	805,050	2,432,690	4.0
2015	538,585	1,244,550	861,675	2,644,810	4.3
2020	531,630	1,407,000	943,300	2,881,930	4.6
2025	543,000	1,581,000	1,030,000	3,154,000	4.9
2030	567,000	1,765,000	1,130,000	3,462,000	5.3
2035	586,000	1,960,000	1,215,000	3,761,000	5.8
2040	600,000	2,170,000	1,295,000	4,065,000	6.2
80–00	+2.2%	+4.7%	+2.2%	+3.0%	
00–20	–0.1%	+3.1%	+1.7%	+1.9%	
20–40	+0.6%	+2.2%	+1.6%	+1.7%	

Pop = Population

Figure 12.14
Active Members of non-Christian Religions, 1980–2040

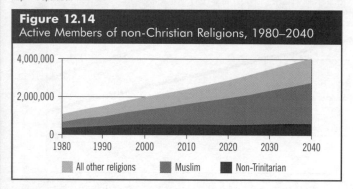

All other religions — Muslim — Non-Trinitarian

Table 12.14.2 Patterns of Religious Involvement in the United States

In a typical week …	1991 %	2000 %	2010 %
Prayed to God	88	83	78
Attended church service	49	40	35
Read the Bible	45	40	32
Attended a small group	15	17	19
Volunteered at church	27	21	18
Used Internet for religious purposes	~	3	6

Source: Boiling Point, George Barna, Regal, 2001, Page 213.

Table 12.14.3
Top five Descriptive Statements

"Spiritual"	
Exploring the inner self	63%
Meditating	59%
Searching for the meaning of life	53%
Praying privately at home	31%
Upholding humanistic values (eg justice, equality)	29%
"Religious"	
Participating in church rituals (eg Eucharist)	77%
Subscribing to religious doctrines	71%
Sharing in worship at church	69%
Studying the Bible at home	23%
Respecting nature	18%

Source: Predicting Religion, Edited by Grace Davie, Paul Heelas and Linda Woodhead, Ashgate, Hampshire, 2003, Page 138.

Other religions

The majority of **Table 12.14.1** is taken from the figures given in Section 10 in this *Religious Trends*, but the 1990 and 1995 figures come from *Religious Trends* No 4, and the 1980 and 1985 figures from *Religious Trends* No 2. These figures are for active membership, which is usually taken as about half the community. The figures are graphed in **Figure 12.14**. The percentage of the population which these groups occupy is shown in **Table 12.14.1**. The Muslims are separated from the other non-Christian religions as they are more than half the total from 1995 onwards, and growing much faster than the rest. If this rate of growth continues, and that given in **Table 12.4.1** for Christians also continues, then active Muslims will outnumber Christian church members by 2049. The non-Trinitarian churches are included here for simplicity, following the pattern which has been used in each edition of *Religious Trends*.

It is obvious that the number of active people in the non-Christian religions is growing, and quite rapidly, when active Christians are declining. While part of their growth comes from immigration, it does not solely come from this source. In general those of other religions tend to have a higher birth rate than Christians, so some of their growth is biological. Other growth comes from people converting to the relevant religion, often because of marriage. The rapid increase suggests that all three factors will be more important in the decades ahead.

Others on the future church

Other people have written about the future of the church, such as Michael Moynagh in *emergingchurch.intro* and other publications from his experience with The Tomorrow Project, Stuart Murray-Williams, Rt Rev Graham Cray who was Chair of the Emerging Church Working Party which produced *The Mission-shaped Church*, Tom Sine, Nick Page in *The Invisible Church*, Alan Jamieson in *A Churchless Faith*, *Predicting Religion* edited by Grace Davie, Paul Heelas and Linda Woodhead, to name but a few. Some of the descriptions are quantitative, but most are qualitative. This page surveys a small selection of this kind of literature.

1) Paul Woodman in an MBA Thesis "An Evaluation of the Role of Strategy in UK Churches", 2003/2004, projects church attendance forward to 2100. The number attending in the year 2040 was just under 2 million, dropping to under half a million by 2100 (Page 5). His conclusion is that larger churches will survive, growing even larger, but at the expense of closure of many smaller churches.

2) George Barna in *Transforming Children into Spiritual Champions* (Regal, California, USA, 2004) identifies the spiritual upbringing of children as the topmost critical factor in the church's survival. He shows that many churchgoing parents believe they are providing a suitable culture for their children's relationship with God despite only 5% having a biblical worldview, fewer than 10% of parents reading the Bible or praying together as a family, and under 5% having any devotional time together during the week (Page 125).

3) Wolfgang Grulke in *Ten Lessons from the Future* (@OneCommunications, South Africa, 2000) writes "Businesses are defined more by their relationships than by their products!" Should the same be true for churches? He further says, "If you have an existing successful business, built up over many years, you may no longer be able to afford the luxury of change. The historic baggage of your past success may lie so heavily on your back, that you will not be able to stare the future firmly in the face.

"You may not be nimble or determined enough to change. You may have to create a few radical new businesses that will seriously cannibalise your existing cash cows. The new economy tsunami is coming." (Page 143). The structure of some denominations inhibits their ability to move radically forward. Could a plethora of new ways of doing church, based on people's values not on services, succeed?

4) Reginald Bibby in *Restless Gods*, a survey of Canadian religious renaissance, (Stoddart, 2002) states categorically that secularism is dead, but that spirituality in its various forms is alive. In a totally different survey, some of the descriptors of "religious" and "spiritual" were identified, and these are given in **Table 12.14.3**. Insofar as the religious/ spiritual debate increases, and it would appear that it is likely to do so in the future, these descriptors may become of increasing use.

13

Alphabetical Index

This cumulative index uses the style Edition/Section/Page. Thus "4/6.3" means *Religious Trends* No 4, Section 6, Page 3, "n" = Footnote, so 4/6.3n5 means *Religious Trends* No 4, Section 6, Page 3, Footnote 5. "NRM" = New Religious Movement.

The previous editions of *Religious Trends* have been No 1, 1998/1999; No 2 2000/2001; No 3 2002/2003; No 4 2003/2004; and now No 5 2005/2006.

This index cumulates all entries for editions Nos 2, 3, 4 and 5, but only retains entries for No 1 where the data given in it was unique to that edition and not updated subsequently.

See also Subject Index for Research Reports on Page 7.10.

13

13

13

13

13

13

13

13

13

13

13

13